Engaging Archaeology

Engaging Archaeology

25 Case Studies in Research Practice

Edited by Stephen W. Silliman

WILEY Blackwell

This edition first published 2018
© 2018 John Wiley & Sons, Inc.

Registered Office(s)
John Wiley & Sons, Inc., 111 River Street, Hoboken, NJ 07030, USA
John Wiley & Sons Ltd, The Atrium, Southern Gate, Chichester, West Sussex, PO19 8SQ, UK

Editorial Office
9600 Garsington Road, Oxford, OX4 2DQ, UK

For details of our global editorial offices, customer services, and more information about Wiley products visit us at www.wiley.com.

Wiley also publishes its books in a variety of electronic formats and by print-on-demand. Some content that appears in standard print versions of this book may not be available in other formats.

Library of Congress Cataloging-in-Publication Data

Names: Silliman, Stephen W., 1971– editor.
Title: Engaging archaeology : 25 case studies in research practice / edited by Stephen W. Silliman
   (University of Massachusetts, Boston, MA, US).
Description: First edition. | Hoboken, NJ : Wiley, 2018. | Includes bibliographical references and index. |
Identifiers: LCCN 2017030730 (print) | LCCN 2017031283 (ebook) | ISBN 9781119240525 (pdf) |
   ISBN 9781119240532 (epub) | ISBN 9781119240501 (cloth) | ISBN 9781119240518 (paperback)
Subjects: LCSH: Archaeology–Research–Case studies. | Archaeologists–Case studies. |
   Archaeology–Philosophy–Case studies. | Excavations (Archaeology)–Case studies. |
   Antiquities–Collection and preservation–Case studies.
Classification: LCC CC83 (ebook) | LCC CC83 .E54 2018 (print) | DDC 930.1–dc23
LC record available at https://lccn.loc.gov/2017030730

Cover image: © LOWELL GEORGIA/Gettyimages
Cover design: Wiley

Set in 10/12pt Warnock by SPi Global, Pondicherry, India

Printed in Singapore by C.O.S. Printers Pte Ltd

10 9 8 7 6 5 4 3 2 1

Contents

List of Figures

List of Tables

Notes on Contributors

Anna S. Agbe-Davies is an Associate Professor in the Department of Anthropology at the University of North Carolina, Chapel Hill. She holds a PhD from the University of Pennsylvania (2004). Prior positions at DePaul University and the Colonial Williamsburg Foundation led to research on sites of colonialism and plantation slavery in the US Southeast and Caribbean and post-Emancipation lives in the rural and urban Midwest. The results appear in a range of articles, technical reports, books, and online resources.

Elizabeth Arkush is an Associate Professor at the University of Pittsburgh, where she has taught since 2010; prior to that time she taught at the University of Virginia. She obtained her PhD in Anthropology from the University of California, Los Angeles in 2005. Her field research in the south-central Andes has been published in her book *Hillforts of the Ancient Andes* (2011) and several articles and book chapters. She also co-edited *The Archaeology of Warfare* (2006).

Jane Balme obtained her PhD from the Australian National University in 1991. She has taught at the University of Western Australia since 1996. She has published over 70 articles on subjects such as the human colonization of Australia, the archaeology of gender, and archaeology education. She has worked with Indigenous groups on Australian archaeological projects in northern and western New South Wales, southern Arnhem Land, the Kimberley, and southwest Australia.

Juan A. Barceló is Professor of Quantitative Archaeology and Head of the Quantitative Archaeology Laboratory at the Universitat Autònoma de Barcelona (Spain). His teaching and research activities deal with theoretical and methodological developments in archaeology and in digital humanities, notably in the domain of artificial intelligence, advanced statistics, and virtual reality and computer visualization. He has published extensively about those subjects, and is also the author of *Computational Intelligence in Archaeology*.

Douglas J. Bolender received his PhD in Anthropology from Northwestern University in 2006. He has held postdoctoral positions at SUNY Buffalo and the Field Museum for Natural History and is currently a Research Assistant Professor in the Department of Anthropology at the University of Massachusetts Boston. His research focuses on the Viking Age North Atlantic, where he has conducted fieldwork since 1998. He has published an edited book and several articles and book chapters.

Brian N. Damiata received his PhD in Geological Sciences-Geophysics from the University of California, Riverside in 2001. He is a Research Assistant Professor with the Andrew Fiske

Memorial Center for Archaeological Research at the University of Massachusetts Boston and also an Assistant Researcher with the Cotsen Institute of Archaeology at UCLA. He has conducted fieldwork in Barbados, China, Dominica, Egypt, Guatemala, Greece, Greenland, Iceland, Turkey, and the United States. He has authored more than 35 articles and book chapters and more than 100 technical reports.

Neal Ferris (PhD, McMaster University, 2006) is Lawson Research Chair of Canadian Archaeology at the University of Western Ontario, cross-appointed between the Department of Anthropology and the Museum of Ontario Archaeology. He is also Director for Sustainable Archaeology: Western. Prior to his faculty career, Ferris served as a provincial archaeologist for the Ontario Ministry of Culture for 20 years. His research primarily focuses on archaeology of the last 1000 years in Eastern North America, British global colonialism, and the contemporary practice of archaeology.

Ben Fitzhugh received his PhD in Anthropology from the University of Michigan in 1996. He has taught in the Department of Anthropology at the University of Washington since 1997, where he is Associate Professor. He studies the North Pacific Rim from Kodiak Alaska to northern Japan and the Kuril Islands in Russia, with other fieldwork in north Alaska, northeast Canada, eastern United States, Peru, and Ukraine. Publications include one book, four edited books/special issues, and 40 articles, chapters, and essays.

Ted Goebel received his PhD in Anthropology from the University of Alaska Fairbanks in 1993. He has held faculty posts at Southern Oregon University, University of Nevada Las Vegas, University of Nevada Reno, and Texas A&M University, where he is currently the Endowed Professor of First Americans Studies and Associate Director of the Center for the Study of the First Americans. His field-based research in the western United States, Alaska, and Siberia investigates the dispersal of modern humans.

Rosemary A. Joyce received the PhD in Anthropology from the University of Illinois-Urbana in 1985. A curator and faculty member at Harvard University from 1985 to 1994, she moved to the University of California, Berkeley in 1994, where she served as Director of the Hearst Museum of Anthropology until 1999 and is currently Professor of Anthropology. She conducted fieldwork in Honduras from 1977 to 2009. She is the author of nine books and editor of nine others.

Jennifer G. Kahn received her PhD in Anthropology from the University of California, Berkeley in 2005. She has taught in the Department of Anthropology at the College of William and Mary since 2012, where she now holds the rank of Associate Professor. She has conducted fieldwork in the Pacific Island region (East Polynesia, Melanesia) and the Southwestern United States. She has published one co-authored book, three edited books and journals, and more than 45 articles and book chapters.

Lisa J. LeCount received her PhD in Anthropology from the University of California, Los Angeles in 1996. She has taught in the Department of Anthropology at the University of Alabama since 1999, where she now holds the rank of Associate Professor. She has conducted fieldwork in the American West, Peru, and currently, Belize. She has published two edited books and more than 32 articles, book chapters, and other essays on political dynamics, identity, and pottery.

Matthew Liebmann is the John and Ruth Hazel Associate Professor of the Social Sciences in the Department of Anthropology, Harvard University. He served as Tribal Archaeologist and NAGPRA Program Coordinator for Jemez Pueblo from 2003–2005, and received his PhD from the University of Pennsylvania in 2006. He has conducted fieldwork in New Mexico, Arizona, Israel, and Guatemala, and his research interests include historical archaeology, the American Southwest, collaborative archaeology, and the archaeology of colonialism.

Oriol López-Bultó obtained his PhD in Prehistoric Archaeology in 2015 from the Universitat Autònoma de Barcelona (Spain). He specializes in the study of wood technology (timber objects, structural elements, and unworked wood) and functionality using different methodological approaches including dendrology, 3D scanning, tool marks and use-wear analyses, and experimental archaeology.

Diana DiPaolo Loren received her PhD in 1999 from SUNY Binghamton, arrived at Harvard University in 1999, and is currently Museum Curator of North American Archaeology at the Peabody Museum of Archaeology and Ethnology. She specializes in the colonial period American Southeast and Northeast, with a focus on the body, health, dress, and adornment. She is the author of *In Contact: Bodies and Spaces in the Sixteenth- and Seventeenth-Century Eastern Woodlands* (2007) and *The Archaeology of Clothing and Bodily Adornment in Colonial America* (2010).

Diane Lyons has a PhD in Archaeology from Simon Fraser University (1992) and is currently an Associate Professor in the Department of Anthropology and Archaeology at the University of Calgary. She has participated in archaeological research in Canada, Australia, Hawaii, and South America. Her ethnoarchaeological research focuses on how social identities are constituted in vernacular architecture, spatial order, culinary practice, and craft production in rural communities in Cameroon, Sudan, and Ethiopia.

Vera Moitinho de Almeida is a postdoctoral researcher, and honorary collaborator at the Quantitative Archaeology Lab, at the Universitat Autònoma de Barcelona (Spain). She obtained the PhD from the Universitat Autònoma de Barcelona, focusing on technological and functional analysis of archaeological objects, using 3D digital models and reverse engineering processes. She has authored more than 40 publications in the field of 3D applications to research on cultural heritage.

Eduardo G. Neves received his PhD in Archaeology from Indiana University in 2000. He is Professor of Brazilian Archaeology at the Museum of Archaeology and Ethnology, University of São Paulo, Brazil. He has been working since the 1980s in the Brazilian Amazon and has supervised more than 30 master's theses and PhD dissertations on Amazonian archaeology. He has published one authored book, two co-authored books, one co-edited volume, and more than 100 articles, book chapters, and other essays.

John William Norder is an enrolled member of the Spirit Lake Tribe and received his PhD in Anthropology from the University of Michigan in 2003. He is an Associate Professor in the Department of Anthropology at Michigan State University and currently serves as the Director of the Michigan State University Native American Institute. He has conducted fieldwork in the western Great Lakes Region on issues of Indigenous knowledge and cultural and environmental resources management.

Akinwumi (Akin) Ogundiran received his PhD in Archaeological Studies from Boston University in 2000. He is currently Professor of Africana Studies, Anthropology, and History at the University of North Carolina at Charlotte where he also serves as Chair of the Africana Studies Department. He has led several interdisciplinary research projects in Nigeria and has been part of archaeological research teams in Ethiopia and the United States. He has published widely, including authoring or editing five books.

Tadhg O'Keeffe completed his PhD in Archaeology in 1991 at University College Dublin. He is now Professor of Archaeology there, having joined its academic staff in 1996. He is a specialist in medieval European architectural history, but he also maintains research interests in landscape archaeology, "post-medieval" archaeology, urban history, heritage politics, and intangible heritages. His published work includes nine books (two co-authored) and more than 100 articles in journals and books.

David Orton received his PhD from the University of Cambridge in 2008. He has subsequently held postdoctoral positions at SUNY Binghamton, Cambridge, and University College London, before taking up his current lectureship in zooarchaeology at the University of York in 2015. He has worked on faunal assemblages from England, Scotland, Serbia, Croatia, Bosnia, and Turkey, and has interests ranging from Neolithic farming in the Balkans to (post)medieval fish trade around the Baltic.

Antoni Palomo received his PhD in Prehistoric Archaeology from the Universitat Autònoma de Barcelona (Spain) in 2012. He has taught in the Department of Prehistory there since 2013, where he now holds the rank of Associate Professor. He studies Neolithic process in the Mediterranean and has conducted fieldwork in the Iberian Peninsula and Syria. He has published eight authored book, two edited books, and 56 articles, 32 book chapters, and other essays.

Megan A. Perry completed her PhD in Anthropology at University of New Mexico in 2002. She has been a faculty member in the Department of Anthropology at East Carolina University since 2003, where she is now a Professor. Her research focuses on paleopathology, isotopic analyses, and mortuary practices in first-century BC to sixth-century AD Jordan. She is the editor of one book and has authored more than 30 journal articles and book chapters.

Uzma Z. Rizvi received her PhD in Anthropology from the University of Pennsylvania in 2007. She has taught in the Department of Social Science and Cultural Studies at Pratt Institute of Art and Design, Brooklyn, New York, since 2009, where she now holds the rank of Associate Professor. She has conducted fieldwork in Syria, India, Pakistan, and the United Arab Emirates. She has one authored book in press, and has published three edited books, and more than 40 articles, book chapters, and other essays.

John Robb received a PhD in Anthropology from the University of Michigan in 1995, and is now Professor of European Prehistory at the University of Cambridge. He has published on Central Mediterranean prehistory, prehistoric art, and human skeletal remains.

Stephen W. Silliman received his PhD in Anthropology from the University of California, Berkeley in 2000. He has taught in the Department of Anthropology at the University of Massachusetts Boston since 2001, where he now holds the rank of Professor. He has conducted fieldwork in the Northeastern United States, the American West Coast, Bermuda, and Japan. He has published one authored book, two edited books, and more than 40 articles, book chapters, and other essays.

John M. Steinberg received his PhD in Anthropology from UCLA in 1997. He has worked at the Andrew Fiske Memorial Center for Archaeological Research at the University of Massachusetts Boston since 2006. He is interested in economic problems of colonization, both in New England and across the North Atlantic. As a principal or co-principal investigator, he has received over a million dollars in National Science Foundation funding.

Kathleen Sterling received her PhD in Anthropology from the University of California, Berkeley in 2005. She joined the faculty at Binghamton University in New York in 2009 where she is Associate Professor of Anthropology and an affiliate in Women, Gender, and Sexuality Studies. She is currently co-director of research at Peyre Blanque, an open-air Pleistocene site in the French Pyrénées. Her published work addresses learning, landscapes, and intersectional feminisms in the past and present.

Xavier Terradas is currently Research Scientist at the Spanish National Research Council (CSIC-IMF, Barcelona, Spain). He has mainly worked on the study of socioeconomic strategies in the Mesolithic–Neolithic transition as well as its dynamics of change in the western Mediterranean. He specializes in the study of technological innovations and technical skills in prehistory, especially those related to quarrying activities, raw materials sourcing, and stone tool production.

Heather B. Trigg is a research scientist with the Andrew Fiske Memorial Center for Archaeological Research at the University of Massachusetts Boston. She received her PhD in Anthropology from the University of Michigan in 1999. Her research interests include Spanish colonialism in the American Southwest, paleoethnobotany, and environmental archaeology. She is the author of *From Household to Empire: Society and Economy in Early Colonial New Mexico*, and has also published articles on foodways, demography, and human parasites.

Acknowledgments

This volume, and the project chapters contained therein, could never have happened without the involvement of many others. Space is limited for extensive expressions of gratitude, but this section provides some by the editor himself about the overall volume and includes acknowledgment sections from those chapter authors who included them.

The editor appreciates the assistance of Natasha Leullier Snedeker with copy-editing and thoughtful comments on his own chapters and with overall encouragement with this book project. He thanks Kelton Sheridan for her initial copy-editing, Rosemary Morlin for the final copy-editing work, and Erica Hill for the indexing. He also appreciates that all of the contributors were willing to take up the challenge of writing about their research in such unique and personal ways and were patient with the sometimes heavy editorial intervention to achieve the volume's objectives.

Chapter 2. The field research discussed in this chapter was supported by grants from the National Science Foundation, UCLA's International Studies and Overseas Program, and several small grants from UCLA and the University of Virginia. My thanks to Peru's Instituto Nacional de Cultura and the regional directorate in Puno, CARI (Programa Collasuyo), Chip Stanish, and too many colleagues and crew members to list by name.

Chapter 4. We thank Tim Earle and Antonio Gilman for helping us implement the project. E. Paul Durrenberger, a co-PI for several of the grants, was invaluable in helping refine the project. Over 70 different crew members have helped on the project, and we are grateful to all of them. This work was funded by the US National Science Foundation (BCS-9908836, -0107413, -0453892, -0731371, and ARC-0909393) and the Wenner-Gren Fund for Anthropological Research. This work was done in conjunction with Sigríður Sigurðardóttir of Byggðasafn Skagfirðinga Glaumbæ and Ragnheiður Traustadóttir of the Hólar Research Project. The SASS project operated under permits granted by Þjóðminjasafn Íslands & Fornleifavernd ríkisins.

Chapter 7. The Kuril Biocomplexity Project was supported by the US National Science Foundation (ARC-0508109, ARC-1202879) and NICHD research infrastructure grant, R24 HD042828. I thank Stephen Silliman and William Fitzhugh for helpful suggestions on manuscript drafts. Any remaining errors are, of course, my own.

Chapter 8. As always, my sincere thanks to the members of the Lake of the Woods First Nations communities who have shared their time, knowledge, and wisdom over the years. My prayers and thanks go to those ancestors who placed these sacred places on the world for me to learn from and the privileged opportunity to teach others with. Lastly, my deep gratitude to the late C.S. "Paddy" Reid who pioneered community-engaged research with First Nations communities in Ontario and inspired me to continue to do so.

Chapter 9. Thanks to all participants of the Central Amazon Project and Urucu-Manaus pipeline survey for their commitment to Amazonian archaeology and their enduring friendship as well. Unfortunately, for matters of space, their names could not all be presented here.

The more than 30 master's theses, PhD dissertations, and reports produced with data from these projects can be found at http://www.arqueotrop.com.br. Thanks also to FAPESP and Petrobras for their funding of these projects and to Stephen Silliman for the invitation to write this chapter and his superb work as editor.

Chapter 11. With thanks to Jim Wilson and the crew at the time of Archaeologix, Brandy George and the Kettle and Stoney Point First Nation, and all the students who have worked with me and others to help shape a "borderlands" archaeology from these sites. Many thanks to all my colleagues and friends who have helped support this research, and a special shout out to Dr. Christopher Watts who has been involved since the beginning and in effect is really a co-PI on the project. Research support provided by the University of Western Ontario, Anthropology Department, and the Museum of Ontario Archaeology. Core funding provided by Canada's Social Sciences and Humanities Research Council.

Chapter 12. I wish to acknowledge Dr. Nicholas David for the opportunity to first conduct eth-noarchaeology as a member of the Mandara Archaeological Project. Thanks also to Dr. A.C. D'Andrea with whom I worked in Tigray between 1996 and 2006. The Tigray Pottery Project was generously funded by the Wenner-Gren Foundation Post-PhD Grants 7934, 8449, and 8956; the National Geographic Society Committee for Research & Exploration Grant 9065-12; Killam Enhancement Award; and the University of Calgary. Permission for research was kindly provided by the Authority for Research & Conservation of Cultural Heritage in Addis Ababa, especially Ato Desalegn Abebaw and ARCCH field inspectors Ato Degene Dandena Gulti and Ato Gezahegne Girma. This project was a team effort of the work of Dr. Andrea Freeman, Dr. Temesgen Burka Bortie, Dr. Bula Wayessa, Getachew Nigus Meressa, Michael Soboka Embaye, Temesgen Tadessa, Tedros Girmay, Mulubrhan G/Sellassie, Degol Fissahaye, Daniel G/Kidane, Goitum Fitsom, Zelealem Tesfay G/Tsedik, Diana Harlow and Autumn Whiteway. I especially thank Joanna Casey for making this a great adventure. However, my deepest thanks goes to the female market potters, the smiths, and the farmers who graciously gave their time and knowledge to this project.

Chapter 14. The Upper Osun Archaeological and Historical Project has been funded by the Wenner-Gren Foundation for Anthropological Research; National Endowment for the Humanities; Dumbarton Oaks-Landscape and Garden Studies; and the Office of the Dean, College of Liberal Arts and Sciences at the University of North Carolina-Charlotte. I am grateful to these institutions and to the National Commission for Museums and Monuments for granting the permission for the fieldwork in Osun Grove. My appreciation also goes to all the field assistants and research collaborators.

Chapter 15. Stephen Silliman expresses his deepest gratitude to the Eastern Pequot Tribal Nation members, councilors, interns, elders, youth, and friends who have made the field school possible all these years. He also thanks the more than 100 students, both graduate and under-graduate, who have participated in the field and laboratory components as hard workers, team players, and politically astute archaeologists-in-training. He apologizes that they cannot all be named individually. The project has been supported by the US National Science Foundation (BCS-0623532), the Wenner-Gren Foundation for Anthropological Research Post-PhD Grants (7151, 8526), and various units at the University of Massachusetts Boston.

Chapter 20. Thanks to Sara DiPasquale, Matt Liebmann, Steve Silliman, Danielle Spurlock, and Dana Thompson Dorsey for careful and kind criticism of earlier drafts of this chapter.

Chapter 21. Lisa LeCount wishes to acknowledge funding from the US National Science Foundation (BCS-0923747), the National Geographic Society: Committee for Research and Exploration (9279-13; 9658-15) and the University of Alabama's College Academy for Research, Scholarship and Creative Activity (2014-58), as well as others, for fieldwork at Actuncan.

Chapter 23. I extend my sincere gratitude to my colleagues at the Peabody Museum, Harvard University, and Peabody Essex Museum for their support in my research of colonial button molds and for their continued guidance and insight on the topic of colonial dress. As always, any mistakes in this paper are entirely my own.

Chapter 24. We thank Stephen Silliman for inviting us to contribute to this volume and Raquel Piqué for her support and contributions. We thank the Ajuntament de Banyoles and the Centre d'Arqueologia Subaquatica for their support of the work at La Draga, and to the students, researchers, and professionals who have participated in the excavation since the 1990s. All research has been funded by projects HAR2009-13494-C02-01, HAR2009-13494-C02-02, HAR2011-25826, HAR2012-38838-C02-0, HAR2012-38838-C02-02, HAR2012-31036, CSD2010-00034 from the Spanish Ministry of Economy and Concurrence, 2015ACUP 00191 from Fundació la Caixa, and SGR2014-1169 from Generalitat de Catalunya. Archaeological excavation has been funded by Departament de Cultura (Generalitat de Catalunya) (2014/100822). The 3D structured light scanner used on this study has been provided by the Spanish National Research Council (CSIC-IMF, Barcelona). This research also benefited from Vera Moitinho's PhD Grant (2009-2013) from the Fundação para a Ciência e Tecnologia (FCT), Portugal, co-funded by the European Social Fund.

Chapter 25. Kathleen Sterling would like to thank Meg Conkey and Sébastien Lacombe for their support and feedback for the project described in her chapter, and Robert Bégouën and Jean Clottes for access to collections.

1

Engaging Archaeology: An Introduction and a Guide

Stephen W. Silliman

Introduction

This book is about how archaeologists actually do research. Don't expect the stories to always be clean, pretty, or graceful; but do expect them to be revealing and beneficial. What you are getting here is the real deal, the rare sighting, the "flaws and all" perspective, the backstage pass. The book presents a cadre of mid-career and senior archaeologists reflecting honestly on major projects in their professional lives that collectively span many regions, periods, and issues. As candid and sometimes gritty reflections, these chapters intentionally diverge from the standard story that one usually encounters in professional publications – elegant research projects devoid of the personal and frequently laid out in a smooth linear sequence of theory-method-data-results-conclusion. These chapters are about what things worked, or didn't, in actual archaeological projects. They are about how to engage archaeological research and how to do so in an engaging manner.

Why do the archaeologists featured in this volume want to reveal the often circuitous routes, false starts, bumpy travels, denied funding, and "things they wish they had known" that characterize their projects? Well, some of them probably didn't and likely preferred to keep such complexities to themselves until I pitched this book idea to them. These "reveals" aren't for their own edification, as the rough patches and personal takes don't tend to offer the same glory and intellectual traction as the otherwise cleaned-up journal articles and successful grant applications do. Rather, they are designed to offer real-world insights and tips for those ready to embark on projects, whether advanced undergraduates, graduate students, early-career professionals, and perhaps even veteran researchers looking for a fresh take.

As anyone who has attempted archaeological research – or any research – knows, making it happen in successful and rewarding ways can be a delicate craft and often involves an unpredictable set of events and discoveries that need reining in to create a reasonable story of interpretation. All know the value of "the research design" that sets up the projects, outlines the process, develops expectations, and charts the way; these remain indispensable foundations to archaeological research. Yet, how often do we get to hear how research designs *really* came about and what archaeologists might have done to correct them mid-stream? How did theory, method, region, place, material, politics, and circumstance actually play out in a given project? What is it like for these intersections of life and the real world to inform actual archaeological practice? Admittedly, many who have already undertaken archaeological research know how this tends to go, but those thinking about research for the first time or those already finding themselves overwhelmed in a new or even ongoing project might find a little reassurance, a bit of advice, or a reality-check useful. Welcome to that rough guide.

Engaging Archaeology: 25 Case Studies in Research Practice, First Edition. Edited by Stephen W. Silliman.
© 2018 John Wiley & Sons, Inc. Published 2018 by John Wiley & Sons, Inc.

Archaeological Practice

To conduct research means to draw together a question needing an answer or a problem need-ing resolution with a conceptual or theoretical framework to give it meaning, a body of litera-ture that informs the issue, a set of methods to gain access (or rather produce) the necessary information, the data themselves, and the analytical links to pull them all together into reason-able interpretations or conclusions. All of these aspects are required in some form for any research, but projects use components at different strengths and have particular entry points.

Equally important, but frequently left out of anything except perhaps lectures or one-on-one discussions with students and colleagues in the field or over drinks, are the personal and politi-cal dimensions of research – the passions that lead archaeologists to the regions that they love, the materials they enjoy, the questions that inspire them, and the politics that concern them or that they try to avoid. Remarkable published exceptions can be found in the Atalay *et al.* (2014) volume on activist archaeology, where "engaging archaeology" takes on yet another meaning as "engaged scholarship," or in the short reflections in the "Special Forum: I Love Archaeology Because…" in the May 2013 issue of *The Archaeological Record*. Archaeologists are frequently archaeologists because something in the process calls to them or satisfies them in a very personal way, and not because they sought a lucrative career and decided archaeology would do the trick compared to other options like accounting or computer science. We know the flaws in that reasoning! Notably, these passions, politics, and personal aspects are not as secondary to the research process as the overly scientific, aseptic take on them would argue. Doing archaeology, or any kind of intellectual inquiry or research endeavor, is very much a human affair in the present, not just an empirical pursuit of a long-gone past.

To engage research, archaeologists mobilize theory, method, and data in innumerable con-figurations to practice their craft, but understanding those requires a sense of where archaeolo-gists draw their inspiration, why they chose a particular approach, how they frame various project components, and whom they hope to impact with the results. As a consequence, routes into archaeological research are numerous. Some archaeologists and their projects are driven by theory, dedicated to finding the best way to engage a cherished or troublesome model, whereas others are grounded in the development and application of methods that can draw out new data. Some thrive on empirical and physical sciences, some are drawn to evolutionary frameworks, and some find their grounding in the social sciences and humanities. Some have a burning question to answer and will seek whatever data or methods they can to address it; others may have a site or a collection that needs study, and they must figure out what they can learn from available materials. Some work in regions that have inspired them for as long as they can remember, some chose areas of the world that could answer their most exciting research questions, and some developed expertise in geographic regions due to the vagaries of their graduate school experiences. In addition, some seek to acknowledge and often impact the politics of the present, whereas some try to focus mainly on a good-faith rendering of the past.

Similarly, some archaeologists have a real affection for certain kinds of materials (e.g., projec-tile points, pottery vessels, dirt itself) and can follow them from project to project, and might even have a hobby built around them such as flintknapping or pottery making, while others delve into whatever materials are necessary to produce the desired outcome and might require the incorporation of specialists. Some projects span many years and multiple sites, whereas others may be completed in relatively short order and concern only one site or even only one set of materials (e.g., animal bones, ceramic sherds, lithic objects) recently excavated or long-held in a collection. Some projects lend themselves to multiple articles and a book or two, others might generate just enough information for a thesis or an article, and others still might produce a technical report on file in a state archive read mainly by the occasional professional.

And, finally, some projects require time in the field with extensive survey or excavation, but others are entirely based in laboratories or museum collections.

All of these are valid ways to practice archaeology. Some may have heard the adage from Sir Mortimer Wheeler (1954: 1): "There is no one right way of digging but there are many wrong ways." The contributions to this book make this point poignantly (and also demonstrate that archaeology is way more than just digging), but thankfully by representing the former rather than the latter half of that maxim. In addition, these various entry points into archaeology should put to rest any concerns that a recent arrival to the joys of archaeology might feel. Are the best archaeologists those who have known their "calling" since they were five years old and enjoyed digging in a sandbox for their lost toys? Are the most successful archaeologists those who love everything about the geographic region in which they work and have felt that affinity for most of their lives? The answer to both of these is no, contrary to what some personal statements written for graduate school applications might lead you to believe. It is easy to look back in our childhoods to find something to presage our future directions because it is even easier to not include in that story all of the things that lead us nowhere close to our careers. You may have stacked up blocks as a child, but didn't become an engineer, and you likely wrote on someone's wall with a colored pencil but never became an artist.

How someone reaches archaeology as an educational or professional pursuit remains highly significant, especially for the personal connections and sustainable ambitions, but the time of arrival is not as important as what one does with it upon arrival. The key is to produce high-quality research, both in the process and in the product, and to make that research useful to other archaeologists, descendent communities, the general public, and/or students trying to make their way to becoming archaeologists themselves. This book explores that process with a bit of flair.

Finding and Filling a Gap

For those wanting to understand how archaeologists conduct research and practice their craft and especially for those ready to attempt it themselves in a senior project, a master's thesis, a PhD dissertation, a major grant proposal, a bid for a contract, or even a post-PhD major new project, few real guides exist. One can read a host of textbooks or more advanced handbooks on research methods to gain a sense of how the techniques work – survey methods, radiocarbon dating, soil analysis, Geographic Information Systems (GIS), petrography, statistics – and when one might apply them (e.g., Banning 2007; Maschner and Chippindale 2005; Sutton and Arkush 2014; see also the "Manuals in Archaeological Method, Theory, and Technique" now published by Springer). Similarly, one can consult a variety of highly-recommended, quality treatments of theory in archaeology and how it is developed and applied (e.g. Bentley, Maschner, and Chippindeale 2009; Cipolla and Harris 2017; Johnson 2010; Praetzellis 2015). These kinds of resources remain indispensable when teaching students (and often reminding ourselves) about method and theory. However, where does a reader, especially an eager student, turn to see how archaeologists link together methods, theories, practices, and passions in a project?

Of course, one can read any major research article and see the cleaned-up narrative of how an idea led to a method, which led to some data that could then feed back to the original issue, but how many of those articles provide insight into how that project *really* worked ... or didn't? Or how many publications talk about how one actually formulated a doable project from the very beginning? Admittedly, major monographs often, but certainly not consistently, have the page space and some of the honesty necessary to recount how a research endeavor came together, but these are widely dispersed, often costly, and not packaged well for conveying take-away messages about the research process. Some notable, affordable, and very readable exceptions do exist, though (Newman 2014; Spector 1993).

Otherwise, only two published resources have come close to offering the full picture of research process. First, the only offering similar to what the current volume attempts is *Archaeology: Original Readings in Method and Practice* commissioned by Peregrine *et al.* (2002) at the turn of the millennium. This is still an invaluable resource for undergraduates relatively new to the discipline trying to learn about theories, methods, and issues, but the very expensive book only offers seven case studies and hasn't been updated since the original publication. Second, undergraduate and casual readers could refer to books in the now-defunct (as of 2005) but useful "Case Studies in Archaeology" series, edited by Jeffrey Quilter (e.g., Hayden 1997; Sheets 2005). These offered some important and readable insights, but a student in an archaeology course could never be assigned more than one, or maybe two, of these to provide an example of research process. These case studies also require a bit of commitment to specific projects for even a short book-length treatment. In the end, though, both of these teaching resources outlined here were written more for a relatively novice undergraduate audience and likely haven't served graduate students or even advanced undergraduates when they begin to think about how to do a project of their own.

I have become acutely aware of this missing piece of the archaeological puzzle after almost two decades of teaching and advising undergraduate and graduate students. I have regularly felt disappointed that I couldn't find readings to cover the research process, from inspiration to development through implementation to completion. In the undergraduate archaeological method and theory course I offer, it has been easy enough to teach students about methods for finding, excavating, dating, and analyzing sites and about the historical development of theory to interpret them, but I have wanted something else to anchor those components in real projects by real archaeologists. In addition, I craved these in a language that was accessible, revelatory, and directed not at peers who evaluate published research but rather at the next generation of archaeologists who are trying to figure out where to start and what to do. Original research articles can do the former, but rarely the latter. Similarly, after many years of assisting with and evaluating master's thesis proposals, I began to realize that the same gap in undergraduate education exists in graduate education as well, especially at that moment when students need a project of their own.

Students, in particular, need to hear more about how research was inspired, conceptualized, implemented, altered, analyzed, revised, and disseminated in cases that may mirror some of their own challenges and potentials. One of the biggest difficulties for both advanced undergraduates and beginning graduate students is figuring out how a project even begins, much less how it is carried out and ultimately ends. Some students recognize major concepts or issues that they would like to study, but cannot quite grasp the ways that methods and data might be mobilized to address them. In other words, they can "talk the talk" with the right references and buzzwords, but they often assume that data will just fall into place once they start a laboratory or field project. Other students have a particular artifact category such as ceramics, stone tools, or plant remains, or a specific analytical technique like GIS (Geographic Information Systems), remote sensing, or chemistry that they want to engage, but sometimes need guidance in finding the larger research issue in which to situate those. They tend to think that once they have examined artifacts or quantitative data, they can just inductively build up an interpretation without much theoretical accountability or, worse, that they need not (or cannot) aim for the "bigger questions." Finally, some students are handed a collection from their advisor, or boss in a cultural resource management firm or government agency, or local museum curator to pursue as a project, and they struggle with how to develop a viable research question for the materials. How much do they need to understand the collection to formulate that question, and how much happens along the way versus at the outset? They often don't realize that advanced researchers also confront these questions when they inherit collections or when data are generated in contract projects that weren't able to follow an intellectual lead or grand question.

A Guide to Engaging Archaeological Research

This book aims to fill these gaps in a creative and useful way. It uses the tried-and-true case study approach to ground research reflections in real, not hypothetical, projects. In addition, it offers readers those adventures in the words of the ones who made them happen, spanning 25 different chapters, concisely and engagingly written, that can appeal to a wide range of reader, student, and instructor interests. These chapters cannot be found anywhere else, and the authors produced them to meet the specific objectives of this volume – to teach and inform, and to provide both aspirational projects as well as cautionary tales. No chapter is a methods-only or a theory-only contribution; these kinds of treatments are available elsewhere and would not serve the purpose here of showing readers how archaeologists themselves (not archaeology broadly speaking) blend, use, or are inspired by these in actual projects. In addition, unlike the case study volumes noted above, no chapter provides a "go-to" resource for final results or grand contributions of the projects covered. Those are available in other places and easily found in the chapter references. However, to facilitate that accompaniment, each chapter highlights one key already-published reading as a "pairing" to help readers develop a robust context for understanding the choices, challenges, and considerations in those projects and how the research stories provided in this book result in a professional article, book chapter, or book itself.

Authors had quite a bit of freedom to represent their personal paths through research projects, so each chapter has a unique flow, voice, and set of circumstances and project components. However, each author had to address, in one way or the other, seven key issues to provide some consistency, even if they didn't follow this order or provide a series of explicit headings other than the "project summary" that opens each chapter. These include:

1) *Short biographical account.* This contextualizes the researcher in terms of interests, background, and aspirations. Some chapters foreground this personal view, while others weave it in more subtly.
2) *Source of project.* The chapters address whether the associated project was a graduate thesis, a long-term interest, a request from a community, a cultural resource management (CRM) project, a specialist contract, an unexpected and somewhat accidental opportunity, an inherited collection, a collaborative effort, a response to other work in the literature, or other type.
3) *Theoretical framework.* Each contribution relates, at least in part, the conceptual frameworks that inspired or guided the project. Some emphasize the core importance of this, whereas others only address it more obliquely.
4) *Methods.* Chapters relate how they acquired data, and how their methodological choices related to other issues.
5) *Nature of the data.* With this target, authors inform about the kind of data that they used and whether such data were enough, surprising, fully useable, and so on.
6) *Reflections.* To meet this requirement, chapters needed to address whether or not the project ended up where it should have and connected the theory-method-data as originally hoped.
7) *Lessons learned.* In the final section, the authors extract some take-away messages from their experiences that they think would be useful for someone embarking on their own archaeological research project.

Readers might be interested to know, too, that many of the contributors found their writing task much more challenging than they originally expected, although a couple found it profoundly easier to do than their regular academic writing. Either way, engaging archaeology in an engaging way isn't necessarily straightforward or simple. This frequent difficulty speaks – or so I would like to believe – not only to the quality of thoughtful reflections available here as they represent hard-won efforts, but also to the relative rarity of this kind of discussion and style of reflection among even established archaeologists. We talk about these things casually, but don't usually commit them to writing and in an organized manner. Turning stories we share casually among ourselves into useful parables for other researchers takes some thoughtful reflection.

The 25 projects recounted here serve to provide substance and coverage while keeping the book's size manageable and the book's price accessible when compared to the burgeoning, over-priced textbook market. Fortunately, having more than two dozen projects in the roster permits a reasonably good sampling of periods, places, methods, datasets, and issues around the world, which was an explicit goal. The volume also showcases a range of archaeologists with varied backgrounds, subject positions, and perspectives to highlight the many paths into and through archaeology in the twenty-first century as an educational pursuit, a professional career, and a personal passion. Still, the collection couldn't cover everything by a long shot, and I anticipate some questions about the holes: why is this site, this archaeologist, this specific region, this theoretical perspective, this type of technique, or other "this" options not included? I can answer in advance by reiterating that the book needed to be affordable and manageable, and some tough – but I think quite reasonable – choices had to be made.

Across the numerous chapters, there should be much to inform and satisfy (Table 1.1). Readers can find chapters spanning most of human history, from the Pleistocene through the Holocene to the medieval and "modern world" periods initiated in and from Europe, or for those inclined to call them such: from deep prehistory to historical archaeology. Chapters cover most major regions including Australia, the Pacific, Northeast Asia, South Asia, the Middle East, East Africa, the West African coast, Europe (including France, Spain, Italy, and Ireland), Iceland, tropical and highland South America, Mesoamerica, and several North American regions (New England, the Mid-Atlantic, the Great Lakes region, the Southwest, and the Great Basin) (Figure 1.1).

Readers can also encounter projects covering a variety of datasets and specializations: zooarchaeology, paleoethnobotany, bioarchaeology, ethnoarchaeology, ceramic analysis, lithic analysis, pipe studies, metal analysis, geochemical sourcing, soils, stratigraphy, seriation, absolute dating, classification and typology, sampling, computer modeling, remote sensing, Geographic Information Systems, rock art, and architecture. Chapters cover an assortment of survey (e.g., pedestrian, geophysical, subsurface), surface collection, and excavation options in the field but also emphasize research in the laboratory and in museum collections. Project scopes range as well, from those oriented to households to those focused on landscapes and settlements, and from those involving only the author in the laboratory, to a handful of researchers conducting moderate-scale surveys and excavation, to a large team conducting extensive fieldwork. I intentionally avoided too many of the latter so that this book better shares modestly-sized projects that students might find themselves doing.

In a similar array of coverage, the chapters represent decent theoretical spreads and "big issue" commitments. Readers can find chapters on many hot topics of contemporary archaeology: social inequality, colonialism, warfare, landscape, foodways, identity, race, gender, age, bodies, craft production, domestication, mobility, interaction, colonialism, and culture change and continuity. Again, all options are not represented in a mere 25 offerings, but these chapters represent a rather robust sample. On the theory front, some authors herein find their inspiration

Table 1.1 Chart of major topics (other than regions – see Figure 1.1) covered by all chapters. Recommended for those who want personalized sequences of reading or seek to build chapters around a course syllabus. NOTE: "Historical archaeology" is used in the section on temporal periods to try to identify those who (often) describe what they do as "historical archaeology" and not to suggest that the other periods are not historical nor to perpetuate any kind of prehistory-history divide. For this reason, the other periods are not called "prehistoric" and are instead situated in larger divisions of absolute time.

Topics	Chapter																								
	2	3	4	5	6	7	8	9	10	11	12	13	14	15	16	17	18	19	20	21	22	23	24	25	26
PERIOD																									
Pleistocene																	x								
Holocene	x	x			x				x	x			x	x	x			x	x	x	x		x		x
Historical Archaeology			x															x	x			x			x
THEME																									
Inequality	x		x						x		x			x	x				x						x
Political Economy			x	x		x																			
Households							x		x	x	x	x	x	x	x			x		x	x				
Identity				x			x		x	x	x	x	x	x	x	x		x	x			x			x
Gender/Age											x														
Environment/Ecology																	x								
Landscape	x	x	x	x	x	x	x		x		x	x	x					x							
Foodways						x	x		x												x				
Colonialism				x								x	x	x					x			x			
Craft/Technology					x						x	x	x				x		x	x		x	x		
Practice/Agency										x	x	x		x	x	x			x	x		x	x	x	
Critical Social Theories				x										x	x		x		x			x		x	
METHODS																									
Field survey	x	x	x	x		x	x	x						x	x		x	x							
Remote sensing	x	x	x																						
Surface collection	x	x																							
Excavation			x		x	x		x	x			x	x	x	x	x	x	x	x	x	x		x		x
Collections									x			x						x	x	x	x			x	x

(Continued)

Table 1.1 (Continued)

Topics																	Chapter								
	2	3	4	5	6	7	8	9	10	11	12	13	14	15	16	17	18	19	20	21	22	23	24	25	26
Experimental/Ethnoarchaeology											x														
Classification							x												x	x	x	x	x	x	
Dating		x	x		x	x											x	x		x	x				
Sourcing		x				x			x		x			x			x			x	x		x		
Sampling			x			x	x		x																
DATASETS																									
Lithics		x			x	x			x						x		x						x		
Ceramics				x	x	x				x	x	x	x	x	x					x					
Metals				x																					
Pipes/Adornment													x						x			x			
Wood/Fiber																	x						x		
Plants/Animals			x			x			x			x	x	x			x				x				
Human Remains																x									x
Soil			x					x																	
Architecture	x								x	x		x	x	x	x			x							
Space/GIS	x	x	x			x	x		x		x			x		x				x	x				
Rock Art							x																		
RESEARCH DESIGN																									
PhD Project	x	x		x		x	x		x	x	x	x		x	x	x	x		x	x	x		x	x	x
Post-PhD Project	x	x	x		x	x		x	x	x	x	x	x	x	x	x	x		x	x	x	x	x		
Emphasis on Grants			x			x			x	x	x			x	x	x		x			x				
Emphasis on Chance													x		x	x									x
Scholarly Collaboration			x		x			x	x		x	x	x			x	x		x		x		x		x
Community Engagement		x		x			x	x	x	x	x			x											x
Cultural Resource Management/Heritage							x	x		x		x	x		x			x							x

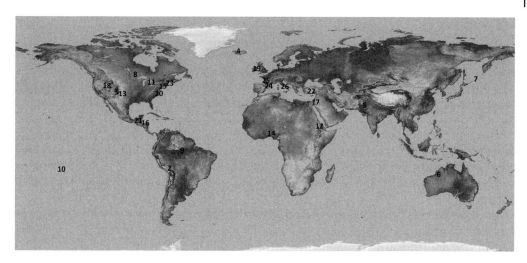

Figure 1.1 World map showing locations of research projects discussed in the volume, marked by chapter number.

in cultural ecology, population dynamics, settlement systems, and environmental stress; some situate their work in agency, communities of practice, the *chaîne opératoire*, social learning, information processing, and regional interactions; and still others ground their research in postcolonialism, decolonization, indigenous perspectives, feminism, critical race theory, and collaborative epistemologies.

With these parameters in mind, readers can find a variety of ways to engage these chapters. The book can be read front to back for a full appreciation of contemporary archaeology, or it can be read piece-meal and easily out of the current chapter order to access a variety of places, times, methods, or issues as needed for a course syllabus or a set of reader interests. I considered ordering all chapters alphabetically by author, forcing readers to pick their way through the chapters based on a variety of parameters using Table 1.1. This strategy could have initiated a more personalized engagement with the material as readers would have to tailor the book to their own interests at the outset. If not, they would end up on a seemingly random stroll through archaeology. As intriguing as that "choose your own path" method was, it was not a formula for success since most readers – especially casual, unfamiliar, and student readers – appreciate some sense of structure. Actually, we probably all appreciate some structure in our first foray into new material, and many prefer to read a book cover to cover rather than jump around. Besides, I don't want any false accusations of being a lazy editor without a vision!

Therefore, the chapters are organized into three sections based on project scale: those focused on larger scales like regions, settlements, and landscapes; those dealing with medium scales of households, sites, and communities; and those emphasizing specific material classes or collections. The order within those three sections is relatively arbitrary, other than trying to keep places, periods, and processes reasonably well distributed rather than clustered. Differentiating chapters by project scope seemed far superior to dividing them into somewhat bland geographical and temporal categories or forcing artificial separation and coherence depending on whether one selects method, theory, or something else. Even still, these categories based on scale have their own blurriness, but I encourage you not to look too closely at those edges, for this classification system is merely organizational and not foundational. That said, for the more adventurous, the more focused, or the more inclined to fit these readings into existing course syllabi, Table 1.1 remains the go-to resource for charting your own path. Mix and match as you see fit.

Conclusion

My hope, which is shared by all contributors, is that this book reveals and advises while offering an enjoyable and fun read. It should make readers comfortable at times with their own projects, whether envisioned or underway, but it should also make readers wary and concerned at other times as they think about the pitfalls or dead-ends lying ahead on their particular research path. This is an enjoyable profession, but it isn't always the easiest, the most action-packed, and most romantic one despite rumors and movies to the contrary. We should remember this humorous, rather than ominous, take on our discipline: "Archaeology is rather like a vast, fiendish jigsaw puzzle invented by the devil as an instrument of tantalising torment" (Bahn 1989: 5). Yet, we revel in picking up those pieces and wouldn't have it any other way.

Finally, we have all heard that we need no "cookbook" approach to archaeology, but perhaps we have taken that metaphor too far to mean the rote application of instructions to create desired end results. Maybe this volume is actually a kind of cookbook for archaeology if we realize that tried-and-true formulae are good places to start for those needing familiarity with the process, that cookbooks have many recipes covering a range of menu options rather than a one-size-fits-all approach, and that interesting and successful recipes are great foundations for experienced chefs to start experimenting with different ingredients, spice palates, and brand-new dishes. Most projects are not created entirely anew, but rather materialize *uniquely and contextually* from what researchers have learned already from those who have tried out some of the same theories, methods, and datasets in different regions, contexts, or time periods.

So, let's dig in....

References

Atalay, Sonya, Lee Rains Claus, Randall H. McGuire, and John R. Welch, eds. 2014. *Transforming Archaeology: Activist Practices and Prospects*. London: Routledge.

Bahn, Paul. 1989. *Bluff Your Way in Archaeology*. London: Oval Books.

Banning, Edward B. 2007. *The Archaeologist's Laboratory: The Analysis of Archaeological Data*. New York: Springer.

Bentley, R. Alexander, Herbert D. G. Maschner, and Christopher Chippindale, eds. 2009. *Handbook of Archaeological Theories*. Walnut Creek, CA: Altamira Press.

Cipolla, Craig N. and Oliver J. T. Harris. 2017. *Archaeological Theory in the New Millennium: Introducing Current Perspectives*. London: Routledge.

Hayden, Brian. 1997. *The Pithouses of Keatley Creek*. Toronto: Harcourt Brace.

Johnson, Matthew. 2010. *Archaeological Theory: An Introduction*, 2nd ed. Oxford: Wiley-Blackwell.

Maschner, Herbert D. G. and Christopher Chippindale, eds. 2005. *Handbook of Archaeological Methods*, vols. 1–2. Walnut Creek, CA: Altamira Press.

Newman, Elizabeth Terese. 2014. *Biography of a Hacienda: Work and Revolution in Rural Mexico*. Tucson, AZ: University of Arizona Press.

Peregrine, Peter N., Carol R. Ember, and Marvin Ember, eds. 2002. *Archaeology: Original Readings in Method and Practice*. Upper Saddle River, NJ: Pearson.

Praetzellis, Adrian. 2015. *Archaeological Theory in a Nutshell*. London: Routledge.

Sheets, Payson. 2005. *The Ceren Site, A Prehistoric Village Buried by Volcanic Ash in Central America*. 2nd ed. Belmont, CA: Wadsworth Publishing.

Spector, Janet. 1993. *What This Awl Means: Feminist Archaeology at a Wahpeton Dakota Village*. Minneapolism MN: Minnesota Historical Society Press.

Sutton, Mark and Brooke Arkush. 2014. *Archaeological Laboratory Methods: An Introduction*, 6th ed. Dubuque, IA: Kendall Hunt Publishing.

Wheeler, Sir Mortimer. 1954. *Archaeology from the Earth*. Oxford: Clarendon Press.

Part I

Landscapes, Settlements, and Regions

2

Climbing Hillforts and Thinking about Warfare in the Pre-Columbian Andes
Elizabeth Arkush

Project Statement

Between 2000 and 2007, I investigated late pre-Columbian hillforts in the highlands of southern Peru, starting as a doctoral project and continuing for two years afterward. The project targeted a larger-than-normal region by restricting the fieldwork to hillforts identified in advance through air photos and other methods. We mapped the architecture of hillfort settlements using a handheld GPS unit, made surface collections, and dug test pits to obtain carbon samples for dating. GIS software was especially useful in analyzing patterns of hillfort distribution, defensibility, and visibility on a regional scale. Ultimately, the project shed light on how society was structured at the time and on possible causes for the rise of defensive settlement patterns.

The Hillfort Project: Version One

I could tell the story of this project in at least two ways: there is what happened, and there is what I think was going on underneath.

At the beginning of my graduate school years I went to the Titicaca basin in the highlands of Peru to work with my new advisor, Charles Stanish, and there I became obsessed with hillforts (Figure 2.1). They belonged to a time after the collapse of an earlier state, Tiwanaku, and before the expansion of the Inca empire. This period is called the Late Intermediate Period (LIP, AD 1000–1450), and in the highlands of the Andes, it's a bit of an ugly duckling. The periods right before and after teem with temples and kings, colorful pottery and gorgeous stone carving, human sacrifices, and llama caravans loaded with valuables. But the LIP in the highlands doesn't have much in that vein. The pottery is cruder. The public architecture is just smallish plazas (if that), and kings are nowhere to be found. There are instead hundreds of villages and towns, whose architecture sometimes still remains on the surface: many sites and many sherds, since the highlands were densely populated in this late phase. Aboveground tomb structures and graves often remain visible on the surface. And, at least in the high-altitude plain or *altiplano* around Lake Titicaca, multiple large walls surround hilltop settlements where many people began to live at that time. Some obvious questions about this age between empires were there for the asking: Why the walls, why the hillforts? How were groups organized politically and socially in this time of apparent fear?

I developed a project on these questions for my doctoral research and did the fieldwork in the summers of 2000, 2001, and 2002. After I completed my PhD at UCLA in early 2005, I continued

Engaging Archaeology: 25 Case Studies in Research Practice, First Edition. Edited by Stephen W. Silliman.
© 2018 John Wiley & Sons, Inc. Published 2018 by John Wiley & Sons, Inc.

Figure 2.1 The western walls at Pucarani, the biggest hillfort in the northwestern Titicaca basin. This was the first hillfort I climbed as a graduate student in 1999. It had never been mapped or published.

and expanded the project in the 2005 and 2007 field seasons, ultimately publishing the results in book form (Arkush 2011). (Since then, I've directed other kinds of projects on hillforts that I will not discuss here.) I started out with a basic assumption that hillforts were a response to warfare or at least the fear of attack. So, these were really questions about warfare, and hence they were part of a bigger conversation in anthropology about non-state warfare, its causes, and how it might shape societies and their histories. It was a conversation in which archaeologists were participating more and more.

But first I had to figure out what was going on in the altiplano in the LIP. Fairly little research had been done, and the state of knowledge was limited. I could borrow insights from better-studied regions, but actually answering my research questions was a challenge. The first question, the "why hillforts, why warfare, why then?" question, could turn on better chronology – whether the hillforts came right on the heels of the collapse of Tiwanaku, or developed gradually throughout the LIP as populations rose and hostilities grew in scale, or emerged later as a response to Inca aggressions from farther north. The second question about social and political organization could be tackled in different ways. On a regional scale, patterns of hillforts might reveal the political landscape of hostile borderlands and spheres of integration. But the stand-ard regional methodology used in the Andes, a full-coverage pedestrian survey, couldn't hope to cover enough ground to capture a political landscape of warring polities and buffer zones. On a local scale, it seemed fruitful to study large hillfort settlements: maybe they were planned and centered around leaders' houses or plazas, or maybe arranged in more equitable ways. Potentially, excavation could reveal wealthy elite houses with fancy goods and poor commoner houses. But it made no sense to do an excavation project and collect deep, detailed information about one site, in a vacuum of regional knowledge.

In the Field

Fortunately, a great deal of the architecture at these late sites shows above ground on the grassy, open hilltops of the altiplano (Figure 2.1). It even shows far above ground, in air and satellite photos, as Dr. Stanish had noticed during an earlier survey. There was no Google Earth yet, so I spent several days at the office of Peru's National Air-photo Service on the Air Force base in Lima, with the help of a friendly colonel combing over air photos with a loupe for concentric walls on hilltops, and marking the spot on my photocopied maps. I'd already marked, in a different color, the place-names containing the word "fort" (or *pukara*, in Quechua and Aymara, the native Andean language), and in the altiplano I added anything that looked like a fort through binoculars from the ground or from other hillforts. From the multicolored messes of my maps, I eventually selected forty-four hillforts spread across the northwest altiplano to visit and map the defensive walls and the internal layout. With my crew, I drove Dr. Stanish's project truck over a few paved roads and more dirt tracks to the foot of these hills, and hiked the rest of the way. A small crew of three or four good-humored friends and helpers was enough, always including at least one experienced Peruvian assistant to explain our work in Quechua and extricate us from difficulties. But aside from the occasional truck break-down and an ice storm, the fieldwork went without a hitch.

Working on hilltops at 13,000 feet has big advantages, despite the obvious disadvantage of having to go up them. Walls, tombs, storage platforms, and house foundations are usually still visible on the surface: the hilltops are not subject to deposition, and they lie above the effective range of agriculture. Since the land is not valuable, the nearby farmers didn't mind us poking around up there. The hills also had excellent satellite coverage, and I realized the walls and domestic sectors could be mapped with a handheld GPS unit. The results were less precise than a Total Station map, but much quicker and still informative. At first I just made sketch maps marked with GPS coordinates: crude efforts, and I knew it. Later I started mapping directly onto big sheets of millimeter graph paper with coordinates on the axes, which would flap furiously against the clips on the clipboard. Then, shortly after completing my doctorate, I purchased a second-hand Trimble GeoExplorer, a high-precision GPS with a customizable interface. The Trimble could digitally record points and lines and any extra information you wanted, like measurements and notes. You could download the data right onto the computer and, by comparing the records for the same time frame from a fixed base station with a known position, correct it with differential GPS for extra precision. I adored my new toy, which easily generated high-precision maps embedded with notes and data, and exported them right into ESRI ArcGIS. Trimble in hand, we revisited many of the larger hillforts to make better maps.

My crew and I did other things on the hills, too, like measuring and photographing walls, entrances, and other features, and making surface collections of ceramics. In neither of these were we very systematic, which I regretted later. As a graduate student I was somewhat overwhelmed by these amazing sites and how to record them adequately without having to hike up the damn things umpteen times each. Fieldwork is all about trade-offs: I traded more hillforts for less detailed and systematic data, and by the time I knew I could do better, I didn't want to start over. For instance, we just made grab-bag collections of ceramics. (In later projects I was careful to use more robust methods, like surface collections on a grid for large sites, and found that when they were prudently designed, they were hardly more time-consuming.) Still, I believe these early collections were adequate and not misleading for what I was mainly doing with them: mapping regional distributions of ceramic styles. We also dug small test pits at ten sites for carbon samples from house occupation contexts. Following a clever tip from Michael Moseley, we looked for grass in the mortar in some defensive walls, which could also be dated.

With funding from a National Science Foundation (NSF) Dissertation Improvement Grant, I sent off the samples for radiocarbon dating.

Back in the lab, I had gotten intrigued by GIS. No class on it was offered yet at UCLA, so I taught myself ArcGIS software, borrowing at times from the expertise of friends. GIS was useful for displaying maps and data in space so that you could see the patterns, and also for systematically calculating things like: which hillforts could see and be seen by which other hillforts? How hard were they to get up to (going by the terrain, not our field times, which depended on where we could park the truck)? Did the hillforts on the steepest hills have smaller walls?

Theory and Interpretation

Meanwhile, I was reading a great deal on warfare in ethnography and archaeology, starting with Keeley's book *War Before Civilization* (1996), which influenced me profoundly. I developed a theoretical perspective planted firmly in the processual tradition. It went something like this. Pre-industrial warfare can and should be studied comparatively, across cultures, because it is patterned: there were kinds of warfare that happened a lot, surrounded by empty unoccupied spaces of things that *didn't* happen. To be sure, people were active agents in war, and warfare took on a unique flavor depending on its cultural, historical, and geographic terroir, so there were variations on the patterns, but they were limited. In part these patterns were simply the result of rational-choice behavior (i.e., they followed a fairly simple logic of costs and benefits). A rational-choice model doesn't work for all human behavior, but I considered that it does work for choices related to the outcome of violent conflict, especially when the conflict was fierce and people were really afraid, because the stakes were too high to allow any kind of random cultural wackiness. At the end of the day, people had to fight to win, and if they didn't – well, they didn't last long.

This allowed all sorts of interpretive arguments in my work. The patterned nature of warfare meant I could interpret what I found with reference to cross-cultural analogs half a world away. Concentric walls and parapets could be interpreted as defensive; it was no great leap to believe people in many different regions had independently discovered the worth of these structures. Hillfort settlements could be interpreted as a response to actual warfare, not just a state of fearful hostility, because in the ethnographic record, other societies that fortified their settlements waged war frequently. Furthermore, the patterns might extend beyond the immediate nitty-gritty of defense to more complicated realms; for instance, archaeologists elsewhere were amassing good evidence for correlations between environmental crisis and episodes of prehistoric warfare. Hence the case I was studying might speak to questions of broad interest beyond my regional specialty: for example, what caused warfare in general, and whether warfare was good for building states or not. These two larger questions furnished the theoretical "hook" for my project. The first I had used in proposal writing from the start, but the second I arrived at later, after analyzing and thinking about my data.

Working from the data we collected, and supported by this interpretive framework, I wound up with some interesting conclusions. First, the hillforts were late, with carbon dates mostly around or after AD 1300. So they were not an immediate response to the fall of Tiwanaku around AD 1000. Nor did they seem to be a very gradual development. On the other hand, they started too early and were too widespread to be a response to Inca aggression. I came to think they were somehow related to climate, particularly a very arid patch in the early LIP. (I originally believed that this drought directly spurred the onset of fortification (Arkush 2008). Now that more paleoclimate data has become available, I suspect the aridity of the early LIP inhibited dense permanent settlement until the middle of the LIP, but set the stage for societies emerging in the wake of this resource crisis to be bellicose in the extreme.) Second, the internal organization of hillforts echoed what researchers had found in other parts of the Andean highlands at this time: some settlements could be quite large, but they just did not look very hierarchical. Third, the large-scale regional pattern was "clumpy": a political landscape of clusters of hillforts sharing visual links and ceramic styles, which might have corresponded to confederations or alliance groups. In this region, warfare did not seem to have encouraged the building of states.

All this shed significant light on altiplano society. At least in retrospect, it did what a field project was supposed to do: it used appropriate methods to obtain data to answer an interesting research question, interesting because it investigated a broader process or theme through a particular case in a way that felt fresh. To be fair, the freshness was none of my own doing. As I was working on my doctorate, warfare and violence were becoming trendy topics in archaeology, and by luck I graduated at the crest of that wave. I was also something rather rare and piquant at the time, a woman studying warfare. My career had started.

This is all true, but is it the whole truth? There is a more complicated story about how I arrived at this project and its methodology, and how I arrived at a theoretical approach to warfare.

The Hillfort Project: Version Two

First, the project. I went to the Titicaca basin because I got into UCLA, and my advisor worked there. I planned, with his encouragement, to work on the Inca period. But then hillforts sucked me in. It was my own idea; no one else really wanted to study them. Why were they such a source of curiosity to me? Behind the research questions in grant proposals, what was my real question? It is hard to put my finger on this. It had to do with climbing a difficult hill step by step, gasping embarrassingly in the thin air, and getting to a place hardly anyone went anymore, a place where dozens of house foundations lay half-hidden in the long grass. (I can recognize this is an experience steeped in Romantic European notions of ruins and landscape, but I still find it wholly captivating.) It had to do with making maps: I had always been intrigued by city maps, atlases, and even the imaginary maps on the first page of a fantasy novel. I would stare at them, feeling that they held great knowledge if you could only unlock it. Then, there was the alluring sense of freedom and power that comes from looking down at the world from above, even in black-and-white photos viewed through a loupe in an ill-lit office. There was satisfaction, too, in constructing and solving clever puzzles in GIS (and impressing people of a less technical bent). All these things appealed to me on a visceral level. Finally, I was intrigued by war, so alien to my own life experience.

Practical considerations also shaped my methods. I hadn't done much digging, and felt unequal to the task of running an excavation as my dissertation project. But by climbing dozens of high-altitude hills, maybe I could earn enough macho credibility to outweigh that inadequacy and convince the world I was a bona fide archaeologist. And here is the big one: I had a serious boyfriend, who became my husband. Shortly after finishing my PhD I had a baby, too (and I don't mean the Trimble). Every day I spent in the field was a day away from home. I couldn't afford to mess around. I had to collect data with maximum efficiency, and I cut corners in the places where it didn't seem to matter much. How I envied the great male archaeologists of the 1940s, with their stalwart wives to do the child-rearing and labwork and painstaking, beautiful ceramic studies!

In a sense, then, my project was first a method. I needed to make my time in the field count. I was fascinated by hillforts, the more the better; each one was different and intriguing in its own way. I liked making site maps and playing around in GIS. I defined a project that would reasonably justify doing these things. The methodological cart came before the research question horse.

Theory and Interpretation: Under the Hood

What about the theoretical underpinnings? As I matured as a scholar, warfare was gaining the interest of archaeologists with very different perspectives. Among them were some who felt that pre-Columbian conflict in the Andes could not be compared productively to other world regions. Some of this I could discount as romanticized Andean essentialism, but not all – not the Amerind seminar I participated in, organized by Axel Nielsen and William Walker, and their resulting edited book, *Warfare in Cultural Context* (2009). Nielsen and Walker argued that warfare should be viewed as a culturally specific practice. Ripping cases out of their cultural context to try to place them in universal patterns was absurdly reductive. I liked these guys and could see they were very smart; their viewpoint had to be taken seriously. Were my ideas as well-founded as I assumed? Where did this theoretical position of mine come from, anyway?

Most obviously, it had come from my education at UCLA in a department where archaeologists of a certain stripe had shaped the intellectual culture, people like Lewis Binford, Jim Sackett, Jeanne Arnold, Tim Earle, and of course my advisor, Chip Stanish. Their examples implicitly defined the normal and acceptable ways of thinking, so that by the time I finished, it was as natural as breathing. Perhaps my views also owed something to my Midwestern upbringing: I was allergic to bullshit, and suspicious of postmodern pirouetting. My reliance on GIS also subtly reinforced a certain standpoint. GIS software does certain things well and not others. It is quantitative rather than qualitative. It deals well with "objective" environmental factors and constraints rather than subjective factors or "culture." It encourages the user to measure and optimize, using properties of the land. Using GIS nudged me towards some ways of thinking and away from others.

But there was something else going on. Warfare, particularly the warfare of indigenous non-Western people, is a tricky topic in anthropology. Discussions about it are strongly colored by their political implications. How do you approach past violence in a way that is both respectful and accurate, that neither sensationalizes nor trivializes it? By arguing that warfare was waged mainly for material and political ends, strongly shaped by resources and demography, and driven by the need to not lose, my perspective implicitly claimed warfare followed the same basic logic in any culture. That logic might be brutal, but it was universal. Westerners and non-Westerners and people everywhere were trying to cope in a difficult world of trade-offs; they were morally equivalent. This argument is one way through the intellectual minefield of indigenous warfare, one way to avoid racism and accomplish cultural relativism. Or is it?

In the new millennium, North American archaeology was increasingly shifting towards "pull" rather than "push" explanations, emphasizing agency and negotiation rather than conditions and pressures. Our vision of the past was subtly changing to one of relaxed constraints and flourishing human creativity – a sense of *options*. Fluidity, contingency, and possibility were reintroduced to old histories. From my office in my first tenure-track job at the University of Virginia, in a department where archaeologists engage closely with the perspectives of the cultural anthropologists, I could see the appeal of these ideas. Recognizing the agency of people in the past, especially non-Western people, felt like a way to restore some credit to them for their histories. From this angle, a theoretical approach concerned with grand patterns looked too mechanistic, reducing people and their life choices to unimportant pawns in a game whose outcome was already mostly determined from the start.

Indeed, perhaps there was something overdrawn about the hard-core processual literature on warfare, by Keeley and others of his ilk. This body of scholarship laid tremendously important groundwork by establishing that warfare really existed, early and often, in the deep past, and really affected peoples' lives. But by now, that refrain was starting to feel wearisome in its relentless emphasis on unforgiving environments and harsh choices. It seemed to imply that other concerns – leadership roles, gender, decisions about storage, mortuary treatment, social affiliations, and all the other things bound up with war – were peripheral, the "soft" stuff. This hawkish strain of scholarship, always written by men, was (to me at least) faintly reminiscent of small boys gleefully smashing action figures together in combat. By contrast, the new fashion of emphasizing the cultural meanings embedded in indigenous warfare sounded more, well, *tasteful.* Maybe that was a better way through the minefield.

Or maybe not. What did it mean to consider warfare something as varied and inexplicable as religion? Didn't that open the door to some old-fashioned notions of indigenous warfare as a primitive, picturesque, feather-waving sport – a footnote of history, eventually crushed by the juggernaut of battle-hardened Europeans who really knew their stuff? So claimed Victor Davis Hanson (2001), influential military historian of classical Greece and occasional advisor to George W. Bush. (Ivory-tower arguments about ancient war are not so removed from contemporary politics as you might think.) Hanson argued that a uniquely effective, culturally distinctive "Western way of war" had inevitably led to global Western domination. No: that way danger lies. Maybe there is no safe way through the minefield after all.

I kept worrying about how to think and talk about warfare, after most of my colleagues had moved on. I could see that, ethical and political considerations aside (while conceding they can never truly be put aside), there was empirical *truth* on both sides. Nielsen and Walker were right: warfare, like any other behavior, *is* enculturated. It is full of rituals of preparation for battle, white flags of surrender, triumphal marches, and even rules and conventions that actually diminish military effectiveness: counting coup (Mishkin 1940), marking off places of asylum (Kolb and Dixon 2002), or abiding by the Geneva Conventions. That said, these practices are cultural, but not "irrational." They have their uses, like showing off mettle in battle, emphasizing solidarity, intimidating enemies, proclaiming victorious leadership to an awed populace, and limiting the damage when neither side wishes to risk out-of-control casualties. And there was also something to the idea that warfare can only be understood as a historical development: it emerges from regionally specific histories of injury and amity, land-use and land-claims, affiliation and identity. That idea was high in my mind as I finished writing my book (2011), which ultimately couched the results of the project as a particular regional history, but also one with broader lessons about warfare and fortification.

I still believe that there are certain general patterns and principles to how warfare works. And I have come to think there is no contradiction here: the kind of explanation archaeologists emphasize has much to do with the nature of their data. Some archaeologists work on iconography and the sacrifice of captured warriors; others pay attention to the design of forts and weapons. Some are concerned with what happened in a community over a couple of generations, a scale commensurate with ethnographic studies and historical records. Others chart phases of more intense warfare and more peaceful interludes over a thousand years and over half a continent. At one scale, you see patterns; shift the lens and you see diversity and uniqueness. This makes ancient warfare more fascinating to me than ever.

Looking Back

Projects and their principal investigators (PIs) evolve in sometimes unexpected ways, responding to luck, difficulties, convenience, connections, and the shifting tide of an intellectual culture. The story told in grant proposals and job letters leaves this out: not just the happenstance and serendipity of any archaeological project or career, but also the funny, often unexamined ways we come to a topic that interests us, a set of methods that work and that suit us, and a theoretical standpoint where we feel comfortable. Over the course of this project, my research took a winding route. I tried to learn from early mistakes and be honest about what methods and questions the hillforts deserve. I pondered how to envision past violence, and how that affects my archaeological interpretation. This too sometimes felt like toiling uphill, but it has been very stimulating. Looking back, I think the parts of this project that worked best were motivated by genuine curiosity, an openness to new ideas and new technology, and a willingness to notice what wasn't working.

By now, we've figured out some important things about the people of the hillforts, though the questions have multiplied faster than the answers. I hope other researchers will tackle these wonderful sites with fresh ideas (and fresh legs). As for the question behind the question, the thing that first drew me to hillforts, I recognize by now that it can't be answered. It is an experience rather than a question – one I count myself extremely lucky to have had. It is to come to the top of a windswept hill, seeing the land open below like a vast map, and walk along a remnant fortification wall spanning the shoulder of the hill. It is to witness emerge on the page or the screen a village you can no longer see when you are standing in it. It is the sense of emptiness and distance, the palpable absence of the owners and dwellers, who are 500 years dead. It is to piece together maps and sherds and concepts into the constructions of paper that academics produce, hoping that in them I might capture impossibly foreign lives lived long ago in a hilltop stronghold. It is always getting it wrong, but a little less wrong than before.

Paired Reading

Arkush, Elizabeth. 2011. *Hillforts of the Ancient Andes: Colla Warfare, Society and Landscape.* Gainesville, FL: University Press of Florida.

References

Arkush, Elizabeth. 2008. "War, Chronology, and Causality in the Titicaca Basin." *Latin American Antiquity*, 19(4): 339–373. DOI: 10.1017/S1045663500004338.

Arkush, Elizabeth. 2011. *Hillforts of the Ancient Andes: Colla Warfare, Society and Landscape.* Gainesville, FL: University Press of Florida.

Hanson, Victor D. 2001. *Carnage and Culture: Landmark Battles in the Rise of Western Power.* New York: Doubleday.

Keeley, Lawrence H. 1996. *War Before Civilization.* New York: Oxford University Press.

Kolb, Michael and Boyd Dixon. 2002. "Landscapes of War: Rules and Conventions of Conflict in Ancient Hawai'i (and Elsewhere)". *American Antiquity*, 67(3): 514–534. DOI: 10.2307/1593824

Mishkin, Bernard. 1940. *Rank and Warfare Among the Plains Indians.* Seattle, WA: University of Washington Press.

Nielsen, Axel and William Walker. 2009. *Warfare in Cultural Context: Practice, Agency, and the Archaeology of Violence.* Tucson, AZ: University of Arizona Press.

3

Losing Control in the American Southwest: Collaborative Archaeology in the Service of Descendant Communities

Matthew Liebmann

Project Summary

This chapter details a collaborative research project initiated at the request of a Native American tribe (Jemez Pueblo) in the Southwest United States, conducted over the course of three field seasons from 2010–2012. The tribe was interested in documenting their ancestral ties to the Valles Caldera National Preserve, a place of sacred importance. However, this landscape is largely devoid of artifacts harboring a clear ethnic signature. Our solution to this conundrum was to conduct a study of obsidian artifacts found in association with ancestral Jemez Pueblo villages dating to AD 1200–1700. We used a methodology of surface collection and x-ray fluorescence to establish links between the archaeological record and this sacred landscape. This research serves as an example of one of the primary challenges facing archaeologists engaged in collaboration with descendant communities: giving up control over the research process. If we view this loss of control not as an obstacle but as an opportunity, archaeology stands to benefit from collaboration in ways we cannot yet imagine.

Introduction: The Meeting

I gnawed my lower lip as I closed my laptop. It was the summer of 2009, and I'd just received an email from the tribal administrator at Jemez Pueblo in northern New Mexico requesting my presence at a meeting of the Jemez Cultural Resource Advisory Committee (CRAC) the following evening. The message didn't mention what would be on the agenda. I was simply instructed to show up at the Tribal Administration building at six o'clock the next night. I had been conducting archaeological research in collaboration with the tribe for nearly ten years, but I knew that there were good reasons to be nervous. Jemez Pueblo has earned its reputation as one of the most staunchly conservative and traditional tribes in the American Southwest. CRAC meetings are conducted largely in their native language of Towa, a tongue spoken exclusively by members of the Jemez Pueblo tribe. Moreover, their community often eschews contacts with outsiders, who are banned from attending many traditional rites and from residing within the Pueblo. This reticence to allow outsiders access to their community extends particularly to academics from big fancy universities back East. I had heard stories of *bilagáanush* [white people] banned from the Pueblo entirely after writing books about Jemez culture and history. Anthropologist Elsie Clews Parsons was threatened with bodily harm if she ever returned to Jemez after publishing her ethnographic study of the Pueblo in 1925. More recently, a Franciscan

Engaging Archaeology: 25 Case Studies in Research Practice, First Edition. Edited by Stephen W. Silliman.

priest working on his PhD ran into trouble in the 1980s. When tribal leadership discovered that he had been transcribing their language (a taboo at Jemez, where the study of the Towa language by non-Natives is strictly proscribed), they carried his bags to the reservation border and asked him not to return. Now I worried that a similar fate was in store for me. I had just signed a contract for the publication of my first book, based on my PhD dissertation and a decade of research about ancestral Jemez archaeology (Liebmann 2012). While I collaborated with Jemez people on this research, I feared that some tribal members might have become offended at the idea of this publication.

The next day I trudged to the Tribal Administration building. I entered the conference room – a fluorescent-lit chamber with a large U-shaped table surrounded by office chairs. Around the table sat six of the Pueblo's religious leaders, drinking Diet Cokes, eating corn tamales, and cracking jokes in their native language. I sat down and joined in the joking as much as I could, using the few Towa words I knew (mostly dirty ones). But inside, my stomach churned as I waited for the meeting to begin. Around 6:15 one of the tribal officials spoke softly in English, saying "Well I guess we can get started. Will the war captain please lead us in prayer?" When the prayer finished, I tensed in anticipation of what would come next.

As it turned out, they hadn't asked me there to excoriate me or to tell me that I couldn't publish my book. I exhaled as the nervous storm in my belly subsided. Much to my relief, it turned out that the CRAC had asked me to the meeting to hear a request. The Pueblo was interested in documenting their tribal history, and they wanted me to collaborate on a new archaeological research project. Would I be willing, they wondered, to investigate their ancestors' use of an important locale that had recently been transferred into federal ownership?

The prospect of this new collaboration electrified me. I had been working in the Southwest United States for more than a decade, lured there initially because of my PhD advisor's interests. But I quickly became entranced by the Jemez culture and the rugged beauty of their homelands. For years I had hoped that my archaeological research might prove useful to the tribe. Now they were asking me to apply my expertise to pressing, real-life concerns. This work would be relevant to tribal members in the present day, not just to academic debates inside the ivory tower. While my previous investigations as part of my dissertation research on ancestral Jemez archaeology had been collaborative, the agenda for that project had followed my own academic interests. But this research would be different. It would be driven by the interests of the tribe.

The project that the CRAC had in mind was an investigation of their ancestors' relationship with the remains of a dormant volcano known today as the Valles Caldera. To the Jemez this place is better known as *Wavema* (sometimes translated as "the father of all northern mountains"). For hundreds of years, the crater has served as the focal point of Jemez religious life. When the US government purchased Wavema from private landowners in the year 2000, federal land managers encouraged the tribe to provide information that could aid in culturally appropriate methods of preservation and management. As part of this effort the CRAC wanted to document ancestral Jemez interactions with this place using the tools of archaeology. I enthusiastically accepted their invitation, and we dubbed our collaboration the Wavema Archaeological Research Project (WARP).

Just one problem loomed on the horizon: I had no idea how to accomplish this research.

I had never conducted investigations in the Valles Caldera myself. The little I knew about this place included the fact that there isn't much visible archaeology there. No Pueblo villages, no middens full of ceramics, and nothing that I knew of that would address the CRAC's research agenda. Its material assemblage is sparse, with one major exception: lithics. The Valles Caldera is home to some of the most abundant sources of artifact-quality obsidian in the Southwest. Yet, I had never before worked with lithics. My previous research focused on architecture, ceramics, and rock art – not on projectile points, scrapers, and debitage. I was stumped about how we could even begin to address the CRAC's question about ancestral Jemez use. After all, flakes of obsidian don't normally lend themselves to the sorts of fine-grained study of ethnic identity needed to address our research questions. I left the meeting at the Tribal Administration building that night the same way I had entered: gnawing on my lip. What had I gotten myself into?

I didn't know it then, but by agreeing to collaborate on the WARP I had taken the first step in one of my most satisfying and important experiences as a professional archaeologist. At the time I was worried about how I would bring my knowledge to bear on the problem, but what I didn't realize was the fact that my willingness to investigate new questions and learn new things was far more valuable than my previous expertise. Saying yes to this collaboration forced me to put aside my own agenda and commit myself to that of the tribe. By dedicating myself to research serving the needs of others, I had opened the door to worlds of knowledge that I never would have known existed – and forced myself to learn things that I never would have dared to learn on my own.

The Setting: The Valles Caldera/Wavema

Located about 32 kilometers (20 miles) north of Jemez Pueblo (Figure 3.1), the Valles Caldera is a landscape of breathtaking and incomparable beauty, a verdant oasis in the midst of the dry northern New Mexican deserts. The volcano's crater forms a vast basin of grass-covered meadows, termed *valles* by the Spaniards who stumbled into this region in the sixteenth century AD, interlaced by clear mountain streams. The emerald hues of the caldera contrast with the desiccated tans and reds of the mesas that form the volcano's flanks. Ringing the edge of the volcanic bowl are high mountain ridges bristling with Ponderosa pines. Beneath this prairie a fitful geothermal world simmers and steams, spilling out into hot springs that mist the surrounding hills on cool mornings. In order to preserve the unique geology, ecological diversity, and cultural importance of this landscape the federal government purchased 89,000 acres in 2000, naming the area the Valles Caldera National Preserve (VCNP). Fifteen years later that property became part of the National Parks system.

For centuries the Jemez have utilized Wavema to sustain their unique way of life. Within the caldera the Jemez hunt, collect plants and herbs, gather minerals, pasture livestock, and perform some of their most important ceremonial and spiritual activities, including prayer, pilgrimages, retreats, and ritual initiations. Given the astonishing beauty of the Valles Caldera it is no wonder that the Jemez hold this place in particular esteem. Their primary shrine – a stone structure where tribal members communicate with the spirit world – adorns the top of Redondo Peak, the highest summit in the caldera (Sando 1982: 11). The importance of this place is rooted deep in Jemez history, stretching back to their ancestral migration into northern New Mexico more than 700 years ago.

In the Jemez worldview Wavema is the source of all life and the heart of Jemez culture, the place from which vital forces emerge and flow. Wavema provides life to newborns and a place for spirits to return after shedding their earthly skins (Parsons 1925: 125). As one contemporary tribal member noted, "Wavema is Jemez heaven. That's the place where the ancestors live." Its Judeo-Christian equivalent would be something like the Garden of Eden and Heaven all rolled into one: the place where life began, from which life springs forth today, and to which the spirits of the deceased eventually return.

The Jemez people revere Wavema because it is home to spirits, ancestors, and supernatural creatures. These beings interact directly with people through a relationship of mutual cooperation, and humans can access them directly at various "portal" locations in the landscape. For the Jemez, many of these portals are located at springs that well up out of the ground. Spirit

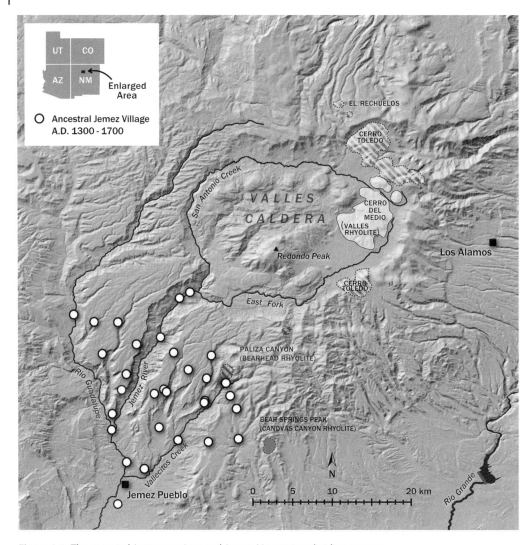

Figure 3.1 The ancestral Jemez province and Jemez Mountains obsidian sources.

beings dwell on Wavema's mountain peaks as well. These summits provide homes to the *katsinas* (masked spirit beings) and *dyasa* (cloud or rain people), creatures associated with moisture and precipitation in all forms: rain, snow, fog, mist, and clouds.

One of the singular resources of Wavema draws particular attention from archaeologists: superior-quality obsidian. In the northeast quadrant of the caldera a literal mountain of obsidian rises up from the grassy plain. Known to the Jemez as *Gee way kia shin* (Shining Rock Hill), and as Cerro del Medio to the non-Pueblo world, its sheer bulk makes this the largest obsidian source by volume in the Southwest United States (Shackley 2005: 72). Today as in the past, Jemez people seek stone from Shining Rock Hill specifically for use in prayer and religious ceremonies because obsidian carries special meanings for Pueblo people. Traditional Pueblo belief holds that obsidian "is formed by lightning striking the ground" (Ford 1992: 122). Lightning, in turn, is believed to endow the land with fertility. Through this link to lightning, Jemez people associate obsidian with fertility, rainfall, and the life-giving powers of Wavema.

Finding the Right Data

When we began to plan our research for the WARP, it quickly became clear that the biggest obstacle was the sparse nature of Wavema's archaeological remains. Compared with the kinds of sites I had investigated in my previous research – large, stone-masonry Pueblo villages with clearly visible middens chock-full of ceramics – the archaeological record within the Valles Caldera could charitably be described as lacking in diversity. With a narrow assemblage consisting primarily of obsidian debitage, hammerstones, and chipped stone tools, the artifacts thinly scattered throughout this landscape lack a clear ethnic signature. Determining who exactly left these lithics on the mountain slopes and grassy meadows of Wavema is difficult, if not irresolvable. Furthermore, ancestral Pueblo farmers did not build any of their characteristic plaza-oriented, stone-masonry pueblos within Wavema's confines. Instead they chose to inhabit lower elevations where their crops could flourish.

Instead of looking for traces of the Jemez at the VCNP we decided we would look for traces of the Valles Caldera where the Jemez lived. This meant we would have to search outside of Wavema's grassy bowl. Luckily for us, between AD 1200–1700 the Jemez constructed more than 35 large villages of 50 rooms or more and thousands of small, one- to four-room field-houses on the mesas that flank the dormant volcano. When the first Europeans entered this region in 1541, they wrote that the occupants spoke a common language (Towa) and identified themselves as ethnically "Hemes," which the Spaniards later transliterated as *Jemez*. The region's inhabitants also shared a penchant for the same characteristic pottery, favoring black matte-paint designs applied over a chalky, oyster-white slip. Known as Jemez Black-on-white, this distinctive style dominates the ceramic assemblages of archaeological sites throughout the region. By focusing WARP investigations on these sites we were confident that the evidence we would collect had been produced by ancestral Jemez people, and not the ancestors of one of the other 18 Pueblo tribes in the state of New Mexico. The middens at Jemez pueblos brim not only with Jemez Black-on-white pottery, but also with lithic debitage. Chipped black obsidian is scattered on the ground at these sites like glassy leopards' spots. This obsidian forms the link we needed to trace ancestral Jemez use of Wavema.

Five primary sources of obsidian issue from the peaks and domes surrounding the Valles Caldera. All five of these obsidian sources exhibit unique trace element compositions, which can be differentiated using x-ray fluorescence (XRF) spectrometry. The elemental makeup of obsidian artifacts acts like a fingerprint, revealing the location from which that obsidian was originally mined. The idea for the WARP study was deceptively simple: collect obsidian from ancestral Jemez sites and perform XRF analysis on this obsidian to ascertain its original location. By determining how much of the obsidian came from Valles Caldera sources, we could establish links between the people who lived at those villages and Wavema itself.

Not all of the obsidian artifacts in our study proved useful for determining ancestral Jemez interactions with the Valles Caldera, however. Deposits from four of the five local sources erode into adjacent river drainages, resulting in what geologists call "secondary deposits." These secondary deposits mean that flintknappers in the past could have harvested this type of obsidian at a variety of locations throughout central New Mexico. In fact, nodules from some of these sources have been discovered in river gravels as far away as Chihuahua, Mexico – more than 540 km (340 miles) to the south. Finding obsidian from sources with these secondary deposits thus offers no conclusive evidence regarding flintknappers' interactions with the Valles Caldera in the past, as they could have collected that obsidian from many different locations.

However, the fifth of these sources is the Cerro del Medio source, and that source tells a different story. Unlike the aforementioned four other sources in this region, Cerro del Medio obsidian does not erode into any of the surrounding canyons and river valleys. In order to obtain Cerro del Medio obsidian, someone had to journey directly into the Valles Caldera to procure it. They couldn't pick up a nodule mixed in with the river gravels of the Rio Grande or one of its tributaries. This unique quality establishes a direct link between artifacts made of Cerro del Medio obsidian, the sites where those artifacts are found, and Wavema itself. It allowed the WARP project to use the Cerro del Medio obsidian found at ancestral Jemez pueblos as a proxy for the inhabitants' interactions with the Valles Caldera.

Methods

The first step in our study involved the collection of obsidian. I began by gathering four assistants, members of the tribe in their late teens and early 20s, and we set off to visit 30 ancestral Jemez archaeological sites over the course of two field seasons in the summers of 2010 and 2011. This group of 30 sites included nearly all the large Jemez pueblos with occupations spanning AD 1200–1700. Fortunately, these sites generally exhibit a high degree of artifact visibility, so we were able to collect samples directly from the surface (within midden contexts) at each village, avoiding the need to excavate. The tribe preferred this non-invasive strategy because it ensured that we would not disturb any burials. Surface collection also allowed us to sample a larger number of sites than we would have been able using invasive techniques, because excavation is both costly and slow-going by necessity.

After collecting an average of 75 obsidian flakes at each site, we analyzed a total of 2,222 artifacts from 30 Jemez sites using a portable XRF spectrometer, colloquially known as an XRF gun, or simply pXRF. We received training in how to use this instrument from the manufacturer, the Bruker Corporation. Sample sizes ranged from 15 to 170 artifacts per site, with lower numbers collected at sites with limited surface visibility, usually due to a thick carpet of pine needles covering the ground. Our sample included unmodified primary and secondary obsidian flakes, debitage, and lithic shatter. We deliberately selected artifacts from the early stages of production (rather than finished projectile points, scrapers, or knives) to better represent patterns of acquisition. In other words, we looked for obsidian that showed signs of being knapped at that location, rather than finished artifacts. Knives and arrowheads are more likely than debitage to have traveled from the place they were originally produced, either through trade or movement during their use-life. While it is theoretically possible that "raw," unworked obsidian could have made its way to these villages through exchange, the proximity of these sites to the Valles Caldera sources negates the likelihood of down-the line trade. In short, the presence of Cerro del Medio obsidian at these sites suggests that at some point in the formation of these artifacts, a Jemez person had to venture into the Valles Caldera in order to quarry obsidian at *Gee way kia shin*/Cerro del Medio.

Results

After subjecting all 2,222 individual artifacts to XRF analysis, we discovered that Cerro del Medio obsidian was the most common of the five local sources of obsidian utilized by ancestral Jemez villagers. Jemez flintknappers made more artifacts out of Cerro del Medio obsidian (n = 1173) than from obsidian derived from all other sources combined. In total, 52.8% of the artifacts analyzed were made of obsidian derived from Cerro del Medio. In addition, when we compared the assemblages from these 30 sites to one another, Cerro del Medio obsidian emerged as uniquely ubiquitous. It is the only quarry among the five local sources appearing in the lithic assemblage of each and every site we sampled. Each of the four other local sources appeared at some of the 30 sites we sampled, but not others.

The use of the Cerro del Medio quarry by ancestral Jemez people clearly varied through the centuries, however. If we break down the WARP sample chronologically we can see distinct temporal trends, with obsidian acquisition increasing dramatically from the 1200s through the 1600s (i.e., the pre-Colonial period). At pueblos settled during the first three centuries of this era, Cerro del Medio obsidian accounts for just under a third (29.2%) of the assemblage, but the middens at sites occupied after 1500 are bursting with more than twice as much obsidian from Wavema (72%). While much of this increase has to do with the proximity of these early sites to closer, alternative sources, this intensification nonetheless demonstrates a surge in the use of the Valles Caldera landscape by Jemez people through the first four centuries of settlement.

The abundance of Cerro del Medio obsidian at ancestral Jemez pueblos attests to the extensive ties between the residents of these villages and Wavema. Its presence and quantity indicates that ancestral Jemez people made frequent trips into the Valles Caldera landscape, procuring Cerro del Medio obsidian along the way. Jemez interactions with Wavema began shortly after their migration into the region around 1200. As time passed the Jemez utilized the Cerro del Medio obsidian quarry with increasing frequency and intensity, peaking in the sixteenth century. This upward trend of Cerro del Medio exploitation suggests that ancestral Jemez familiarity with this landscape grew during pre-Colonial times.

In a few cases, villages we sampled are located closer to an alternative source of artifact-quality obsidian, yet their residents still preferred Cerro del Medio obsidian in greater quantities. Yet all of these sources provide excellent flintknapping material. Why would the people at these villages choose to journey *farther* to obtain obsidian from Cerro del Medio, rather than simply going to their neighborhood obsidian source nearby?

One possibility is that obsidian obtained from within Wavema retained special meanings – possibly tied to the associations of life, fertility, and power with the Valles Caldera landscape. Another possibility is that this obsidian was collected opportunistically, while Jemez people were in the Valles Caldera tending to other tasks such as retreats, pilgrimages, and hunting expeditions. In either scenario the presence of Cerro del Medio obsidian suggests the special meanings that the Valles Caldera landscape held for the site residents.

Reflections and Lessons Learned

The results of the WARP analysis clearly demonstrate that ancestral Jemez people used the Valles Caldera landscape routinely and continually over the course of 400 years. Furthermore, the intensity of their use of Wavema increased through time, at least until access was curtailed first by Spanish colonialism and later by private landowners in the eighteenth, nineteenth, and twentieth centuries. Our study shows that not only was Wavema important to Jemez people between AD 1200–1700, but that Cerro del Medio was *the most* important source of obsidian for four centuries.

Looking back on the WARP, I'm pleased with the results. Luck and geography were on our side, and we were fortunate that Cerro del Medio obsidian has the unique quality of not being distributed in secondary contexts. Then, too, we were lucky to stumble onto this question in 2009, when the techniques of XRF had become relatively affordable and well-established. In the end, the ability to link a well-defined research question with a robust dataset through the use of an appropriate methodology produced satisfying results. Theory didn't play a significant role in our research design, in part because the results of this project needed to be understood by non-anthropologists and non-archaeologists and came from a community's directive. Of course, we were challenged by the sparse archaeological record of the Valles Caldera and had to re-focus research to the adjacent villages when it became apparent that we could not identify a clear ethnic signature among the artifacts scattered about Wavema. While some archaeologists might view not being able to excavate as a limitation, the use of non-invasive surface collection was a boon to our project, allowing just five of us to sample a far greater number of sites over the course of two field seasons than would have been possible using standard sub-surface techniques. But again, we are lucky to work in contexts with superlative surface visibility and easily dated surface contexts thanks to well-studied local ceramic styles.

More importantly, my tribal collaborators at Jemez are understandably thrilled with the results. To them, the science we employed in the WARP reaffirmed what they already knew – namely, that Wavema has always been an important sacred place to the Jemez people. While many constituencies might find such an outcome maddening (if archaeology only tells us what we already know, why spend the time and money to do it?), to the Jemez this was exactly what they sought. The WARP provided another link between the tribe and Wavema, the kind of scientific evidence recognized in a court of law and among professional archaeologists. Ultimately, the Pueblo hopes that the WARP data will help them to reassert their ownership over Wavema. Whether or not the Jemez will get their day in court – and whether or not the WARP data will play a role in the proceedings – remains to be seen. At the end of the day, however, the research we conducted stands on its own, as sound science testifying to the enduring relationship between the Jemez people and Wavema.

For me personally, the greatest lesson I learned was the importance of leaving yourself open to new research questions. Had I walked into the meeting at the Jemez Tribal Administration building with a preconceived agenda about what my next research project should be, I would have missed out on multiple opportunities: the opportunity to serve those who had aided me in my previous research; the opportunity to learn about entire areas of archaeological investigation and techniques that I knew nothing about; the opportunity to make my archaeological interests relevant outside of academia. One of the primary challenges facing archaeologists who endeavor to engage in collaborative research is giving up control over the research process. However, if we can allow ourselves to conceive of this loss of control not as an obstacle but as an opportunity, we stand to benefit in numerous ways. Ultimately, giving up control forces us to open ourselves to the investigation of new questions, producing archaeology that is less partial, more balanced, and more innovative.

Paired Reading

Liebmann, Matthew. 2017. "From Landscapes of Meaning to Landscapes of Signification in the American Southwest." *American Antiquity*, 82(4): 642–661. DOI: 10.1017/aaq.2017.39.

References

Ford, Richard I. 1992. *An Ecological Analysis: Involving the Population of San Juan Pueblo, New Mexico*. New York: Garland Publishing.

Liebmann, Matthew. 2012. *Revolt: An Archaeological History of Pueblo Resistance and Revitalization in Seventeenth Century New Mexico*. Tuscon, AZ: University of Arizona Press.

Liebmann, Matthew. 2017. "From Landscapes of Meaning to Landscapes of Signification in the American Southwest." *American Antiquity*, 82(4): 642–661. DOI: 10.1017/aaq.2017.39.

Parsons, Elsie. 1925. *The Pueblo of Jemez*. Papers of the Southwestern Expedition Number 3. Phillips Academy, Andover, MA: AMS Press.

Sando, Joe S. 1982. *Nee Hemish: A History of Jemez Pueblo*. Albuquerque, NM: University of New Mexico Press.

Shackley, M Steven. 2005. *Obsidian: Geology and Archaeology in the North American Southwest*. Tucson, AZ: University of Arizona Press.

4

Getting It Wrong for All the Right Reasons: Developing an Approach to Systematic Settlement Survey for Viking Age Iceland

John M. Steinberg, Douglas J. Bolender, and Brian N. Damiata

Project Summary

This chapter describes the history of the Skagafjörður Archaeological Settlement Survey (SASS) and how we were able to systematically investigate a small part of a valley in North Iceland. With the help of several grants from the National Science Foundation (NSF), we sought to understand the initial Viking Age colonization of the region and the subsequent development of the medieval manorial state by combining systematic regional archaeological survey and small-scale excavations to produce comparable data from collections of adjacent farmsteads. Good archaeology depends on setting up a project that allows for the rejection of assumptions and the revising of methodology – but we had no idea that the successful survey would require such profound rejection and revising. We are now delighted that our assumptions were so easily refuted because that refutation helped us to adjust our methods to work at the proper scale. The ugly truth is that so much of archaeology advances in that backward way – where being wrong is a critical step in getting it right.

The Idea: The Easy Part

Two of us, John Steinberg and Douglas Bolender, had worked together on a Bronze Age archaeological project in northwest Denmark in the 1990s and were interested in the sources of political power in pre-industrial, hierarchical, family-based polities. These intermediate societies between simple family bands and complex states are sometimes called chiefdoms by anthropologists. Two of our mentors had spirited discussions about the nature of productivity in these chiefly societies. Specifically, they argued over whether elite leaders added to the productivity of a society (Earle 1991) or whether a rich and powerful class could emerge by simply taking resources (Gilman 1981).

Iceland presented an intriguing place to explore these issues. For about 400 years after it was first settled in the ninth century AD, the politics seemed to reflect a stable chiefdom, one of the last in the European sphere. Also, previous research suggested that the settlement of Iceland had resulted in widespread environmental degradation and that political consolidation could have happened while overall productivity went into decline. How was the chiefdom instituted by the newly arrived settlers, how did it survive for so long, and how was it consolidated into a medieval manorial state? Even at the beginning of our project, it struck us that we were asking very basic questions. Looking back, we realize that this was one of the real strengths of the

Engaging Archaeology: 25 Case Studies in Research Practice, First Edition. Edited by Stephen W. Silliman.
© 2018 John Wiley & Sons, Inc. Published 2018 by John Wiley & Sons, Inc.

project: we were trying to answer questions that could be asked in an undergraduate introductory anthropology course.

To answer these questions, we knew we had to do a settlement pattern study. Gordon Willey (1953) defined settlement patterns studies, saying they provided a "strategic starting point for the functional interpretation of archaeological cultures," and in previously uninhabited Iceland, we thought it not only a starting point, but perhaps a final goal. Fundamental to anthropological archaeology is the idea that increases in site size and site complexity (and in some cases the appearance of specialized administrative, religious, trade, and production centers) are a proxy for increasing economic and political power (e.g., Flannery 1972). A settlement pattern study, chronicling the location, size, establishment date, and complexity of households and farmsteads, would help us answer our basic questions about these Viking Age and medieval societies.

The basic outline of Icelandic history comes from the sagas, a body of literature written in the thirteenth century that describes the Viking Age settlement of the island and the succeeding developments. These texts depict a massive migration to this North Atlantic island over about 50 years, primarily of Norwegians. The sources explain how many of the earliest settlers, who had claimed or taken large areas, gave or sold partitions of their land to their children, later settlers, or individuals who were part of their settlement entourage, which included workers, relatives, and slaves. In AD 900, a general assembly (Alþing) was established by the chiefs to set law and resolve disputes. The resulting society, called the Commonwealth, lasted for over 300 years. In addition, in about AD 1000 at the Alþing, Icelanders decided to abandon their Norse religious practices and adopt Christianity. At the time there were no church institutions, but by AD 1096 a tithe was introduced and soon thereafter Christianity was fully institutionalized.

Commonwealth Iceland was comprised of independent landowning farmers with an underclass of enslaved household workers and a chiefly elite who vied for control over the districts where they lived. By the thirteenth century Icelandic society was developing institutionalized inequalities between manorial landlords who owned multiple farmsteads and tenant farmers. While the family sagas single out some farmers and chieftains as wealthy and powerful, what that wealth or power was, where it came from, and how it was maintained are not clear from the texts. Even less clear are the factors that gave rise to the church and other large landowners who ended up controlling so much of the society. This led us to settle on two goals: define the timing of the rise of inequality and identify the factors that caused it. Thus, before we even put a shovel into the ground, we knew what we wanted to know. This is perhaps the only aspect of the project that has not changed since its inception.

The Data: The Hard Part

While the theoretical question of chiefdoms and the methodological approach of a settlement pattern study were straightforward, the actual necessary datasets proved more difficult to obtain, especially the main one of systematically identifying Viking Age farmsteads. The two material mainstays of archaeological survey and hence site identification, ceramics and lithics, are largely absent from Viking Age material culture which otherwise consisted primarily of wood, textiles, and metals. In fact, surviving artifacts of any kind are relatively rare in Icelandic archaeology.

The farmsteads themselves were also unusual. Icelanders constructed their buildings with a driftwood frame surrounded by substantial turf walls, sometimes with a dry-laid stone foundation. Turf is the root mass cut from the upper portion of a bog, and once dried, it becomes a light, flexible, and durable building material with good insulating properties. Viking Age farmsteads were dispersed throughout the inhabitable areas of Iceland, and until the modern era the island had no urbanization. These farms consisted of a central concentration of turf structures, the immediately surrounding infields, outfields, and pastures. In the pre-modern era, as probably in the Viking Age, hay served as the main crop to fodder animals through the winter. While most farms appear to have engaged in basic subsistence activities, we were also interested in identifying signs of economic specialization in products such as metals, charcoal, cereals, fishing, or even specific animal husbandry strategies (e.g., dairying, meat, wool) outlined in McGovern's (e.g., 1990) work.

The problems and possibilities of conducting a systematic settlement survey in Iceland had been outlined by Smith and Parsons (1989). In addition to the absence of surface artifacts, these problems included a settlement pattern made up solely of small and dispersed farmsteads and extensive land modification due to erosion, landslides, flooding, and modern land leveling. On the other hand, if sites could be systematically identified, a relatively complete household pattern could be reconstructed, as could the changing hierarchies over time and the history of individual farms from initial settlement to today. Perhaps most beneficial to archaeological investigation is the presence of multiple volcanic ash or tephra layers in the soil that result from Iceland's active volcanoes. These can be traced to specific eruptive events and provide fine-grained stratigraphic markers to date and phase sites across the landscape. With these parameters in mind, Smith and Parson's work became our roadmap. As they suggested, we needed to combine regional and site-specific archaeology, but first, we needed to know if sites from the Viking Age in a given region were still preserved and if we could find them all. We needed an archaeological methodology to find settlements and identify the various activities that went on at them.

Our work in Iceland began with an opportunity to collaborate with Jesse Byock, a historian and saga specialist. Byock wanted to expand his research on the Viking Age and was interested in collaborating with archaeologists. Byock wanted to better understand the sagas, and we wanted to know if it was possible to overcome the problems outlined above and take advantage of the benefits of the archaeological record in Iceland. In 1998, the same two of us joined Byock in Iceland, with Steinberg embarking on a major post-PhD project and Bolender in the early stages of his own dissertation project at Northwestern University. After some initial experimentation, and some long conversations with archaeologists working in Iceland, we realized that not just alluvial processes were changing the landscape, but also widespread aeolian (wind-based) erosion and deposition had completely denuded some highland areas and had blanketed lower fertile areas with substantial sediment. The resulting landscape has notably uneven conditions of archaeological preservation and surface visibility: abandoned farms in marginal regions were likely to be visible on the surface, but well-preserved farms were likely to be deeply buried under aeolian deposition, later occupations, or leveled modern fields. Previous surveys had taken advantage of these conditions to focus on patterns of highland abandonment, but the Viking Age settlement pattern in the most productive lowland areas was largely unknown.

We settled on two methods to achieve our site-detection goals: geophysical survey and a program of extensive coring and soil sampling for phosphate analysis. Both methods had been used in other parts of the world, but neither had been systematically applied in Iceland. Soil sampling had been used effectively to discover medieval villages in Scandinavia. We figured it should work in Iceland too. In our plan, once we identified areas of old settlement we would follow up with geophysical survey to identify different structures and activity areas. This basic two-pronged strategy would also allow us to collect crucial negative evidence so that we could say where settlements were and were not located.

In 1999, we applied for a "High Risk" NSF grant to find out if we could do a settlement pattern study using these two methods of coring and geophysics to identify sites from the Viking Age. It was granted, but when we took cores and ran the phosphate tests and when we processed the magnetometer and ground conductivity readings and began test trenching, the results looked grim. Most of the excavations revealed unremarkable soil sequences or natural features like rocks from landslides. We did find areas with high soil phosphates, but these appeared to be associated with manured agricultural fields rather than farmstead architecture. We thought NSF was going to ask for their money back. However, in one of the excavation trenches, we had bisected a small charcoal pit overlain by an AD 1500 black tephra layer. We needed to find, date, and qualify or quantify the nature of multiple sites, and that one pit demonstrated that we, in fact, had the basic tools to do it. We were thrilled.

The Grant: The Best One Might Be a Rejected One

So, in 2000, we applied for a standard NSF grant based on what we had accomplished in 1999. We proposed a three-year study of the entire Mosfell Valley in western Iceland not far from Reykjavík using ground conductivity and phosphate testing. Small excavations, based on the geophysical and phosphate results, would then allow us to look at the economic activities at each of the discovered farms to understand if there was any specialization and if so, how much and what kind. From that, we would then figure out how the chiefdom became territorial and how inequality developed. The grant was rejected, and the reviews were brutal.

Interspersed with the problems that the reviewers rightly identified, we found a new roadmap. We had made a classic mistake, and the reviewers pointed it out starkly: we were trying to adjust our methods for a settlement survey to fit the Mosfell Valley and what it had to offer. That is, they found our questions and methods satisfactory, or at least on the right track for the general problems of Icelandic archaeology and questions about social evolution, but the location was wrong. Mosfell potentially had chiefly residences, used an important nearby harbor, and served as a gateway to the Alþing, and we thought it a perfect area to study the nature of chiefly society. But, as the reviewers pointed out, Mosfell did not have any of the amazing volcanic tephra layers between AD 871 and 1225, the time period we were most interested in. The reviewers recognized that volcanic tephra layers are the key to making a settlement pattern survey work. Why work in Iceland if you are not going to take advantage of the tephra layers that can blanket large regions, the reviewers rightly asked? Where else can you date a landscape and the associated settlement pattern with such precision? If we wanted to do the project we envisioned, we were going to have to find a location with a better tephra sequence.

In the summer of 2000, we set out to find the perfect region, where the tephra was just right and the archaeological preservation good. We traveled across Iceland, volunteering on as many projects as we could, attempting to figure out how to answer the NSF reviewers' critiques. The south of Iceland had too many tephra layers, the west too few, which left the east and the north. An Icelandic archaeologist we were working with, Guðmundur Ólafsson, suggested that we explore the region of Skagafjörður in the north of Iceland.

Skagafjörður is a large and productive region. It was one of the centers of early power consolidation in Iceland. It contained one of Iceland's two bishoprics, which was also one of the largest medieval manors. It also has a good sequence of early tephra layers. Interestingly, Skagafjörður is rarely mentioned in the Icelandic family sagas – apparently no family feuds or other events inspired lengthy descriptions of the people and places in the region – but it is the area where the family who returned from the Vinland colony in North America came to after their voyages and suggested that it might have been connected to international trading networks in the Viking Age. Furthermore, Skagafjörður was extensively described in a later series of stories, called the Sturlunga sagas, which detail the accumulation of power in a number of chiefly families in the twelfth and thirteenth centuries and provided us with a historical description of the political system for the end of our archaeological study period. We had found a place that suited our methods and questions.

The reviewers also recognized that the refinements necessary to make a survey based on geophysical methods work were not minor. We needed a genuine geophysicist, not just an archaeologist walking back and forth with various instruments, to develop and test methods that could be applied in Iceland and beyond. We needed to be more collaborative. Brian Damiata, a geophysicist with interests in how to apply geophysics to archaeological problems, agreed to join the project. While his primary interest was Classical and Hellenistic Greece, Viking Age Iceland presented problems and possibilities that made the work intriguing and worth the adventure in much colder climes.

The Scale: Right Methods, Wrong Organization

With Brian Damiata on board, we re-applied to NSF for a survey project based in Skagafjörður. This time we were successful. Skagafjörður is a huge region, far too large to be systematically surveyed in its entirety. We needed a representative sampling strategy, and we took our best guess at what might work. According to the *Book of Settlements* (Pálsson and Edwards 1972), Skagafjörður was initially claimed by 22 named individuals. These claims were very large and consisted of a wide variety of landscapes and environmental situations: coastal, inland, lowland, highland, and riverine. In historical times, those 22 claims had been divided into approximately 400 farms. In an attempt to assess this huge region, we adopted a stratified sampling approach. We proposed to investigate five farms each in five different distinct environmental areas for a total of 25 farms. We thought that this approach would tell us about specialization and regional variation: were highland areas settled before or after lowland ones, and did riverine and coastal areas make different investments in their fields? While reasonable on paper, the stratified sampling strategy failed in the field for three clear reasons.

First, the five areas had dramatically different levels of archaeological preservation and, more specifically, tephra preservation. It quickly became clear that differences in preservation would dominate any inter-area analysis and would complicate a comparison of site chronologies among regions. Second, five farms in a given area provided too small of a sample. We detected substantial differences in farmstead sizes, but these differences were found in all regions. There were big and small farms everywhere. In other words, site variability within regions was greater than the variability among regions, and five farms were simply too few to compare regional settlement pattern hierarchies. Our choice of the farms to sample in each region would inadvertently dictate what we found. Third, we discovered that at our 25-site scale we could only gather enough data from each farmstead to compare basic metrics like size and establishment date and produce a basic characterization of farming strategies.

Ultimately, a strategy based on regional comparisons was not accessible to our methods. We could not expand the number of sites surveyed in a region without sacrificing the limited comparative metrics we were producing, and we could not gather more data without decreasing our already-too-small regional samples. So we changed the sampling strategy. Rather than continuing to look at several different environmental areas, we focused on one region where preservation seemed to be the best, an area called Langholt that corresponded to one of the original settlement claims in Skagafjörður. We significantly expanded our sample in that region to include all of the 20 pre-modern farms. The new strategy resulted in a complete survey of the region, including good negative evidence that helped establish that we were not missing hidden farms in our survey, and eliminated any bias introduced by our choice of sites.

The Middle Range: Incomplete Data, Incomplete Theory

While the complete single region strategy seemed perfect for providing answers to our questions, the right mix of methods – coring, geophysics, and excavation – that could outline the critical data of the region still needed to be developed.

The first mix was too dependent on coring for phosphate samples. Plotting areas of high phosphates could be correlated with the general area of buried farmsteads. The phosphate samples themselves could be roughly dated using their relationship to the tephra layers visually identified in the cores. Then, the results of geophysical surveying over the high phosphate areas could be used to identify buried structures on those sites, which would then be excavated. Unfortunately, the phosphate-enriched areas from different time periods were very large and sites themselves were difficult to identify, and the act of removing and recording the soil samples from the cores and then processing them was very slow. That being said, phosphate sampling has proven to be an excellent method for comparing patterns of field management and comparing intensification strategies between farms (Bolender 2006).

Our second mix depended too much on geophysics. Plotting anomalies in the geophysical surveying could be correlated with buildings and structures. Covering large areas with widely-spaced ground conductivity transects could give us areas to investigate with a power auger and follow-up backhoe trench excavations. A backhoe seemed appropriate because our previous experience suggested that many of the anomalies would be natural stratigraphic sequences. Unfortunately, the geophysical grids were hard to set up and the areas to be surveyed were too extensive. Furthermore, rather than indicating site boundaries and site edges, several of the geophysical anomalies were located in and at the edges of buildings, where power auger holes and backhoe trenches were not appropriate.

We soon realized that turf debris and ash associated with buried farm buildings and middens were readily apparent in the cores, even in the marginal deposits at site edges. Furthermore, the cores were very reliable for visually identifying signs of buried human activity, such as charcoal, peat ash, turf, and other anthropogenic deposits and even roughly dating them using the tephra layers. By no longer taking soil samples for phosphate analyses, hand coring became incredibly rapid. Once a site's edges were identified, intensive multi-instrument geophysical results, as well as further coring, yielded details that made placing excavation units routine and remarkably productive.

Our third mix was much better. It involved rapid coring for initial site reconnaissance, targeted geophysical survey to identify and map buried structures, and then more intensive coring in combination with the geophysical data to place hand-excavated test pits in specific midden deposits. The well-placed hand excavations were used to refine settlement sequences, collect paleoethnobotanical and zooarchaeological samples, and most importantly, identify the earliest deposits, from which a date for the establishment of the farmstead could be obtained. With the new protocol we were able to expand our survey area and collect more and better targeted data from each site.

In subsequent NSF grants, many of which were rejected the first time, we refined and expanded this protocol. In 2005, we, along with the insightful Paul Durrenberger, tested ground-penetrating radar (GPR) to see if we could get an even finer level of detail from the buried farms. In 2007, we implemented the new GPR protocol to see if we could use it to map the earlier layers of still-occupied farmsteads (Figure 4.1). We learned that GPR provided useful results on abandoned and relatively simple sites, but not on more complex sites with more recent deposits. Finally, by plotting cores with cultural material of any type and dating them using the tephra layers, the area of a farmstead at a given time could be calculated. This

Figure 4.1 Fieldwork in Glaumbær and Meðalheimur, Iceland. Top: Brian Damiata (left) and John Steinberg experiment with GPR at Glaumbær with the grass removed. Surveying over the de-turfed surface dramatically improved the geophysical results. Bottom: Douglas Bolender excavates substantial turf architecture at Meðalheimur. The site, based on historical sources, was assumed to be small and late, but turned out to be early and large. Photographs by the authors.

approach allowed us to compare both abandoned sites and current mounded sites at multiple periods in history. While the data were of a low quality (a gross estimate of farmstead size), we could collect comparable data on every farm in the region.

The Conclusion: The Right Way To Be Wrong

When we started our project we had clear ideas about how to conduct a systematic settlement survey of Viking Age Iceland. These ideas ended up being wrong not because they were bad in concept – they were all derived from standard archaeological survey protocols – but because they did not fit the specific and unusual conditions on (and in) the ground in Iceland. We certainly learned that by starting with an experimental one-year grant, that explained both the long-term theoretical justification and the immediate methodological problem to be solved, we could integrate feedback about the scale necessary to take on the project in the next round. By explaining what worked, and more importantly what did not work, in the follow-up multi-year grant application, the whole grant application process was not only successful, but became an integral part of the actual research program.

Many of our assumptions about what we would find ended up being wrong, too. We imagined that the first settlers would go through a period of trial and error as they adapted to the new environment and that we would discover a large number of early abandoned sites. Moreover, as the society went from a Viking Age chiefdom to medieval manorial state, we expected to see a wholescale reorganization of the settlement system. After all, as our anthropological ancestors had told us, chiefdoms and states don't have the same settlement system. Moreover, in a marginal environment like Iceland, specialization and intensification should be the hallmarks of the reorganized settlement system. Even more interesting would be if that were not the case.

In the end, by collecting negative evidence and comparing the size and establishment date of the farms in the study region, we found that the Viking Age settlement pattern was far more stable than we expected. Few early farms had been abandoned, and the determining factor in a farm's size at the end of the Viking Age was how early in the settlement sequence it had been established. This suggests that, at least in Langholt, a major factor in the creation of inequality was settlement order, with earlier farms enjoying a substantial advantage and that this advantage was remarkably enduring (Steinberg, Bolender, and Damiata 2016). We never did identify much in the way of differences in farmsteads relating to economic specialization; all farms, big and small, seemed to engage in the same basic economic activities.

However, the detailed archaeological and geophysical examination of the sites did identify a difference in function in several of the large farmsteads: some had early Christian churches. Fortunately for our ongoing geophysical methodology, specific graves within a churchyard could be identified using GPR (Damiata *et al.* 2013). That discovery complemented the work being conducted by Guðný Zoëga on the distribution of churches in the Skagafjörður area (Zoëga and Murphy 2016). Our current work, with Zoëga, is a three-year project that seeks to understand the relationship between the settlement pattern of farmsteads and the geography of churches in the nearby region of Hegranes, which is a more marginal region then Langholt. Again, this project was preceded by several seasons trying to determine how to reliably identify churches and graves. And, already, we seem to be making just as many errors and have had to revise much of our approach. The take-away lesson? It is good to be wrong – at least for the right reasons.

Paired Reading

Steinberg, John M., Douglas J. Bolender, and Brian N. Damiata. 2016. "The Viking Age Settlement Pattern of Langholt, North Iceland: Results of the Skagafjörður Archaeological Settlement Survey." *Journal of Field Archaeology*, 41(4): 389–412. DOI: 10.1080/00934690.2016.1203210.

References

Bolender, Douglas J. 2006. "The Creation of a Propertied Landscape: Land Tenure and Intensification in Medieval Iceland." PhD Dissertation. Chicago, IL: Northwestern University.

Damiata, Brian N., John M. Steinberg, Douglas J. Bolender, and Guðný Zoëga. 2013. "Imaging Skeletal Remains with Ground-Penetrating Radar: Comparative Results over Two Graves from Viking Age and Medieval Churchyards on the Stóra-Seyla farm, Northern Iceland." *Journal of Archaeological Science*, 40: 268–278. DOI: 10.1016/j.jas.2012.06.031.

Earle, Timothy K. 1991. *Chiefdoms: Power, Economy, and Ideology*. Cambridge: Cambridge University Press.

Flannery, Kent. 1972. "The Cultural Evolution of Civilizations." *Annual Review of Ecology and Systematics*, 3: 399–426. DOI: 10.1146/annurev.es.03.110172.002151.

Gilman, Antonio. 1981. "The Development of Social Stratification in Bronze Age Europe." *Current Anthropology*, 22: 1–23.

McGovern, Thomas H. 1990. "Archaeology of the Norse North Atlantic." *Annual Review of Anthropology*, 19: 331–351. DOI: 10.1146/annurev.an.19.100190.001555.

Pálsson, Hermann and Paul Geoffrey Edwards. 1972. *The Book of Settlements; Landnámabók*. Winnipeg: University of Manitoba Press.

Smith, Kevin P. and Jeffery R. Parsons. 1989. "Regional Archaeological Research in Iceland: Potentials And Possibilities." In *The Anthropology of Iceland*, edited by E. Paul Durrenberger and Gisli Pálsson, 179–202. Iowa City, IA: University of Iowa Press.

Steinberg, John M., Douglas J. Bolender, and Brian N. Damiata. 2016. "The Viking Age Settlement Pattern of Langholt, North Iceland: Results of the Skagafjörður Archaeological Settlement Survey." *Journal of Field Archaeology.* 41(4): 389–412. DOI: 10.1080/00934690.2016.1203210.

Willey, Gordon R. 1953. *Prehistoric Settlement Patterns in the Virú Valley, Perú*. Bureau of American Ethnology. Washington, D.C.: Government Printing Office.

Zoëga, Guðný and Kimmarie A. Murphy. 2016. "Life on the Edge of the Arctic: The Bioarchaeology of the Keldudalur Cemetery in Skagafjörður, Iceland." *International Journal of Osteoarchaeology*, 26(4): 574–584. DOI: 10.1002/oa.2446.

5

Archaeological Projects in India: Decolonizing Archaeological Research, Assessing Success, and Valuing Failure

Uzma Z. Rizvi

Project Summary

The Ganeshwar Jodhpura Cultural Complex (GJCC) Survey in northeastern Rajasthan, India (2000–2003) is a community-based archaeological project that developed a decolonized approach to archaeological research in collaboration with various local stakeholders. The research question at the core of this project focused on locating and understanding the political economy of third-millennium BCE settlements of copper mining communities in northeastern Rajasthan. As the principal investigator (PI) of this project, the results of the survey became the core of my PhD dissertation (2007, Department of Anthropology, University of Pennsylvania), but the project was made possible by ten additional team members, all of whom worked collaboratively with local communities. Major funding was provided by the Fulbright-Hayes Doctoral Dissertation Research Abroad, and institutional support was offered by the University of Rajasthan (Jaipur), Rajasthan Vidyapeeth University (Udaipur), Deccan College (Pune), and the American Institute of Indian Studies (AIIS).

Retrospective Origins

I have been working in South Asia for almost two decades, but as an undergraduate in the early and mid-1990s, my archaeological interest was focused on the Classical Greek world. The questions that rooted me there had to do with a desire to understand political frameworks and relationships to architecture, which led to my interest in the agora and iconographic representation of public life in Greek vase painting. The Classical Greek world is well excavated, with a finely tuned chronology allowing for nuanced considerations of the ancient political landscape. It was only in my final year (1995) that I was introduced to the archaeology of South Asia, which seemed to be diametrically opposite: it was an ancient landscape with muddled chronologies and not nearly enough excavated materials. There was no way to ask the questions I would have wanted to without foundational archaeological work first. In retrospect I think I considered moving research interests from the ancient Greek world to ancient South Asia because it also held the promise of an epistemic change. As an undergraduate student working in the Classical Greek world, the ways of knowing were already quite set, and so it was exciting to think that perhaps in ancient South Asia, how we know what we know might also constitute some foundational change and that we might be part of that change. And so, I began my graduate career in 1998 with similar questions as in my undergraduate work about ancient political

Engaging Archaeology: 25 Case Studies in Research Practice, First Edition. Edited by Stephen W. Silliman.
© 2018 John Wiley & Sons, Inc. Published 2018 by John Wiley & Sons, Inc.

urban landscapes, but this time, with a key interest in "first cities," political economy, and a focus on South Asia.

As an American student with South Asian heritage, it was tricky because there was almost too much expected and at stake. When I was greeted in South Asia at any archaeological site, the people did not see an archaeologist first – what they saw was a young South Asian woman – and so the politics of practice were completely different from what my white male professors in the United States had taught me based on their own field experiences. Recognizing those politics as distinct proved to be key in developing a decolonized archaeological practice. Listening to and assessing what sorts of expectations people had for me that differed from what they expected my advisor to do was also important. I also needed to know the history of colonization in these regions, as reference to colonial projects were constant. My prior experience working on archaeological excavations in both Pakistan and India helped shape my methodology and approach to my dissertation topic.

To be honest, when I was developing this methodology and practice, I recall feeling very confused because everything seemed overlapping without a clear sense of how things connected. What I was doing, but unaware of at the time, was simultaneously enacting multiple layers of what ended up being the project: first, how decolonizing a methodology might have an epistemic impact; second, how community-based archaeological practice might impact public and museum policy; third, how the significance of counter mapping acts as a form of colonial resistance; and finally, how the survey data would provide the ancient landscape with foundational archaeological information. Throughout this process, however, I stayed true to my core research questions that had to do with understanding the political economy of the ancient landscape during the third millennium BCE in a region that was associated with, but not, the Harappan Civilization. Given the scope of ancient interaction I needed to document, I knew I would have to conduct a survey. I had also decided that in order to put the postcolonial critique into action through community-based practices, I would have to direct my own project. Given my prior experience excavating at the site of Gilund in Rajasthan, I decided to focus my attention in a known area.

As I conducted preliminary surveys in Rajasthan in 2000, I met with many communities and different officials. Ultimately, my dissertation proposal resulted from those conversations; that is, it reflected the concerns of the communities. I believe it was these processes and conversations that led to an official invitation letter for a collaborative archaeological project by the Indian Administrative Services (IAS) officer, Dr. Lalit Panwar. Prior to sending me that letter, Dr. Panwar, a historian, had spent a number of hours with me talking through my ideas of community-based work and what I thought a decolonized archaeology could do. In retrospect, I now see the significance of that sort of mentorship and trust and how he saw the promise and potential of this sort of project. At the time, I was just grateful for the help, a sounding board, and the advice.

Setting Up the Survey: The Ganeshwar Jodhpura Cultural Complex (GJCC) Survey

As I began my dissertation fieldwork in Rajasthan, I became acutely aware that I required a new set of standards that acknowledged neocolonial frameworks while critically engaging with the context. I have written about this elsewhere (Rizvi 2006, 2008) and present some of the more relevant material in this chapter. Perhaps one of the most important starting points was to situate my practice at multiple scales from global to local. This meant simultaneously understanding interactions on individual levels based on intersectional understandings of self/ other (class/caste, race, gender, and religious affiliation), and each of these variables within a larger understanding of how colonial history and the present simultaneously operate to influence decision-making, interpretation, and relevance for archaeological stakeholders.

All archaeologists construct and enact our own identities in the field, negotiated repeatedly in relation to whatever "home" culture and society we originate from and choose to identify with and how we choose to perform those identity formations. The politics of performance are active on all scales of interaction and, although often mundane, inextricably alter the ways in which we conduct, imagine, and re-imagine ourselves in the field. These locations of practice often serve as nodes of activity that mark the articulation of what is considered obvious archaeology, for example, picking up material from the ground during a ground survey. The "obvious" is constructed through a negotiation of identity; that is to say, based on one's identity, multiple possibilities for what is or is not considered "obvious" exist. For example, while working in India, it may be obvious for some to ask permission from the landowner or farmer to conduct a survey on that land, and for others it may be just as obvious to assume that with government permission, no other permission is required unless direct interaction should take place. I chose the former.

I may choose to identify myself in multiple ways, but during the 2003 field season in Rajasthan, others introduced me with certain qualifiers in a sequence that I could not always control: female, Muslim, American, South Asian, archaeologist. Albeit formulaic, once created without active intervention on my part, the repetition of that statement continued to establish my identity, ascribing me to a very specific position within the village social structure. I renegotiated that identity by focusing on the performance of archaeological research, including, but not limited to, my use of technological instruments and my attire that, in addition to a generic *shalwar, kameez,* and *duppatta* (traditional Indian/Pakistani pants, shirt, and long scarf), consisted of a large backpack and hiking boots. These interactions suggested two things. First, enacting archaeological "competence" did not alter the social hierarchies in place, and second, performing archaeology fitted seamlessly with the combination of identities presented in a manner that was acceptable and believable. My practice and performance were affected by both the rigid nature of the sociocultural hierarchies prescribed by my cultural heritage and a simultaneous flexibility that allowed for multiple combinations and renegotiations of my identity.

Decolonizing Archaeological Survey Methods: The GJCC 2003 Survey

Being self-reflexive about your own subject position and identity within the social and cultural spaces that one inhabits during archaeological and cultural work is an absolute must in any decolonizing project. That self-awareness was important to activate one of the key components to a methodology I employed, which was both community participation and collaboration and which I have consequently considered to be alternating between community-based archaeology and public archaeology. A collaborative, community-based model worked very well in the village-to-village survey.

Preliminary survey work took place in the summer of 2000, and in 2003 the full survey project commenced with (in total) ten team members, including doctoral students from the University of Rajasthan, Jaipur, and the New School University, New York. In addition to these team members, I formed smaller collaborative projects with participating villages and communities in order to conduct the archaeological survey. These collaborative spaces were often realized through practices that documented the presence/absence of ancient artifacts on the surface during survey, but also included eight after-school programs, 64 *panchayat* (or village council) meetings, and countless discussions with individuals of all ages who would join us on our surveys, communities who chose to engage in discussions about copper mining, and publics that formed around the discourse of tourism, heritage management, and the use of archaeology in the contemporary world.

Each new survey began with a visit to the village *sarpanch* (village council head) to discuss the overall project. This would often result in a discussion with other *panchayat* members and interested community leaders, including farmers. Such discussions made each of them individual stakeholders in the overall project, each with a particular point of view and specific interests in collaboration with the survey project. In most cases, local history teachers would also join in the efforts and their classes would join our surveys. In some instances, these students would actually become part of after-school programs in which the GJCC Survey team would teach the students survey techniques and lessons in the general archaeology of South Asia.

The survey was conducted primarily in three districts: Sikar with 48 sites documented, Jaipur with 51 sites, and Jhunjhunu with 30 sites, and additional sites located in the districts of Tonk with four sites and Alwar with two sites. In total 135 sites were documented during the survey (Figure 5.1). Roughly spread over 34,000 sq km, with an estimated settled area at 12.51 sq km, the GJCC sites documented during the 2003 survey include settlement sites, vitrified metal waste sites, mining sites, and raw material processing sites, often found in close proximity to

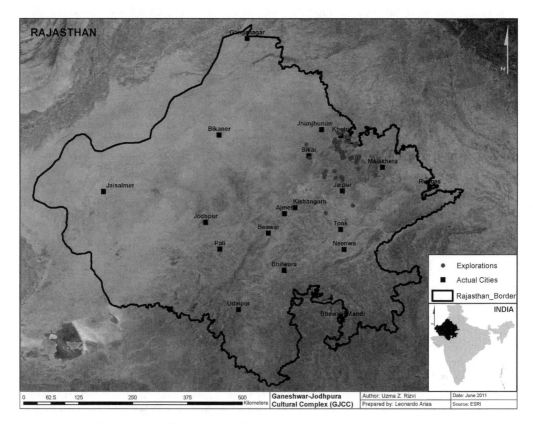

Figure 5.1 Map of Ganeshwar Jodhpura Cultural Complex survey sites based on 2003 survey. Reprinted with permission from SAGE Publishing and Left Coast Press.

each other, with each providing a different specialized activity or resource. Although a basic ground survey methodology was employed in which we walked $5 \times 5\,\text{m}$ transects in high density artifact regions and $10 \times 10\,\text{m}$ transects between those areas, the community involvement led to new research questions and a dialogic interpretation of the region.

Our work involved interacting with a range of persons including officers of the Archaeological Survey of India (ASI), the State Government of Rajasthan, Secretary of Tourism, Art and Culture, the Directorate of Archaeology and Museums, the District Magistrate, the Assistant District Magistrate, *tehsildars* (tax inspectors), *patwaris* (land recorders), police officers at the stations where artifacts were stored after a chance find, the *panchayat* (the village council), individual *sarpanch* (village council head), school teachers (particularly history teachers), community leaders, elders, head of households and farmsteads, interested individuals passing by, and most of all, children. These methods were developed through our interactions with these individuals and groups as an active mode of decolonization by incorporating community-based archaeology, public archaeology, and a change in the education and training of archaeologists (Atalay 2006; Marshall 2002).

These discussions and interactive spaces were crucial for the types of methodological interventions I had in mind. I felt it important for the village and community to invite us to conduct the survey, rather than our team demanding this as a service. However, this constant dialogue complicated each process – and invariably, our workday did not always reflect the "plan" established at the start of the day. This was difficult, as it took control out of my hands (as director of a project) and placed decision-making abilities into multiple hands, shaped by others' schedules, moods, and ideas, which *theoretically* is the point of collaborative, interactive (as opposed to reactive) work but is difficult to operationalize *practically*. I realized, however, that by giving up control, the survey was open to experiencing and documenting the past in a manner that would not have been possible otherwise. One way to dismantle the colonial control of knowledge production was to give up that very control that continued to reiterate itself in my mind based on my own Western pedagogy.

Working on archaeological projects with communities has proven to be an effective dismantling of research-based power structures (Greer *et al.* 2002; Marshall 2002; Moser *et al.* 2002). Illustrated by the GJCC Survey, a useful point of entry for a decolonizing methodology is community-based archaeology (Rizvi 2006). Such a methodology necessitates the active engagement with community concerns; in other words, simultaneous to archaeological projects is a development of heritage, identity, and in most cases, tourism. The management and public presentation of archaeological and other heritage resources created a situation in which heritage tourism might have been able to put money into the pockets of local communities rather than multinational corporations and develop local heritage resources in ways that are sensitive to the needs and interests of the people (Marshall 2002; Moser *et al.* 2002; Rizvi 2006).

Based on the experience of this survey project, I would argue that all archaeologists interacting with locals necessarily change the stakes for those reformulations and political negotiations for both the locals and the archaeologists. The methodology developed for the GJCC Survey work was inspired by a desire to decolonize and deconstruct field techniques while keeping in mind the negotiations of a relatively new state (established in 1947) and extant social systems, such as caste. For example, as a Muslim, I operated outside the Hindu caste system but was placed very specifically within the corollary Muslim caste system, expressed most prominently as limits on access to certain spaces and demands to occupy others – although I occasionally chose to subvert such systems, depending on the context. This awareness of religious affiliation was heightened due to the sociopolitical climate causing tension between various religious groups.

A Brief Note on the GJCC Survey Results

Having published extensively on the survey results and collections study, I present only a quick synopsis of the project itself below (Rizvi 2007, 2008, 2013, 2017). Located in northeastern Rajasthan, the GJCC is a collection of third-millennium BCE settlements bound together by a shared cultural language that encompass similarities in material culture, production of copper tools, and geographic proximity to copper mines. In geographic and chronological proximity to GJCC is the Harappan culture to the west, the Ahar-Banas Complex to the south west, the Kayatha Culture to the southeast, and at a later date, the OCP-Copper Hoard sites mainly to the east. Located within the regions of the Aravalli Hill Range, primarily along the Kantli, Sabi, Sota, Dohan, and Bondi rivers, the GJCC is the largest copper-producing community in third-millennium BCE South Asia. Archaeological indicators of the GJCC, such as incised ware, reserved slip ware, and copper artifacts are documented primarily in Jaipur, Jhunjhunu, and Sikar districts of Rajashtan, India. This part of India is known for its farming and pastoral resources, as well as for minerals, the most important of which is copper. Khetri, the largest copper source in Rajasthan, has been exploited since antiquity and continues today as one of the major resources for copper production in India.

The GJCC illustrates an indigenous development that sustains a larger regional economic need for copper products. As such, the GJCC defines and is defined by its interactions with and proximity to the Harappan Civilization to the north/northwest and the Ahar-Banas Complex to the south/southwest. By occupying the space between two major cultural forces of the time, the GJCC emerges as a resource specialized community with connections to both. The economic autonomy that resulted from emerging as a resource specialized community based in copper production allowed for enough power to ensure that during the third millennium BCE, at least, the cultural integrity of the GJCC was maintained. It is not difficult to imagine that if the GJCC were economically regressive or in a different political arrangement, either of the two larger contemporary cultural forces, the Harappan and the Ahar-Banas, would have been able to subsume the GJCC and control the resource.

The members of the GJCC community were most likely seen as copper producers in their contemporary landscape. Whether or not each individual actively participated in the processes related to the production of copper becomes of secondary consideration, it is clear that each individual who lived in those communities moved through the spaces within which such bodily practices were being enacted upon the landscape and their lives were enmeshed in the larger industry of copper production through familial or social networks within which they might be situated. The larger social structure provided certain ways of understanding self and community through a lens that was informed largely by copper production (Rizvi 2013).

Assessing Success and Valuing Failure

Most metrics of archaeological success do not have values implicit for community-based or decolonized work that involves much time in workshops, meetings, and negotiating with the myriad of stakeholders invested in the project. Rather than not employing such a methodology, this simply means we now must reassess what successful projects might look like. Not everyone is able or equipped to do public and community-based work. However, everyone is equipped to ensure that whatever praxis they employ does not reiterate colonial mandates in a neocolonial context that maintain certain power relations. Keeping that in mind, it is important for a moment to think about how we might reassess what success is and the significance and value of failure.

I believe the GJCC Survey project was, by and large, a success. However, it had some very clear moments which, in retrospect, I can see as not so successful, such as the Neem Ka Thana Public project (Rizvi 2006) and the publication lag for the copper documentation project (Rizvi 2017). As archaeology changes some of the metrics of success to allow for the cultural vitality of a project to be considered, then we can include the presence of the project, the community involvement and participation, and the continued local support for such projects and for other projects of the same ilk. In all of these criteria, the GJCC 2003 worked well enough. By including local communities and working with school programs we were able to document more sites and create maps, knowledge, and research agendas with local significance to produce relevant archaeological knowledge. Not every archaeological project will have deep political ramifications. But every project does have the capacity to reiterate oppressive structures. Rather than looking to a project to change the world, one might look to their project as ensuring it is not keeping the world the same, as sometimes that sameness adds to the inequity of systems.

Drinking Tea

One of the most useful lessons I learned by watching my PhD advisor, Gregory Possehl, work in India was how to visit people and drink tea. It is counterintuitive if you operate in a Western, capitalist, efficiency-driven mindset, but in fact, it has proven to be one of the most efficient ways to work in most of the world, including the West. Drinking tea is both a metaphor and an action. It is about respecting the person sitting in front of you as a person first; it diffuses the instrumentalization of relationships so prevalent in a capitalist economy. It sets up reciprocity, social networks, and in some cases extended, fictive, academic/research kin.

My experience in India attests to the protection, support, and access that drinking tea has afforded. However, my experience also confirms that at each level of interaction, the coexistence of suspicion and curiosity is a traumatic remnant of a colonial past and a reiteration of an unequal present, in which information, power, and prestige continue to be stolen from the caretakers of the land. It was only at the highest levels of the Indian bureaucracy, and within the company of internationally recognized senior scholars, usually with some Western training, that such a suspicion was not blatant and people expressed an interest in my academic qualifications. At this privileged level, such individuals are recognized, legitimized, and authorized as some part of the elite on the national stage or international stage. In contrast, the vast majority of the middle-class Indian bureaucracy showed less interest in my academic prowess; rather, in order to gain access to locked cabinets, museum records, and information about previous excavations, I had to prove my trustworthiness by locating my spatial practice and performance within their social systems and cultural norms.

During our 2003 survey, it became clear that the power we carried was somewhat transferable. When we were invited to tea in a village household, that household enhanced their cultural capital. A connection was made that often seemed to be very intimate on the part of the host and cautious on our part. Indeed, this may link to rules of hospitality, but perhaps more realistically, these levels of intimacy have to do with the ways in which power and privilege operate. Often our caution articulated a fear of not understanding complex village politics and the tacit knowledge that we, as privileged archaeologists, could not give them everything our power might have suggested. Through our training, we are transformed into vessels of power that signify promise, yet often we cannot live up to that potential. It is a performance of power that we reenact by occupying a specific space that is not local to us, which recalls in collective memory the colonial archaeologists and the power vested in their positions as embodiments of empire. I believe that a shift in methodology – one that accounts for privileged practice, the collective memory of the colonial archaeologist, and the context for any curiosity and suspicion – enables the archaeologist to dismantle the colonial structures upon which she or he stands.

Concluding Thoughts

Between the years of 2000 and 2003, when I conducted my dissertation field work, there were not many sources that dealt directly with decolonizing archaeological methods. I turned to other disciplines, such as history (postcolonial critique) and cultural theory (decolonizing methods), and combined them with community-based archaeology and public archaeology to develop my own methodology. For anyone starting up a research project, the most important step is to situate, understand, and contextualize your own standpoint for entering into your project. In order to conduct research that is true to you, and honors those you are working with, you need to be honest and clear about your relationship to your project. Often our projects develop while we are entrenched within them. This makes sense because as we change through our experiences, our projects, which are articulations of our ideas into the world, also change. It is important to develop a project that has the flexibility to allow for that change, but to also ensure that you are thinking through the ethical and equitable components of your project. If you feel like the theories you are developing are "out there" and no one is writing about it and you are not sure who to cite, cite the work that has helped you get to your place.

An approach cognizant of the postcolonial critique allows for an acknowledgment of what has already happened, the colonial nature of it, and the possible appropriation of it, and it helps identify methods moving forward that allow for a more equitable and just research agenda – one that does not take without giving, one that is dialogic, and most importantly, one that keeps an ethical check on past injustices to ensure they are not replicated. By employing a decolonized approach, archaeological practice has the potential to be a part of reparations.

Archaeological practice in India and Pakistan is necessarily a postcolonial endeavor within a neocolonial space – it is crucial to understand how one might decolonize a practice in order to more rigorously link past archaeological practice to contemporary projects. Decolonization is not presented here as a "feel good" approach; instead, it is an approach that is necessary in order to provide nuance, context, and clear understandings of archaeological work. Although I developed these methods in a specific region, the larger theoretical and methodological concerns may be adapted to any world area. Archaeology is a colonial discipline practiced worldwide, and as such, decolonization is a global project.

Paired Reading

Rizvi, Uzma, Z. 2013. "Crafting Communities and Producing Places: Copper, Settlement Patterns, and Social Identity in the Ganeshwar Jodhpura Cultural Complex, Rajasthan, India." In *Connections and Complexity: New Approaches to the Archaeology of South Asia*, edited by Shinu Anna Abraham, Praveena Gullapalli, Teresa Raczek, and Uzma Z. Rizvi, 315–340. Walnut Creek, CA: Left Coast Press.

References

Atalay, Sonya. 2006. "Decolonizing Archaeology." *American Indian Quarterly*, 30: 269–279. DOI: 10.1353/aiq.2006.0014.

Greer, Shelley, Rodney Harrison, and Susan McIntyre-Tamwoy. 2002. "Community Based Archaeology in Australia." *World Archaeology*, 34: 265–287. DOI: 10.1080/0043824022000007099.

Marshall, Yvonne. 2002. "What Is Community Archaeology?" *World Archaeology*, 34: 211–219. DOI: 10.1080/0043824022000007062.

Moser, Stephanie, Darren Glazier, James E. Phillips, Lamya Nasser el Nemr, Mohammed Saleh Mousa, Rascha Nasr Aiesh, Susan Richardson, Andrew Conner, and Michael Seymour. 2002. "Transforming Archaeology through Practice: Strategies for Collaborative Archaeology and the Community Archaeology Project at Quseir, Egypt." *World Archaeology*, 34: 220–248. DOI: 10.1080/0043824022000007071.

Rizvi, Uzmi Z. 2006. "Accounting for Multiple Desires: Decolonizing Methodologies, Archaeology and the Public Interest." *India Review*, 5: 394–416. DOI: 10.1080/14736480600939223.

Rizvi Uzma Z. 2007. "Configuring the Space In-Between: Redefining the Ganeshwar Jodhpura Cultural Complex in Chalcolithic Northeastern Rajasthan, India." PhD Dissertation. Philadelphia, PA: University of Pennsylvania.

Rizvi, Uzma, Z. 2008. "Decolonizing Methodologies as Strategies of Practice: Operationalizing the Postcolonial Critique in the Archaeology of Rajasthan." In *Archaeology and the Postcolonial Critique*, edited by Matthew Liebmann and Uzma Rizvi, 109–127. Walnut Creek, CA: Altamira Press.

Rizvi, Uzma, Z. 2013. "Crafting Communities and Producing Places: Copper, Settlement Patterns, and Social Identity in the Ganeshwar Jodhpura Cultural Complex, Rajasthan, India." In *Connections and Complexity: New Approaches to the Archaeology of South Asia*, edited by Shinu Anna Abraham, Praveena Gullapalli, Teresa Raczek, and Uzma Z. Rizvi, 315–340. Walnut Creek, CA: Left Coast Press.

Rizvi, Uzma Z. 2017. *On the Affect of Crafting: Third Millennium BCE Copper Arrowheads from Ganeshwar, Rajasthan*. Oxford: ArchaeoPress.

6

Lifeways of the First Australians: Regional Archaeology in the Remote North of Australia

Jane Balme

Project Summary

In 2011 my colleague, Sue O'Connor, and I began a project in northwest Australia to examine the timing, technologies, and social behaviors of the first Australians. Although much had been said about these issues, previous work had been based on small samples and controversial dates. The project took a very long time to develop and is still in progress, but importantly for such a project, we have been able to provide a chronological framework with precise dates and have begun to understand the variation in sequences in the region. While we have been able to identify a new colonizing technology, our understanding of the overall technology has been hampered by the lack of preservation in the deepest part of the deposits and the unrealized large samples that we had been hoping for.

Introduction

In the early 1990s, my colleague, Sue O'Connor, excavated three cave/rockshelter sites in land traditionally owned by the Bunuba people in the southern Kimberley region of north-west Australia. Two of these shelters contained Pleistocene archaeological deposits, one of which extended to over 40,000 years. A few years later I excavated a cave site of similar antiquity about 250 km east of her excavations and in the traditional lands of the Gooniyandi people. All of these caves and rockshelters are in the same ancient limestone reef system and, because the deposits are alkaline and generally dry, organic remains are well-preserved.

At the time of these excavations both of us were interested in questions about the antiquity, technologies, and other behaviors that were associated with the first colonizers of the Pleistocene continent of Sahul (consisting of present-day Australia, New Guinea, and the Aru islands). My interest in this area developed from a lot of happenstance, such as changing my undergraduate course from science to anthropology and being lucky enough to get a job at the Western Australian Museum (I did a lot of volunteer work there as an undergraduate) where I worked on the excavations at the cave site of Devil's Lair, one of the oldest archaeological sites in Australia at the time. Then, for my PhD I worked in western New South Wales where again, the sites were mainly Pleistocene but this time preserved in sand dunes bordering lakes and rivers and containing evidence for intense exploitation of these environments. The different technologies and resources used in these widely different environments but both representing some of the first human occupation of Sahul, made me think about the relationship between

Engaging Archaeology: 25 Case Studies in Research Practice, First Edition. Edited by Stephen W. Silliman.
© 2018 John Wiley & Sons, Inc. Published 2018 by John Wiley & Sons, Inc.

people and their environment and the different social, technological, and economic trajectories that could be used to successfully adapt to their different environmental circumstances. In this I was greatly influenced by Human Behavioral Ecology (HBE) perhaps because at the time I was doing my PhD in the early 1980s, this approach had become increasingly important in the discipline. HBE's concern for how behavior changes in relation to both physical and social environmental circumstances makes it a useful way to understand why behaviors vary. With the dramatic difference between Wallacea and Sahul, and the great diversity of environments that were rapidly occupied within Sahul, the principles of HBE can help identify different social environments and why different groups adopted particular behavioral strategies.

Two of the pervading archaeological questions about the first occupation of Sahul have been how long people have been in the continent and what behaviors were associated with the apparent very rapid dispersal of people throughout the various environments (Balme *et al.* 2009). Dates of up to 60,000 years have been suggested for the earliest evidence of occupation in Australia, but this and many other early dates have been controversial (O'Connell and Allen 2015). This controversy is a result of problems with the accuracy of the radiocarbon and luminescence-based dates, along with the poor precision of the dates in the order of ±5,000 years and the reliability of the context and association of artifacts with dated materials.

The question about the behaviors associated with the first colonizers has been especially prevalent since the flurry of publications about what constitutes "modern human behaviour" in the early 2000s. As Sahul was only ever occupied by our species (*Homo sapiens sapiens*), evidence from this continent is important for understanding the variation in such behavior. In particular the behavioral qualities associated with our species, planning depth, information exchange, and language no doubt helped the ancestors of Australian Aboriginal people move from island Wallacea to a new continent (Balme *et al.* 2009). The early evidence from Wallacea suggests that people largely exploited deep-sea fish and other marine resources because the region was depauperate in land-based fauna but rich in marine resources. However, once in Sahul, they apparently dispersed into all environments, including the arid center, within about 10,000 years. This was done with a tool kit apparently consisting almost entirely of percussion-flaked artifacts. The simplicity of this tool kit in comparison with the apparently more complex tool kit associated with modern people from the same period in the Old World has been often remarked upon. How could such small groups of people achieve rapid, successful colonization of so many varieties of new environments with such a seemingly simple tool kit? Did people really lose their complex technology en route to Australia as Mellars (2006) and others suggest? Or, did people use this technology as an adaptation to their new environment, and was it not possible to invent their own tools – a possibility that seems to be denied by the arguments suggesting loss of complexity? In our view, too much emphasis was being placed on inferring technology only from direct evidence – stone artifacts. Because retouch on identified Pleistocene stone artifacts from Sahul suggests that they were primarily used for wood work, and Wallacean sites include pelagic fish probably caught with hooks and lines, we hypothesized that organic technology, including fiber, was most likely very important in the colonization of Sahul (Balme and O'Connor 2014).

One of the difficulties in answering these questions is that the number of Pleistocene archaeological sites investigated so far remains very small and geographically widely distributed. In addition, the sizes of excavations in each site are typically small – usually one or two 1 m squares. There are a variety of reasons for these "telephone boxes" including a priority interest in "getting old dates," but other factors, such as heritage legislation that has specified how much of a site can be excavated and the often short time spans associated with research grants, have also been an influence. Thus, although we had many dates converging on about 50,000 years ago from different parts of the continent, the samples of archaeological material recovered from each site are small. Some of the Pleistocene sites have been rich in faunal remains, but few of these assemblages have been studied in detail. The upshot of all of this is that our knowledge of the first occupants of Sahul is based primarily on small samples of stone artifacts that, while ubiquitous, convey limited information about the cognitive abilities, technologies, and symbolic behaviors of the first people.

In 2007, Sue and I got together at a workshop, organized by a philanthropic group, for people who had worked, or were thinking of working, in the Kimberley region of Australia. We didn't know each other all that well then, but as the philanthropic group would provide seed funding to begin new research projects and we had similar interests, we thought it a good opportunity to return to the southern Kimberley. The sites we had worked on in the 1990s indicated that the area had great potential, not just for antiquity and well-preserved organic remains, but also for fine-grained age resolution of the deposits as the sites that we had worked on individually had good stratigraphic integrity. These characteristics would make the southern Kimberley area an excellent prospect for providing large samples of material that could contribute to questions of antiquity, technology, and social behaviors associated with the colonization of Sahul.

In addition, the sites had the potential to contribute to another related question about the first Australians – their ability to respond to environmental stress. All of the sites we had excavated had hiatuses or periods of slow deposition within the deposits at around the time of the Last Glacial Maximum (LGM), but the precise timing of these depositional changes varied between sites. Breaks in deposition had been recorded in many arid zone sites in Australia, and several researchers had suggested that these indicated abandonment of sites by people during the arid glacial period – often citing the sites excavated by Sue and myself in the southern Kimberley amongst the evidence (see summary in Veth 2005). Such ideas suggest that people were not sufficiently flexible to deal with the LGM aridity. However, very few sediment studies and next to no micromorphology had been undertaken at any of these sites to understand the causes of the deposition breaks. Although the Kimberley region is in the tropical north, with a monsoonal climate of hot wet summers and cooler dry winters, the southern Kimberley is semi-arid and lies on the edge of the desert and would have been much drier during the LGM.

The Project

Following the 2007 meeting we began to devise a project informed by the questions discussed above. The remoteness of the research area makes it is a very expensive place to work. This meant that we had to apply for a competitive Australian Research Council Grant to pay for it and these are only open for applications annually with a very long review process of eight months. However, before we could apply we had to consult with, and receive approval from, the two Aboriginal Traditional Owners groups of the area. This was also a time-consuming process and involved attending several community meetings over a period of about two years, but we were fortunate in having the seed money to pay the transport costs. Traditional Owners have many issues on their plate, and we cannot expect them to prioritize our interests. Also an archaeological project has to have benefits for them so we had to make sure that any project met their needs and interests in addition to ours. These meetings went well, and both groups were very interested in the proposed work. They were keen for us to provide opportunities for their young people to obtain experience in excavating, mapping, and recording rock art. They also wanted all information to return to communities so that they can use it for management and education purposes.

In 2009 we applied for a grant and heard of its success in 2010. We called the project the "Lifeways of the First Australians," defining our research area as the part of the ancient limestone reef system in the southern Kimberley between the two localities where we had worked in the 1990s. The overall aim of the project was to produce a more holistic picture of the first Australians by recovering a large sample and a wider range of materials than had been previously recovered from Pleistocene deposits in any region in Australia. We wanted to investigate the technologies, evidence for subsistence, symbolism, and other social and economic behaviors in more detail to both characterize them and consider how they were used in the colonization of a new continent. The project also had many sub-questions, including interpreting the deposition hiatuses identified in the sites that had previously been excavated. The regional approach to the work was to provide an understanding of the different expressions of people's behavior in different places and the role of differences in local environment on the sequences recorded in archaeological deposits.

Approach

Such broad ranging research questions required multiple methods and excavations of several site in the region. One of the first steps was to apply for an excavation permit from the State government – a process that we knew would take several months.

For this project it was critical to produce a sound and detailed chronological framework to assess the timing of first occupation, identify periods where there were changes in occupation intensity, and compare the results between different sites. Identification of discontinuities in sediment deposition and human occupation also required a detailed analysis of the sediments. Given the problems in dating discussed above, we decided to use radiocarbon techniques where possible and to compare the results to those obtained from luminescence techniques. To help produce our chronological framework we teamed up with Zenobia Jacobs, an optically stimulated luminescence (OSL) dating expert who had a fellowship to re-date early Australian sites, and Rachel Woods, a radiocarbon dating expert. A PhD student with a background in micromorphology was appointed to analyze and interpret the sediments.

We gathered together specialists in faunal analysis, uranium series dating for assessing its potential for dating coatings over rock art, and a team of other people, including PhD students, to analyze and interpret stone artifacts, charcoal, and the rock art, which occurs in great abundance in most of the caves and rock shelters in the region but had never been systematically recorded or interpreted.

Neither Sue nor I had done a great deal of survey during the 1990s. In fact, the sites that we had previously excavated were not found by us but had been drawn to our attention by Traditional Owners. However, we suspected that there would be many more such sites in the reef complex, perhaps with even greater potential. What we were looking for were sites that might be attractive to live in – that is, with enough space for more than one person to move about in without hitting their head, and with good potential for deep, undisturbed sediment deposits. In our first field season in 2011, we spent a lot of time surveying the region looking for such sites; however, at the end of several weeks of this survey we concluded that the sites we had previously excavated were probably the best prospects in the area. We therefore decided to expand our previous excavations in two of these previously excavated sites, Riwi and Carpenter's Gap 3 (CG3), and to excavate at two other large sites, one of which was particularly rich in rock art and had numerous archaeological materials on its surface, and the other was close to a deep, water-filled gorge. We also began a rock art recording program.

Because the project has several components, I restrict my discussion here to interpreting the chronological sequences and our views from this work about the technology associated with first Sahul colonization.

The Excavations

In the second year of the project we commenced excavations, beginning with extensions of one of the previously excavated sites (CG3) by digging to its base in two squares. We also excavated two new rock shelters. In the following year we extended the 1 m square excavated in 1999 at Riwi to its bedrock and excavated three new 1 m squares in the site to bedrock. To ensure fine resolution in all sites, we excavated in 2 cm excavation units separating identifiable features, such as hearths and pits, and observable stratigraphic changes. To provide spatial resolution, each 1 m square was divided into four 50 cm quadrants and separately excavated. Stone artifacts and some large charcoal samples for dating were recorded in three dimensions.

To allow for later comparisons of changes in density of material over time, we recorded the weight and volume of all material recovered on previously prepared standard excavation recording forms. The sediments in each bucket were passed through 3 mm and 1.5 mm mesh screens. Samples of unsieved material were also collected to test whether very small material was present. Although we tried flotation to recover macrobotanical material at one site, preservation at most of the sites is dependent on desiccation and they are too fragile to be immersed in water. In situ charcoal samples for dating were taken, especially from hearths to ensure that dated charcoal was demonstrably anthropogenic. Samples for OSL dating were also taken, after first checking for background radiation.

Interpreting the Chronological Sequence

In the 1 m square excavated at Riwi in 1999 there appeared to be a marked discontinuity in the deposit between about 34,000 and 6,000 years ago. While this discontinuity covered the critical LGM period, if it did represent a time of no human occupation, it was a very long time. Some 250 km further to the west, CG3 appeared to have a hiatus in occupation during the LGM between about 25,000 and 15,000 years ago. Another site previously excavated, Carpenter's Gap 1 (CG1), only 3 km from CG3, had no hiatus but apparently reduced evidence for occupation during the LGM (O'Connor *et al.* 2014).

Clearly more dates were required to provide a finer-grained resolution that might help explain the differences between the sequences of the sites in the region. One site, Riwi, was selected for a particularly detailed dating program to examine differences between radiocarbon and OSL results. Because the base of the site is archaeologically sterile, it also had the potential to provide information on first occupation of the region.

The excavations in 2013 showed a similar sedimentary sequence to those exposed in 1999. A total of 12 stratigraphic units were identified, and 37 new radiocarbon dates were obtained (Figure 6.1). A vertical sequence of 37 OSL samples was taken down the wall of the 1999 square. The results of each method were modeled using Bayesian statistical techniques (Wood *et al.* 2016). A Bayesian analysis helps to reduce the uncertainty of ages estimated from the ranges provided by the error margins in the dating results. Only seven outliers were identified in the radiocarbon dates, one of these came from an area identified in the micromorphology as being affected by bioturbation, and the remaining six were all on small pieces of charcoal found

Figure 6.1 Section of Riwi, Square 1, East and South Walls, Kimberley, Australia. Picture shows the positions of some calibrated radiocarbon dates (bold) and optically-stimulated luminescence (OSL) dates (italicized). The dotted black line marks the main stratigraphic discontinuity. The vertical trench in the corner is where OSL samples were removed. Photograph by the author.

outside of hearths, suggesting minor movement in the sediment. This highlights the importance of sampling from discrete charcoal lenses or hearths. Once these were excluded, there was close agreement between the two dating techniques, suggesting that, for at least this area, the two techniques are comparable.

The model provided a date of 46.4-44.6 kcal BP for the oldest hearth and, although a handful of artifacts were recovered from up to 10 cm below this hearth, we could not be confident that these had not moved down the deposit through trampling. Thus this date is presently the most precisely dated secure age for human occupation of Sahul.

The remaining major question about the sequence interpretation concerned the hiatuses in the sites. This was at least partly answered by the better dating and the interpretation of micromorphology of the sediments in the context of cave morphology and other evidence of environmental change (Vannieuwenhuyse *et al.* 2017). At Riwi, the extension of excavations revealed that some sediments representing the LGM were present in the new squares near the cave wall and at the front of the cave. Interpretation of the sediments suggested that the long hiatus observed in the squares within the cave was the result of the cave reaching its maximum capacity at about 34 kcalBP which resulted in a shift to an erosional environment. The LGM deposits in the square in front of the cave contain much hearth residue and many stone artifacts suggesting that people did indeed occupy Riwi during the LGM. These findings are in contrast to the CG1 and CG3 sequences. The absence of deposition in CG3 at the critical period, and the generally small archaeological signature on either side of the LGM period, makes it difficult to identify whether or not the site was abandoned during that time. At CG1 there is evidence of occupation during the LGM but, like the other Pleistocene deposits in all sites, the low level of archaeological materials suggest infrequent occupation. The observed differences between all three sites are mainly related to the morphology and hydrologic regime of each shelter (Vannieuwenhuyse *et al.* 2017).

We could conclude from all of this that it is dangerous to interpret regional occupation sequences from one or two sites. Sites that are geographically close can have very different sequences, and even within a single site, sequences can vary dramatically. However, we could say that the southern Kimberley sites cannot support abandonment of the arid zone during the LGM and that the causes of discontinuities in other sites should be investigated more closely.

The Technology

The low numbers of retouched stone artifacts in the Pleistocene deposits made it difficult to answer our questions about Pleistocene colonizing technology. Because Australian Pleistocene stone artifacts are relatively undifferentiated, the approach to analysis was to characterize the reduction sequences (Hiscock and Tabrett 2010) to see whether there were any identifiable changes in the way in which people made artifacts. Like previous Australian studies we found no significant changes in the Pleistocene contrasting dramatically with Holocene changes. However, in CG1 a single flake with polish on it was found from sediments dated to between 44 and 49 kcal BP (Hiscock *et al.* 2016). This flake was found not in the sieves but by a student sorting the artifacts excavated during the 1990s. Close analysis of the flake suggested that it was from an edge ground axe and was probably discarded when re-sharpening the axe. Because this flake was then the oldest evidence for edge ground axes in the world, we had to be sure that the flake had not moved from further up the deposit. If that had occurred we would expect smaller specimens in the low levels including the axe levels, than in immediately higher ones. We therefore examined the relationship between depth and artifact size for specimens in excavation units and established that there is no significant relationship between depth and artifact mass. There are at least two other northern Australian sites with similar evidence from the deepest part of the deposit and fragments of edge ground axes frequently occur in Pleistocene sites in northern Australia, including in other sites investigated for this project. As edge ground axes do not occur anywhere else in the world (apart from Japan) until the Holocene, they must be a novel adaptation by the first Australian colonizers. Ethnographically such objects are used to chop hard woods from which wooden artifacts are made, supporting our hypothesis about the importance of organic technologies in the colonization of Sahul.

Discussion

Perhaps the biggest take-home message about undertaking a regional project in a remote area is that nothing happens instantly. Don't expect to be able to dream a project and begin work straight away. This is especially so when other groups of people have interests in the region in which you want to work; therefore, you need to be prepared to be flexible in your approach and schedule. Also, you can't expect to do it all yourself. Individuals do not have the expertise to cover all aspects of the work so it is important to gather a team of experts, all of whom have to have the personality to cope with trying field conditions in remote areas (no cell phones to stare at in this area).

Of course a lot more has come out, and is still coming out, of this project than discussed here, but we have already answered the fundamental chronological questions. We have found good correspondence between radiocarbon dating and OSL, at least for this region of Australia, and by modeling the dates using Bayesian techniques, we were able to obtain a much more precise date for first occupation of Sahul than has been previously available. While our results suggest that first occupation was after 50 kcal BP, sequences from elsewhere in Australia need to be analyzed in a similar way to produce secure, precise dates.

This analysis, together with detailed analyses of the stratigraphy, sediment, archaeological features, and materials, provided us with a good lesson in not drawing grand conclusions from single sites, or even in making pronouncements about the sequence in a site from a small excavation. The regional approach we used allowed us to understand why there is variation and to conclude that in the Pleistocene, evidence for human occupation in the southern Kimberley is sporadic and fluctuates in ways that seem to be largely independent of local climatic variation. This indicates the adaptability of the first colonizers and suggests that arid zone sites need to be individually examined before regional conclusions about abandonment can be made.

Unfortunately, despite our extensive excavations we did not recover as large a sample of Pleistocene artifacts as we had hoped. However, what we did find supported our suspicion that organic technology was especially important in the colonization of Sahul. In particular, the world's first invention of edge ground axes in northern Australia represents an innovation associated with the production of organic technology in this new environment. It doesn't matter what time period you are working in, but don't forget that the "invisible" technology may be much more important than what is preserved in the sites.

It is possible that the small samples recovered may be because we have confined our excavations to caves and rock shelters and, as in the recent past, people might have lived more often in open areas. Our future plans are to excavate open sites and, while it is unlikely that organic artifacts will be preserved in such sites, at least we know that OSL dating will be reliable. The project has led me in entirely new directions. For example, the role of symbolic behavior by the first Australians, in particular beads, which are common in these sites, and their distribution far from their original source, has directed my interest to the different meanings of beads in different contexts in Australia. In addition, the independent invention of new technologies in a new environment (in this case the edge ground axe) has led me to think about the effect of the arrival of new technologies within established societies. Recently I have begun a project on the effect of the sudden appearance in the mid-Holocene of a living technology – the Australian dingo.

Paired Reading

Balme, Jane and Sue O'Connor. 2014. "Early Modern Humans in Island Southeast Asia and Sahul: Adaptive and Creative Societies with Simple Lithic Industries." In *East of Africa: Southern Asia, Australia and Human Origins*, edited by Robin Dennell and Martin Porr, 164–174. Cambridge: Cambridge University Press.

References

Balme, Jane, Iain Davidson, Josephine McDonald, Nicola Stern, and Peter Veth. 2009. "Symbolic Behavior and the Peopling of the Southern Arc Route to Australia." *Quaternary International*, 202: 59–68. DOI: 10.1016/j.quaint.2008.10.002.

Balme, Jane and Sue O'Connor. 2014. "Early Modern Humans in Island Southeast Asia and Sahul: Adaptive and Creative Societies with Simple Lithic Industries." In *East of Africa: Southern Asia, Australia and Human Origins*, edited by Robin Dennell and Martin Porr, 164–174. Cambridge: Cambridge University Press.

Hiscock, Peter, Sue O'Connor, Jane Balme, and Tim Maloney. 2016. "World's Earliest Ground-Edge Axe Production Coincides with Human Colonization of Australia." *Australian Archaeology*, 82: 2–11. DOI: 10.1080/03122417.2016.1164379.

Hiscock, Peter and Amy Tabrett. 2010. "Generalization, Inference and the Quantification of Lithic Reduction." *World Archaeology*, 42: 545–561. DOI: 10.1080/00438243.2010.517669.

Mellars, Paul. 2006. "Going East: New Genetic and Archaeological Perspectives on the Modern Human Colonization of Eurasia." *Science*, 313: 796–800. DOI: 10.1126/science.1128402.

O'Connell, James F. and James F. Allen. 2015. "The Process, Biotic Impact, and Global Implications of the Human Colonization of Sahul about 47,000 Years Ago." *Journal of Archaeological Science*, 56: 73–84. DOI: 10.1016/j.jas.2015.02.020.

O'Connor, Sue, Tim Maloney, Dorcas Vannieuwenhuyse, Jane Balme and Rachel Wood. 2014. "Occupation at Carpenter's Gap 3, Windjana Gorge, Kimberley, Western Australia." *Australian Archaeology*, 78: 10–23. DOI: 10.1080/03122417.2014.11681994.

Vannieuwenhuyse, Dorcas, Sue O'Connor, and Jane Balme. 2017. "Settling in Sahul: Investigating Environmental and Human History Interactions through Micromorphological Analyses in Tropical Semi-Arid North-West Australia." *Journal of Archaeological Science*, 77(172): 193. DOI: 10.1016/j.jas.2016.01.017.

Veth, Peter. 2005. "Between the Desert and the sea: Archaeologies of the Western Desert and Pilbara Regions, Australia." In *Desert Peoples: Archaeological Perspectives*, edited by Peter Veth, Peter Hiscock, and Michael Smith, 132–141. Malden, MA: Blackwell.

Wood, Rachel, Zenobia Jacobs, Dorcas Vannieuwenhuyse, Jane Balme, Sue O'Connor, and Rose Whitau. 2016. "Towards an Accurate and Precise Chronology for the Colonization of Australia: The Example of Riwi, Kimberley, Western Australia." *PLOS ONE*, DOI:10.1371/journal.pone.0160123

7

The Kuril Biocomplexity Project: Anatomy of an Interdisciplinary Research Program in the North Pacific
Ben Fitzhugh

Project Summary

The Kuril Biocomplexity Project (KBP) was an interdisciplinary field survey of the Northwest Pacific Kuril archipelago, undertaken to explore settlement history and associated human-environmental dynamics in a remote, island region. We conducted archaeological survey in parallel with studies of volcanic, tsunami, climatic, and ecological histories. Interdisciplinary collaboration revolved around island biogeography theory and ecological anthropology, tuned to what little was known about the islands. After several seasons of field and lab work, we answered some of our initial questions and moved on to explore new questions raised. It sounds simple, but it was not so easy or so straightforward. We faced logistical, methodological, diplomatic, and conceptual challenges we did not anticipate. Some were overcome, some remain to be resolved, and others we can chalk-up as lessons in humility. This chapter presents the story of a complex research program that is anything but a model for an early career project, but one that can provide insight into how a research career might expand beyond a "first" project.

Introduction

The volcanic Kuril Islands stretch from Hokkaido, Japan to Kamchatka, Russia – almost 1100 km (Figure 7.1a, 7.1b). They stand sentry over foggy passes connecting the northwest Pacific and Sea of Okhotsk. Most of the islands are covered by subarctic tundra, and – except for the northernmost and southernmost islands – terrestrial faunas are limited to voles and foxes. The waters surrounding the Kurils are seasonally productive, feeding seabirds, fish, and sea mammals. Seasonal variability is extreme, with dense fog and relatively calm seas for a couple of months in summer, while winter brings snow, pack ice and intense storms.

The Kurils were occupied for thousands of years by a succession of marine-oriented hunting-fishing-gathering cultures. The core archaeological research goals of our project were to understand how people were affected by and managed the remoteness and environmental vulnerability of island life, especially in the more insular (and smaller) central islands. To do this, we needed a record of human settlement history, population change, natural hazards, and climate/ecological change.

I was in my second term as an assistant professor when I was asked to take a look at a photograph of some pit features in the Kurils. The photo had been taken the summer before during a biological survey project. We agreed that the features looked like house structures and an

Engaging Archaeology: 25 Case Studies in Research Practice, First Edition. Edited by Stephen W. Silliman.
© 2018 John Wiley & Sons, Inc. Published 2018 by John Wiley & Sons, Inc.

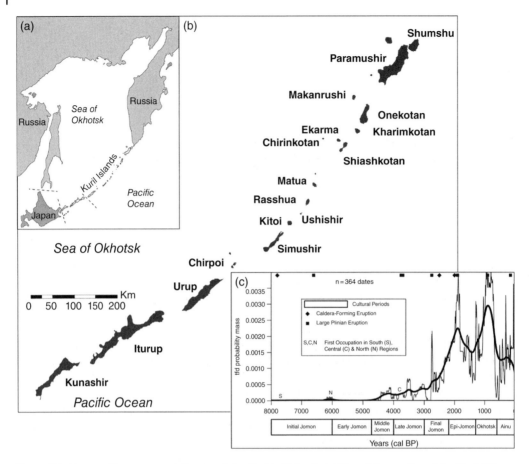

Figure 7.1 Maps and human population trends for the Kuril Islands. (a) Map of the northwest Pacific; (b) Close-up map of the Kuril Islands; (c) Human population reconstruction trend reconstruction (see text and Fitzhugh *et al.* 2016).

archaeological survey of the islands might provide anthropological context for contemporary island ecology. That was in the spring of 1998. We visited the islands with the biologists in the summers of 1999 and 2000, gaining a better handle on the archaeological potential. But it took eight years before a full-scale archaeological and paleoenvironmental expedition could be initiated.

For some of us there is nothing more satisfying (and sometimes frustrating) than working collaboratively and comprehensively on "big picture" questions with colleagues who bring different skills and perspectives. KBP was intensely collaborative. There were roughly 35 scientific personnel from three countries and five disciplines in the field each of the three main seasons (2006–2008). Many others participated in the lab and seminars. Every aspect of the endeavor was more complex than anything I had organized before.

Biographical Account

I was raised on subarctic coastal archaeology. Some of my earliest memories come from summers spent traveling the coast and islands of northern Labrador, Canada, surveying and excavating sites of past maritime cultures with my archaeologist father, family, and crew.

That lifestyle convinced me to pursue archaeology as a career. In 1987 I helped excavate an amazing, well-preserved "wet site" on Kodiak Island, Alaska, a project that got me to the Pacific and led to dissertation and subsequent research in Alaska.

I went to the Kurils for the first time in the summer of 2000. Biologist Ted Pietsch invited me to assemble a small group to consider prehistoric human influences on island biogeography and biodiversity. We discovered that the Kurils had been occupied by maritime hunter-gatherers for millennia, though by the time we got there, the islands were largely abandoned (Fitzhugh *et al.* 2002). Japanese and Russian archaeologists had previously documented the outlines of this history, mostly from the more accessible southern and northernmost islands. The more remote, central Kuril Islands were poorly known, and no one had yet approached the region holistically, to document changing settlement distributions, zooarchaeology, or the environmental context of occupations. While interdisciplinary "environmental archaeology" is not new, it was a novelty in the region, where archaeological research has focused primarily on culture historical description and change.

In three weeks in 2000 we tested 11 sites on as many islands and found evidence of significant human occupation throughout the islands. More sustained research would be needed to unpack the relationships of natural and human history in the Kuril chain. We would require a substantial team of archaeologists, geologists, geographers, oceanographers and paleoecologists working together, sharing observations, and collaborating actively. Such a project confronts two fundamental challenges: 1) building an effective interdisciplinary team and 2) finding substantial funding to pay for what would amount to multiple, simultaneous research activities *and* the cost of ship-based logistics in a remote region. Given the need to move between islands each field season, we needed a ship, a floating research platform for summer field seasons. Ship-time, even in the Russian Far East in the early 2000s, is expensive!

As it happened, pulling together a team was not difficult. Two of my colleagues had ongoing collaborations with Russians in the Russian Far East and Eastern Siberia, studying paleo-earthquakes and tsunamis, pollen, and paleoclimates. They were eager to work in the poorly known Kurils. We each had additional colleagues in the United States, Japan, and Russia who would bring technical and regional expertise in areas such as volcanology/tephrochronology, paleoceanography, climate, and demographic modeling. We needed Russian hosts to help coordinate logistics and permits for the work. Fortunately, the archaeologist we worked with in 2000, Valery Shubin and volcanologist Alexander Rybin, were willing to help organize logistics, including arranging research ships each summer and getting the necessary permits for research. With prospective partners engaged, we had to negotiate collaborative agreements with several research institutions in Russia, essential to any international work.

Funding was a bigger challenge – a normal situation even for small-scale projects. The National Science Foundation is the standard funding agency for US research, including archaeology at both the dissertation and professional levels. Indeed, every PhD student should plan on submitting an application for dissertation funding to the relevant agencies in their country. This serves several purposes beyond, hopefully, providing necessary funding. It ensures a well-reasoned and vetted research plan that can provide guidance later into the project when the immediacy and reality of research inevitably distracts us from our larger goals – and sometimes confronts us with the need to modify our original plan. Of course, experience in grant-writing is also valuable professional experience that counts when competing for almost any higher-level position in archaeology.

The NSF Archaeology Program is the primary funding source for US archaeology projects. It has modest budgets of roughly US$ 20,000 for graduate student research and US$ 200–300k for professional level grants. Unfortunately, there is nothing modest about conducting interdisciplinary research in remote islands, by ship, for multiple seasons. We needed a budget in excess of US$ 2 million, an order of magnitude greater than budgets available through the usual channels. To fund such a project – at least for those with (generally poorly-funded) social science at the core – researchers often look to special, cross-cutting or thematic programs involving climate, earth, and biological sciences.

The NSF "Biocomplexity in the Environment" Program was just such a program, with targeted budgets of US$ 2 million for projects up to five years. One of the themes of this program was the study of "Coupled Human and Natural Systems." The fit could not be better. Of course, reviewers had different ideas the first, second…and even third times we submitted an application. For us, the fourth time was the charm, and in late 2005, we were granted the funding.

Early career researchers should take note not to give up after one or two rejections, and this rings true for both grant proposals and manuscript submissions. It is the norm, not the exception, to receive multiple rejections before success, even for smaller-scale, "standard" projects. Usually a component of the problem is simply too many high-quality proposals for too little funding. Even so, the review process provides a valuable source of professional guidance for improving the research plan or clarity of presentation. Having served on a number of NSF review panels, I cannot emphasize enough the importance of taking seriously and addressing reviewer recommendations in subsequent submissions of a proposal. Assume that resubmitted proposals will be reviewed by some of the same and some new reviewers. Respect reviewer time and feedback, even if you disagree with it.

Methods

The Kuril Biocomplexity Project began in earnest in the summer of 2006 when our international team steamed out of the port of Korsakov for our first six-week research cruise. Our archaeological field methods were basic: land at as many locations and on as many islands as possible; search for archaeological evidence such as pit houses and eroding archaeological deposits; and use cleaned erosion exposures, test pits, and occasionally larger excavations to sample cultural stratigraphy for datable charcoal, fauna, and artifacts. Our natural science colleagues sampled tsunami deposits on adjacent beaches and terraces and took tephra and pollen samples from a range of archaeological and non-archaeological settings to reconstruct past vegetation, sea level, and climate changes. At times we worked together and at times from completely different camps or the ship for weeks at a time. Sometimes archaeological and geological data could be correlated directly (e.g., tephra layers interspersed with archaeological layers). In other cases, we had to rely on chronological correlations based on radiocarbon and tephra dates.

Theory

The theoretical framework that guided the project had a strongly environmental flavor, derived from biological ecology and the idea that island size and isolation from source populations influence the diversity and fragility of island fauna and flora. This "theory of island biogeography" has been applied in island archaeology before with mixed results, but for our purposes, it set up clear expectations about the interaction between human colonists and endemic faunas. We predicted that human hunter-fisher-gatherers moving into increasingly remote and small islands would be more likely to destabilize endemic faunas that they in turn needed to survive. In behavioral ecology the concept of resource over-exploitation is called *resource depression* – when prey return rates decline due to over-harvesting. The twist for remote islands is that faunal diversity is already low, leaving fewer alternative resource options and making more likely the possibility that loss of subsistence options could undermine the potential for continued occupation. Accordingly, smaller islands, such as those in the central Kurils, with more limited faunal diversity, should have been last settled and most precarious to occupy. This relationship is qualified, but not nullified, when the foragers depend on migratory maritime resources.

In coastal Japan and mainland East Asia south of the Kurils, open-water navigation, deep-sea fishing, and sea mammal hunting appeared by the early Holocene. The subarctic and Arctic coasts north of Hokkaido, including the Kurils, were clearly settled by maritime communities only after 4000 years BP (Fitzhugh 2016).

Once settled, the Kurils – especially the small, central islands – presented unique challenges. This is because small, remote islands commonly support low biotic diversity and high rates of local extinction. Ecosystems with low diversity leave fewer alternatives when an important resource becomes scarce. While marine species are less confined to individual island habitats, maritime foragers should still experience occasional shortfalls due to climatic variability, catastrophic geological events, and/or over-harvesting that would be most devastating in the central islands.

This island biogeography-based model formed the core framework for our research, but was itself insufficient to capture the strategic and social nature of human foraging. Our model was made more suitably "human" with the addition of ideas from ecological anthropology concerning mobility and social networking. People move and use social networks strategically for many reasons, including as "insurance" when hard times hit. Networks are established and maintained through marriage connections, occasional social calls, trade and gifting. Extensive social networks might be particularly desirable for settlers in the remote Kurils. We further reasoned that high travel costs (and dangers) would make imperative the development of local strategies. Accordingly, settlers of remote islands have the greatest need to move and maintained extensive networks at least initially but pay the highest costs to maintain them, providing an imperative to focus on intensive and local strategies to mitigate local hazards. We expected to see shifts between these strategies in consort with environmental and demographic changes. As discussed below, additional theoretical concepts became important during interpretation of results, such as "political economics" and the "core-periphery," or "world systems" perspectives.

Results

Evaluating our predictions required evidence for human population trends throughout the islands, including colonization and abandonment. We needed to measure changes in degrees of mobility and non-local social interactions, the status of subsistence resources, climate and ecological change, and natural hazard frequencies.

Human population trends were estimated using frequency distributions of radiocarbon dates based on 364 charcoal samples from components at 70 sites throughout the island chain (Figure 7.1c). Techniques, assumptions, and limitations of this method have been well-exercised in the archaeological literature over the past couple of decades (Brown 2015 and references). Results of this analysis showed robust cycles of population expansion and contraction – twice, in fact – over the past 3,500 years, with gradual expansion to 2000 BP, attrition until about 1300 BP, explosive growth to 1000 BP, total collapse around 750 BP, with minor resettlement over the past 500 years (Figure 7.1c; Fitzhugh *et al.* 2016).

The strength of the pattern was surprising. However, did environmental factors play a role as our model anticipated, or was something else involved?

We started by looking at the geological data to see if catastrophic events, particularly large eruptions or tsunamis, could have triggered the population declines, especially in the more remote and ecologically "fragile" islands. Surprisingly, we found that populations did particularly *well* during intervals of more frequent and larger eruptions. Large events could be found associated with peak population throughout the islands, which *could* have triggered a chain reaction from ecological and logistic crises to population decline. But even these events appear to have been relatively local. In one of the most extreme cases, the massive caldera-forming eruption of Ushishir about 2100 cal BP dumped over 30 cm of volcanic ash on the neighboring island of Rasshua, 25 km away. A site was buried in the process but reoccupied soon after. While local impacts of large eruptions were likely significant, no evidence suggests that the eruption had any long-term negative consequences on that community or that of the broader population. Thus, even the largest Kuril eruptions appeared to be local events of limited impact. Mobility and reliance on a maritime economy may have helped mitigate volcanic impacts.

Our geological colleagues estimated tsunami frequencies of 10–30 m elevation at intervals of 150 and 500 years (MacInnes *et al.* 2016). Ethnographic analogues suggest that information could be preserved over this interval in oral histories, and even settlers coming from coastal Hokkaido or Kamchatka would have been aware of tsunami hazards. The elevations of Kuril archaeological settlements – typically 20–40 m above sea level and often on the lower-risk, Okhotsk Sea side of the archipelago – provides evidence for evasive practices grounded in traditional experience. Tsunamis could have a more wide-ranging impact on near-shore ecology, arising from scour of shallow subtidal and intertidal habitat and coastal inundation and erosion. We can't evaluate these factors explicitly, lacking relevant information. In any case, like effects of volcanic eruptions, tsunami impacts can be mitigated by short moves to unaffected areas, which could usually be found on the opposite side of any island. We concluded that natural hazards were local affairs that could have had serious impacts for human life, health, and food security at the scale of individual or neighboring communities without undermining broader population dynamics.

The implications of climate change are even more difficult to measure. In general, the lake pollen suggested broad climate stability through the late Holocene (Anderson *et al.* 2015), while peat samples, which are often more sensitive to very local conditions, showed evidence of subtle, but perhaps significant, climate changes (Razjigaeva *et al.* 2013). Near-shore lake cores showed high sand influxes that may relate to increased aridity or storminess (Anderson *et al.* 2015). Coupled with evidence of relative sea level fluctuations, the paleoecological data suggest intervals of coastal stability and intervals of active dune mobilization. The results so far show some environmental changes that correlate with human population changes and some that do not (Fitzhugh 2012).

Food security is best studied with a variety of zooarchaeological and paleobotanical data. While people ate a range of plant products (terrestrial and marine), their primary source of calories, protein, and fats came from fish, sea mammals, and birds. Shellfish were important near Kamchatka and Hokkaido, where intertidal habitats supported a wider variety. While zooarchaeological collections were a primary goal of our sampling strategy – and key to the biogeographical research orientation – we were dismayed to find fauna preserved only from a single time interval (1200–750 BP). In volcanic soils, fauna are usually preserved well only when shells are abundant in the midden matrix, as these provide a counter-balance to the background acidity. Without many shells in middens from the central islands, faunas older than about 1200 BP were lost, a major hindrance to testing our resource depression hypotheses. We are currently trying to mitigate this problem, expanding samples from the northern islands where shell middens are prevalent.

In aggregate and at century scale resolution, comparison of population trends and regional climate proxies argues against simple climate-deterministic impacts on Kuril settlement. Kuril populations thrived and declined equally in both warm and cool intervals. This suggests that climate and ecological changes were not directly, or simply, responsible for population fluctuations. Such comparisons do not rule out climate impacts at the scale of years to decades, but they provide an opening to consider more complex hypotheses.

This returns us to mobility and social networking and how these practices connected Kuril occupants to influences of the larger Northeast Asian social world. We addressed these topics with obsidian and pottery source data. Kuril occupants obtained a variety of lithic materials directly from local beaches, but obsidian, the highest quality tool-stone available, could be obtained only from Hokkaido or Kamchatka. In his doctoral dissertation, Colby Phillips (2011) found that prior to 1300 BP, Epi-Jomon got obsidian from the nearest source (north or south), with overlapping distribution in the central islands. This pattern is expected of "down-the-line" trade connecting communities living more or less permanently within island groups to outside sources. The Okhotsk pattern (1300–750 BP) is different, with most obsidian coming from Kamchatka. Presumably Okhotsk settlers were cut off from access to Hokkaido obsidian. Perhaps they had developed unfriendly relations with cousins in Eastern Hokkaido, which could have motivated their initial movement into the Kurils. If so, the need for social networks elsewhere would have led Okhotsk to seek contacts to the north. But if the northern contacts were unstable, the Kuril Okhotsk might have been less resilient to natural hazards and subsistence failure than their predecessors. This might have played a role in their shorter residence time in the islands.

Pottery analysis allowed us to look more closely at inter-island interactions. In his dissertation, Erik Gjesfjeld (2016) found that pottery composition for both Epi-Jomon and Okhotsk periods clustered into clay source-groups centered in different parts of the archipelago. Such distributions suggest local production and limited transport, though some pots were transported longer distances. These data again support the conclusion that Epi-Jomon and Okhotsk settlers were year-round residents connected more broadly by social networks.

The accumulated evidence suggests resilience to environmental variability and persistent reliance on extensive social networks. These conclusions led me to expand my thinking about how social factors outside of the islands may have affected the welfare of Kuril settlers. For example, the Japanese state formed in the early first millennium CE, and the accompanying demand for raw materials and prestige commodities led to increased interaction and resource extraction to the north, eventually reaching Hokkaido. Simultaneously, markets originating in mainland East Asia (China, Korea, lower Manchuria) inspired trade down the Amur River and into Sakhalin and Hokkaido. The Kurils probably remained peripheral to much of this expanding commodities trade prior to the seventeenth through nineteenth centuries. At that time Ainu groups moved into the Kurils to hunt seal and sea otter for the pelt trade with Japanese and Russians. But earlier trade could have affected Kuril Epi-Jomon and Okhotsk settlers by undermining or destabilizing critical social networks between the Kurils and Hokkaido and/or by introducing epidemics to small, vulnerable Kuril communities.

These ideas remain to be more fully explored and research will continue but represent the fertility of a research program with a comprehensive orientation. I expect to refine, reject, and expand hypotheses and interpretations with future work. This is the nature of archaeological research. Projects start and end, often with cycles of funding and publication (including student dissertations). But in my experience, effective research programs often never really end, or at least not with tidy conclusions. Instead, they evolve with accumulated insights, inevitable obstacles, rejected hypotheses, new analytical technologies, and new ideas!

Reflections

The KBP project was successful in addressing some of the original research questions. While some aspects of the proposed project remain unfulfilled, the results so far are gratifying. Each disciplinary team – and indeed each national team to some extent – had its own research tradition, questions, optimal scales of analyses (spatial and temporal), and terminologies. These differences can create impediments to field communication and logistics, data comparison, and synthesis. Overcoming these issues is vital for successful interdisciplinary research, and it often falls on the shoulders of archaeologists to lead their resolution because of our commonly greater dependence on environmental data than vice versa.

Lessons Learned

The Kuril Biocomplexity Project was an expensive and complicated research endeavor, lasting almost a decade and bringing together a host of collaborators including undergraduate and graduate students, university professors, museum scholars, and other researchers. It led to numerous reports, conference presentations, publications, and educational materials, much not discussed here. It was *not* my first research project nor the first for my peer collaborators. Nevertheless, KBP carries lessons for early career researchers. First, it shares many characteristics with any good project: a theoretically informed model to guide research activities and analyses; a clear set of objectives for generating and analyzing data; and both logistical and intellectual flexibility and open-mindedness. Proposal reviewers for research at any stage expect achievable goals linked to relevant research questions. In our case the relevance was tied to more general questions about the relationship of community vulnerability to environmental and social risks.

Naturally, first projects should be more limited in scope. A common mistake – that I make often – is to propose to do too much. A good advisor will help student researchers scale prospective projects to achievable objectives. But good research, even at the starting level, should connect to larger questions and lead to expanded research possibilities. Distilled to their basics, lessons for early career researchers from KBP include:

1) Interdisciplinary research is challenging and rewarding. Interdisciplinary thinking builds intellectual creativity, flexibility, and proficiency beyond what one can learn through disciplinary specialization, though having a specialty is critical as well. It may seem daunting and contradictory to be expected to become specialized while simultaneously broadening one's interdisciplinary proficiency. It is! But the effort will forge a better scholar, and a better understanding of the world.

2) When engaging in cross-disciplinary collaborations be prepared to learn enough of the collaborating discipline to understand its research objectives, scales of analysis, and limitations. Don't be surprised to discover scale-mismatch problems that need to be acknowledged and circumnavigated.

3) Give specialists space to deal with their own disciplinary needs while finding channels for meaningful collaboration.

4) Invest in good working relations with potential collaborators, including graduate students in cognate fields.

5) Nest achievable goals into a broader research vision, and don't be afraid to let your research evolve in unanticipated directions.

Paired Reading

Fitzhugh, Ben, Erik W. Gjesfjeld, William A. Brown, Mark J. Hudson, and Jennie D. Shaw. 2016. "Resilience and the Population History of the Kuril Islands, Northwest Pacific: A Study in Complex Human Ecodynamics." *Quaternary International*, 419: 165–193. DOI: 10.1016/j.quaint.2016.02.003.

References

Anderson, Patricia, Pavel Minyuk, Anatoly Lozhkin, Marina Cherepanova, Vladimir Borkhodoev, and Bruce Finney. 2015. "A Multiproxy Record of Holocene Environmental Changes from the Northern Kuril Islands (Russian Far East)." *Journal of Paleolimnology*, 54, 379–393. DOI: 10.1007/s10933-015-9858-y.

Brown, William A. 2015. "Through a Filter, Darkly: Population Size Estimation, Systematic Error, and Random Error in Radiocarbon-Supported Demographic Temporal Frequency Analysis." *Journal of Archaeological Science* 53, 133–147. DOI: 10.1016/j.jas.2014.10.013.

Fitzhugh, Ben. 2012. "Hazards, Impacts, and Resilience among Hunter-Gatherers of the Kuril Islands." In *Surviving Sudden Environmental Change: Answers from Archaeology*, edited by Jago Cooper and Payson Sheets. 19–42. Boulder, CO: University of Colorado Press.

Fitzhugh, Ben. 2016. "Origins and Development of Arctic Maritime Adaptations in the Western Subarctic." In *Oxford Handbook of the Prehistoric Arctic*, edited by T. Max Friesen and Owen K. Mason, 253– 278. Oxford: Oxford University Press.

Fitzhugh, Ben, Erik W. Gjesfjeld, William A. Brown, Mark J. Hudson, and Jennie D. Shaw. 2016. "Resilience and the Population History of the Kuril Islands, Northwest Pacific: A Study in Complex Human Ecodynamics." *Quaternary International*, 419: 165–193. DOI: 10.1016/j.quaint.2016.02.003.

Fitzhugh, Ben, Valery O. Shubin, Kaoru Tezuka, Yoshihiro Ishizuka, and Carole A. S. Mandryk. 2002. "Archaeology in the Kuril Islands: Advances in the Study of Human Paleobiogeography and Northwest Pacific Prehistory." *Arctic Anthropology*, 39: 69–94.

Gjesfjeld, Erik W. 2016. "The Compositional Analysis of Hunter-Gatherer Pottery from the Kuril Islands." *Journal of Archaeological Science: Reports*. DOI: 10.1016/j.jasrep.2016.03.049.

MacInnes, Breanyn, Ekaterina Kravchunovskaya, Tatiana Pinegina, and Joanne Bourgeois. 2016. "Paleotsunamis from the Central Kuril Islands Segment of the Japan-Kuril-Kamchatka Subduction Zone." *Quaternary Research*, 86: 54–66. DOI: 10.1016/j.yqres.2016.03.005.

Phillips, Stephen. 2011. "Networked Glass: Lithic Raw Material Consumption and Social Networks in the Kuril Islands." PhD Dissertation. Seattle, WA: University of Washington.

Razjigaeva, Nadezhda G., Larisa A. Ganzey, Tatyana A. Grebennikova, Nina I. Belyanina, Ludmila M. Mokhova, Khikmat A. Arslanov, and Sergei B. Chernov, 2013. "Holocene Climatic Changes and Vegetation Development in the Kuril Islands." *Quaternary International*, 290: 126–138. DOI: 10.1016/j.quaint.2012.06.034.

8

Listen for the Echo of Drums Across the Water: Rock Art Sites as Engaged Community Research in Ontario, Canada

John William Norder

Project Summary

Since the summer of 1998, I have conducted archaeological research in the Lake of the Woods region of northwestern Ontario, Canada. The area is rich in Indigenous rock paintings dating back potentially thousands of years. These sites and the contemporary Indigenous communities that continue to engage them remain central to the broader research that I do, which focuses on the relationships that past and present Indigenous peoples have with their natural and social landscapes. In recent rock art studies, landscape has become a common focus, moving beyond traditional studies that only examine the meaning of images and compositions of rock paintings towards a consideration of these sites as part of larger created social landscapes. In this chapter, I focus primarily on the rock art research I undertook between 2000 and 2005.

Prologue

When paddling a canoe through the wilderness of northern Ontario, it's easy to fall into a state of mind where it's just you moving through a landscape empty of people. Periodically, you encounter beaver dams, ranging in size from small 1- or 2-foot barriers that you can just slide your canoe over to 15-foot-high, quarter-mile wide blockades that leave you speechless and humbled at the scale of their engineering. Between waterways, you portage from lake to lake along narrow animal paths where your only encounters, if any, are with deer, moose, and maybe an occasional bear. Back on the water, the haunting call of loons echoes off the rocky shores and cliffs. It's a place that is filled with life, but truly feels untouched by human hands. However, in the evening, you sit at your camp and idly scrape away a bit of the thin soil and you find a scattering of tiny stone flakes. Nearby, in a crack in the rocky surface you find some more along with some small pieces of pottery. Humans have been here before.

The next morning, the winds blows out of the west, and as you set out on the water for the next leg of your paddle you stay close to the western shorelines to avoid the waves further out. Lichens cover the cliff walls you pass, many a dark green or black but an occasional orange lichen attracts your attention. One such cluster of orange lichens catches the corner of your eye, and as you look closer you notice the orange is more of a red. Suddenly the shape of a human with its arms raised appears to you along with a series of other images including birds, lines, and strange otherworldly figures that provide both a sense of excitement and foreboding.

Engaging Archaeology: 25 Case Studies in Research Practice, First Edition. Edited by Stephen W. Silliman.
© 2018 John Wiley & Sons, Inc. Published 2018 by John Wiley & Sons, Inc.

As you ponder what you are seeing, you hear the gentle lapping of the water against the cliff. It's a soothing rhythm that lends to the serenity of this place where water meets the land meets the sky. It is like the sound of drums, and it echoes across the water.

The Questions of Rock Art

When I encountered my first rock painting site in northwestern Ontario, I had no idea what I was looking at (Figure 8.1). There was a human figure, a bird figure, a bunch of animals, and handprints which were all easily recognizable, but there were lines, shapes, circles, and other images that weren't. All of them were painted at the same spot, and I had to wrap my head around the idea that this "meant" something that I didn't understand but had undertaken the task of researching. As with all the other sites that I subsequently documented, I began with the assumption that these collections of images formed compositions and were placed together at these locations by an individual or group of people for some meaningful purpose. By extension, each place would have served as a "message" of some "type," and each message was important enough to be placed in locations visible to others who might pass by as they either canoed or, in the winter when the water was frozen, walked by. Within the larger Canadian Shield Rock Art Tradition, which include the sites in Ontario, it is estimated that there are probably more than 3,000 rock painting sites stretching from Québec to Saskatchewan. Of these, perhaps a dozen are not found on or overlooking bodies of water.

In any interpretive endeavor, the first question we need to ask is "who are the makers?" To do this we also need to know how old the paintings are; however, paintings in the Canadian Shield are notoriously difficult to date. The reason is that the sites are almost exclusively open-air

Figure 8.1 Cliff face with pictograph, northwestern Ontario. Can you find it? Photograph by the author.

sites, which are exposed to the elements year-round. In a region of pronounced seasonal variation this means that a good deal of the "paint" weathers away over time, particularly any of the potentially organic, and therefore easily dateable, components. However, there are some rock painting sites that have a mineral drip that accretes over the rock surface on which the paintings are found due to water seepage from cracks above. Organic materials, in this case, are sealed in and can and have been dated on paintings at one site in Québec, which yielded a result of ca. AD 0 (Arsenault *et al.* 1995). However, this method has not been replicated at other sites in the Canadian Shield.

Within my study area, people have made educated guesses about the time period that these sites originated. In this case, it is the Laurel Culture (300 BC to AD 1000) (Rajnovich 1994) and is coincident with the one dated site in Québec. However, in the broader region, paintings have been documented to have been made at least as recently as the eighteenth or nineteenth century (Conway and Conway 1991). As a result, rock painting originated and has endured in its production for up to 2,000 years. This span of time includes up to three other post-Laurel archaeological cultures: Blackduck, Selkirk, and Sandy Lake. In turn these archaeological cultures are ancestral to today's Algonquian and Siouan language-speaking peoples who currently inhabit the Canadian Shield, specifically the Algonquian-speaking Anishinaabeg, Saulteaux, and Cree and the Siouan-speaking Assiniboine. So, we have a complicated web of four different archaeological cultures, two major contemporary descendant groups, and, anomalously, one rock painting tradition that temporally, spatially, and culturally is relatively homogeneous across all of these.

However, this isn't as much of a concern as it might seem. The Canadian Shield Rock Art Tradition, as noted above, is both time-transgressive and transcultural in its expression. Rather than think of the makers as a specific individual culture or group, we need to focus on the type of communities we find in the Canadian Shield. In this case, we are looking at boreal hunter-foraging communities, who for almost the entirety of the last 5,000 years have changed very little in terms of their subsistence economies, trade and exchange networks, and, more importantly, use of symbols. What changes we have are the adoption of ceramics roughly 3,000 years ago, and a slow increase in the number of archaeological cultures leading up to European contact. In terms of cultural and religious practices, the post-contact ethnohistoric and ethnographic literature supports a strong shared cosmology among Algonquian and Siouan-speaking cultures across the entirety of the Canadian Shield including views of the landscape and the production of images – two of the key components for the framework I developed concerning the function of rock painting sites in my original thesis work (Norder 2003).

Images and the Experience and Meaning of Place

Back in 1998 when I encountered that first site, in addition to the mystery of what these sites meant, I was also just in awe. I was familiar with the imagery from my reading of books by Selwyn Dewdney and Kenneth Kidd (1967) and Grace Rajnovich (1994), but to encounter them in person, floating in a canoe, I was speechless. It was magic. It was mystery. It was the "other." In this encounter, I was joined by a French-Canadian colleague who had visited other sites before, and at our first stop he immediately got his camera out and started taking pictures of the site. However, my response was completely different. I reached into my bag, and, rather than a camera, I took out a small tobacco tie and leaned forward and placed it on the stone shelf in front of the rock art site.

To provide a reason for the different response, it's important to understand that I am American Indian – an enrolled member of the Spirit Lake Dakota Nation. My mother was raised on the reservation there, but I was not. Rather, I was raised in the suburbs of Minneapolis/ St. Paul, Minnesota, during the 1970s and 1980s. I learned about my history and culture through school, visits to family on the reservation every year, and spending time with other American Indian kids in my school. Cultural education was loose, given we came from different tribal communities and backgrounds, but since we grew up during the time of protest and pride in one of the heartlands of the American Indian civil rights movement we were all "Indians." As a result, we were always aware of the political, cultural, historical, and spiritual world that surrounded and defined us as Indian peoples.

So, when I scattered that tobacco, it was because I knew from people that I had met over the course of my life that when you encounter a place that feels sacred you leave an offering. I could feel the spiritual when I saw those images, and while I didn't know what the images meant, I knew that this was a powerful place and it was one to be approached respectfully. To give my French-Canadian colleague the benefit back at that first site, he eventually produced a bag of tobacco and scattered some on the stone shelf after he was done taking pictures. We talked about it after I had taken a couple of pictures, and the discussion was interesting because he talked about it is a *requirement* for visiting the site and taking pictures while my understanding of it was as a *responsibility*. It was food for thought as the encounters with sites progressed over that first summer and then onward into my formal research, which began in the summer of 2000.

Based on my experiences in the field, where I documented more than 60 rock art sites across the province of Ontario, I came to understand several things about Canadian Shield rock art. First, as I had conversations with local First Nations people familiar with these sites, all of whom were Cree or Anishinaabeg, they rarely talked about the images at these sites. They generally provided two reasons for why when I asked further, which were 1) that they didn't know what the images meant, or 2) that knowing what the images meant was part of a deeper religious responsibility that had to be earned, something I had not done. The second was that people generally emphasized the importance of the place the images were found. The images were important, but they were almost secondary to the place itself, which was understood to be the place where spirits dwelled. Third, and following on the first two, these places marked locations people went to offer prayers or to seek aid from the spirits of these places. Last was that many times, when looking for a rock art site, I would see a cliff face where I thought I spied images, but when I paddled closer, I found it empty or covered with red-orange lichens instead of images. It began to niggle at me that there were a lot of places that rock paintings *could* have been placed but weren't.

The Social Landscape of a Sacred World

It was while I was working at a book store in Ann Arbor that I was introduced by the store manager, of all people, to the book *Rock Art and the Prehistory of Atlantic Europe: Signing the Land* by Richard Bradley (1997). It ended up providing one of the theoretical cornerstones of my dissertation. Bradley's overall argument was that as population densities increased over time among hunter-gatherer societies, the ability to maintain informational networks through face-to-face communication becomes difficult and so information begins to become inscribed or "signed" onto the land in some manner that helps to communicate information, particularly regarding boundaries. In this case, the inscriptions were rock art sites.

Bradley's research was further refined by the hunter-gatherer research of Tim Ingold (1987), which provided a definition of boundaries and territories. To start, Ingold proposed that hunter-gatherers viewed landscapes as a series of interconnected "sites and paths" rather than large flat surface areas (1987: 153). Within this perspective, boundaries were not carved out chunks of a landscape like plots of land. Rather they would occur at points along paths or at sites where paths crossed. For Bradley, this explained a good portion of the siting of rock art on the landscape. When you looked at the distribution of rock art sites placed on exposed cliff or rock faces on a map, he noted that they occurred in clusters and along lines that connected those clusters. Oftentimes the placement was overlooking or placed near sites with various resources or along trail systems. For Bradley, rock art sites had a "sign-post" function that helped guide movement across the land.

For me, this was revolutionary because, to start, it introduced a secular function for rock art that the literature generally ignored in favor of sacred, or religious, interpretations. No one would argue that hunter-gatherer rock art sites were not religious or spiritual in nature. Even Bradley didn't make this argument, and my own experience and teachings regarding rock art sites preclude such an assertion. However, it is important to observe that a secular function of rock art sites does exist within the social, political, and economic spheres of hunter-gather societies that complements the religious. To further clarify, and as Bradley concluded, the division of the sacred and the secular in archaeological studies represents a social construction of modern thought that may have been irrelevant or non-existent among the hunter-gatherer societies that produced rock art. Rock art sites were and are inherently multi-functional and polysemous in nature.

In the Lake of the Woods, rock art sites seemingly were placed in manners that reflected Ingold's theories regarding hunter-gatherer landscape perception and territoriality, but I wanted to evaluate this, myself. To achieve this, I did something no one else had done, which was to go out and conduct a survey to identify places not only where rock art sites were placed, but also where rock art sites could be but weren't. This involved extensive shoreline survey throughout the northwestern Lake of the Woods region, which in addition to the main lake possesses over 300 smaller lakes in a roughly 400 sq km area. Given the time frame, it wasn't feasible to visit every lake, so the survey was designed to maximize the amount of shoreline covered, which in this case was roughly 65%. Overall, 51 rock art sites were documented within the study area out of over 600 potential places available to place rock art images where they would be clearly visible to people paddling by. The implications of this were staggering, as I discuss in greater detail below.

Speaking to Strangers

In addition, I could not ignore the rock art images themselves. However, the challenge I faced here was that I wanted to examine rock art images in a manner that avoided a lot of the biases of standard stylistic analyses. A straightforward image or stylistic analysis was possible, of course, like one would do with ceramics, but I wanted to avoid the pitfalls of classification and try for an approach that provided a measure that focused on this idea of rock art sites as communicating something. In this effort, I was aided by the work of Hartley and Vawser (1998), who used the framework of "Information Theory." In their work, rock art sites were viewed as *messages* that were either easy or difficult to understand. The images within the composition helped to facilitate the ease of understanding based on both the number of images and/or the repetition, or lack thereof, of images in a composition.

To elaborate, a rock art site with one image would be as easy to understand as a rock art site with a dozen copies of the same image. In fact, the greater the replication, or redundant use of the same image, the clearer the message would be. For example, if I said "stop" once, you might or might not stop depending on if I caught your attention. However, if I kept saying "stop" repeatedly you would almost certainly get the message at some point and stop. Alternatively, a message would become more difficult to understand when the number of different images increase and the replication of images goes down. So, to take our example a different direction I might start off with "stop" and you may or may not catch it the first time, but if I continued and said "stop, go, jump, stay, walk, circle, whistle, clap, stomp" you would probably tell me to repeat or translate the message until it made sense. In "Information Theory" a numerical value is calculated on a scale from 0 to 1, where 0 represented messages that are difficult to understand and 1 represent easy.

In Hartley and Vawser's work, they discerned two possible site functions. In my research, I found three, although I had originally proposed four. For both studies, the site types were defined not just by their information content, but also by their placement on the landscape. However, I also added a qualitative element to the analysis, which was based on a cultural distinction. Among the Anishinaabeg there were two types of image classes: *kekeewin* and *kekeenowin* (Vastokas and Vastokas 1973). *Kekeewin* images were those that were known by all members of the community, with the exception of children since producing images was considered to be potentially spiritually harmful, while *kekeenowin* images were those restricted to shamans, other religious practitioners, and to specific ceremonial and ritual contexts. Rock art images of the first type consisted of simple representations of people, animals, body parts, and simple geometric images like lines and circles. The second type consisted of more elaborate representations of people, anthropomorphs, spiritual beings, and complex geometric images.

In terms of overall research outcomes for the image analysis, as noted above, I found three sites types based on the clustering of numbers alone. The largest category of sites had values of 1, or seemed unambiguous in terms of the message they communicated. It's important to note that most these sites consisted of single images. The next category of sites fell into a range of .80 to .60, or sites with messages that were not overly difficult to understand. Images at these sites generally fell into the *kekeewin* cultural category. The last category fell into a range of .40 to .10, or sites with messages that were relatively difficult, if not almost impossible, to understand. As you might guess, most of the images at these sites fell into the *kekeenowin* category.

Maps and the Meaning of Locative Experience

For the landscape analysis, I had two goals: first, to address the issue of the disparity between the number (51) of rock painting sites vs. the high number (>600) of potential places for siting rock paintings, and second, to see how sites patterned out on the landscape, if at all. The structuring principle I used for both question links us back to Ingold's observation regarding hunter-gather landscape engagements via lines and clusters. In this case, if rock painting sites serve as a means of constructing the social landscape of the region, then it is possible that they are sited in a manner that reflects this perception. To test this idea, I and a colleague employed multiple GIS methodologies to address the two goals (Norder and Carroll 2011). For the first, in regards to the disparity, we first had to establish that the numbers and distribution were not just artifacts of random choice. For this we employed a Monte Carlo simulation, which furnishes an agent with a range of potential outcomes and their probabilities of occurrence for any choice of action. In this case, it looked at the choices already made and examined the probability that they were random. They were not, which is what we had hoped.

For the second goal, we used least cost path analysis, which has become a standard tool for human mobility studies, and posits that humans typically choose routes of travel with the least energetic costs. Based on superficial observations of the distribution of sites, and the three site types, it was apparent that the three site types occurred in relatively discrete clusters in terms of their placement on the landscape. Type II sites tended to be found in clusters at two locations in the study area that could be considered boundary zones as per Bradley (1997). The images at these sites tended to be *kekeewin*. Type I sites tended to be strung out across the landscape between Type II sites, suggesting that they might be associated with Ingold's "paths." Type III sites were relatively random in their distribution, but they were also the ones that consisted of primarily *kekeenowin* imagery and were often quite spectacular in their compositions. Once again, all sites were located on or immediately overlooking bodies of water, so accessibility was not an issue and, as a result, they were all located on a least cost path through the study area. The interesting part, is that, as with the siting of rock paintings, not all the available paths through the region had rock painting sites on them.

This leaves us with a remaining challenge in terms of how we situate these sites in the context of the worldview of ancestral Algonquian and Siouan peoples as they encountered this landscape. We can infer that they approached this land in a way that was meaningful and carefully expressed through the selective inscription of landscape with these painted sites. With less than 10% of the available "canvases" for rock paintings used over a span of possibly 2,000 years, the action of image making, as stated above, was clearly socially proscribed. However, this still doesn't fully address the patterning. There was intentionality to the placement, and, at least for the Type I and II sites, reflects a view of the world of "sites" (Type II) and the "paths" (Type I) between them. The Type III sites seem anomalous, but even though I have not done an empirical study using GIS for them, they do share a characteristic of being located at places where travel is more hazardous, particularly over larger lakes and expanses of open water where extreme wind and weather make travel virtually impossible. But why not use or mark all potential routes in some manner?

For this last question, I could posit a variety of different theories relating to population increase, mobility, communication strategies, territoriality, and cultural continuity, and these very likely have a role in the overall argument, and I've addressed them somewhat in the preceding, but I would like to leave you with a more humanistic answer and also a conclusion. To a certain extent these theories take a secondary role when we revisit the time-transgressive and transcultural nature of rock art in the Canadian Shield. As the landscape was settled, rock art came to be a tool for making people visible to each other as a proxy for regular face-to-face communication, but it also gave the world greater agency in how people engaged with it. Past or present, rock paintings in the Lake of the Woods are evocative encounters and are memorable to anyone who encounters them, and this extends to the routes people would travel. They create familiarity through their place-making, and this serves as a guide for people who expect to see them in terms of how they should respond both as engagement with the sacred world but also to move through the social one, as well. They exist as metaphorical and enduring sign-posts that descendants will continue to understand, adopt, and produce. They guide people to where they need to go and how to behave, and their absence means you have gone off the beaten path.

Epilogue

The last time I was in the Lake of the Woods in 2014, I went out to visit several sites I'd documented in previous years. The irony wasn't lost on me that I motored and paddled from one site to the next without stopping to look in any of the side bays or explore the various other routes through the complex web of lakes and rivers. I'd surveyed them all before, and so the paths from site to site were known to me at this point. The mystery of something around a hidden corner no longer beckoned me. However, I remained cognizant of the enormity of the world beyond those corners.

I continued on, leaving my offerings of tobacco at each site, and as I looked closely at these still mysterious compositions, I understood that I didn't need to know what they meant. The compositions spoke to me in their own specific ways, and my response to them, as I had learned from my time with various Anishinaabeg people from the local First Nations' communities, was both private to me but part of that growing internalization of the world I was engaged with while there. The lessoned learned? Rock art sites, as archaeological phenomena existing in their primary contexts of production and consumption, make them as much an artifact of the present as much as one of the creators of the past.

Paired Reading

Norder, John and Jon Carroll. 2011. "Rock Art in the Lake of the Woods Region of Ontario: An Applied Geospatial Approach." *International Journal of Applied Geospatial Research*, 2: 77–92. DOI: 10.4018/jagr.2011100105.

References

Arsenault, Daniel, Louis Gagnon, Charles A. Martijn, and Alan Watchman. 1995. "Le Projet Nisula: Recherches Pluridisciplinaires Autour d'un Site a Pictogrammes (DeEh1) en Haute-Côte-Nord du Québec." *Archéologies québecoises*, edited by Anne-Marie Balac, Claude Chapdelaine, Norman Clermont, and Françoise Duguay. 17–57, Montreal: Recherches amerindiennes au Québec.

Bradley, Richard.1997. *Rock Art and the Prehistory of Atlantic Europe: Signing the Land*. New York: Routledge.

Conway, Thor and Julie Conway. 1990. *Spirits on Stone: The Agawa Pictographs*. Echo Bay, ON: Heritage Discovery Books.

Dewdney, Selwyn and Kenneth Kidd. 1967. *Rock Paintings of the Great Lakes*, 2nd ed. Toronto: University of Toronto Press.

Hartley, Ralph and Anne Vawser. 1998. "Spatial Behavior and Learning in the Prehistoric Environment of the Colorado River Drainage (Southeastern Utah), Western North America." In *The Archaeology of Rock-art*, edited by Christopher Chippendale and Paul S. C. Taçon, 185–211. New York: Cambridge University Press.

Ingold, Timothy. 1987. *The Appropriation of Nature: Essays on Human Ecology and Social Relations*. Iowa City, IA: University of Iowa Press.

Norder, John. 2003. "Marking Place and Creating Space in Northern Algonquian Landscapes: The Rock-Art of the Lake of the Woods Region, Ontario." PhD Dissertation. Ann Arbor, MI: University of Michigan.

Norder, John and Jon Carroll. 2011. "Rock Art in the Lake of the Woods Region of Ontario: An Applied Geospatial Approach." *International Journal of Applied Geospatial Research*, 2: 77–92. DOI: 10.4018/jagr.2011100105.

Rajnovich, Grace. 1994. *Reading Rock Art: The Indian Rock Paintings of the Canadian Shield*. Toronto: Natural Heritage/Natural History.

Vastokas, Joan and Roman Vastokas. 1973. *Sacred Art of the Algonkians: A Study of the Peterborough Petroglyphs*. Peterborough, NH: Mansard Press.

9

The Heart of Lightness: Doing Archaeology in the Brazilian Central Amazon

Eduardo G. Neves

Project Summary

From 1995 to 2010, I ran two large archaeological projects in the Brazilian Amazon: the Central Amazon Project and the Archaeological Survey of the Area of Influence of the Urucu-Manaus pipeline. Both projects involved the participation of students and professionals from Brazil and abroad and made a substantive contribution to the development of Amazonian archaeology. Their goal was to understand the patterns of social and political organization of the Amerindian populations that occupied the Amazon in the last centuries prior to European colonization. Although I do not work anymore in the Central Amazon but elsewhere in Amazonia, this chapter presents some thoughts on how to carry out research in areas with poor infrastructure. Working in such conditions means being methodologically flexible: logistics are not always easy, and a huge gap exists between textbooks and actual fieldwork. The attempt to understand past patterns of nature management and transformation means one needs to be interdisciplinary. Indeed, the collaboration with natural scientists has been one of the most intellectually rewarding parts of my research, as has collaboration with Indigenous and local populations where we do fieldwork.

Doing Archaeology in the Amazon in the Early 1990s

In the late 1980s few people were interested in Amazonian archaeology. In Brazil most research centered on the 150-year-old Goeldi Museum, and it was done by Vera Guapindaia, Maura Imázio, Marcos Magalhães, and Edithe Pereira. In the United States, Betty Meggers from the Smithsonian Institution and Donald Lathrap from the University of Illinois, both leading figures of Amazonian research from the 1950s onward, were no longer active in field research and rather involved in a bitter dispute that would last until the end of their lives. Aside from them, Anna Roosevelt from the University of Illinois – Chicago and Clark Erickson from the University of Pennsylvania conducted important research at mound sites at the mouth of the Amazon, late Pleistocene and early ceramic sites in the lower Amazon (Roosevelt *et al.* 1991, Roosevelt *et al.* 1996), and earthworks in Bolivia (Erickson 2000). Thomas Myers, Scott Raymond, and Warren De Boer, former Lathrap students, were no longer active in field research there as well. In coastal French Guiana, Stéphen Rostain was working alone on PhD research that would later revolutionize the archaeology of this area (Rostain 2013). In Colombia, Santiago Mora was part of a multidisciplinary project investigating the geneses of anthropic dark soils in Araracuara on the Caquetá River (Gnecco and Mora 1997). Despite the lasting

Engaging Archaeology: 25 Case Studies in Research Practice, First Edition. Edited by Stephen W. Silliman.
© 2018 John Wiley & Sons, Inc. Published 2018 by John Wiley & Sons, Inc.

impact of these scholars' contributions, their joint effort amounted to less than ten projects in an area, the Amazon basin, which is roughly the size of the continental United States. If the Amazon is still an archaeologically uncharted land today, it was even more so in the late 1980s.

I am part of a wave of South American archaeologists who left their countries to do their PhDs in the United States in the 1980s and 1990s. After receiving my BA in History from the University of São Paulo, I won a scholarship and came to the United States to pursue a PhD in Archaeology at Indiana University. At that time there were no graduate programs in archaeology in Brazil, but I already wanted to do my research in the Amazon. When I designed my PhD research, I had few options but to work on my own: there were few large excavations or projects going on in the Amazon. Moreover, I was more interested in doing research among Indigenous people, in this case among the Tukanoan speakers of northwest Amazonia, and to combine archaeology and ethnography to understand the impact of colonization on the history of multilingual Indigenous social networks found in this area. A pre-doctoral grant from the National Science Foundation provided me with the funds to come to the field in 1993 and 1994. At the same time, Michael Heckenberger, then a graduate student at the University of Pittsburgh, and now at the University of Florida, was developing a similar approach for his own research among the Kuikuro Indians of the Upper Xingu River, also in the Brazilian Amazon (Heckenberger 2005). Coming from very different backgrounds we both arrived at the same notion that the way for archaeology to move forward in the Amazon was through partnerships with Indigenous communities.

To arrive in the northwest Amazon, I would either travel from Manaus by boat (four days) or fly (three hours) to São Gabriel da Cachoeira, near the mouth of the Uaupés river. From there it was another two-day-long boat trip up the Uaupés to my base at Iauaraté, the old Salesian mission and frontier military post. The early 1990s was a wild time to work in the northwest Amazon: the ongoing gold rush there, and rampant inflation in Brazil, together with the impossibility of wiring money to remote places, made me resort to using my grant money to buy gold and exchange it for food, services, and fuel.

One of the shortcomings of working alone in a place where no previous archaeology has been done within a radius of several hundred kilometers is that one needs to start from scratch: there are no available chronologies, no sites mapped, no settlement pattern data, and no crews of trained archaeologists available. In the middle Uaupés, with no roads, travelling is done by boat or foot. Delays are common, and one has to be flexible with schedules, goals, and targets. This kind of approach for a PhD in archaeology is dying out in graduate programs overall. It takes too much time, and the results may not be worth the effort and funds invested. On the other hand, the possibility of working with the Tukanoans, to partake of their superior intelligence and their refined sense of humor, to drink their pepper soup followed by big cigars for breakfast, and to learn from them and from their expectations about archaeology offered a unique experience. The experience in the Uaupés was fundamental for my training as an archaeologist.

The Central Amazon Project

The Central Amazon lies midway between the Upper Xingu and the Upper Rio Negro, and archaeologists (such as Lathrap and Oliver 1987) have suggested it to be an ancient center of cultural development, including early pottery and plant domestication in the whole New World. Aside from previous work in the 1950s and 1960s by Peter Hilbert and Mario Simões, no one had worked systematically there for the previous 20 years. The Central Amazon Project developed as a natural outcome from Heckenberger's and my own previous isolated initiatives at the time. Our assumption was that these areas had stratified societies that occupied large and sedentary settlements, and who, through their management strategies, had altered the tropical settings where they lived. If we were correct, the image of a pristine wilderness sparsely populated that fits general contemporary notions about the Amazon would have to be revised, because they result much more from the decimation of European colonization than from an inherent, atavic tropical pattern (Clement *et al.* 2015). Addressing these questions is today the main research agenda of Amazonian archaeology, and it continues to generate much debate among social and natural scientists alike.

We established a triangular research area roughly 30×30 km that covered a veritable "Mesopotamia" between the Amazon and Negro rivers, across from Manaus. Manaus lies at the mouth of the Rio Negro, next to its junction to the Amazon. It is an extraordinary city of more than 2,000,000 people surrounded by tropical rainforests and isolated from most of the rest of Brazil, from which it can be reached only by plane or boat. It is known, among other things, for its beautiful opera house built in the early 1900s at the peak of a rubber boom that brought wealth for a few and disgrace for many throughout Amazonia.

A generous grant from the William Hilman Foundation gave us the funds to conduct a preliminary 50-day field season in September and October 1995. The slight watershed that cuts across the research area was already crossed at the time by a paved road, from which secondary dirt roads led to the banks of the Negro and Amazon. Our research design was straightforward, and the aims were simple. First, we would produce a preliminary map and open a few test pits at Açutuba, a large open-air multi-component site identified by Heckenberger in a visit to the area in 1994. Second, we would travel by boat and car to perform an unsystematic survey of other sites in the research area. September is the peak of the dry season in the Central Amazon and, therefore, the time when the rivers' floodplains begin to be exposed. In the case of the Rio Negro this meant beautiful white sand beaches that in some cases stretch beyond the horizon. Already during my PhD research, I had given up doing controlled sampling for surveys. In a place where so little is known, such as the Amazon, opportunistic strategies bring better results at the end of the day. We spent the 1995 field season camping in a straw hut at Açutuba beach. After a few days, we were joined by Jim Petersen, who had a lot of experience working in the Caribbean and New England as well. Jim's contributions were fundamental for the grounding of the project.

After 50 days we left the field with good samples of the test pits excavated and a coarse topographic map (Açutuba is 900 ha in size, full of mounds and other topographical features and it would take us a full month in 1999 to map it with a total station. The site is unfortunately destroyed today). In 1997, once more due to Heckenberger's effort, we received a grant from the Wenner-Gren Foundation that enabled us to return to the field. By that time, we already had two publications (Heckenberger *et al.* 1999) and had also defended our PhDs. This time, in a 40-day-long season we were joined by Robert Bartone, bringing experience of fieldwork archaeology in the United States and the Caribbean. With Bartone along, we began a more consistent survey of sites in the hinterland areas and along the shores of the Amazon. It was during this season we identified sites that were to be further excavated by the project, such as Osvaldo, Lago Grande, and Hatahara. It became clear that we needed to increase the size of our crews working in the field to have more people involved in the general effort for the project to grow and do justice to the archaeology of the area of confluence.

In 1998, I met Carlos Augusto "the Brick" da Silva in Manaus. Born in 1956 in a village close to the Amazon River, the son of a rubber tapper and a housekeeper, he moved to Manaus as a boy to attend school, pursuing a trajectory that would culminate with him receiving a PhD in Amazonian studies in 2016. Carlos is descended on both sides of his parentage from the Indigenous people who had been mass-transported and uprooted by the Portuguese in colonial times and the Brazilians at the time of the rubber boom in the late 1800s and early 1900s. Although phenotypically an Amerindian, he does not speak any native language nor does he claim direct affiliation or ancestry to any of the native Indigenous societies of the contemporary Amazon. Like many of his peers, he has an encyclopedic knowledge of the plants and animals of the forests and the maze of rivers and lakes that make up the Amazon. Carlos was not a trained archaeologist but had a natural aptitude and talent for it. An important dimension of teaching and learning archaeology happens away from the classroom, either in the field or in labs. Part of that teaching and learning experience is silent and is done more through gestures than words. Already with a background in social sciences, and with an above-average intelligence, he learned fast and eventually became an accomplished archaeologist with a major role in the further history of the project, helping to organize and lead the several field schools we held in the early 2000s and conducting research on his own as well.

The First Field School Years (1999–2005)

In 1999 I received a grant from FAPESP (São Paulo State Foundation for the Support of Science), a Brazilian agency. FAPESP grants are very competitive, but at the time had no upper limit for the amount of money requested. Besides funding research, it also funds fellowships for graduate and undergraduate students. Public education is still free in Brazil, but these grants allow archaeology students to fund, for instance, their fieldwork.

The late 1990s and 2000s were an important period for graduate and undergraduate public education in Brazil. From 2004 to 2016, 17 new public federal universities were opened, most of them in remote places, and some of them with undergraduate programs in archaeology. In the Amazon alone, three new such courses were opened. In the same way, new graduate programs in archaeology started throughout the country. The University of São Paulo hosts one of them, out of the seven currently working in the country today. The possibility of teaching in a graduate program, together with the regular influx of grants from FAPESP and the continuous participation of US-based colleagues, brought the right ingredients for the Central Amazon Project to grow.

In the Brazilian Amazon, many of the archaeologists who have taken up positions in the newly-formed archaeology departments during the last few years went to the field schools of CAP and received their PhDs from the USP with FAPESP grants. In hindsight, what happened with archaeology in Brazil in the 2000s was similar to what happened, on another scale, in the United States in the 1960s and 1970s: a massive expansion of public education and the opening of numerous new academic positions.

In 1999, Heckenberger accepted a position at the University of Florida, and moved away from work on CAP to continue his Xingu research. At the same time, we had 11 people for the 1999 field season, allowing us to work at more than one site simultaneously. From 1999 to 2009 I supervised directly or indirectly eight field schools in the Central Amazon. The smallest in 1999, had 11 people, the largest, in 2007, had 57. Anyone who has run a field school knows the ups and downs of it. The greatest up is the joy of teaching and seeing new vocations manifesting themselves on the ground. The downs relate to the challenges of coordinating the activities, housing, and feeding large groups of students. CAP research area is located almost beneath the equator. Fieldwork was normally done in the dry season, from July to September, which meant no rain but also working under a scorching sun. As the project grew we began to receive students from outside the Amazon and other parts of Brazil and abroad: Argentina, Bolivia, Colombia, Peru, France, the United Kingdom, and the United States. Some of the students were not used to the climate of the Amazon. One was bitten by a boa constrictor (nothing serious happened). Several had bouts of diarrhea, and I had a chronic thyroid ailment that made me very weak during the 2007 season.

Over time we developed partnerships with other colleagues, mostly soil scientists, as general interest in Amazonian archaeology grew. Among the subjects receiving greater attention were

Anthropic Dark Earths (ADEs) or *Terras Pretas*, dark and fertile soils associated with archaeological sites across the Amazon. Owing to these traits, it is not uncommon that contemporary Amazonians use archaeological sites as farming grounds, mostly for small-scale agriculture, which poses interesting challenges for the partnerships with local populations for the preservation and stewardship of this patrimony. Besides their fertility, terras pretas are also known for their stability; that is, contrary to other tropical soils, they retain their nutrients over time, despite the intensive lixiviation. While known since the nineteenth century, the anthropic origin of these soils remained open to debate until the 1990s, when the independent work of Dirse Kern and Bill Woods showed the clear association between their chemical properties and past human activities. I am far from being a geoarchaeologist, and neither was I initially interested in studying terras pretas, but the significant amount of ADE sites found in the Central Amazon made it almost inevitable not to work with them. Moreover, their widespread distribution shows the inherent capacity of ancient Amazonians to modify nature, a strong argument against environmental determinism. Thanks partially to work done in the Central Amazon, it is known that these soils formed initially as trash middens behind houses (Schmidt *et al.* 2014).

In 2005 we held another field school at CAP. This time we were based at the village of Lago do Limão, where we had lived and worked before. Some of the local inhabitants were permanent members of the project. We had by the time developed an outreach and education initiative, coordinated by Carla Gibertoni, which regularly brought children and teachers of local schools to the accessible sites to visit excavations and see how archaeologists work (Figure 9.1). We were already publishing in international peer-reviewed journals and edited volumes.

Figure 9.1 Photograph of fieldwork during the Central Amazon Project. Helena Lima (squatting), Carol Caromano (taking notes), and Anne Py-Daniel (standing at the pit edge and supervising the project, well into her second trimester) receive public school students from Iranduba in their visit to excavation of Hatahara site, 2006. Photograph by Val Moraes, Central Amazon Project.

Besides USP students, graduate students from universities such as Binghamton, UC-Berkeley, and Cambridge were doing their PhDs with CAP data.

The year 2005 was the tenth anniversary of CAP. Petersen and I were finally talking about writing an NSF proposal with a view of increasing the reach of the project. The day after we had a party to celebrate the anniversary on August 13. We stopped for a beer after work at a local family-owned restaurant. One hour later Jim was dead, shot in the stomach, during a freak robbery. Jim was also an anchor to the project, a solid rock to back the exciting work we were doing. His violent death a few days after turning 51 was a terrible blow to everyone, including the more than 30 people who were in the field with us in 2005. By that time, we were moving to another scale of presence in the area. We had just rented a large house in Manaus, which would serve as a laboratory and lodge and were about to combine the funds from FAPESP together with even larger resources from Petrobras, the Brazilian National Oil Company. We were all devastated and called off fieldwork for 2005, just to jump intensely into the pipeline project for the coming years and dividing our attention with CAP.

The Pipeline Years (2005–2009)

The 2000s were a time of intensive economic growth in Brazil and the Amazon Basin, and its native populations were to suffer the impact of several large-scale infrastructure projects. One such project was the Urucu-Manaus pipeline, designed to bring natural gas from the Urucu area, deep under the jungle of central Amazonia, to the city of Manaus. Despite its size and population, most of the energy of Manaus in the mid-2000s (and unfortunately still today) comes from the burning of oil. The remainder was electricity generated by the ill-fated, large, and wasteful Balbina dam, built in the 1980s 200 km north of the city. We were approached by Petrobras to conduct the archaeological work prior to the construction of the pipeline because the planned trajectory of the pipeline cut across the CAP research area.

The decision to work on the pipeline was not easy: on the one hand it meant adhering to the security norms and field procedures of Petrobras, a radical change from the easy-going and careless, albeit sometimes reckless, ways we were used to working. It also meant taking part in a project deeply criticized by NGOs and parts of civil society within and outside Amazonia. On the other hand, it meant replacing oil burning and hydroelectric damming by a less damaging, although far from perfect alternative. The tipping point was the possibility of building a permanent education and research center with Petrobras funds at Iranduba, where most CAP activities took place. In 15 years, from 1995 to 2010, I watched Iranduba grow from a rural county with large forested areas and a small county seat into a fast-growing Amazonian town. Until 2011, connection to Manaus was made by ferry and fast boat. Nowadays, a three-mile-long bridge connects both sides of the Rio Negro, transforming Iranduba into a neighborhood of Manaus. We felt that resources from the pipeline project would give us the money to build the education and research center and could cater as much to students from the Amazonian interior as to people from Manaus.

Working for the pipeline project provided us with resources we never had before. The best luxury was to have a ca. 600 km long transect cut mostly through forest areas that we would never have the chance to visit. We recruited to the project many of the students who had attended the previous field schools as well as hiring permanently some of the people who had worked for us in previous excavations. We could use some of the money to cover our own ongoing work in the Central Amazon. At times we had fully furnished boats available to us for weeks, allowing for hosting crews in sparsely inhabited areas where archaeological sites were found. A large house was rented in Manaus, and it served as a laboratory and storage area for the collections made in the field. More important, we had an agreement that by the end of the project there would be resources to start an institute called CABA (Center for the Archaeology of Amazonian Biomes), based in Iranduba, and associated with the then new undergraduate program in archaeology at Amazonas State University, which I helped to design. Many months were spent discussing this new program and adapting that vision into the requirements of the Brazilian Ministry of Education. Countless hours were spent in meetings with architects to provide a plan for the construction of a series of buildings hosting classrooms, a library, storage areas, laboratories, and an exhibition center, which would be built on an abandoned lot located at a bluff at the edge of the Amazon. Without realizing, I was slowly changing from a field archaeologist into an administrator. However, as a result of the global economic crisis in 2008, the whole project crashed. Money for the construction was withheld, and the lot was never bought. At least the undergraduate program in archaeology survived, albeit functioning in precarious conditions in a space lent by a public high school. In December 2011, with no more money to cover rent, the laboratory in Manaus was closed, and after long and difficult negotiations, the collections were handled by the Federal University of Amazonas. This signaled the end of the Central Amazon Project.

Reflections and Lessons Learned

I still hold an academic appointment at Federal University of Amazonas, which brings me back to Manaus quite often. I like to think that my engagement with the archaeology of the Central Amazon went through a metamorphosis. I am not longer directly active in research there, but some of my former students are. After a legal battle with the help of federal prosecutors, the Federal University received funds from Petrobras to build a state of the art laboratory on campus, currently under the leadership of Carlos Augusto da Silva. I am still very active in fieldwork in the Amazon, but in the last years I changed my research area to the current border of Bolivia and Brazil. There, as with Manaus, one faces the same structural conditions: lack of proper laboratories and recent archaeological programs struggling to consolidate themselves academically in areas with a wonderful potential for research. On the other hand, one sees there again the strength of partnership with young and bright scholars and a wonderful group of students, eager to learn.

As someone who is based and works in the Global South, I feel a silent revolution happening in archaeology. As new data from previously unknown places are revealed, a different picture of the deep human past is emerging, distinct from the established canonical traditions still derived from nineteenth-century evolutionist thinking. Amazonian archaeology is part of this general movement, and doing archaeology there brings many pains and pleasures. Traditional, detached, research-only commitments are clearly not enough to do justice to the demands presented to those willing to follow such engagement. Indigenous populations threatened by large development projects and logistical limitations are part of the history. Another part, much more rewarding, is to use archaeology to bring a voice to these silenced pasts.

Paired Reading

Clement, Charles R., William M. Denevan, Michael J. Heckenberger, André Braga Junqueira, Eduardo G. Neves, Teixeira, Wenceslau G., and William I. Woods. 2015. "The Domestication of Amazonia before European Conquest." *Proceedings of the Royal Society B*, 282 (1812): 32–40. DOI: 10.1098/rspb.2015.0813.

References

Clement, Charles R., William M. Denevan, Michael J. Heckenberger, André Braga Junqueira, Eduardo G. Neves, Teixeira, Wenceslau G., and William I. Woods. 2015. "The Domestication of Amazonia before European Conquest." *Proceedings of the Royal Society B*, 282 (1812): 32–40. DOI: 10.1098/rspb.2015.0813.

Erickson, Clark. 2000. "An Artificial Landscape-Scale Fishery in the Bolivian Amazon." *Nature*, 408, 190–193. DOI: 10.1038/35041555.

Gnecco, Cristobal and Santiago Mora. 1997. "Late Pleistocene/early Holocene Tropical Forest Occupations at San Isidro and Peña Roja, Colombia." *Antiquity*, 71: 683–690. DOI: 10.1017/S0003598X00085409.

Heckenberger, Michael J. 2005. *The Ecology of Power: Culture, Place and Personhood in the Southern Amazon, 1000–2000*. New York: Routledge.

Heckenberger, Michael J. and Eduardo G. Neves. 2009. "Amazonian Archaeology." *Annual Review of Anthropology*, 38: 251–266. DOI: 10.1146/annurev-anthro-091908-164310.

Heckenberger, Michael J., James B. Petersen, and Eduardo G. Neves. 1999. "Village Size and Permanence in Amazonia: Two Archaeological Examples from Brazil." *Latin American Antiquity*, 10: 353–376. DOI: 10.2307/971962.

Lathrap, Donald and José Oliver. 1987. "Agüerito: el complejo policromo más antiguo de America en la confluencia del Apure y el Orinoco (Venezuela)." *Interciencia*, 12: 274–89.

Roosevelt, Anna C., R. A. Houseley, M. Imázio da Silviera, S. Maranca, and R. Johnson. 1991. "Eighth Millennium Pottery from a Prehistoric Shell Midden in the Brazilian Amazon." *Science*, 254: 1621–1624. DOI: 10.1126/science.254.5038.1621.

Roosevelt, Anna C., M. Lima da Costa, C. Lopes Machado, M. Michab, N. Mercier, H. Valladas, J. Feathers, W. Barnett, M. Imázio da Silveira, A. Henderson, J. Silva, B. Chernoff, D. S. Reese, J. A. Holman, N. Toth and K. Schick. 1996. "Paleoindian Cave Dwellers in the Amazon: The Peopling of the Americas." *Science*, 272: 373–384. DOI: 10.1126/science.272.5260.373.

Rostain, Stéphen. 2013. *Islands in the Rainforest: Landscape Management in Pre-Columbian Amazonia*, Walnut Creek, CA: Left Coast Press.

Schmidt, Morgan J., Anne Rapp Py-Daniel, Claide de Paula Moraes, Raoni B. M. Valle, Caroline F. Caromano, Wenceslaur G. Texeira, Carlos A. Barbosa, João A. Fonseca, Marcos P. Magalhães, Daniel Silva do Carmo Santos, Renan da Silva e Silva, Vera L. Guapindaia, Bruno Moraes, Helena P. Lima, Eduardo G. Neves, and Michael J. Heckenberger. 2014. "Dark Earths and the Human Built Landscape in Amazonia: A Widespread Pattern of Anthrosol Formation." *Journal of Archaeological Science*, 42: 152–165. DOI: 10.1016/j.jas.2013.11.002.

Part II

Sites, Households, and Communities

10

Household Archaeology at the Community Scale? Refining Research Design in a Complex Polynesian Chiefdom

Jennifer G. Kahn

Project Summary

My project set out to test models of emerging social and political complexity, and increasing centralization of elite power, with material evidence recovered at household and community scales. The project in the 'Opunohu Valley, Mo'orea Island (Society Islands, East Polynesia) emphasized the linkage between production and social organization. Excavated sites spanned the Development Period (AD 950–1250) to the Classic Period (AD 1550–1750) just prior to European contact. This three-year project involved two field seasons of site mapping and excavation. This chapter documents a shift in research design, specifically how to move from a detailed household archaeology study of a handful of house sites with extensive, horizontal excavations, to a broader coverage model at the community scale, whereby house sites, temples, and other types of structures are excavated to provide larger comparative datasets of residential and ritual landscapes. In effect, can a household archaeologist successfully carry out research at the community scale without compromising the detail needed for micro-scale analyses?

Introduction

This is my story, one of an archaeologist who completed "traditional" household archaeology for her PhD in East Polynesia, with large horizontal excavations of five pre-contact house sites in the 'Opunohu Valley, Mo'orea, Society Islands. I then successfully modified my field methods and research design for a post-dissertation research project focused on social relations at the community scale in the same valley where I completed my dissertation work. More broadly, I have worked as an archaeologist in the beautiful islands of East Polynesia (Hawai'i, Marquesas, Society Islands) since 1993, completing field research as a CRM archaeologist in Hawai'i, and then embarking on MA and dissertation field research in French Polynesia. My research interests include household archaeology, monumental architecture, ritual and religion, lithic technology, foodwebs, and human-environment interactions.

Here I discuss how I moved from a detailed and tightly focused dissertation project based at the micro-scale and then took what I learned from that project to generate new research questions and a new research design at the community scale. As I have progressed as a researcher, I have learned some important lessons, such as not all of your research projects have to be as detailed or as involved as your dissertation research! Once you become a full-time academic, if that is your goal, you generally have less time to focus solely on research. Thus, having trusted

Engaging Archaeology: 25 Case Studies in Research Practice, First Edition. Edited by Stephen W. Silliman.
© 2018 John Wiley & Sons, Inc. Published 2018 by John Wiley & Sons, Inc.

collaborators (graduate students, undergraduates, specialists) with whom you share fieldwork duties, or laboratory analyses, or write up tasks, is key. I have also learned that I am the type of researcher who likes to engage in new projects, using different theoretical insights and new field and laboratory methodologies, every few years. Even though I have engaged in many forms of research in the last decade, many of my post-dissertation studies have been situated in the 'Opunohu Valley, the location of my initial dissertation research. This provides an anchor and continuity to my multi-scalar research.

Project Management for Multi-Year International Collaborative Research

The field site, the 'Opunohu Valley, is owned by the Territorial Government of French Polynesia. The land is managed by the SDR, the Service de la Développement Rural, which is a branch of the Ministry of Agriculture. In order to complete archaeological survey or excavation in the valley, a letter of support had to be acquired from both the local head of SDR as well as the mayor of the island. In addition, as with other international locales, research visas and permits had to be acquired. Local research permits had to be obtained from two different agencies, the Ministry of Culture and the Haut Commissaire/Delegation of Research. Obtaining all the necessary research permits and visas for each team member took a substantial amount of time.

As the field work portion of the project required intensive excavation during a three-month period (the duration of our research permits), it was necessary to have a large field crew. During the two field seasons, we paid an experienced archaeologist to serve as Assistant Field Director, while undergraduates (two each field season) were funded partially by their universities and partially by our grant to gain field experience. The bulk of our field crews were made up of local Tahitians, who were hired, trained, and paid with NSF funds. Eight Tahitians were hired each field season. Hiring local workers serves varied purposes: it gives back to the community in a meaningful way (via monetary support and training), and it integrates our research into the Tahitian community in an explicit manner.

Given that this was a large-scale, three-year project, there just was not enough time for me to carry out all the lab-based analyses myself. Consequently, I had to identify appropriate specialists as collaborators. This was another departure from my dissertation research, where by and large, I carried out all the post-excavation lab analysis myself. Three specialists were brought on as project collaborators including two geochemists specializing in Hawaiian geology who completed the XRF analysis and interpretation, and a Pacific Island biological scientist who completed the micro-fossil analysis and interpretation.

Research Questions and Theoretical Framework

This project, focused on residential and ritual landscapes, was my first large-scale National Science Foundation (NSF) funded research after my dissertation. I used unanswered questions generated from my dissertation as a springboard for a new project, which was funded for three years by NSF. I used my expertise in identifying rank and status in 'Opunohu Valley house sites to shift to a broader approach, looking at spatio-temporal variability in rank and status across two ritual and residential communities within the valley. The project required landscape-style mapping of stone surface architecture in addition to extensive excavations at a range of site types (e.g., temples, houses, terraces). I teamed up with my former dissertation advisor and now colleague, Patrick V. Kirch, who is an expert plane table and alidade mapper. We generally divided our labor into two camps. He would direct the GIS mapping and the more detailed mapping of all extant stone architecture in the two communities identified for study, while I would direct the site excavations and laboratory analyses, in addition to applying for all necessary research permits, visas, and export permits.

In my dissertation, and in the current project, I applied a *house society* ("*sociétés à maison*") model, originally introduced by Lévi-Strauss (1979). House-based studies in archaeology have linked changes at the micro-scale level of households to macro-scale, society-wide processes (see Plog and Heitman 2010), a key element of my study. While the house society literature, including ethnographic studies of Austronesian societies (such as those in East Polynesia), proposed material correlates of house societies, I had to read through the Society Island archaeological, ethnographic, and ethnohistorical literature to develop material correlates for Society Island house societies. Developing these "linking arguments" (see Wylie 2007) for how I would investigate house societies materially, on the ground, was a real challenge but one of the most enjoyable elements of the project.

Linking Arguments: Material Correlates of House Societies

Previous archaeological survey demonstrated pervasive patterning in clusters of residential sites and temples, which I reasoned were material correlates of "landed estates" of house societies (Kahn and Kirch 2013). Rectangular and oval-ended house sites, grouped on land whose inheritance from the ancestors I contend was validated by use of shared ritual spaces (temples), are inferred to represent ranked kin groupings or "houses" (Kahn 2007). I argued that common investment in these landed house estates through time, grounded in both genealogical relationships and communal interests, should produce material patterns for investigating shifts in social organization at the local scale. I proposed to look at: 1) *Definable estates*, residences occupied over several generations and house clusters with complex site use-lives (multiple building and re-building episodes), 2) *Common investments in the houses' estate*, necessary for its perpetuity, including daily production of material goods and raising of foodstuffs for household consumption, gift exchange, and tribute to the chiefs, (3) *Common investments in the houses' ritual estate*, symbolic of its ancestral claims, including temple construction, use, and re-building episodes, and (4) *Communal participation in ritual and feasting*, including familial rites at simple temples and community-wide rites at elaborate supra-household temples, with the latter including rites performed almost exclusively by chiefs and priests.

Shifting the Research Design and Sampling Protocols

My model of the expected material correlates of Society Island house societies dictated that research be carried out at the community scale. Clusters of residential sites, subsistence sites, and ritual sites, forming communities, became the target of analyses. I chose to intensively analyze two communities in the ʻOpunohu Valley, each with house sites, agricultural terraces, and temples and shrines situated on separate ridge tops, one in a wet sector for wetland agriculture, one in a dry sector for dryland agriculture. But how was I – a traditional household archaeologist who completed large horizontal excavations of house sites, excavating between 60–100% of house interiors for my dissertation with an average ratio of 3:1 of interior house excavation size versus exterior house excavation size (see Table 10.1) – to modify my research design?

In my new project I needed adequate samples of both house interiors and exteriors, in addition to test excavating temples and the residential or agricultural terraces surrounding them.

Table 10.1 Excavation samples sizes at select house sites in the 'Opunohu Valley. Top rows, Sites 120–171C = dissertation; bottom rows, Sites 289–322 = NSF post-dissertation.

Site #	Size house interior (m)	Interior excavation (m)	% Interior excavated (m)	Exterior excavations	Ratio interior to exterior excavations
120	50	47	94	13	3/1
123	13.5	13.5	100	31	1/3
170	72	43	60	10	4.3/1
171B	36	28	78	10	3/1
171C	25	25	100	18.5	1.3/1
289	45	15	33	15	1/1
290	22	21	68	10.2	1/1.4
294	102	22	22	25	1/1.4
322	9	7.5	83	11.5	1/1.5

ScMo-123 was excavated during the second year of my dissertation fieldwork, when I began to establish concrete parameters for determining house function which then allowed me to minimize excavations in house interiors.

During my dissertation research I quickly learned that excavations within both a house interior and exterior were critical to identifying house function, whether the house served as an everyday sleeping house, had a specialized function as a cookhouse, or had a ritual function. Given that residential house interiors were typically quite clean and lacked features other than postholes and perhaps a small hearth for light and warmth (Kahn 2007), I decided to do smaller interior house excavations for my landscape-scale project. This decision derived from field observations during my second year of dissertation research, where I observed that I could reduce the number of units completed in house interiors as I had established concrete parameters for identifying house function. Once dirty deposits had been identified in house interiors or features other than small hearths were identified, a specialized (non-sleeping house) functional designation could be given to a particular house structure. Or alternatively, if clean interior house deposits were encountered in addition to a small hearth along the house midline, a sleeping house designation could be applied to a particular structure. Then excavations could proceed in areas exterior to the house to determine the specific constellation of exterior features and ultimately reveal evidence of the house's function and/or residential status.

Thus, utilizing my on-the-ground experience from my dissertation, I shifted my overall sampling design. I targeted larger excavations in house exteriors rather than interiors, and ultimately excavated closer to a 1:1 ratio of house interior versus exterior (Table 10.1). This shift saved precious time to excavate other types of stone structures, such as temples and terraces, in order to test a greater amount of structures per residential cluster. This shift was key in terms of developing a relative chronology of site construction and more detailed analyses of site use within two large ritual and residential complexes. Ultimately, I excavated only 22–68% of house interiors, with a larger percentage of excavation focusing on other types of structures (e.g., terraces lacking house outlines, agricultural features, temples, and shrines). In no way did I feel that I compromised my credentials as a household archaeologist in minimizing the amount that I excavated per house site; rather, I used my previous experience to determine how much of a house interior I really needed to excavate to determine its use and how much of a house's exterior I really needed to excavate to determine its function.

In many ways exploring the specifics of my excavation methodology, certainly in terms of excavation sample size, forced me to explore the specific manner in which I determined house function both in the field and in the lab. This exercise allowed me to be more rigorous in my sampling regime, so that I no longer over-sampled house sites just to find one more post-hole or just to find a larger amount of artifacts when I likely already had a large enough sample size. My shift in research methodology supports current household archaeology applications whereby both large horizontal excavations as well as smaller block excavations that still use "micro-scale techniques of analyses" fall under the umbrella of accepted household archaeology methods (Kahn 2016; Pluckhahn 2010). This discussion broadly supports how research methodology must be flexible and must closely match the scale of the research questions being asked.

Following the tenets of traditional household archaeology, in my PhD research I set out to compare and contrast sub-surface features, artifacts, and spatial patterning at five pre-contact house sites with the goal of determining how site proxemics, surface architecture, and artifact assemblages could be used to study household status. The goal was to differentiate elite house sites from commoner house sites and residential house sites from house sites used for specialized purposes. In writing my first post-dissertation NSF grant application, I turned to understand how households were embedded in larger social landscapes, namely clusters of house sites, temples, and agricultural complexes which formed communities. The change in research questions forced not only a change in excavation sampling, but a change in the scale of the laboratory analyses. While five house complexes were excavated during my dissertation, ten site complexes were excavated in the landscape-scale study. Block excavations and skip trenches were completed in house interiors and exteriors, while test pits were excavated at the base of agricultural walls and temple walls to retrieve wood charcoal for dating. A suite of 15 AMS radiocarbon dates were used to develop a model of site construction and site use through time, a crucial component in identifying multiple building and re-building episodes in the landed house estates. Therefore, in many ways the theoretical principles of the project, investigating the materiality of house societies and their change and elaboration through time, grounded the choice of methods.

I used presence and absence of sub-surface features (pits, hearths, earth ovens), as well as their size and spatial location, to identify house function and social status, in addition to the presence of ritual attractors such as stone uprights, backrests, and sculpted figures (*ti'i*). These data were integral in documenting common investments in the house's landed estate and ritual estate, as well as for documenting feasting events. Every attempt was made to use "micro-scale" techniques of sampling and analyses (Kahn 2016) in the house excavations to document spatial variability in activities and artifact patterning that could be related to site function and site status. For example, bulk soil samples were collected from each house excavation unit and floated to retrieve micro- and macro-botanical samples and lithic samples. These data were used to identify patterns of daily use, including in-situ activity areas, site maintenance and cleaning, and whether house floors were "dirty" or "clean." Soil samples taken from sub-surface features, such as pits, hearths, and earth ovens, in addition to samples recovered from probable agricultural terraces, were subjected to micro-fossil analyses to obtain data on the types of plants grown in each residential/ritual complex as well as the types of objects manufactured from organic materials (mats, barkcloth, etc.) (Kahn *et al.* 2014). Collectively these organic remains constituted "social production," supra-subsistence production beyond the needs of consumption of individual households (Brookfield 1972).

These suites of information were important for documenting daily production of material goods and raising of foodstuffs (i.e., household consumption), in addition to patterns of gift exchange and tribute to the chiefs which could vary among and between households and communities of differing rank and status. Some of these datasets mirrored those used in earlier household archaeology studies in my region, allowing my new project to be broadly comparable at the regional level. One must always remember that we never have a conversation alone. Our research designs, and in some cases our choice of datasets, have to be a part of broader thematic or regional conversations in order for our own work to add to the greater body of archaeological knowledge.

Finally, in structuring the lithic analysis, I decided to use broad comparisons, such as the density of all lithics at each site (flakes, debitage, tools, as lithics per sq m) in addition to tools per sq m at each site, and percentage of exotic versus local artifacts (as determined by x-ray fluorescence, or XRF, analyses) as broad proxies for access to lithic production and consumption. Rather than subjecting each individual artifact to detailed flake analysis, this generalized comparative approach was deemed sufficient for the scale of my research questions. This contrasted with more detailed analyses that I completed for my dissertation, where every lithic artifact was subjected to detailed, time-consuming individual flake analysis. This decision was a hard one to make, but it was important, as I realized that a broader and quicker analysis of the stone artifacts sufficiently met the needs of my landscape-scale study. All of the lithic artifacts derived from the sites have been curated, and they happily await a graduate or undergraduate student who might come along and complete their more detailed analyses in the future, if such a research design meets their needs.

As I have outlined, shifting the excavation methodology derived rather organically from the theoretical perspective and landscape-scale of analyses, but at times it felt like a struggle. I was used to completing large horizontal excavations of house site interiors and exteriors, and focusing on smaller scale excavations left me sometimes feeling like I was sacrificing detail for broad coverage. But it was the only way to get the job done. Ultimately, the results (see below) highlight how important having a larger data set of excavated stone structures, albeit with smaller scale excavations at each individual structure, was to the success of the landscape-scale study.

Project Results: Successes and a Few Failures

In terms of project results, while our project successfully identified landed estates of two communities, only a single structure, a low-status house, had clear evidence for multiple-use and occupation events. This reflects the difficulty of working in the humid tropics, where bioturbation and rain leaching through acidic soils leave traces of micro-stratigraphy impossible to discern. Yet our project results highlighted interesting variability in residential communities' ability to add to their clusters through time, with new temples built, and new house sites constructed, suggesting differences in social power more broadly across 'Opunohu Valley ritual and residential landscapes.

Perhaps of most interest, I found that in Residential/Ritual Complex A, the first sites to be constructed included an elaborate, high-status house in addition to two temple sites (Kahn and Kirch 2013). This demonstrates that investments in the house's landed estate and ritual estate went hand in hand and were established early on in the inland expansion into the 'Opunohu Valley. Temples, in addition to the "origin houses," or namely high-status house sites constructed in ritually charged elements of the landscape, such as ritual promontories, served dual purposes, as the material foci of daily life and ritual activities, but also as claims of group heredity and ownership. Later on, other high-status residences and commoner dwellings were constructed on the landscape, as house membership grew. The temporally-staged dwelling and temple construction was recovered only through the comparative analysis of many house and temple structures in two residential and ritual landscapes. Such a pattern would not have been evident if the analyses had taken place at the scale of the individual site, as occurred with my dissertation analyses.

Final Commentary

In shifting from intensive house-based analyses to landscape-based analyses, I learned that both scales of analyses have their added benefits. More importantly, it is critical that your scale of analyses fits your research questions. What I learned, and I think this is an important take away message for undergraduates, graduate students, and junior researchers alike, is that often one's dissertation (or honors thesis, or MA thesis) solves some questions, leaves others unanswered, and then opens up new lines of potential research. It can be quite beneficial to follow these new lines of research, but of course, you cannot replicate what you did for your prior project. Studies that just add to your original dataset in the same manner, using the same theoretical perspective and the same methodologies, rarely, if ever, are funded in the ever increasing context of US grant competitions and rarely, if ever, are rewarded by student placement in competitive graduate departments. Yet being flexible, and learning from the project you just completed, to develop something new, but perhaps related, with a new theoretical perspective, and perhaps a new scale of analyses or a new analytical perspective, can be quite successful in terms of grant funding and your ongoing graduate and postgraduate career.

Ultimately with my landscape-scale project I wanted to more broadly impact the archaeological community, not just those interested in household archaeology, but those interested in the development of social complexity, house societies, and landscape-scale analyses. My project was able to do so with its close fit between research questions, scale of analysis, and methods of analyses. Clearly, I have learned the benefits of having a well-crafted research design. I have also learned that one must be flexible in terms of scale of analysis in the lab and in the field. It is always tempting to feel you have uncovered the one correct way to excavate a particular type of site, but in the end, research design must dictate site sampling and laboratory analyses.

I certainly learned there is more than one way to excavate ʻOpunohu Valley house sites. Not all household archaeology needs to be of the "traditional" kind with huge horizontal excavations. In some cases, it can be more important to examine what has been done in your region and modify excavation design to fit a broader landscape- or community-scale approach (see discussion in Lee and Wright 2016), even if you started out as a "traditional" household archaeologist. You can study households at the community scale; this process just gives you different data, including larger samples in terms of number of structures excavated, which fits well with a landscape approach. In such landscape-scale studies, micro-scale approaches to house excavation can provide consistency with more traditional large horizontal household archaeology data sets, which can be key to comparative analyses. Another important take-home lesson is that not all projects post-PhD, in fact, probably none, will get your undivided and long-term attention like your dissertation assemblages. This is okay. You can still learn a lot from analyses that are less detailed as long as they fit well with your research design. It is also key to identify partners and collaborators, be they undergraduate and graduate students working in your lab, or specialists working in their own labs, to take part in large multi-year projects. Even so, keep up to date with innovations in archaeometry, geoarchaeology, and other related sub-fields, so that you can be an "educated consumer" and an educated collaborator (Killick and Young 1997).

In putting together large field-based, multi-year research projects, there is a special need for a good fit between lab specialists and project principal investigators (PIs). Heading up a large team of collaborators takes some skill and effort and can sometimes feel like you are herding cats, but ultimately can enrich one's professional development in a myriad of ways. Certainly teaming up with collaborators in the field and in the lab requires patience and often a need for cross-disciplinary or inter-disciplinary communication, sometimes with individuals who have a tempo to their work or theoretical perspectives entirely different from your own. Remember that multi-year projects typically continue for three to five years after the excavations have been completed. So choose your collaborators wisely as this long-term relationship and its health determines in many ways how successful the outcomes of your project will be. When working with collaborators it is also essential to develop structured publication agreements (what they will be, when they will be done, and how authors will be ordered) from the outset. PIs and specialists alike are busy and juggling multiple projects; therefore having a generalized publication plan from day one makes the expectations of the lead PIs clear and transparent from the start. Such plans are extremely important for graduate students as well as junior researchers who are managing their publication strategies as they move towards finding an academic position and eventual tenure evaluation.

Finally, in terms of unexpected surprises related to the project, my choice of using the house society model was a bold one, as there had been few studies of this kind in Polynesia or even world-wide at the time the project was funded in 2006. In some ways, using an original theoretical outlook likely led to the funding of the project via NSF. NSF reviewers always like to see some sort of innovation, and my theoretical perspective, and certainly aspects of the project's methodology (some discussed here, but others not) were pioneering. So choosing an "out of the box" theoretical perspective likely gave my project a leg up. But in the long term, I have found that scholars outside of the Polynesian region are sometimes resistant to the notion of house societies. This has led to some difficulties in publishing some of the data from this project, an unexpected and frankly unwelcome surprise, but one that is not unsurmountable. Through conversations with colleagues using the house society perspective in other parts of the world, I have concluded that it will make the most sense to publish much of the house society interpretations as a stand-alone book. What will be key is finding the right publisher and editor to nurture that book to its fruition to accompany the other publications that have derived already from the project. For my first post-dissertation project, the study was ultimately a broad success, but not without its moments of doubt and difficulty.

Paired Reading

Kahn, Jennifer G. and Patrick V. Kirch. 2013. "Residential Landscapes and House Societies of the Late Prehistoric Society Islands (French Polynesia)." *Journal of Pacific Archaeology*, 4: 50–72.

References

Brookfield, Harold C. 1972. "Intensification and Disintensification in Pacific Agriculture: A Theoretical Approach." *Pacific Viewpoint*, 13: 30–48.

Kahn, Jennifer G. 2007. "Power and Precedence in Ancient House Societies: A Case Study from the Society Island Chiefdoms (French Polynesia)." In *The Durable House: House Society Models in Archaeology*, edited by Robin Beck, 198–223. Carbondale, IL: Southern Illinois University.

Kahn, Jennifer G. 2016. "Household Archaeology in Polynesia: Historical Context and New Directions." *Journal of Anthropological Research*, 24: 325–372. DOI: 10.1007/s10814-016-9092-9.

Kahn, Jennifer G., Mark Horrocks, and Michael Nieuwoudt. 2014. "Agriculture, Domestic Production, and Site Function: Micro-fossil Analyses and Late Prehistoric Landscapes of the Society Islands." *Economic Botany*, 68: 246–263.

Kahn, Jennifer G. and Patrick V. Kirch. 2013. "Residential Landscapes and House Societies of the Late Prehistoric Society Islands (French Polynesia)." *Journal of Pacific Archaeology*, 4: 50–72.

Killick, David and Suzanne M. Young. 1997. "Archaeology and Archaeometry: From Casual Dating to a Meaningful Relationship?" *Antiquity*, 71: 518–524. DOI: 10.1017/S0003598X0008529X.

Lévi-Strauss, Claude. 1979. "Nobles Sauvages." In *Culture, Science et Développement: Contribution à une Histoire de l'Homme*, 41–55. Paris: Edouard Privat.

Lee, Rachel J. and Joshua Wright. 2016. "Household Archaeology in East Asia: Introduction to the Special Issue." *Journal of Archaeological Research*, 72: 129–132. DOI: 10.1086/686299.

Plog, Stephen and Carrie Heitman. 2010. "Hierarchy and Social Inequality in the American Southwest, AD 800–1200." *Proceedings of the National Academy of Sciences*, 107: 19619–19626. DOI: 10.1073/pnas.1014985107.

Pluckhahn, Thomas J. 2010. "Household Archaeology in the Southeastern United States: History, Trends, and Challenges." *Journal of Archaeological Research*, 18: 331–385. DOI: 10.1007/s10814-010-9040-z.

Wylie, Alison. 2007. "The Constitution of Archaeological Evidence." In *The Archaeology of Identities: A Reader*, edited by Timothy Insoll, 97–18. New York: Routledge.

11

Research Spaces from Borderland Places – Late Woodland Archaeology in Southern Ontario
Neal Ferris

Project Summary

The Late Woodland Borderlands project is an ongoing research program involving colleagues, students, and myself at a number of Canadian universities. The focus of the project is a cluster of circa twelfth- to thirteenth-century village-like communities in southwestern Ontario that were located at the time within a borderland between distinct material archaeological traditions. This project really began through the happenstance fortune of a cultural resource management (CRM) company's excavation of these sites in advance of opening up quarries and my personal association with the company president. How we managed to go from those CRM findings to a funded, reflexive, theoretically-informed academic research program supporting several graduate students, scholars, and Indigenous community research is reviewed in this chapter, with special emphasis on both successes and failures.

Introduction

For most of my career I have worked as a government archaeologist, regulating commercial archaeology (i.e., CRM) in that area of Canada located between Lakes Erie and Huron. Known locally as southwestern Ontario, this area adjacent to the Great Lakes is about the size of Ireland, is currently home and/or traditional territory for various Haudenosaunee and Anishinabeg Indigenous peoples, and tells the human material history of people living rich and diversified lifeways, uniquely tailored to the local region and yet connected to broader continental social developments through the millennia (e.g., Munson and Jamieson 2013). This region has also experienced close to a century and a half of archaeological activity and continues to sustain an active practice today, the vast majority of which undertaken by commercial archaeologists hired to mitigate the impacts to sites as a result of a wide array of land development and construction activities.

I mention this because during my time as a government archaeologist all that archaeological activity for southwestern Ontario came through my office. So my experiences developing a "research program," if it could be called that, arose exclusively from the spaces I found within the massive array of sites uncovered and archaeology practiced locally, either by my office as salvage or by consultant archaeologists only too happy to hand off a collection for research. I certainly had research "tendencies" towards the archaeology of the last 1,000 years or so and on

Engaging Archaeology: 25 Case Studies in Research Practice, First Edition. Edited by Stephen W. Silliman.
© 2018 John Wiley & Sons, Inc. Published 2018 by John Wiley & Sons, Inc.

how archaeology was being practiced and differently understood, but that was all reactive to what I was being exposed to, day in and day out. Beyond developing archaeological policy and programming, I never really had the luxury of developing an idea, research question, or anything remotely looking like a hypothesis to then go out to test or explore. Rather I took what fell in my lap and ran with it: puzzling over site findings or the absence of sites where expected because these sites or locales were in the way of a subdivision or quarry, not because they were selected to test a particular research project's design.

To be honest, my experiences have left me with a healthy skepticism on the merit of intellectual curiosity and rigorous research design directed at excavating simply to address that curiosity. In my world, shaped by massive scales of ongoing CRM activity, and the fact that, as a government regulator, I was continually confronted with archaeology as a contested heritage beyond archaeological sensibilities, pursuing intellectual curiosity feels a bit self-indulgent if not balanced with the realities that our practice creates and faces in the wider world (Ferris and Welch 2014). Tens of thousands of archaeological sites are excavated in the name of preserving the past for the future, often poorly known and rarely accessed. So finding research spaces within what the practice of archaeology has become, to archaeologists but also to the descendant groups and anyone else in society who draw value and meaning from that heritage, seems to represent a more sustainable way of doing archaeology in the twenty-first century than pursuing status quo curiosities.

Finding a Space for Research

All that said, in the spring of 2008, not long after being newly minted as a university professor at Western University, I was grappling with the very dilemma of how to make research: where should I focus my interest, and should it "look" academic, or continue what I've always done?

It wasn't long before that question was being answered, and in the fashion I had always experienced in the past. In April, I received a phone call from a colleague, a CRM archaeologist excavating a series of archaeological sites, all dating to the same period (ca. AD 1100–1250), and located in a tight 3,000-m radius of each other. Jim Wilson's company was excavating these sites on behalf of a client planning a series of sand quarries. Jim had called me because he knew I had an interest in this period, an archaeological manifestation referred to locally as the Western Basin Late Woodland Tradition (Murphy and Ferris 1990).

To back up a bit, I have found the material record from this period and region to be an intriguing topic, because it reflects the lifeways of ancient communities that are inconsistent with the overwhelmingly dominant Late Woodland (ca. AD 900–1400) archaeological record known for southern Ontario, and referred to as part of the Ontario Iroquoian Tradition. Indeed, the history of Ontario archaeology through the twentieth century is dominated by the cultural historical pursuit of tracing back in time the ancestry of Iroquoian-speaking peoples first encountered by Europeans at the start of the seventeenth century. Interest in this more westerly Late Woodland record didn't attract the same research curiosity, and this manifestation tended to be dismissed as a peripheral part of that better-known archaeological construct. So most of the basic cultural historical ordering of material from AD 900 to 1400 around the western basin of Lake Erie came from Michigan and Ohio (e.g., Fitting 1965), and was applied rote to Ontario material.

But archaeologists came to know Ontario manifestations of this record much more directly through the 1980s, primarily as a result of CRM-generated salvage excavations. The local record came to be characterized by what appeared to be a distinctive ceramic craft tradition (Watts 2008) and settlement patterns that tended to lack evidence of residential structures, but included concentrations of deep, circular storage pits. The data suggested a fair amount of seasonal mobility and a diversified subsistence less focused on the maize agriculture archaeologists had documented for the adjacent archaeological tradition to the east. However, subsequent academic and CRM-generated human skeletal research undertaken with Indigenous community consent (e.g., Watts *et al.* 2011) added further complexity to that picture. It suggested that people following these diversified subsistence practices and mobility were, at about the same time, consuming as much maize as their neighbors to the east, confounding archaeological notions of the determinacy of agriculture in triggering sedentary village life, and underscoring the critical value that caching technology, reflected in those large clusters of storage pits, played in Western Basin lifeways.

Despite the increased understanding of this period in southwestern Ontario, settlement patterns, both in Ontario and in adjacent States, remained elusive. Prior to 2008 only three relatively complete and a couple of partial house structures had been documented for this 500-year period, and all those sites with large clusters of storage pits lacked any defined indication of residential space. So any sense of ordered settlement or spatial use of locales was lacking.

This lack of settlement data fits well with archaeological assumptions about these communities being seasonally mobile prior to about AD 1400. It also fits assumptions that the Western Basin Late Woodland record was left by ancestral Anishinabeg peoples who spoke Algonquian languages, and reflected lifeways archaeologists were familiar with for the Great Lakes region in seventeenth- and eighteenth-century historical accounts. Thus the focus of early research on this Late Woodland manifestation in southwestern Ontario was on the apparent differences in the archaeology for this area, and immediately east, and the implications that the more easterly archaeological manifestation represented ancient lifeways of historically-documented northern Iroquoian-speaking peoples. Indeed, while the boundary between these two traditions had never been documented in the field, the area of Jim's findings near the modern-day town of Arkona was understood to be very close to where those archaeological traditions transitioned (see Cunningham 2001). In other words, the sites Jim was finding fell within a material transition generally imagined by local archaeologists to reflect ethno-linguistic cultural differences or ethnicities.

The thinking about the Western Basin material record that emerged through the end of the twentieth century tended to reflect the way archaeology, and especially cultural historical archaeology, draws historical narratives and explanations from limited datasets. We tend to generalize and over-emphasize particular material traits and attributes, and we want to assume these "mean" something as profound to the people who left that record as the record appears to us to be. The socio-linguistic ethnicity of pots and sites were the historically-rooted tendency that archaeologists in the Northeast and Great Lakes invoked to explain the archaeological record centuries prior to written records of Europeans ever being generated for this region about Indigenous peoples (see Ferris 1999 for further discussion).

Given this background context, and my colleagues knowing my interest in that record, it was not a surprise that Jim Wilson would want to share his crew's findings. He knew I would be interested because his excavations were uncovering clear settlement patterns, including evidence of houses and a palisade, something not previously documented for the Western Basin Late Woodland. I ended up visiting the Figura site and assisted his crew in their excavations, in particular in recording the settlement patterns. The site revealed four small houses, each around 7 m long by 5 m wide and aligned in an ordered pattern along the interior of a single-rowed palisade, which itself was shaped in an oval oriented north-south, and encompassing the houses, feature concentrations and a large more open space (Figure 11.1). Exterior to the palisade was an additional house and more concentrations of features. In all, the settlement pattern was relatively clean and ordered, with little feature overlap or evidence of rebuilding. It also nearly tripled the number of documented houses known for this period, and revealed a

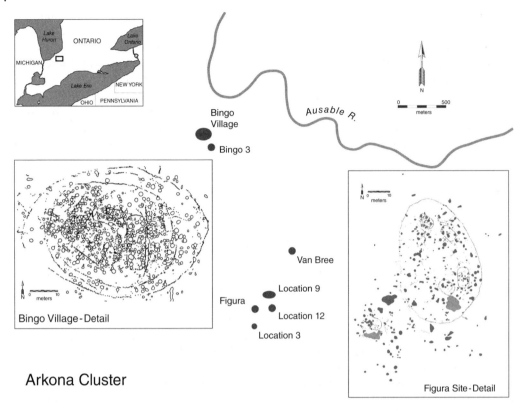

Figure 11.1 Arkona Site Cluster, southern Ontario. This map depicts the cluster of Late Woodland sites excavated in the Arkona area by CRM archaeologists, and the focus of the research program discussed in this chapter. Inset are settlement plans for the two larger sites excavated from this cluster. Map courtesy of Chris Watts.

more formal settlement expression than previously seen from this time anywhere between northwestern Ohio and southwestern Ontario. Color me intrigued!

But as important as Figura appeared to be, it was only part of the story. Jim's crews had been working on a number of other sites within this same area. In all, his company documented eight sites dated to the same time period as Figura. The Bingo site (named after the quarry pit) also included a palisade encompassing feature concentrations and houses. But unlike Figura, with its tidy ordering of small houses, the settlement pattern at Bingo included a massive concentration of cultural features densely clustering and overlapping each other in open areas, and aligned along both sides of the interior of longhouse structures that each measured about 20 m in length. The palisade consisted of two to three rows of posts. This messy and busy settlement pattern at Bingo was also reflected in a much more substantial material culture assemblage than recovered from Figura, including around ten times as many projectile points (34 at Figura; 425 at Bingo); smoking pipe fragments (22 at Figura; 227 at Bingo); along with substantial ceramic rim differences (226 vs 553). Clearly basic material representation at Bingo was more intensive than at Figura, for reasons only research could begin to explore.

Beyond Figura and Bingo, Jim's company had also documented several smaller sites consisting of one or two small houses or a scattering of features only. They also documented sections of additional sites that seemed to be Bingo-like or Figura-like settlements. Incredibly, Jim's company had generated, over the course of two field seasons, a massive dataset for the Late Woodland archaeology of this material tradition from a small radius that, on the face of it, appeared to significantly add to and revise understandings of this period. I could readily see many dimensions of the findings that could sustain research. Now, how to go about and create that research space from Jim's CRM efforts?

Making that Research Space

By the second half of the summer of 2008 and with Jim's support, I had decided to build a research focus. To me, the research potential was readily evident straight from the out-of-the-field findings: a cluster of sites the likes of which had not been previously documented in south-western Ontario, all found in a tight area and apparent very close chronology, exhibiting variable settlement patterns that would allow for extensive intra- and inter-site comparisons. Additionally, and critically, while the material recovered reflected the temporality of these communities, it also reflected variation in design and form that suggested engagement with broader material, settlement, and subsistence trends known to the west and to the east of the Arkona area.

The obvious option I had was to pull together a grant application for the Social Sciences and Humanities Research Council (SSHRC), the principal source of research funding in Canada for archaeology. In fairness I did not give myself a lot of time to pull together an application, but since the data were so compelling, at least to me, I felt it worth the effort. In the 2008 application I suggested the following goals:

> to advance our knowledge of the complex social processes within and between First Nations communities dating to circa AD 1000–1300 and associated with the Late Woodland Younge phase of the Western Basin Tradition in southwestern Ontario ... to document the archaeological processes that are manifest in the record as a result of individuals being within and evolving along a cultural frontier in the ancient past through a period of significant social change ... undertaking detailed, science-based materials analyses on the extensive collections generated as a result of commercial excavations of these sites ... Collaboration will also extend to the Kettle and Stony Point First Nation...

This excerpt from the summary of my application highlights what I thought were the strengths of the project, namely: 1) this dataset represented a community at a point in time between archaeological material traditions, and thus worth exploring for how those findings were and were not consistent with the culture history in the region; 2) this research would be about value-added material studies conducted on the already documented data by the CRM firm; 3) by virtue of working with Jim's company, I would be demonstrating the strengths of collaborating with CRM to reflect the value that academic scholarship can bring to the dominant form of archaeological practice in North America; and 4) by seeking Indigenous collaboration, I wanted to also demonstrate how the community could develop its own way of interpreting the record, relevant to them, and bring a greater robustness to archaeological ways of knowing the past.

The application spent most of the limited space provided for detailing the planned research describing archaeological understandings of the Late Woodland in this region, and the implications the Arkona data would have to what I characterized as a "frontier zone" between the

Western Basin material record and the better-known record to the east. I spent a fair bit of time framing this period as the emergence of agriculturally-based societies that created stress on both innovation and tradition in material and lifeway crafts, and the implications this may have within a frontier zone. And to convey a sense of the spectacular nature of the findings, I spent a lot of text describing them, simply because the limited space in the application precluded using maps or images.

I concluded by arguing that the project would be situated within global archaeological research on the emergence of agricultural societies and social complexity and that the archaeological record I wished to explore in southern Ontario could readily contribute to that cutting-edge research. A rather ambitious assertion, and one ultimately I failed to make the case for, since in the spring of 2009 I found out that the application was turned down. Why it failed, I feel, is because I had overly emphasized how the research would advance understandings of local archaeology. Despite alluding to broader theoretical trends and global implications of the findings, I had only poorly made the case, managing to avoid citing much research beyond the regional literature connected to the local Western Basin Late Woodland. The trap I had fallen into was the risk that comes from working with known data and thinking about research on these data already wrapped up in an initial layer of interpretation generated during discovery. I may have known in my head the wider implications for this research, but I had written the application as if I was working out the local cultural historical importance, as I had been talking to Jim and his crews about all summer.

Despite being unsuccessful I was not dissuaded from trying again, and set out to write a second application in 2009. One useful comment received from the reviewers first time out had been a concern for the lack of a more overt and clear theoretical approach to frame the research, so I focused on correcting that deficiency in the second attempt. As such I intended to provide a broader context for interpreting the data, one that only incidentally would also advance knowledge of local traditions. Beyond this conceptual revision, I felt that the focus on collaboration with CRM archaeology and the Kettle Point and Stony Point First Nations, and making knowledge from existing collections were still all strengths of the proposal, albeit framed within that new, broader theoretical orientation.

The orientation adopted for the project expanded on the notion that the site cluster falls within a transition between archaeologically-defined material traditions. In other words, does difference in material culture mean something beyond cultural historical classification? Exploring whether these classifications reflect some kind of social material reality could best be done by considering the site cluster as an archaeological borderland between such classifications, or so I argued in 2009:

> This proposal seeks to advance our knowledge of the complex social processes that were at play among a series of archaeological "borderland" communities ... Moreover, this borderland will allow us to consider archaeologically how such material practices worked to shape family and community identity, and how that heightened sense of material expression connected to a landscape of neighbors with diverse material inventories variably facilitating revision to community and personal identity.

In other words, I was proposing to build from local cultural historical trait classifications of variable archaeological traditions of this period and region to explore ideas that more broadly interrogated archaeological materiality. So in this version of the application I spent much less time detailing local understandings of the archaeology, and more arguing why these data would be ideal for exploring the implications of a material archaeological borderland:

theoretically informed research programs can focus on the implications of that material existence and how individuals' engagement with that material repertoire – or network of human and material agencies – reflects patterns of social organization and perceptions of the world both inside and outside the community ... And since with the early Late Woodland of southwestern Ontario we have a record clearly pertaining to an archaeological frontier or border, we in effect have an archaeological laboratory here to test archaeological constructs while exploring differential development of materially recognized social change and subsistence innovation, and the ways in which the presence of a border – or borderland – did or did not contribute to that change.

Important in this revised proposal were the notions that the local archaeological record presented a "laboratory" to test the theoretical construct, and that this notion of a material "borderland" could serve as a construct from which ALL of the findings could be interpreted. This approach afforded me a cohesiveness to the proposed research beyond local culture history, while nonetheless building from as well as examining implications of those material conceptions identified locally. It also would allow me, and the various colleagues and students participating, to engage with a range of theoretical constructs around material difference and similarity, innovation, and tradition, all from the datasets already in hand reflecting variable local and regional community patterns, material craft traditions, and subsistence. In effect, I gave the proposal reviewers every chance to see how all the various strands of the project could readily be achieved as value-added research arising from already existing findings the funding agency would not have to pay to be excavated in the first place – this project could go beyond documentation because that had already been done through CRM.

To be clear, the adoption of a theoretical construct to frame the proposed research was not because I had a specific theoretical orientation to impose. While I tend to embrace contextual, interpretive orientations and a relativity in my own work, the particular construct I emphasized was more a pragmatic use of a conceptual approach that seemed to "fit" the kinds of research questions the data could best engage with. In the case of the Arkona cluster, that notion of material difference in a place of transition between distinct archaeological manifestations led me to consider notions of community material identity as they played out over very few generations. How did these communities – communities of practice making choices about artisan craft and livelihood and internal understanding of themselves and their neighbors further afield – differently negotiate notions of tradition and innovation reflected materially over those few generations? So whether the analysis of this data was to be based in material science (thin sectioning and CT scanning of ceramics; maize DNA studies), ceramic attributes, inter- and intra-site contextual comparisons of material and foodways, or a contemporary Indigenous archaeological approach, the social processes of identity maintenance and revision (and how we can get at these archaeologically) were clearly well-suited concepts to be researched. For me, adopting a particular theoretical construct here was a kind of eclectic pragmatism ratcheting together interpretive concepts to best fit the data in hand, rather than overlaying a theoretical model and seeking to make the data fit that model.

One other important distinction of the 2009 application is worth noting. As I felt the data recovered for the Arkona sites were spectacular, I wanted to illustrate, rather than describe, those findings. But the convention of an application precluded me from including site maps or images. So, in perhaps a slightly cheeky way around that limitation, and saving precious writing space, Jim and I wrote a basic article on the findings, which included lots of maps and images, and posted that online. I was then able to cite that source, and its URL, in the application. I don't know if reviewers felt compelled to look at the article during their review, but at least I had provided them with that chance to see those findings directly, if they wanted.

Research Spaces in Borderland Places

As my narrative implies, I was successful second time out, receiving full support for the research proposal. While this project will continue for many more years, to date, beyond myself and four colleagues, five MA students and three PhD students have worked or are continuing to work on these materials, all from the framework of exploring the implications an archaeological border-land construct has for interpreting the findings from those CRM excavations. As with most theoretical constructs, the elegance of the borderland model has worked most effectively when used as a metaphor for looking at materially lived life through this period and has validated the appearance of intensive social innovation shaping and revising material expression across the Arkona cluster of sites. Extensive dating has confirmed all these sites existed within 100 years of each other, while limited survey indicates settlement was minimal in the few centuries prior, and absent afterwards.

Research on these sites has invited researchers to consider communities of practice in the formation of ceramic vessels as agents of change and continuity within the borderland, and social management of space across individual sites as a negotiation of family and broader social units. Some of the initial findings in particular are suggesting that the generations of ceramic artisans who created ceramics in the Arkona community developed a craft that was "coherently incoherent." Vessel form and construction appears to reflect the logics and conventions of what archaeologists would refer to as Western Basin-like ceramic production, but with more of a collage of decorative attributes commonly found to the west and to the east. In so doing, these communities appear to have been in the process of creating a distinct material expression of that time and place. These findings are also encouraging us to consider that material practices reflected within this community of sites may have been so innovative and engaged with mate-rial trends beyond the borderland as to change over time from "Western Basin-like" in classifi-cation to "Ontario Iroquoian-like" in classification, especially after this community departed from the Arkona area. This notion underscores how cultural historical constructs of trait lists translate poorly into the self-definitional and always revising notions of self and group identity. And it has allowed Indigenous community research to move beyond archaeological constructs altogether and consider a historical narrative for these sites that better aligns with oral tradi-tions of migration and travels across the Great Lakes through that time, regardless of what archaeological interpretive constructs also brought to bear on this record.

In retrospect, the metaphor of "borderland" also characterizes the space between CRM and academic scholarship. The recovery of archaeological sites as resources that need to be docu-mented and removed before development occurs is the overwhelmingly predominant form of archaeological practice today. It is where most students who study archaeology in university will end up pursuing careers. And the rhetorical intent of that work to preserve this record for future study is the principle we assert to justify this practice as broadly relevant. But collectively archaeology pays minimal lip service to that aim, with academic research largely ignoring as well as being unable to access the bulk of the record harvested within CRM. Yet, as I learned developing this research program and through my transition from CRM to academic scholar-ship, rich and robust research spaces exist to explore within that accumulated record. As archaeologists we just need to meet in the borderland between those forms of our practice to help make real the promise in that record recovered in the name of archaeology.

Paired Reading

Ferris, Neal. 1999. "Telling Tales: Interpretive Trends in Southern Ontario Late Woodland Archaeology." *Ontario Archaeology*, 68: 1–62.

References

Cunningham, Jerimy. 2001. "Ceramic Variation and Ethnic Holism: A Case Study from the 'Younge-Early Ontario Iroquoian Border' in Southwestern Ontario." *Canadian Journal of Archaeology*, 25: 1–27.

Ferris, Neal. 1999. "Telling Tales: Interpretive Trends in Southern Ontario Late Woodland Archaeology." *Ontario Archaeology*, 68: 1–62.

Ferris, Neal and John Welch. 2014. "Beyond Archaeological Agendas: In the Service of a Sustainable Archaeology." In *Transforming Archaeology: Activist Practices and Prospects*, edited by Sonya Atalay, Lee Rains Claus, Randall McGuire, and John R. Welch, 215–238. Walnut Creek, CA: Left Coast Press.

Fitting, James. 1965. *Late Woodland Cultures of Southeastern Michigan*. Anthropological Papers, 24. Ann Arbor, MI: University of Michigan.

Munson, Marit K. and Susan M. Jamieson. 2013. *Before Ontario: The Archaeology of a Province*. Montreal and Kingston: McGill-Queen's University Press.

Murphy, Carl, and Neal Ferris. 1990. "The Late Woodland Western Basin Tradition of Southwestern Ontario." In *The Archaeology of Southern Ontario to A.D. 1650*, edited by Chris Ellis and Neal Ferris, 189–278. Occasional Publications of the London Chapter, OAS Number 5: Ontario Archaeological Society.

Watts, Christopher. 2008. *Pot/Potter Entanglements and Networks of Agency in Late Woodland Period (c. AD 900–1300) Southwestern Ontario, Canada*. British Archaeological Reports, International Series 1828. Oxford: British Archaeological Reports.

Watts, Christopher, Christine White, and Fred Longstaffe. 2011. "Childhood Diet and Western Basin Tradition Foodways at the Krieger Site, Southwestern Ontario, Canada." *American Antiquity*, 76: 446–472. DOI: 10.7183/0002-7316.76.3.446.

12

Ethnoarchaeology of Pottery in Tigray, Ethiopia: Engaging with Marginalized People
Diane Lyons

Project Summary

Ethnoarchaeology contributes to the understanding of people's relationship with the materials and spaces of everyday life. Presented here is advice for researchers considering their first ethnoarchaeology project. While drawing on experience from a long career in ethnoarchaeology, specific issues that arise in a project are discussed using the Tigray Pottery Project in Tigray, Ethiopia (2007–2015) as an example. This project's objective is to determine how marginalized identities of female market potters are materially and spatially constituted in daily practice. The results of the study are relevant to understanding material expressions of complex societies and the resilience of contemporary potters in the face of rapid market change. Ethics, the need for long-term study, working with tight budgets, the value of team-based projects, and shifting circumstances over the course of a study are explored.

Starting Out: Lessons in Patience

Ethnoarchaeology is the study of the relationships between contemporary people and material culture, places, and spaces in ways that can inform archaeological and other social science research. Recognizing that the present is different from the past, ethnoarchaeological research is never intended to be imposed directly onto the past as its explanation. Instead, ethnoarchaeological and archaeological contexts should be compared to determine how these contexts are similar *and* different and to then investigate why they are so using multiple lines of evidence.

Doing ethnoarchaeology is different from archaeology in that our research largely depends upon the kindnesses of strangers. Regardless of how carefully we craft field objectives and methodologies, the success of any ethnoarchaeological project ultimately depends on who will agree to participate in our projects and what they will decide to tell or show us. The opportunity to learn from these strangers is both a privilege and a test. People have opinions. Their actions often run contrary to cherished archaeological theories, and while we observe them, they observe and measure us. To actually learn something from people who are generous enough to participate in our projects takes time, ethical practice, and commitment. Trust must be earned. People need to know what you are doing, have time to observe you at work, to talk with you over coffee, to see if you are serious.

Engaging Archaeology: 25 Case Studies in Research Practice, First Edition. Edited by Stephen W. Silliman.
© 2018 John Wiley & Sons, Inc. Published 2018 by John Wiley & Sons, Inc.

Ethnoarchaeology cannot be done in brief forays to the local village to answer questions for a larger archaeological project. A few archaeologists have approached me for tips to do this kind of research. I caution them that short-term study is unreliable, but they usually do the study anyway. But what would they say if I asked them for a few tips to do a little archaeology as a sideline to a major ethnoarchaeology project? Would two or three small test pits in a large geographic region provide enough information to generalize about the relationship of the past with the present in any substantive way? Would you dare to build a people's history with those data (see Lyons and Casey 2016)?

The concern with short-term ethnoarchaeological study is that it is virtually guaranteed that some of its information is wrong. For example, when I was working on my doctoral research in northern Cameroon, I observed small pots under granaries in compounds of lineage heads. I suspected that they were for ritual. Everyone told me that they were just pots – but I was warned not to touch them! Six months into my research a senior lineage head, whom I had visited several times previously, took me over to his granary and lifted each pot explaining to me that these were his ancestor pots and how he ministered to them, and he answered my many questions. Similar interviews with other lineage heads followed in quick succession, along with a flood of social and ritual information. When I asked why I was being given this information now and not before, I was told that the lineage heads had decided together that they could trust me. I felt deeply honored – and I learned to be cautious. People's first answers can be guarded, even purposefully misleading. The rich data that eventually I received were critical to my final interpretation, an interpretation that would have been woefully simplistic if based on earlier observations.

I had similar experiences in other projects as have most of my ethnoarchaeology colleagues. I have learned to wait while I collect quantifiable data: making maps, measuring pots, asking standard questions. Quantitative data still require people's cooperation, but qualitative data take much longer to acquire. Qualitative data are often personal, and they require not only people's willingness to impart this kind of information but also that I have become familiar with the material context under study. It is only when I reach this point in a project that the information that people tell me about social relationships begins to mesh with what I observe them doing. Understanding the relationship between people and the material is a physical-spatial language of action or doing that is hard for people to articulate into words. But this engagement is the essence of how people constitute themselves in the material and how the material constitutes us. This kinetic-material language takes time to see and to start to interpret. Do not expect to achieve full fluency, I never have, but we must acquire a basic vocabulary. So my best advice to anyone attempting their first ethnoarchaeology project is that good research takes time, tenacity, and patience. Ethnoarchaeology is "slow science" (see MacEachern and Cunningham 2016).

The Tigray Pottery Project

The example of research that I will use here is the project that I directed in Tigray Regional State in northern highland Ethiopia between 2007 and 2015 (Figure 12.1). The purpose of the Tigray Pottery Project is to determine how practices of marginalization of Tigray's female market potters are materially and spatially constituted. The study began with a short pilot project in 2007, and was followed by four field seasons of ethnoarchaeological research between 2009 and 2015. Foreign researchers working in Ethiopia are only provided a permit for a $100\,km^2$ area, which makes regional studies difficult. I got around this problem by doing three independent and separately funded research projects: one in Eastern Tigray near the market town of Edaga Hamus (2007–2010), a second in Central Tigray in and near the town of Yeha (2012), and a third in Northwestern Tigray in the town of Selekeleka (2015). The result is the first regional study of contemporary pottery production in northern Ethiopia.

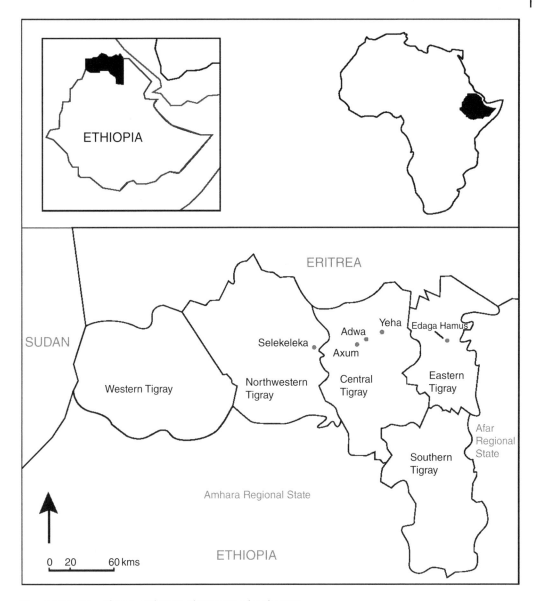

Figure 12.1 Map of Tigray, Ethiopia. Places named in the text.

This was a team-based project. Geoarchaeologist, Dr. Andrea Freeman (University of Calgary) participated in the pilot project. I persuaded Dr. Joanna Casey (University of South Carolina) to work with me in 2009, 2012, and 2015. Joanna has conducted ethnoarchaeology in Ghana since the 1980s. Her research interests include the role of women's small-scale market trade in household provisioning. Ethiopia offered Joanna an opportunity to compare her study in Ghana with women traders in Ethiopia, including pottery trade. Her study substantially expanded our understanding of pottery and other products in household economies in all three study areas. We collected data through interview, observation, documentation of the potters' *chaînes opératoires*, materials analysis (x-ray diffraction (XRD), neutron activation analysis (NAA), thin-section analysis), and mapping of villages and domestic compounds. The project supported two MA theses and an honors thesis, and it has provided field experience for two

Ethiopian doctoral students. All three projects were funded generously by the Wenner-Gren Foundation, and the Yeha study was also funded by a grant from the National Geographic Society. Additional funds were provided by the Killam Foundation and the University of Calgary. But first, it is instructive to explain how I came to study these potters.

The Path to the Potters

The common thread running through more than three decades of my research is an interest in how social identities are constituted and mediated through domestic and community spaces and places and through the mundane material things of everyday life. That trips off the tongue more readily today than it did 30 years ago, but in retrospect I was drawn to ideas about social identity that were becoming central to both processual and post-processual theories in the early 1980s when I was a graduate student. I first explored this interest in my MA thesis (1982), an archaeological study of regional variation in Dorset art style in the Canadian Arctic and Greenland. I had never considered doing ethnoarchaeology or working in Africa until an opportunity arose to do a doctoral project in 1986 in northern Cameroon as a member of Dr. Nicholas David's (University of Calgary) Mandara Archaeological Project (MAP). This opportunity was extended because of the interests explored in my MA thesis. MAP was investigating material culture style and its meaning in multiple ethnic contexts in the northern Mandara Mountains and adjacent plains. My doctoral project was an 11-month investigation of how gender, social status, and ethnic identities were configured in domestic and community buildings and spaces in a multi-ethnic community. While I enjoy archaeological research, ethnoarchaeology offered me a greater personal challenge: trying to understand the material from cultural perspectives and practices that are markedly different than my own. These perspectives and practices cannot be imagined without this human engagement. I wanted to learn more; I wanted to do more ethnoarchaeology.

In 1996 after my doctorate, I began a decade of work in Tigray Regional State in northern highland Ethiopia with a colleague, Dr. Cathy D'Andrea (Project Director, Simon Fraser University). My ethnoarchaeological research in Tigray was to provide social context for interpreting early farming societies. Most of the region's archaeology is focused on the formation of complex societies in the early first millennium BC and the Christian Aksumite Kingdom in the first millennium AD (Phillipson 2012). There is almost no archaeology in northern Tigray for the period following the decline of the Aksumite kingdom. Nevertheless, the northern and central highlands were governed by the Solomonic Dynasty from 1280 to 1974, its kings claiming direct descent from Aksum's first king Menelik I, fabled son of the Queen of Sheba and King Solomon. The Abyssinian empire was a tributary and hierarchical society of aristocrats, nobles, clerics, peasants, artisans, and slaves under the authority of the Emperor. The last emperor, Haile Selassie, was overthrown by the Derg regime in 1974 and civil war followed. Since the Derg's defeat in 1991, the country has been governed by the Federal Democratic Republic of Ethiopia.

In 1996, Tigray was in the early stages of rebuilding after the war in which the region experienced active fighting, famine that killed 25% of the population, and economic collapse. Development of Tigray's infrastructure and commerce generated rapid material culture change. My early research focused on rural material practices, specifically vernacular architecture, land tenure, village social, economic and political organization, and household economies. I interviewed farmers, former nobles, and administrators for information on changes in practices that occurred before, during, and after the war. The study of vernacular architecture demonstrated that perceptions of gender were literally built into domestic compounds using gender-specific technological practices and building materials in different spatial areas of rural farms (Lyons 2009). In addition, domestic buildings were used to make statements of power including a man's ambition, his status in the community, and formerly as a household's claim to land (Lyons 2007a). Through the years I undertook an investigation of cuisine and culinary technologies to determine what they might tell us about the origins of agriculture in Tigray and the development of regional and local identities (Lyons and D'Andrea 2003; Lyons 2007b). It was the study of cuisine that brought me to the potters, but it was my immersion in rural material culture that gave me the foundation for the pottery project.

There were almost no market potters to be found in the farm villages in the Gulo-Makeda district in northeastern Tigray where I worked with D'Andrea. Farm women purchased pots from potters from Edaga Hamus, a market town about 35 km south of Gulo-Makeda. Despite the fact that potters make a necessary product for rural farms, making pots for a living was perceived as deeply shameful. Some Gulo-Makeda women referred to the Edaga Hamus potters as "*buda*."

In many societies in Africa, certain types of artisans are socially marginalized either because their craft is demeaning or because artisans are perceived to have dangerous occult powers that can harm other people. People's fear of being polluted or harmed by these artisans is controlled through practices of marginalization. Practices can include segregation of artisans into separate communities, and some artisans are prohibited from owning land, holding political office, and from sharing food, drink, and sex. In Tigray, metal workers, hide workers, potters, and weavers are called *buda* in Amharic or "*tabib*" in Tigrinya. These individuals and their kin are believed to have "evil eyes" that allow them to enter into their victim's body resulting in illness and/or death, and the capacity to turn into hyenas at night and consume the dead (see Lyons 2014). Using the term *buda* is now illegal in Ethiopia and prejudicial treatment of artisans is prohibited. Nevertheless, these beliefs and practices are deeply entrenched, and they continue to affect actions in daily life.

Although there is considerable anthropological and ethnoarchaeological study of craftworker marginalization in Africa, we still do not know the range of variation of these practices, the reason that certain crafts are marginalized, and the history of the phenomenon in different parts of the continent. Similarly, Boivin (2005) has argued that occupational caste is well studied in South Asia, but that archaeologists have made little headway in studying this practice's past because the material expressions of caste are unknown. This poses a problem. Marginalized craft is important to theories of the development of complex societies, but how do we study marginalization if we don't know what it looks like in contemporary societies? Until recently, theorists focused on the role of elite consumption of specialized craft in creating unequal social relations: a top-down view of power and inequity. But increasingly, researchers have come to recognize that we need to understand craft producers and their social relations in a range of social contexts. I felt that a study of Tigray's potters could contribute to this discussion. I set out to answer some basic questions: how are Tigray's potters perceived and marginalized, how are practices of marginalization constituted materially and spatially, and how are marginalized identities changing with globalizing markets?

Theory

Theories based in agency, practice, and embodiment make the most sense to me in understanding social identity. People learn social identities and their roles as members of social groups, and they consciously and unconsciously practice, perform, and modify these roles in daily life. Some identities are fluid and change during a lifetime, but marginalized identities are hard to shake. This may be because artisans in some societies are perceived by others to be made of different stuff because of what they do. In particular, many social identities, including gender, class, and social status, are constituted in technological practice. In Tigray, learning certain types of technological knowledge and the performance of technological skills transform artisans into different types of people with dangerous and polluting capacities (for a fuller discussion see Lyons 2014). The embodiment of dangerous knowledge and skills can happen in two ways in this region: through inheritance in bloodlines or by taking up craft for economic reasons. Those who inherit skills in a bloodline, which includes all metalworkers and their kin, are always perceived to be *buda*, and they form endogamous castes. People in severe economic circumstances can choose to learn a craft to survive. These people are despised for practicing a disgusting occupation and marriage with such people is shameful, but they do not form strict castes and they may or may not be perceived as *buda*. Most of the female market potters that we interviewed fell into the latter category. Very poor women took up pottery as a strategy of economic survival. This was a conscious choice, and they knew that making pots for a living exposed themselves and their families to verbal insults, social avoidance, political insignificance, and sometimes violence.

Types of Data

The field team was small, and I was active in all stages of research and project administration. I had relatively small grants so the team's size was restricted by the number of people that could legally ride in the vehicles. Some years the budget covered one vehicle so we had a team of up to five; other years we could afford two vehicles with a team of eight. The team included me, Joanna, two interpreters, driver(s), the government inspector, and one or two students. These constraints required that Joanna and I shared interviews with students mainly because the budget could not provide more interpreters. This was not ideal, but we made it work. The three study areas were selected for two reasons: there were large communities of potters in each location, a fact confirmed by making enquiries in local markets, and these locations were near areas where archaeology had been conducted. Ultimately the ethnoarchaeological data can be compared with local archaeological records to determine longer-term histories and relationships among and within these areas.

Despite some variation in goals of individual team members, we collected comparable quantitative and qualitative data on social, material, and spatial practices using similar methods that included interviews, observation, documentation of pottery *chaîne opératoire* (e.g., technological style), and mapping of houses and villages. These social, material, and spatial practices were shown to contribute to the creation of unequal social relationships among potters, farmers, traders, and other artisans in daily life.

Interview and observation are standard methods of ethnoarchaeological research and are part of all types of data collection. Most archaeological societies and universities have ethical standards in field work that involves human participants. My university has a review that issues a certificate for each project. In the field, I disclose the purpose of my research to people when asking for their participation and assure them that participation is voluntary and that their identity will remain anonymous. People are allowed to withdraw at any point from the study without penalty. I am not fluent in Tigrinya so I work through local interpreters who can ask questions with the intonations of respect in the local language. We interviewed potters, farmers, merchants, and administrators to determine practices of pottery production, distribution, and consumption as well as the histories of potters and their experiences. Whenever possible I interviewed metalworkers as a source of comparison with the potters' experience of marginalization. We observed daily life, and we participated in village events.

While it is illegal to call someone *buda*, it is not illegal to talk about it. Many people were quite willing to discuss the topic, but others found it uncomfortable. When people were uncomfortable, we skipped the questions on marginalization and discussed other things including pottery consumption practices and consumer needs, and we documented their *chaînes opératoires* and mapped their houses. Sometimes, people who decided not to answer questions on marginalization would initiate conversation on the topic later in the interview. I usually conduct several repeat visits to potters to document firings and raw material collection. These visits afforded additional opportunities to return to the discussion of marginalization. If a participant did not return to it, that was their right. As people became comfortable with us and the project, they talked more about their experiences.

A new issue arose in 2012. While I did not encounter problems in photographing potters in Edaga Hamus, Yeha potters did not want to be photographed for fear that the pictures would be circulated and make it difficult to find husbands for their daughters. This was a problem because images are essential to document *chaînes opératoires*. After some discussion we agreed that I would photograph the potters making pots as long as I did not take pictures of their faces. We received similar requests in Selekeleka. This was easily accommodated, and people could check the images in the camera play-back mode.

A major objective was to document the ceramic *chaînes opératoires* in the three study areas. *Chaîne opératoire* is used widely in African archaeology to determine material identities of past and contemporary communities and to determine their relationships and histories. *Chaîne opératoire* recognizes that artisans' technological choices at each stage of craft production are also social choices learned as members of a social group of producers and consumers. A particular artisan community's suite of technological choices is their technological style: a material identity of that community (Gosselain 2001). Because artisan choices are affected by consumer needs and tastes, aspects of technological styles are impacted by broader societal identities and interactions, including ethnicity, local identities, and forces of globalization. *Chaîne opératoire* is an appropriate methodology for data collection using theories of agency and practice. While change in technological styles is anticipated, researchers have found that some elements are more resistant to change than others, particularly fabrication practices (Gosselain 2001).

Data included collecting a sample of pottery from potters in each area. XRD and NAA analyses were conducted to determine types and sources of raw materials used by different potter communities, and thin-section analysis was performed to determine if stages of the *chaînes opératoires* were detectable. I was surprised at how much of the *chaîne opératoire* was affected by potter marginalization, including paste recipes, firing, and distribution practices. Expertise in NAA analysis was provided by Dr. Michael Glascock's team at Missouri University Research Reactor (MURR), and we were assisted in XRD analysis by Diane Caird at the University of Alberta. On Dr. Glascock's advice we modified the pottery sampling strategy after the first season. We stopped collecting raw clay samples and only collected fired clay from potters for the reason that raw clay is modified in paste preparation. Fired clay is more representative of the potter communities' technological styles. Analysis is also a lesson in patience. It took all four seasons to collect these data. However, two MA students have worked on some of the materials analysis in eastern and central Tigray providing some early results, but the full regional NAA analysis is only now completed and we are preparing the material for publication.

I collected spatial data by mapping domestic compounds. This information will help to define regional variation in vernacular architecture and differences in categories of compounds whose owners have different occupations and status. I have a database of over 200 domestic compounds in these regions for comparison. However, mapping compounds became increasingly difficult as we moved west, possibly because of increased military security in 2015 along Ethiopia's northern and western borders. Many potters would allow me to map their compounds but not to enter their buildings, a very rare problem in earlier studies. While these data are less rich, the information still provides comparative information on the scale of the compound, number, size, and type of buildings. We also mapped two potter villages to determine if and how potters and smiths were spatially segregated within communities.

Reflections

I am happy with the results of this study. Despite limited budgets, we compiled a very rich database of interviews, domestic compounds and village maps, and materials analyses that provide the first regional study of ceramics in Tigray and the first substantive study of pottery and its variability in this region. Writing and analysis are ongoing, but I can say that each area produced a distinct *chaîne opératoire* that will be useful in developing the region's social and ceramic history. The project's theoretical and methodological frameworks were consistent in all three projects in order to obtain comparable data. Nevertheless, interview questions were modified over time. Standard types of information were obtained, but individuals contribute new perspectives/variability that requires exploration. Certainly my understanding of how marginalized practices are constituted in material and spatial practice became much more nuanced over the course of the study.

Lessons Learned

What lesson can I impart to a researcher beginning their first project in ethnoarchaeology? I realize that this is a bit of cheat: I have logged thousands of hours talking and watching people engaging with material and spatial contexts in Tigray, Sudan, and Cameroon. Starting out, you won't have that experience or foundation, but it will come. Be patient.

Contexts of research can change in the course of a project, change that is worth following. We talk about rapidly globalizing markets, but actually witnessing the speed of change is astounding. In 1996 I rarely observed industrial products in rural farms. Craft still thrived. In 2005, I visited large healthy pottery markets in Eastern Tigray on market day. Dozens of potters could be found selling the full range of the domestic pottery assemblage: jars, bottles, griddles, pots, braziers, incense burners, and basins. By 2010 these same markets were overwhelmed by cheap Chinese plastics and enamelware. The vessel market shrank to a fraction of its former size. Big vessels for beer brewing, serving and storage, water carrying jars, and washing basins were only made for special order, if at all. As the project moved to Yeha and Selekeleka, the same events had already overtaken these markets. I was worried: pottery making is a strategy of very poor women, so what would they do now? I learned that these women are resourceful, and the study has followed their progress in changing markets. While vessel markets shrank, some potters expanded into new markets and the process is still unfolding.

Finally, as my colleague Joanna has reminded me, ethnoarchaeology is best as a team pursuit. It is a lot more fun working with a team than spending evenings alone writing notes, and it is much more fruitful to bounce your ideas and experiences off one another at day's end. I still find it surprising how much variability there can be in a practice from one community to another but also comforting to realize that other team members are getting similar information in different locations. But even a team still depends upon the kindnesses of strangers. Some important initial strangers included our local interpreters and field assistants. We were so fortunate to find a group of excellent local men who became valued field assistants, facilitators, and friends. Make sure that you take time with field workers, especially interpreters, to ensure that they understand the project and the type of data that you need, and to get their opinions on your field approach. Eat some of your meals or have refreshments with your crew. In the vehicle and over drinks these men offered their perspectives of potters and smiths from the standpoint of the young, university educated, and emergent urban middle class. They introduced us to new contacts through their network of friends and family, expanding the breadth of our understanding of Tigray's pottery production and life. They made the project work in ways that we could not have done on our own. Find good colleagues to work with, build your network, and enjoy the adventure.

Paired Reading

Lyons, Diane and Joanna Casey. 2016. "It's a Material World: The Critical and On-going Value of Ethnoarchaeology in Understanding Variation, Change and Materiality." *World Archaeology*, 48: 1–19. DOI: 10.1080/00438243.2016.1214619.

References

Boivin, Nicole. 2005. "Orientalism, Ideology and Identity: Examining Caste in South Asian Archaeology." *Journal of Social Archaeology*, 5: 225–252. DOI: 10.1177/1469605305053368.

Gosselain, Olivier. 2001. "Globalizing Local Pottery Studies." In *Ethno-archaeology and Its Transfers*, edited by Sylvie Beyries and Pierre Pétrequin, 95–112. BAR International Series 983. Oxford: Archaeopress.

Lyons, Diane. 2007a. "Building Power in Rural Hinterlands: An Ethnoarchaeological Study of Vernacular Architecture in Tigray, Ethiopia." *Journal of Archaeological Method and Theory*, 14: 179–207. DOI: 10.1007/s10816-007-9031-7.

Lyons, Diane. 2007b. "Integrating African Cuisines: Rural Cuisine and Identity in Tigray, Highland Ethiopia." *Journal of Social Archaeology*, 7: 346–371. DOI: 10.1177/1469605307081393.

Lyons, Diane. 2009. "How I Built My House: Gendered Technical Practice in Tigray Region, Highland Ethiopia." *Ethnoarchaeology*, 1: 137–161.

Lyons, Diane. 2014. "Perceptions of Consumption: Constituting Potters, Farmers and Blacksmiths in the Culinary Continuum in Eastern Tigray, Northern Highland Ethiopia." *African Archaeological Review*, 31: 169–201. DOI: 10.1007/s10437-014-9149-4.

Lyons, Diane and Joanna Casey. 2016. "It's a Material World: The Critical and On-going Value of Ethnoarchaeology in Understanding Variation, Change and Materiality." *World Archaeology*, 48: 1–19. DOI: 10.1080/00438243.2016.1214619.

Lyons, Diane and A. Catherine D'Andrea. 2003. "Griddles, Ovens, and Agricultural Origins: An Ethnoarchaeological Study of Bread Baking in Highland Ethiopia." *American Anthropologist*, 105: 515–530. DOI: 10.1525/aa.2003.105.3.515.

MacEachern, Scott and Jerimy Cunningham. 2016. "Ethnoarchaeology as Slow Science." *World Archaeology*, 48: 1–14. DOI: 10.1080/00438243.2016.1260046.

Phillipson, David. 2012. *Foundations of an African Civilisation: Aksum & the Northern Horn 1000 BC–AD 1300.* Rochester, NY: James Currey.

13

Integrating Paleoethnobotany in Investigations of Spanish Colonialism in the American Southwest

Heather B. Trigg

Project Summary

This chapter examines the integration of paleoethnobotany into projects of larger scope using two projects in which I have been involved. Both investigate aspects of seventeenth-century Spanish colonialism in the American Southwest. The first project, my dissertation, was a bottom-up project in which the samples for macrobotanicals were given to me by the project's principal investigators (PIs). I had limited opportunity to set sampling strategies, and I received the samples before I had a research agenda in mind. In my most recent project, I am the PI, and I determined the questions, methods, and theories prior to fieldwork. The differing approaches in the projects contrast the relative ease with which top-down and bottom-up projects develop.

Introduction

"Have I got a project for you!" Paleoethnobotanists, particularly those early in their careers, may hear this from project directors who have taken matrix samples for macrobotanicals and need someone to analyze them. I did, and those conversations sometimes generated anxiety because they were commonly accompanied by boxes of dirt and little else. The provenience may have been written on the bags, but generally information about the archaeological context was lacking. Sometimes the samples were rich with plant materials, but often not, but even when rich, the lack of contextual information made the archaeobotanical remains a challenge to interpret and often intellectually unsatisfying for a research program.

One problem with have-I-got-a-project-for-you samples is that data are typically in hand before a research question about them is formulated. Granted, having samples in hand allows the analyst to assess preservation and therefore the potential for addressing any question, but when the question comes first, one can develop sampling strategies – select sites and contexts and determine the size and number of samples – to address that question. When one is given samples, excavations may be complete with no possibility of additional collection. Under these circumstances, questions that may be interesting might not be addressable with the available materials.

A have-I-got-a-project-for-you conversation was the way I began research that laid the foundation for my dissertation and which still bears fruit years later. I have approached paleoethnobotanical research both from the perspective of the analyst whose only role in a

Engaging Archaeology: 25 Case Studies in Research Practice, First Edition. Edited by Stephen W. Silliman.
© 2018 John Wiley & Sons, Inc. Published 2018 by John Wiley & Sons, Inc.

larger project was to analyze the botanicals and from the position as the PI of a National Science Foundation-funded project. As the PI, my responsibilities have shifted from simply identifying and interpreting the botanicals to developing research questions, theoretical approaches, and excavation strategies for a project in which paleoethnobotany is but one method being brought to bear on issues of colonialism and environmental change.

I have heard colleagues say that paleoethnobotanists are atheoretical and cannot be PIs on projects because we are more like technicians than archaeologists. Certainly paleoethnobotanists who do not have information about archaeological context or the opportunity to create research designs and implement them – issues that frequently come with "have-I-got-a project-for-you" samples – may have trouble addressing questions of importance. I mention this not to complain, but to challenge still-held notions of paleoethnobotanists as technicians, and I argue that the more engaged the paleoethnobotanist is in the research planning and execution, the more robust the data, the interpretation, and ultimately the theoretical significance of the work will be. With contextual information, or better yet, with the ability to make decisions about what samples are collected, how they are collected, or even the freedom to direct projects with collection of plant materials in mind and combine those data with other information, paleoethnobotanists can develop research programs that address important anthropological issues.

Having approached paleoethnobotanical information from both the bottom-up, data-driven and top-down, question-driven perspectives, I know some of the advantages and pitfalls of each. In this chapter I contrast the have-I-got-a-project-for-you samples that characterized my dissertation with my current research in which I have control over the overall direction of the project. Both projects investigate Spanish colonialism in the American Southwest from the perspective of the colonizers' households, and they both use materials from the same site, LA 20,000, a seventeenth-century Spanish ranch located about 12 miles southwest of Santa Fe, New Mexico.

My Dissertation

My dissertation project started in the mid-1990s when I was a student at the University of Michigan. As an undergraduate and then a PhD student of paleoethnobotanist Richard I. Ford, I had been interested in and performed analyses of plant remains, mostly on prehistoric sites in the American Southwest, since the early 1980s. I was well trained in the identification and analysis of plants and in the methodological strengths and pitfalls of paleoethnobotany. I also had field experience in the Southwest. For a dissertation project, I was interested in the indigenous Pueblo peoples' response to Spanish colonization in the 1600s, especially the social circumstances under which Pueblo people incorporated plants that they associated with colonizers, such as wheat, watermelons, and peaches, into their foodways and considered them part of their traditional cuisine. (Barbara Mills (2008) has since explored this issue in her paper on the adoption of wheat by the Zuni).

I had identified a Pueblo village dating from the mid-1400s to the late 1600s that had deposits available to address this issue. The site was very large, complex, and multi-component. When discussing my ideas with my dissertation advisor, he would ask questions – some pretty fundamental ones – but ones that I did not have answers to. That sent me back to consider more fully how I was approaching my project. My inability to quickly address his questions made me feel that I was far from actualizing this field project. In retrospect, had I done a bit more reading about that site and the ceramic sequences in the Southwest, I probably could have identified areas that would have addressed my question.

But like many early-career paleoethnobotanists, I was approached by a project director who had taken many flotation samples, and I was told that these samples would make a great dissertation project. The samples came from LA 20,000, the largest, most complex Spanish ranch from early colonial New Mexico (Trigg 2005). The site had been excavated periodically for about 12 years from the 1980s into the 1990s, and the PIs, David Snow and Marianne Stoller, had taken botanical samples but not had any of them examined. The samples he was offering, clearly, would not address the research question I had envisioned, so I would need to abandon that top-down project. My decision was not based solely on research issues. As a single parent with two small children, I did not have the time or luxury of developing the project I envisioned, finding funding, and negotiating permission to excavate to obtain samples, all of which would probably have added a couple of years to my dissertation. I saw this as an opportunity to graduate more quickly. Still, when I told Dave Snow that I was really interested in the Pueblos, he said rather scathingly, "Oh yes, **everyone** is interested in the Pueblos. Those poor Spanish colonists – no one is interested in them." Challenge accepted.

LA 20,000 is a single-component ranch located at the juncture of several Puebloan ethnic groups and near large Pueblo villages. Excavations had uncovered a nearly 1 m deep midden, a large house, a barn, a corral, *horno* (bread oven), and perhaps additional outbuildings. The numerous artifacts include a large quantity of Pueblo ceramics, smaller quantities of imported *majolicas*, olive jars, indigenous Mexican ceramics, and porcelains, some lithics, but only small quantities of metal, glass, and other material culture. Ceramic types and dendrochronology of two beams recovered from the site indicated an occupation from about AD 1629 to 1680. The deep midden and extensive and well-preserved architecture suggested this would be a good location to begin to understand the activities of Spanish colonists during the early colonial period (1598–1680).

I began by looking at the samples I was given, which were from the fill and floors of the house, barn, and some adobe bricks. These samples were not particularly rich, thereby providing a somewhat limited number of plant remains from a limited number of taxa. Given this, I received permission from Snow and Stoller to undertake very limited additional excavations of the midden to obtain more samples. Middens are often good sources of concentrated plant remains because of their association with food debris disposal. While these samples cannot answer all questions relating to the use of plant foods, such as uses in different spatial contexts, this feature afforded the best opportunity to recover information about all people at the site. I analyzed 122 samples totaling 244 liters of original matrix, identifying both the seeds (and related plant parts) and a sample of the charred wood.

A fellow graduate student who had been working in the area for years told me about excavations in Santa Fe at LA 54,000 – the La Fonda Garage Project. Excavators had found pits filled with burned trash possibly from the Pueblo Revolt and had taken flotation samples. LA 54,000 was excavated in the 1980s, and samples had been stored as matrix until 1995 when I obtained permission to float and use them – only eight samples totaling 43 liters. (I am frequently asked if "old" samples are useful. Yes, these were extremely productive.) The plant remains from this site were among the best preserved charred materials I have seen. These eight samples contained more seeds and related plant parts than the 122 samples from LA 20,000. From LA 20,000, I recovered 1,500 specimens and 24 taxa, whereas LA 54,000 generated more than 5,500 specimens and 40 taxa.

The differences between the botanical assemblages at these two sites illustrate a point that I have come to appreciate – that the types and quantities of archaeological plant remains we recover are strongly structured by preservation, which depends on both environmental conditions and peoples' activities. Unless plant materials are deposited in conditions that limit activities of decomposers, such as at waterlogged or very dry sites, they quickly decay. Charring is one major way in which archaeological plant remains are preserved because they become resistant to decay. Plants char when processing or preparation brings them into contact with fire or heat such as when they are used as fuel, during kitchen accidents, when seeds are parched, or with the catastrophic burning of structures. Some plant parts are used or processed in ways that never expose them to fire, and some parts, such as leaves and fruits, even if exposed to fire are unlikely to survive the charring process. These leave little trace in the macrobotanical record of many archaeological sites. Thus the number and types of plants may be highly skewed. Paleoethnobotanists have developed analytical methods to try to address this (Hastorf and Popper 1988), but preservation does strongly structure what we can know and the robustness of our interpretations.

I knew my data were biased and that taxa were missing. The people at LA 20,000 were certainly eating more than maize, wheat, peas, apricots, and goosefoot seeds. To add to our knowledge about plants, I combed documents for any references to what plants were used and who produced them. The documents were extremely limited because all that were held in the colony were burned during the Pueblo Revolt. Some mentioned crops that the colonists might have been growing, but nothing about individual households. I had data, some of which was rich, and I knew some of the standard questions that paleoethnobotany can address – (production and consumption), but I had no question and no theories to help frame the data in this cultural context. I flailed around with what might I do with these data.

I read case studies about foodways incorporating paleoethnobotany and provisioning using faunal remains written about other colonial settings in the Spanish Southeast, New England, and the mid-Atlantic. I tried to envision how I would use my data and what specific analyses would be used (ratios, diversity indices, ubiquity, etc., see Hastorf and Popper 1988; Marston *et al.* 2014), and I failed to see how these specific analyses might be useful. Because of preservation and sampling issues, I knew my data could not be used to address interesting questions about cross-cultural food use, production, land use, or landscape change – issues that are typically investigated with plant remains. So, I struggled with trying to frame these data within an anthropological question.

I also read research about New Mexico written by historians and archaeological investigations of Spanish New Mexicans from this period. Two things were quickly apparent. Snow was accurate when he said that academic archaeologists were generally not interested in the Spanish in New Mexico; at that time, scholars focused much more problem-oriented research on the Pueblos than Spanish colonizers. Also, a significant gap seemed to exist between issues the historians were discussing and those interesting the archaeologists, which was not unusual. This led me to expand my focus from paleoethnobotany to building a framework for how Spanish households functioned and how they articulated with other households, with Pueblo peoples, and with people in Mexico. At first, this was just for my own edification. Then it became clear that it would be helpful to other archaeologists to have an outline of how the different scales of activity were linked.

In New Mexico during the seventeenth century, there were missions within Pueblo villages, one Spanish city – Santa Fe, and rural farms and ranches. Most households were based at these farms, which were portrayed as self-sufficient. Archaeological investigations of these households are limited but suggest that they required goods and services from other colonists and Pueblo peoples. The economy was based on barter, and subsistence goods were among the main items exchanged. The production of subsistence goods served as a critical way Pueblo peoples engaged in Spanish households. As a result, I became interested in understanding the social and economic practices that facilitated exchange among households and with the homeland in Mexico.

Botanical data could be helpful to understand an economy based on subsistence items, but it alone would not address this issue. I broadened the data I used and incorporated the material culture I recovered during my limited excavation of LA 20,000 including the ceramics, lithics, glass, and groundstone. Much of this involved basic information that did not require special analytical skills. I also used information published in CRM reports of excavations of other seventeenth-century ranches, missions, and Santa Fe. I used all of these data to build my framework of the relationships between households, the production and flow of goods, and the relationships at different levels, especially the relationship between laws governing these relationships and the ways they were enacted.

As I developed this project, I moved back and forth between the data, issues, and theories. I viewed theory as providing structure to the inquiry and a framework for organizing and interpreting the data and articulating with other anthropological research. I still did not have a well-defined question, rather it was a goal, but I was reading a wide range of theories, most focusing on economic activity: household economies, formal versus informal economies, wealth finance vs. staple finance, domestic vs. empire economies, theories about frontier economies, and world systems models. The scale and scope of most of these seemed wrong for the data I had and my own goals. I sought out more general anthropological theories of the way things work rather than focusing on economies. I read historical anthropologists focusing on colonialism, and I found practice theory. This appealed to me because, in a way, it allowed me to look at the ways the economy developed in the colony, despite laws regulating it. As a more general theory about the ways people act, it allowed me to think about the different scales of economy rather than only one, a limitation of most other theories I had been considering.

This conceptual model of interactions at different scales provides insight into the dynamic relationships among colonizers, between colonizers and indigenous peoples, and with the homeland in Mexico. It allowed me to view the colonizers not as a unified whole, but rather as composed of different groups with different goals, and it provided a context for understanding the effects of colonization on the Pueblo peoples. This was a far cry from what the PIs envisioned when they gave me the samples.

My Current Research

After my dissertation, I began investigating plant-human relationships at historical sites in New England, the mid-Atlantic, and Iceland. I began seeing commonalities and differences in the colonialism of different regions. More recently I have returned to these issues for seventeenth-century New Mexico. Snow and Stoller had done a great deal of archaeology at LA 20,000, but they had never written it up. Snow knew that ethics required someone to publish the work, and when I told him that I was interested in continuing research on Spanish colonialism during the early colonial period, he asked me to take up the work on LA 20,000. I knew I did not want to simply write up what he had done; I wanted to conduct my own research.

I have gone back with the freedom to develop my own questions. I have thought a lot about theories of creolization and hybridity and have published on foodways (Trigg 2004), regional economic transactions, and demography and plant-human interactions in other regions. These experiences afforded the opportunity to hone questions and theoretical perspectives that interested me most. I was particularly interested in the way people within pluralistic colonial households interacted. My current project investigates the social and environmental consequences of Spanish colonization. The specific goals are to reconstruct environmental changes, understand the foodways as evidence of the incorporation of indigenous knowledge, trace relationships with Pueblo villages, and understand specific spatial relationships within the site. The project relies on excavation, ceramic and faunal analysis, reconstruction of architecture and GIS, as well as paleoethnobotany.

The work I wanted to do required external funding, so I obtained a National Science Foundation grant. That grant allowed me to make the most of the existing work. I reviewed the previous excavation notes, which included over 100 student notebooks. None of the maps had all the excavation units, so with the assistance of colleagues and the notebooks, we created a single comprehensive site map. My colleagues conducted a shallow geophysical survey. We also developed a database of material culture and samples that had already been collected. Upon completing these activities, I was able to develop sampling strategies that combined existing data with new, targeted excavations. A second grant is allowing me to excavate, collect botanical and faunal samples, and material culture.

I use a combination of theories to guide my work. Investigations of practices in colonial contexts often focus on the differences between colonizers and colonized, playing off introduced practices (presumably reflecting the activities of colonizers) and local, indigenous practices (presumably reflecting the activities of the colonized). This approach does have a place, but it cannot be the end point of the research. Most archaeological models of pluralistic households have built upon the premise that the male and female heads of the household were the major determinants of daily practice. In seventeenth-century New Mexico, others may have had an impact as households were typically composed of extended families along with adult relatives, adoptive children, servants, or slaves. Individuals who were not permanent residents of the household, such as day laborers, may have contributed to the nature of a household's practice.

Native peoples had a well-developed understanding of environmental conditions and the distribution of resources across the landscape, and this information would have been useful to colonizers. However, the political nature of intra-household interactions, particularly in the context of colonialism, made the transmission of knowledge and establishment of practices complex. Dual inheritance theory suggests that a person's practices are a product of two processes: one that broadly replicates the culture's existing practices and a second that incorporates new practices. Situated learning theory complements this idea and proposes that learning takes place in social contexts characterized by power dynamics that can either enable or constrain learning. These two models of the way learning is achieved and passed on are particularly useful for analyzing colonization because together they acknowledge the power differential within these households, and they provide a mechanism for the creation of new practices.

In this project, I am supervising the excavations and data collection. Ceramics that will be used to trace economic connections with Pueblos will be sent to ceramic analysts. A colleague will supervise the analysis of the faunal remains. I am also supervising the analysis of the small amount of other material culture – the lithics, groundstone, glass and small finds – and the reconstruction of the site architecture and use of space. Graduate students are assisting with these analyses and are able to develop master's theses from their work. And, of course, I am looking for and aiming to study the additional plant remains secured from this site.

In this project, I use paleoethnobotany in several ways. European colonization frequently brought about major transformations in the environment as new plants, animals, and agricultural technologies were introduced. These transformations are important because they both reflect and influence the physical context in which colonialism is situated. I used palynology to examine these changes. In sampling for pollen, we were limited by contexts in which it might be preserved. A marsh approximately 2 miles from the site provided an excellent context for studying regional vegetation changes that accompanied colonization. We cored the marsh and were lucky that pollen was preserved and sediments dated to the time periods of interest. The results were somewhat surprising in that we did not find any evidence of Eurasian crops, such as wheat, that were introduced and grown nearby. Even more surprising, forest cover may have increased in extent after colonization, not the typical pattern under European colonization (Edwards and Trigg 2016). Major vegetation changes did not seem to be the result of first colonizers, as it was in the eastern United States, but seems to have occurred only after Spanish population increased in the middle to late 1700s. Due to these surprising results, I have altered the strategy and taken additional pollen samples from the area immediately adjacent to LA 20,000 because wheat pollen rarely travels far from its source and is particularly prevalent in areas where it is processed. While I have yet to analyze these samples, I hope the pollen record will reflect agricultural activities at the ranch.

Foodways is another way in which paleoethnobotany is fundamental to the project. I am incorporating the data I collected in 1995, but I have expanded focus to take additional samples in areas where there appear to be charred plant remains and will analyze samples taken during the excavations in the 1980s and early 1990s. These samples come from the structures, and while they might have fewer plant remains, they will provide comparative spatial data with respect to the midden. To address foodways, I am combining analyses of botanicals with that of material culture, specifically cooking implements and serving vessels. These samples and artifacts suggest the meals are complex mixtures of Spanish and Pueblo foods and cooking techniques. We are investigating this further with the faunal remains, particularly the butchery marks and disarticulation patterns. Some models of cuisine in multicultural households focus on the contrast between indigenous people and colonizers, assuming that each brings the practices of their natal community to the household. However, the complexity of foodways at LA 20,000 suggests a more creative approach.

For me, this project is much more intellectually satisfying. I can pose the questions that I have regarding colonialism, and I can select the theories and methods that seem most appropriate.

Lessons Learned

Articulating paleoethnobotanical data with research questions and theory – actually making the data speak in a way that is rigorous and not simply facile – is difficult, especially with a bottom-up, inductive approach. Paleoethnobotanical data are messy and complicated to interpret because of preservation biases and the potential for modern contamination.

To develop a research project from existing samples, one must have information about the site and the samples – archaeological context, dates, sampling strategy, sample size, and presence of other samples. One must also know what sorts of questions can be addressed from such samples. Through the years, paleoethnobotanists (Ford 1979; Hastorf 1999; Wright 2010) have discussed the types of issues we investigate. Research frequently relates to foodways and the larger anthropological questions that can be developed from understanding the role of food in everything from nutrition to identity. Botanical data also can be used to investigate resource acquisition and environmental change, which can address landscapes and resource procurement. These specific issues articulate with questions of broader anthropological significance. Given the importance to many cultures of plants as medicines, foods, and symbols and their inclusion in a wide spectrum of other activities, they afford a window on past behavior that other archaeological materials may not. The extent to which these questions can be addressed relates to adequate sampling of appropriate contexts and also to the preservation and recovery of relevant plant parts (Gallagher 2014). Working closely with project directors prior to or during excavation, or even conducting one's own excavations, can help ensure that sampling is adequate and mitigate the problems with bottom-up investigations. Addressing preservation issues often comes from luck, extensive sampling, and reasonable expectations of the data.

For most inquiries, moving back and forth between case studies, data collection, questions, and theories is important. Despite how studies may appear in scientific journals, rarely are investigations linear, starting with a question or theory, followed by data collection to address that question. When it appears so, it is likely that the question is formulated after a good deal of background research about cultural context and limitations of data.

I end with a final lesson learned, which I want to share in particular with those researchers who seek or already have a specialty often pertinent to many kinds of projects. Paleoethnobotanists can be PIs and being the PI is more fun.

Paired Reading

Trigg, Heather. 2004. "Food Choice and Social Identity in Early Colonial New Mexico." *Journal of the Southwest*, 46: 223–252.

References

Edwards, Kyle and Heather Trigg. 2016. "Intersecting Landscapes: A Palynological Study of Pueblo, Spanish, and Anglo-American Land Use in New Mexico." *Historical Archaeology*, 50: 135–153. DOI: 10.1007/BF03377181.

Ford, Richard I. 1979. "Paleoethnobotany in American Archaeology." *Advances in Archaeological Method and Theory*, 2: 285–336.

Gallagher, Daphne. 2014. "Formation Processes of the Macrobotanical Record." In *Method and Theory in Paleoethnobotany*, edited by John Marston, Jade d'Alpoim Guedes, and Christina Warinner, 19–34. Boulder, CO: University Press of Colorado.

Hastorf, Christine A. 1999. "Recent Research in Paleoethnobotany." *Journal of Archaeological Research*, 7: 55–103. DOI: 10.1023/A:1022178530892.

Hastorf, Christine A. and Virginia S. Popper. 1988. *Current Paleoethnobotany: Analytical Methods and Cultural Interpretations of Archaeological Plant Remains*. Chicago, IL: University of Chicago Press.

Marston, John M., Jade d'Alpoim Guedes, and Christina Warinner, eds. 2014. *Method and Theory in Paleoethnobotany*. Boulder, CO: University Press of Colorado.

Mills, Barbara. 2008. "Colonialism and Cuisine: Cultural Transmission, Agency and History at Zuni Pueblo." In *Cultural Transmission and Material Culture: Breaking Down Boundaries*, edited by Miriam Stark, Brenda J. Bowser, and Lee Horne, 245–262. Tucson, AZ: University of Arizona Press.

Trigg, Heather. 2004. "Food Choice and Social Identity in Early Colonial New Mexico." *Journal of the Southwest*, 46: 223–252.

Trigg, Heather. 2005. *From Household to Empire: Society and Economy in Early Colonial New Mexico*. Tucson, AZ: University of Arizona Press.

Wright, Patti. 2010. "Methodological Issues in Paleoethnobotany: A Consideration of Issues, Methods, and Cases." In *Integrating Zooarchaeology and Paleoethnobotany*, edited by Amber VanDerwarker and Tanya Peres, 37–64. New York: Springer.

14

Framing Local History with Global Archaeological Lenses in Osun Grove, Nigeria

Akinwumi Ogundiran

Project Summary

This chapter tells the story of my research project in Osun Grove, a World Heritage site in southwest Nigeria; the conceptual framework that shaped the project; my research design and field methods; and the outcome. Between ca. AD 1590 and 1730, the present area of Osun Grove was occupied by a thriving community of traders, farmers, and craftsmen and -women. I began archaeological research at this site in 2003 in order to investigate the impacts of early modern commerce on cultural formation in the mainland Yoruba region of West Africa. I situate the story of my research in Osun Grove within the narrative of how I became an archaeologist, my early archaeological education in Nigeria, and its influence on the theoretical approaches that have since guided my research questions and methodologies.

Short Biographical Account

I was born in the city of Ibadan in the Yoruba region of Nigeria. I came across the word "archaeology" for the first time in the dictionary in early 1983. That was a few months before I graduated from high school. Until that auspicious day, I had not heard anything about archaeology, nor had I been to any museum, although history was my most favorite subject. The sound of the word, "archaeology," captivated me and the Oxford Dictionary definition of the term resonated with my interests in the study of the past. I made inquiries whether it was possible to study such a subject in a Nigerian university. Lo and behold, two universities – the University of Ibadan, Ibadan and the University of Nigeria, Nsukka – were offering the course at degree level, but the entry requirement to both was an Advanced Level (post-secondary) qualification. Since I was planning to apply for university admission with my Ordinary Level (high/secondary school certificate) qualification, both institutions were out of the question. I therefore stuck to my original plan to apply for admission into the history degree program at the University of Ife (now Obafemi Awolowo University).

I was admitted to the University of Ife in August 1984 to begin my study as a history major. Little did I know then that the university had just established a department of archaeology with its own undergraduate degree program. My path would change at the end of my fourth or fifth week on campus when Dr. Omotoso Eluyemi (d. 2006) visited my "History of West Africa" class to publicize and recruit students for the new degree program in archaeology. Within 24 hours of his visit, I changed my major to archaeology, becoming the first of the five pioneering

Engaging Archaeology: 25 Case Studies in Research Practice, First Edition. Edited by Stephen W. Silliman.
© 2018 John Wiley & Sons, Inc. Published 2018 by John Wiley & Sons, Inc.

students to enroll in the archaeology degree program at Ife. The rest, as they say, is history, or is it archaeology? I finished my BA in archaeology in 1988 and moved to the University of Ibadan a year later for my master's degree, also in archaeology (1989–1991). Things were moving so quickly. I crossed the Atlantic in 1993 to enroll in the PhD archaeology program at Boston University. Seven years later, I earned my doctoral degree in archaeological studies with certified expertise in African archaeology.

Although I was introduced to the Anglo-American theoretical perspectives in archaeology during my undergraduate and master's education in Nigeria, my training was primarily oriented towards what we now call historical processualism, rather than to behavioral processualism that was very influential in the United States during the 1980s–1990s. In Nigeria, we did not find the behavioral processualism of New Archaeology (also dubbed the "processualist" or "positivist" school) appealing. Its emphasis on "archaeology as the anthropology of the dead" and preoccupation with model testing were considered sterile and irrelevant to the African situation by Nigerian archaeologists (Ogundiran 2015). My Nigerian teachers, especially Omotoso Eluyemi, Babatunde Agbaje-Williams, and Ade Obayemi did not use the term "historical processualism" to describe their approach to archaeology. But their insistence on a problem-oriented archaeological research agenda driven by questions about the history of local communities, living cultures, practices, and traditions is not that different from what Timothy Pauketat (2001) has labeled and articulated as historical processualism (see also Schmidt and Patterson 1995).

The historical processualist approach seeks to use archaeological methods and materials to write a history that is attuned to the self-awareness, cultural sensibilities, and experience of the subject communities. For this reason, it tends to take what people say about their past, and how they relate to that past, as an integral part of formulating archaeological research questions and research design. Hence historical processualism is interdisciplinary *par excellence*. Methodologically, it intersects or juxtaposes oral historical sources, ethnography, and archaeological methods and data. I built on this foundation at Boston University where I developed my interests in the dialogical relationships between oral traditions and archaeology in the study of the past of present living traditions within the framework of comparative world civilizations. This framework guided the design of my dissertation research which focused on how the ebb and flow of regional interactions shaped the multi-sited settlement practices, social memory, and material records of Ìlàrè, a small principality in southwest Nigeria, over a period of 700 years (Ogundiran 2002).

Project Source

During the research that led to my dissertation, I became fully aware of the sharp differences in the archaeological profiles at Ìlàrè of the period between 1200 and the 1500s on the one hand, and between the 1500s and 1800 on the other. Apart from the usual contrasts in ceramic assemblages, I observed the introduction of new classes of artifacts, especially cowrie shells and clay tobacco pipes, into the post-1500 deposits. In addition, the local extant traditions remember the period between 1500 and 1800 as an era of unstable landscape, intense population mobility, and the rising importance of the Atlantic coastlines in the regional commerce. The new classes of artifacts that I observed in the archaeological record are traced to those Atlantic encounters. For this reason, I called the period between 1500 and 1800 in Yoruba cultural history, the Atlantic period (Ogundiran 2002). I realized that we knew very little about the impacts of the Atlantic commerce on the everyday lives of the Yoruba mainland where the majority of the population lived. I wanted to know more. Hence, following the publication of my revised doctoral dissertation as *Archaeology and History in Ìlàrè District, 1200–1900* (Ogundiran 2002), I decided to focus my next research project on the impacts of the transatlantic trade on the everyday lives of the Yoruba mainland.

Theoretical Framework

My objective was to use archaeological and historical ethnographic data to understand how the pan-regional and global processes of the Atlantic trade shaped the everyday lives and the development of new cultural practices and institutions in Upper Osun, in the central region of Yoruba mainland (Nigeria). In other words, I sought to understand how the local communities in Yoruba mainland were historically constituted within the context of the Atlantic world exchange networks of production and consumption processes. My study therefore belonged to the genre of historical anthropological studies that seek to understand the articulation of local experience in broad regional and global contexts based on the realization that local cultures were often products of pan-regional historical processes of which the local is a determined part.

To achieve this goal, I designed a research program that first sought to identify well preserved archaeological sites that would allow me to combine the materialist archaeological evidence of production, consumption, and social distinctions, with the historical ethnography of social memory and cultural meaning of the Atlantic encounters in Upper Osun region. I identified a number of sites that fit this profile, but I decided to focus my investigations on two of them. One was Ede-Ile, a colony of Oyo Empire strategically located to control the flow of commercial traffic between the mainland and the coast. The second was Early Osogbo, a community founded by a group of professional hunters according to oral traditions. Both Ede-Ile and Early Osogbo, about 20 km apart, were established in the late sixteenth century and were located in the upper reaches of the rainforest. I expected that the different backgrounds of these two contemporaneous communities would enrich our understanding of the impacts of the Atlantic economy on the Yoruba mainland.

Methods

For the purpose of this chapter, I only highlight my work in Early Osogbo. I first heard about this archaeological settlement in 1991 in the course of serving as a research assistant on a documentation of cultural resources project. There are references in the oral traditions that several abandoned settlements are located in Osun Grove, but the exact locations were not known. These settlements are supposedly the precursors to the current Osogbo town nearby. Osun Grove, a national monument in the Federal Republic of Nigeria and a World Heritage site (Ogundiran 2014), is a 75-hectare cultural property valued for its biodiversity resources, sacred sites, and sculptures dedicated to various Yoruba deities, but no one knew about its archaeological resources. Indeed no archaeological work had been conducted in the grove before I initiated my study. I assumed that because the grove had been declared a national monument since 1965, the old settlement of Early Osogbo would be well preserved in the protected confines of the grove. Therefore, I felt my first task was to identify and document the archaeological sites in the grove.

With the aid of a GoogleEarth map of Osun Grove, topographic maps from government sources, and other locally-produced maps, I embarked upon the first archaeological survey of the grove and its precincts (Figure 14.1). I began by dividing the grove into 12 north-south transect lines, each 5 m wide and at 100 m intervals. The ground survey along these transect lines proceeded very slowly because of the secondary forest vegetation that predominated the grove. The thick undergrowth often made mobility and ground visibility very difficult, and many times impossible. But this was the best affordable option we had, so I thought, to document the archaeological resources of the grove. However, we did not encounter many archaeological remains in our initial efforts. Shovel-testing occasionally turned up very few pottery specimens, but we were doubtful of their antiquity because these were often associated

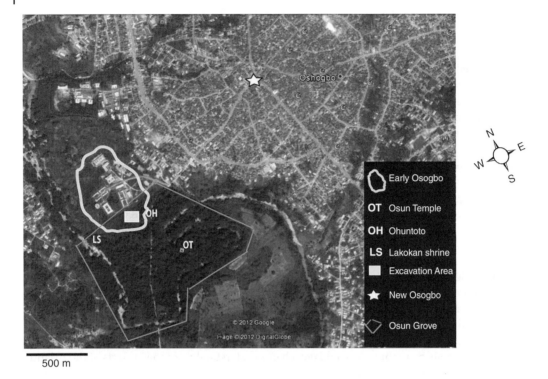

500 m

Figure 14.1 Aerial view and map of Osun Grove, Nigeria.

with tin and plastic products, artifacts originating from twentieth-century mass-produced commodities. Nevertheless, we located substantive archaeological remains in two locations, in the southeast and northwest sections of the grove.

We did not rely only on our transect surveys to identify archaeological sites. We also sought the assistance of priests and priestesses to assist us with the identification of the early sites associated with Early Osogbo. Three places – the Osun, Ohuntoto, and Lakokan temples – were pointed out to us. These are potent sacred sites each demarcated with built structures and are believed in local lore to be associated with Early Osogbo. For religious reasons, archaeological works were not allowed inside any of these sacred places. However, we were allowed to conduct shovel-testing near them. Of the three, only the area around Ohuntoto was found to be archaeologically promising. This is also in the vicinity of the northwest archaeological finds identified during our survey. In fact, we soon realized that the most substantive abandoned settlement in the grove is actually in this northwest area. In the course of our reconnaissance survey, we also noticed that the spatial distribution of the surface finds in the northwest area extended far beyond the delimited boundaries of the grove. So, we decided to conduct a more intensive archaeological survey and mapping of that area. By the time we returned to the field in 2004, however, our intended area of survey was already cleared out by heavy construction machinery, and the digging of the foundation trenches for a government-owned medical school complex was underway. This clearing afforded us a better archaeological visibility, but we soon realized that the school complex was being constructed directly on what we later recognized as the Early Osogbo settlement. It became urgent therefore to recover as much archaeological information as possible before this "modern development" destroyed the site.

Hence, we marked out an area of 450×400 m in this zone for intensive archaeological survey. The area was divided into 20×20 m grids to collect and record surface finds. We plotted only ceramic counts for each grid because these are the dominant and abundant surface finds. Along with 2,596 sherds, a few cowries, animal bone remains, metal objects, and a glass-bead crucible fragment were collected during the survey. Using the surface scatter of ceramic sherds as our guide, we were able to determine that the settlement in the northwest area of the grove was about 18 hectares in size at the peak of its existence. We concluded, based on other converging lines of evidence, that this was the Early Osogbo settlement so well mentioned in the oral traditions and which is memorialized in the traditions of the Ohuntoto temple. Situated on the highest summit in the Osun Grove (304–323 m above sea level), the location of Early Osogbo would have offered the community a commanding view of the river valleys around them, with the meandering River Osun forming a natural defense for the settlement on its southern fronts. We noted elliptical and circular hollows on these southeastern outcrops, showing that the granite surface was used for grinding activities (food and craftwork processing). A refuse mound was also located in that southern edge of the settlement. I decided to concentrate my excavation efforts on and around the refuse mound. Luckily for us, this southern side of the ancient settlement was within the buffer zone of the grove and was not disturbed by the construction of the medical school complex.

Nature of Data

Over the next three field seasons between 2004 and 2012, I supervised the excavation of a total area of 85.5 m^2 in Early Osogbo, with 70.5 m^2 of these focusing on the communal refuse site (Mound A). Such sites are known to yield valuable information on the relations of material life and the diverse socioeconomic activities within a settlement. They are particularly useful for capturing the small details of everyday lives at the local and regional levels, as well as providing deep longitudinal cultural profiles. Overall, the stratigraphic profiles indicate that the settlement history at Early Osogbo did not include any significant demolition and rebuilding of structures. It was a single-phase occupation. Radiocarbon dates, artifact types, and oral traditions demonstrate that Early Osogbo was occupied between the late sixteenth and early eighteenth century.

Three depositional sequences are discernable in Early Osogbo. The first and the oldest deposit consists of the primary deposition of faunal remains of medium and large species, including the crania, mandibles, maxillae, thoracic bones, and teeth of red river hogs and large bovid species. The assemblage was indicative of a butchering or a game sharing site. Accumulated above the *in situ* faunal assemblage is a very diverse range of domestic artifacts deposited in secondary contexts. The assortment of artifacts includes pottery, faunal remains, clay tobacco pipes, iron artifacts, cowries, glass cullet and beads, among others. These artifacts are invaluable for understanding 1) the social scale and character of the formative community; 2) the socioeconomic activities deployed to provision the young settlement; 3) the diverse range of craftsmanship, production, and consumption within and beyond the settlement; 4) long-distance exchanges; and (5) regional flows of peoples and ideas.

The artifacts illustrate the connections of Early Osogbo to the wide Atlantic commerce. About 300 cowrie shells, mostly of the *Cypraea moneta* species, that we excavated were part of the billions of cowries that European traders imported from the Maldives in the Indian Ocean to West Africa where they were used as currency. Tobacco pipes of African manufacture also constitute a dominant class of artifacts, showing that Early Osogbo partook in the novel practice of tobacco smoking that swept across the West African region during the seventeenth century. This followed the initial introduction of tobacco and Native American pipe prototypes into the region about a century earlier by English and Portuguese traders. The diversity of forms and styles in the assemblage of over 80 tobacco pipe fragments and the presence of these same forms in other sites across the Yoruba region indicate that Early Osogbo was connected to the circuits of regional commercial networks. The European ship manifests demonstrate that the tobacco that filled these African pipes was imported largely from Brazil. The tobacco pipes and cowries show that Early Osogbo was firmly within the orbits of the circulation of the new taste and new consumption networks that linked the mainland to the coast during the seventeenth and eighteenth centuries.

A related category of artifacts that is also inspired by the contacts with the Atlantic trading networks and material life are clay oil lamps made in the form of candle stands. This type of lamp appeared in Yorubaland in the early seventeenth century as an adaptation of the European candle stands in the West African littorals. These lamps are characterized by a small shallow bowl joined by a trunk to a similarly hollowed but smaller round pedestal. A brass bracelet, most likely of European manufacture, was also found at the site. This would have been one of the few direct European manufactures that made their way inland along the trading routes for which Early Osogbo served as a crossroad.

The most surprising of the artifacts and finds were a 60-cm deep silo filled with processed pegmatite and a cache of over 138 pieces of glass cullet, frits, and beads. Several of these glass artifacts and pegmatite samples were subjected to Laser Ablation Inductively Coupled Plasma Mass Spectrometry analysis. The results reveal that these glasses were characterized by high lime and high alumina, a unique chemical composition in the world of glass technology. We have since confirmed that these glasses were locally produced in the Yoruba region, and that Early Osogbo participated in one or more segments of the *chaîne opératoire* dealing with primary glass manufacture in the region (Ogundiran and Ige 2015).

Reflections

The suite of archaeological evidence in Early Osogbo made it clear that we need to first locate Early Osogbo within the regional settlement and cultural history before we can effectively understand how it was impacted by the Atlantic commercial revolution. The evidence shows that it was not only the contingencies of the new economic relations pressing in from the coast that impacted Early Osogbo's everyday life but also the sociopolitical transformations originating from the mainland. This realization made me recast my study in Early Osogbo with two overlapping interpretative frameworks. The first focused on the internal frontier migration processes that produced Early Osogbo; and the second is centered on the quotidian material practices that defined the African Atlantic age (Ogundiran 2014).

In this regard, I modified my interpretation frameworks based on the compelling insights offered by the archaeological data. As an internal frontier settlement, Early Osogbo was an experimental site. The fauna assemblage that defined the foundation of the settlement as a hunting camp was succeeded by a density and variability of artifacts showing that the community had a stable residential focus comprising of farmers, hunters, traders, and artisans. The residents relied on hunting to meet their need for meat protein, but they procured their ceramics for cooking and eating meat from diverse sources, especially through what were predominantly specialized economic exchanges. Hence, although the predominance of wild animals in the community's diet gives the impression that it was a formative village community, the diverse range of artifacts in the settlement – cowries, tobacco pipes, locally-produced glass, ceramics, and so on – demonstrates that Early Osogbo was part of a regional system of commerce and a busy crossroads of social, demographic, and political networks.

The archaeological data also show that the models of colonialism and center-periphery are not suitable for framing the local practices in Early Osogbo, even with our global archaeological lenses. The experience in Early Osogbo shows that the Yoruba mainland was not a peripheral automaton unreflexively responding to the interests of the metropolises in the Atlantic basin as world systems and core-periphery theorists tend to suggest. Rather, my data made it imperative that I investigate how local initiatives and agents in the Upper Osun region appropriated the new economic conditions on the coast for their own objectives of self-realization while in the process becoming an interdependent node that was integral to the global network of Atlantic economy. Hence, rather than focusing on the transformative impacts of the Atlantic trade, I find it more insightful to examine how the small community of Early Osogbo integrated the new and few commodities and taste practices coming in from the coast into the local and regional spheres of economic, social, and political interactions.

Lessons Learned

The Nigerian government was working towards nominating the grove as a World Heritage site before we started our fieldwork in Osun Grove in 2003. This nomination was achieved in 2005, and it elevated the interests of the local community and the general public in our subsequent archaeological work in the grove. Given the historical processualism-focus of my work, I saw this as an opportunity to develop a public education program in collaboration with the Osogbo public and the government agency managing the grove (National Commission for Museums and Monuments, NCMM). The public education program was in three parts. First, I organized a workshop for the NCMM staff on how to incorporate the archaeological findings into the museum's public education programs and the interpretation of Osun Grove. Second, I organized a "meet-the-press" day and invited members of the Nigerian press corps to visit the site during our 2011 field season. Journalists from three privately-owned national dailies and two government-owned broadcasting stations visited the site, and each did an extensive story on the archaeological project. This meant that the news of our research was carried across Nigeria. Third, I developed an exhibition of our fieldwork entitled "Ancestral Legacies in Osun Grove: Archacological Exhibition of Early Osogbo History." The exhibition was initially housed in the pavilion of the palace of the king of Osogbo and was declared open by Oba Jimoh Oyetunji, Larooye II, on August 19, 2011. The exhibition ran for two weeks and was then donated to the National Museum, Osogbo for conversion into traveling exhibitions that would target schools and other community centers. I also authored and published a catalog for the exhibition, hundreds of copies of which were given to NCMM for distribution to the public. The electronic version of the catalog is also available online (Ogundiran 2012). All of these outreach events were not originally part of the research design, but they became necessary as the research progressed and public interest in the project mounted.

My experience in field archaeology has taught me that one has to be flexible in the operation of one's goals and one must be clear about the intended audience for a project. These affect the way a research objective is defined, the theoretical framework employed, and the methods used to accomplish the goals. It is always important to start out with a well-crafted fieldwork design that is responsive to the research questions and also anticipatory of the likely logistical challenges. However, one must be willing to adjust the research design once the project starts in order to effectively manage unforeseen circumstances. For example, I was troubled by the destruction of most of the Early Osogbo settlements due to the construction of a medical school campus on the archaeological site. Much more troubling was the fact that the government agencies that owned the land did not carry out archaeological impact assessment before the construction work began. I realized how weak Nigerian cultural heritage laws and their implementation are. Rather than going through government bureaucracy to carry out archaeological salvage work, I found it more productive to obtain the permission and support of the building engineers working at the medical school construction site. Thanks to them, I was able to conduct archaeological survey of Early Osogbo even while construction was ongoing. Nevertheless, I still kept the government agencies supervising my archaeological research in the loop, and I began to advise them on how to be more proactive in protecting the archaeological resources of the grove and its surrounding areas.

Likewise, the encounter of unexpected finds such as the glass artifacts preoccupied my attention more than was originally anticipated and budgeted for. The chemical analysis of these glass artifacts lasted about four years at the end of which we decoded the chemistry of the glass using the most sophisticated laboratory methods available. Looking back, I now think I wasted precious time and manpower trying to implement a traditional survey strategy in the wooded Osun Grove. The method was a good science, but the results were dismal. Rather than speaking mostly to priests and priestesses about the likely areas to find archaeological sites, I should have spent as much time, if not more, speaking to ordinary people such as the maintenance workers and forest guides who worked in different parts of the grove as government staff. Those people had a different kind of relationship with the landscape, and they would have been able to provide a different perspective about site identification at the initial stage of the fieldwork. The research at Osun Grove was full of surprises with some setbacks but also some opportunities. The project has now expanded in a new direction, one that seeks to understand the long-term landscape and cultural history of Osun Grove.

Paired Reading

Ogundiran, Akinwumi. 2014. "The Making of an Internal Frontier Settlement: Archaeology and Historical Process in Osun Grove (Nigeria), Seventeenth to Eighteenth Centuries." *African Archaeological Review*, 31: 1–24. DOI: 10.1007/s10437-014-9152-9.

References

Ogundiran, Akinwumi. 2002. *Archaeology and History in Ìlàrè District (Central Yorubaland, Nigeria), 1200–1900 A.D.* Oxford: Archaeopress.

Ogundiran, Akinwumi. 2012. "Ancestral Legacies in Osun Grove: Archaeological Exhibition of Early Osogbo History." Exhibition Catalog. Charlotte, NC: University of North Carolina. Accessed February 28, 2017. http://africana.uncc.edu/sites/africana.uncc.edu/files/media/OsunGroveExhibitionCatalogue.pdf

Ogundiran, Akinwumi. 2014. "The Making of an Internal Frontier Settlement: Archaeology and Historical Process in Osun Grove (Nigeria), Seventeenth to Eighteenth Centuries." *African Archaeological Review*, 31: 1–24. DOI: 10.1007/s10437-014-9152-9.

Ogundiran, Akinwumi. 2015. "Pioneers of Archaeological Thought and Practice in Postcolonial Nigeria." In *Theory in Africa, Africa in Theory: Locating Meaning in Archaeology*, edited by Stephanie Wynne-Jones and Jeffrey B. Fleisher, 90–110. New York: Routledge.

Ogundiran, Akinwumi and Ige O. Akinlolu 2015. "'Our Ancestors Were Material Scientists': Archaeological and Geochemical Evidence for Indigenous Yoruba Glass Technology." *Journal of Black Studies*, 46: 751–72. DOI: 10.1177/0021934715600964.

Pauketat, Timothy. 2001. "Practice and History in Archaeology: An Emerging Paradigm." *Anthropological Theory*, 1: 73–98. DOI: 10.1177/146349960100100105.

Schmidt, Peter R. and Thomas C. Patterson. 1995. *Making Alternative Histories: The Practice of Archaeology and History in Non-Western Settings*. Santa Fe, NM: School of American Research Press.

15

Rooting in New England: Archaeologies of Colonialism, Community, and Collaboration

Stephen W. Silliman

Project Summary

The Eastern Pequot Archaeological Field School is a collaborative project between the Eastern Pequot Tribal Nation and the University of Massachusetts Boston that I have directed since its inception in 2003. It centers on conducting community-engaged archaeological research on the Eastern Pequot reservation, established in AD 1683 in the northeastern United States and still occupied today as one of the oldest reservations in the country. To date, the project has received external funding from the National Science Foundation and the Wenner-Gren Foundation. The objectives are to study the persistence of this Native American community through centuries of colonialism; to interrogate the ways that culture, community, and identity are lived in the past and represented in the present; and to explore community-driven and participatory archaeology.

Trying to Root in New England

The last day of my "Introduction to Archaeology" course was coming up in mid-December 2002, and we were ending on one of those topics with fun word-plays we love to put in our syllabus: the future of the past. I had my own future "in the past" on my mind that day. I had been hired at the University of Massachusetts Boston with the expectation that I would initiate a new archaeology project in New England, a region where I had never lived or conducted research. I welcomed the challenge (and the job) to continue my commitment to working on important archaeological issues in the proverbial "backyard." However, my third semester on campus was coming to a close without such a project in place. I had taken some appropriate time to acquaint myself with archaeologists, projects, materials, chronologies, histories, and intellectual territories in the Northeast, for I knew better than to overstep my bounds or abilities as a freshly-minted PhD with a background in California archaeology and a penchant for social theory. Still, I knew that I could use core issues and perspectives – more my "thing" than being a material specialist – as the arc that connected my move from the West to the East Coast of North America.

A year and a half in, I was ready to start rooting (in both metaphorical senses) in the dirt of New England. I sought a project that would permit me to do what I had done in California, which was to study Native American responses to and survivals within European colonialism and do so in consultation with an indigenous descendent community, but do it better. I had my sights set on improved theory, longer project duration, more excavation, deeper collaboration,

Engaging Archaeology: 25 Case Studies in Research Practice, First Edition. Edited by Stephen W. Silliman.
© 2018 John Wiley & Sons, Inc. Published 2018 by John Wiley & Sons, Inc.

and stronger political and heritage connotations. I really needed my archaeology to be "doing something" in the present, particularly for Native communities still confronting legacies of colonialism, while also staying true to rendering an accurate picture of the past. This represented some progression in thinking and practice beyond my dissertation and was certainly leagues beyond what I had considered as an undergraduate or even first-year graduate student. I just wasn't sure yet where and how that was going to materialize in New England, and I knew that a stream of publications on my California field and laboratory research would only take me so far. I could hear that tenure clock ticking in the distance.

An email arrived on that fateful day in December that would put me on the path toward something far better than I had imagined. The Eastern Pequot Tribal Nation in southeastern Connecticut was emerging from a federal acknowledgment petition process begun in the late 1970s and had received a positive finding on their case in 2002 (Silliman and Sebastian Dring 2008). They wanted to initiate a cultural and historic preservation program as they transitioned into their new federally-recognized status, and they hoped that this might involve an archaeological survey of their 225-acre reservation, established in 1683 and still occupied today. At the recommendation of Kevin McBride of the University of Connecticut and the Mashantucket Pequot Museum and Research Center, they emailed to ask if I thought that I could be of any assistance to them. Perfect timing! I jumped at the chance and replied before the day was over. I realized that this project not only could permit me to address important anthropological issues and do so over *centuries* of colonialism (rather than the few decades my dissertation had tackled), but also had materialized in the best possible way: a Native community had asked for an archaeologist, and not the other way around. This helped to set parameters of authority, power-sharing, and tribal review that would guide the project for many years.

I admit that I let my researcher excitement and tenure-track mindset get the best of me in my initial response. I wrote a long email – one of my professorial trademarks, I would later realize – proposing all that we might address over several field seasons. Katherine Sebastian Dring, the community liaison at the time and now tribal chair and good friend with whom I have since co-authored publications and presentations, responded with a gentle request to calm down and try a pilot field season first. This was sage advice. The community needed to figure out archaeology's potential contributions and problems on their terms, and we needed to dialogue our way through complex issues and histories and to develop a relationship of trust in a discipline that has often not been a friend to Native communities. We had to figure out if and how archaeology could bring something positive to the Eastern Pequot, and I wanted a shot at some disciplinary redemption. Furthermore, I needed to better assess the potentials of the project to address the research questions that inspired me and to permit the publications and scholarly productivity required of tenure-track life. An email exchange wasn't going to be enough to resolve these lingering questions, but a meeting the following month in their tribal office would put us on the right track.

At that meeting and the close of a mere six weeks of fruitful discussion, we could not have foreseen all of the positive and productive directions this collaboration would take, nor could we have realized the significant mutual benefits that the right mix of community engagement and scholarly research could bring to their community, my career ambitions, and the many students who would participate. These collaborations take time (a lot of time, in fact), plus vigilance, compromise, and an abiding willingness to talk and – more importantly for archaeologists – to listen (Atalay 2012). We also could not have anticipated the terrible turn of their federal acknowledgment bid, as local town residents and public officials would mount an unrelenting campaign to eviscerate their case. This resulted in the Bureau of Indian Affairs rescinding the Eastern Pequot's positive federal acknowledgment decision in late 2005, an unprecedented move of profound negative consequence for the community's hopes for self-determination, elder care, community investment, and economic development. They still contend with this issue today.

Such a disastrous setback easily could have ended the project. However, the positive community benefits deriving from the archaeological project, and the use of research funds external to the tribe to contribute to their historic preservation efforts, kept it going.

Project Implementation

The project essentially began from scratch, but it did so on my end with a strong theoretical orientation to guide it. Theory couldn't determine it, though, because I would need to heed indigenous perspectives and life experiences, not just read social theorists and postcolonial scholars. My commitments to theories of practice, identity, community, and decolonization made me receptive to this project, and they led me directly to the questions that I wanted to address at household and community levels (Silliman 2009). I wanted to explore how the lived, material experience of Eastern Pequot community members could be accessed through archaeology and how those experiences might shed light on how this community, and others like it, survived centuries of dispossession, discrimination, inequality, and historical erasure. Importantly, the project also had to meet the immediate management needs of the Eastern Pequot, but these could all be conjoined rather effectively.

The dual objectives of finding and documenting sites for the tribe and investigating social and material trajectories during the colonial era required that we locate, map, and study Eastern Pequot houses from a variety of reservation periods. We had only a rough map of sites based on a cursory pedestrian survey conducted many years before and some recent locational data generated by an engineering firm on obvious surface sites and a few stone fences. Also, available historic documents, many of which were collected and used as part of the Eastern Pequot's federal recognition petition, offered little help in pinpointing site whereabouts. Certainly no one had ever excavated anything on the reservation, but I had the benefit of consulting years of neighboring work on the Mashantucket Pequot reservation (McBride 1993). Our methods followed rather standard procedure, but they had to be situated in proper Eastern Pequot protocols. For example, a tribal representative placed tobacco offerings in each unit to acknowledge the disturbance of the earth and conducted smudging rituals at the start of the field season to "cleanse" all participants (see Silliman and Sebastian Dring 2008). We also had to negotiate the approval from Tribal Council to remove artifacts from the reservation and to process, study, and temporarily house those in my laboratory in Boston.

The reconnaissance phase of the project was not much influenced by theory, but rather attuned to the physical context and need for discovery and to the Eastern Pequot's request to avoid sacred sites, burial grounds, and, at the outset, current homes. The thick brushy forest across the hilly and rocky terrain created a typical New England situation. Pedestrian survey would only be useful to orient the crew to the landscape and to locate the most obtrusive of sites with collapsed stone chimneys and cellar depressions; anything else would be next to invisible. The pedestrian survey only took a few days with a crew of about ten students and three tribal members. In addition, geophysical survey seemed out of the question with glacial till underlying much of the reservation and hardly a stretch of flat ground without abundant rocks or trees. This was disappointing given my work with magnetometry and electromagnetic conductivity in California during the late 1990s, so I ended up moving away from that burgeoning technical specialty.

This left shovel test pit (STP) surveys, a tried-and-true but ever-uncertain classic in such leaf-strewn environments, as the method of choice to locate sites not visible on the surface and to understand the spread of materials outward from households. The protocol was, and has been ever since, to dig STPs at 10-m intervals with a crew of about a dozen students with the hopes of intersecting and detecting relatively small household sites, but being ready to switch to shorter spacing if we picked up interesting materials or concentrations. Over the years, this method has taken tremendous amounts of time and produced quite a few artifact-empty (but often rock-filled) holes as we ventured across the forested reservation. The latter is important for knowing where things aren't, but you can only repeat that a few times to undergraduates before their glares become worrisome.

However, the STP effort also produced numerous units with artifacts spreading away from obvious houses, and it has landed us two households that had no surface visibility. It is not coincidental, either, that these were wigwam-like structures. In fact, it is testament to the worth of the arduous method, as the STPs detected sites not built in accordance with European-introduced architectural styles that had become common on the reservation in the 1700s and 1800s. Admittedly, I expected STPs to detect more than just these two sites with our comprehensive but not yet exhaustive subsurface survey, but the ephemerality and small size make such sites difficult to detect. And, so, the search continues.

Because I needed to explore different periods and house types to establish trajectories of culture change and continuity, I had to devise a strategy for excavating portions of house sites. Contrary to the systematic sampling strategy employed in the STP survey, I needed to place units where they seemed most likely to provide information on house construction, use, and dissolution through sampling of walls, foundations, cellars, collapsed chimneys, hearths, trash pits, and general sheet midden. The number of units we managed to excavate was not really the result of hitting an ideal target, but usually a function of how many the crew of 12–15 students, plus 2–3 tribal interns, could get done during a five-week field season. More often than not, we had to end the summer wishing we could have excavated more. Since the strategy has been to sample multiple houses across the reservation, only rarely have we returned to a site for a second field season, and the one major time we did was due to our Eastern Pequot field advisor asking that we do so.

At the outset, I assumed that I would find deposits from all reservation eras, both wigwams and framed-style homes, houses with multiple generations of occupation, and some stone tools and indigenous ceramics. All of these assumptions proved problematic. We have yet to find any deposits from the first 50 years of reservation life, thanks to the hard-to-find sites noted above and the fact that many such sites may have current residences on top of them. This has also kept stone tool and locally-made ceramic artifacts known from the seventeenth century mostly out of the narrative I could tell. We have only found two potential wigwam sites, which is not nearly representative of how many had been occupied on the reservation according to historical documents. This biased our sample toward those more visible on the surface, which are remnants of wooden framed houses with collapsed chimneys and either cellars or crawl spaces. Of house sites studied to date, only one – the one we returned to for a second field season – shows a major reconfiguration or household shift during its occupation; the rest seem to be single occupations spanning a generation or two at most.

Making Sense of Things

The data to address the research questions have ranged across a variety of abundant household materials: mass-produced consumer goods like ceramics, glass, pipes, and metal tools; architectural objects like metal nails and window glass; animal bones and shellfish; wood charcoal and some seeds; and various pits, house, and field features for spatial analysis. Lithic artifacts proved to be few in number or often were produced millennia before the reservation was established, which (inconveniently, again) sidelined my previous skills in lithic analysis and sourcing that I had developed in California. Similarly, charred seeds have been frustratingly elusive despite hundreds of soil samples floated to better understand plant use in reservation households.

To manage these diverse datasets, I had to treat this research at two scales – the production of analytical data hovering close to specific materials and the overarching synthesis of household assemblages at the scale of the entire reservation. As the principal investigator (PI) overseeing graduate students, I took on the latter role as I had to spend considerable time advising students pursuing the more technical data analyses, often in collaboration with my university colleagues who had pertinent specialties. This strategy has advanced student careers, produced robust datasets, and permitted project-wide integration of results, but has kept me from being more personally involved in all laboratory analyses – a difficult tradeoff, but an often necessary one for projects that have to meet educational, community, and faculty research needs. One thing is certain: the project would not have been nearly as successful without a graduate program to anchor it and generous colleagues to train students in zooarchaeology and paleoethnobotany. It couldn't have worked solely as a graduate student project given the scope, but a smaller, earlier version might have been possible. On the other hand, the larger project umbrella could certainly shelter and provide data for plenty of master's theses. And it has – 14 completed and 3 underway as of early 2018.

Our discoveries prompted some rethinking, and I believe improving, of the theoretical lens applied to understanding indigenous histories and communities in colonial worlds (Silliman 2009, 2012). I began the project thinking about culture contact, change, continuity, and resistance in ways that had informed my California work, but those frameworks later buckled under pressure of the non-dichotomous nature of the data (that is, artifacts not easily identifiable as European or Native, or as changing or staying the same), my further engagements with postcolonial theory and its routing through practice theory, and the legacies and realities of colonialism in this particular community. In many ways, this was taking to heart some of the key issues raised a decade before by Kent Lightfoot (1995) about multiscalar and diachronic studies across the "prehistory/history" divide.

Without the anchor point of the first half-century of reservation life, I could not reasonably talk about first adoption of many consumer goods and domesticated animals already embedded in household life by the mid-eighteenth century, nor could I talk about the pace or comparative diminution of stone tools or pottery production in household economies. Instead, I needed to account for how materials we did find worked to maintain practices and provide links between generations, those already many decades into reservation living and colonial economies. As a result, I argued that these all be called Eastern Pequot objects to dodge the problematic dichotomies of Native/European artifacts that plagued the discipline (Silliman 2009). Similarly, without more wigwam sites or even a single wigwam site that showed the overlay of a later framed house, I was unable to talk about who changed and who stayed the same and the tempos of either. I had to resituate my interpretation to talk about something that was not simply change or continuity, but rather a state of existence that transcended them or, perhaps more accurately, made them possible: a persistence that we had been trying to recognize as either changing or staying the same (Silliman 2009). That ended up being an epiphany.

In addition, another major revelation in the intersections of field strategies, laboratory analyses, and interpretive efforts was the vital importance of *variation*. I understood this already thanks to a variety of divergent theoretical traditions: Lewis Binford's earliest processualism, evolutionary archaeology's emphasis on anti-essentialism, post-processualism's focus on multiple experiences and multivocality, and feminist critiques of singular narratives and overly logical progressions. However, it did not sink in fully until I began grappling with the "middle period" of reservation history between the missing initial decades and not-currently-researched last century. Rather than continuing to look for sites that "represented" different periods of Eastern Pequot cultural history, I began to pay more attention to synchronous variation between households, as have my students (Hunter, Silliman, and Landon 2014). Therein I could begin to see both the makings of patterns that archaeologists like to identify *and* the ways that these patterns are not homogenous and linear but rather capture – and sometimes suppress – internal community struggles and decision-making. I was not looking at households making constant daily decisions to change or stay the same, but rather households drawing uniquely on shared pasts, present contexts, and future hopes. It is as much in difference as in similarity that real dynamics of community life manifest and lay the foundation for persistence.

Reflections

The project still continues after 15 years, but some reflections are possible. First, I have no idea how this project will end, and this can be unsettling. Will we reach the point of diminishing returns and find that more archaeology would be interesting but not necessary from a preservation standpoint? We have learned much already, but we need to access even more of the variation noted above and the currently missing first years of reservation life for nuanced answers to our research questions. Or, will the community decide at some point that we have done enough archaeology for now or perhaps place one of their community members in the lead on their cultural resource management? I would certainly celebrate the latter.

Second, it has been difficult to sustain the field project annually in the current economic climate, even in a place as logistically accessible as New England. As a result, I had to switch to an alternating year cycle of offering the field school after the seventh field season. The finances required to fund the participation of two or three tribal interns (who, in my opinion, should be paid to acknowledge the time and knowledge they bring to the project) and to feed, house, and transport students outstrips what public university sources can regularly support. Moreover, deeply-settled projects that mainly need to keep doing what they have been doing for years to advance long-term research objectives are harder to sell repeatedly to external funding agencies without a new "hook." In some ways, this constant need to remake oneself or one's project can work against long-term collaborative projects that may need to span a decade or more for the sake of the research and the community members themselves.

Third, the project also ended up being much more about the politics of knowledge production in the present about the past (i.e., heritage) than I had ever anticipated. This is due in no small part to the community engagement woven deeply into the project's fabric, as what we do with site discovery, artifact recovery, earth disturbance, grant-getting, publication, student education, intern training, and public presentations all have real-world effects on the descendants of the archaeological past that drew me to the project in the first place (Figure 15.1).

Fourth, I am pleased with the scholarly products that have come from this project, and it turned out considerably richer than I could have imagined. In this case, the process involves having published work (like this chapter) and master's theses vetted by Tribal Council before they become public, which can be intimidating for many researchers, especially students, but highly rewarding for the ways such a process establishes shared authority, ensures tribal oversight, and holds researchers accountable to the community. In addition, beyond our weekly brief reports during the field season, artifact exhibits at annual pow-wows, and educational sessions with the tribe at the reservation and in my laboratory (which is, incidentally, 100 miles away), I continue to look for more ways to increase the community's access to curated collections and their overall participation. Getting community members into thick, tick-infested forests is not that easy either, even if our archaeological work and the land are valued. The hope is to continue to improve on these fronts. For example, on the ten-year project anniversary I self-published a 35-page, grant-funded commemorative book that included pictures of participants as well as some important artifacts. Eastern Pequot community members provided all captions so that their voices, not mine, narrated the collection. Complimentary copies were provided to all who had been interns, advisors, liaisons, or Tribal Council members during the project period.

Figure 15.1 Photograph of collaboration in the Eastern Pequot Archaeological Field School. Image shows Natasha Leullier Snedeker (left) sharing recently-discovered artifacts with two Eastern Pequot elders, Norma Parrish and the late Robert Sebastian.

Lessons Learned

I offer a few parting thoughts for those pondering their own short- or long-term projects in historical, household, postcolonial, indigenous, and/or community-engaged archaeology.

Find the right balance between diachronic and synchronic emphasis. Archaeologists tend to love the former and proclaim ourselves proficient at the "science of the long-term," but these only emerge from a compilation, sometimes limited in scope, of the latter. This means that a focus on only one house has a lot to offer, especially when time and money are slim, but be cautious what you make that house represent (Silliman 2012). As Jordan (2010) cautions, we need to avoid the problem of thinking of "one site against the world" and instead be attentive to entire networks of life, labor, and political economy – in this case – on and off the reservation.

Collaboration takes time and patience. Plan to settle in for the long haul to do it successfully, realizing of course that the deepest kinds of community engagement are not always possible with new projects or dissertation and thesis endeavors, unless the latter are already situated in an ongoing or larger-scale collaborative effort. However, they are profoundly worthwhile. When working with indigenous communities, in particular, be ready to work with them as collaborators, not as recipients of outreach efforts and not as research subjects (Atalay 2012). You should also be prepared to invest in community products that may not have the same symbolic (and financial) capital as standard academic ones.

Let data and community members challenge you. I could have never applied or reworked postcolonial or decolonizing ideas as I did without confronting material conditions and outcomes of lived experience of people in the past (archaeological data) and in the present (descendent community). Theory can be rather over-determining at times, and it helps to keep theoretical frameworks open for prodding and for asking "what if I am wrong about this?" and "what are the implications of these interpretations?"

Be creative as a project develops and think about publishing on process. This is one way to counteract criticisms often levied at community-engaged research when it does not produce standard academic products at the same pace as more traditional work. It is also one way to start to build trust with a community partner because you are co-producing information rather than using someone's past to simply build a CV. For those in or aiming for academic positions, there is no reason not to generate publications while also being part of other innovative, politically useful, community activities.

Finally, enjoy what you do. Most of us entered archaeology because of a personal passion, or a political commitment, or a material obsession. Even when research is tedious, funding is insecure, advisors or bosses are demanding, and job prospects turn grim, we shouldn't lose sight of ourselves and what anchored us first (and still) to the archaeological process. Keep both changing and staying the same, for together those are the hallmarks of persistence.

Paired Reading

Silliman, Stephen W. 2009. "Change and Continuity, Practice and Memory: Native American Persistence in Colonial New England." *American Antiquity*, 74: 211–230.

References

Atalay, Sonya. 2012. *Community-Based Archaeology: Research with, by, and for Indigenous and Local Communities*. Berkeley, CA: University of California Press.

Hunter, Ryan, Stephen W. Silliman, and David B. Landon. 2014. "Shellfish Collection and Community Connections: Gender and Sustenance in Eighteenth- and Nineteenth-Century Native New England." *American Antiquity*, 79: 712–729.

Jordan, Kurt. 2010. "Not Just 'One Site Against the World': Seneca Iroquois Intercommunity Connections and Autonomy, 1550–1779." In *Across a Great Divide: Continuity and Change in Native North American Societies, 1400–1900*, edited by Laura L. Scheiber and Mark D. Mitchell, 79–106. Tucson, AZ: University of Arizona Press.

Lightfoot, Kent G. 1995. "Culture Contact Studies: Redefining the Relationship between Prehistoric and Historical Archaeology." *American Antiquity*, 60: 199–217. DOI: 10.2307/282137.

McBride, Kevin A. 1993. "'Ancient & Crazie': Pequot Lifeways during the Historic Period." In *Algonkians of New England: Past and Present*, edited by Peter Benes, 63–75. Annual Proceedings of the 1991 Dublin Folklife Seminar. Boston: Boston University.

Silliman, Stephen W. 2009. "Change and Continuity, Practice and Memory: Native American Persistence in Colonial New England." *American Antiquity*, 74: 211–230.

Silliman, Stephen W. 2012. "Between the Longue Durée and the Short Purée: Postcolonial Archaeologies of Indigenous History in Colonial North America." In *Decolonizing Indigenous Histories: Exploring Prehistoric/Colonial Transitions in Archaeology*, edited by Maxine Oland, Siobhan M. Hart, and Liam Frink, 113–132. Tucson, AZ: University of Arizona Press.

Silliman, Stephen W. and Katherine H. Sebastian Dring. 2008. "Working on Pasts for Futures: Eastern Pequot Field School Archaeology in Connecticut." In *Collaborating at the Trowel's Edge: Teaching and Learning in Indigenous Archaeology*, edited by Stephen W. Silliman, 67–87. Amerind Studies in Archaeology 2. Tucson, AZ: University of Arizona Press.

16

Accidentally Digging Central America's Earliest Village
Rosemary A. Joyce

Project Summary

The Lower Ulua Valley Archaeological Project, co-directed with John Henderson, was intended to pursue an archaeology of household life during the period from AD 500–1000 when towns and villages near the site of San Pedro Sula, Honduras, engaged with Classic Maya cities. We targeted sites in danger of destruction for economic development, especially earthen platforms created by rebuilding houses over multiple generations. We intended to spend one season gathering data from each site to form a regional comparison. What we found led us to carry out five field seasons there between 1994 and 2000. Our time frame was redefined as Puerto Escondido's partial destruction made possible excavation of one of the earliest (before 1550 BC) village sites exposed in Central America. Our interest in the face-to-face setting of everyday life remained, but household archaeology was challenging or impossible to implement in a deeply buried village. Nonetheless, the project contributes to our theoretical framework that questions the inevitability of rising inequality in Mesoamerica and examines how strategies and tactics in daily life contributed to creating differences in social authority.

Getting to Puerto Escondido: How Research and Researchers Develop

When I began training as an undergraduate at Cornell University, I already knew I wanted to be an archaeologist. I had worked on a dig as part of a community archaeology project through the Buffalo Museum of Science. I intended to continue doing historical archaeology in the United States, to understand experiences not highlighted in history textbooks and communicate with the public by working in museums. Cornell, a great place to combine anthropology and interdisciplinary archaeology training, did not have a project in North American historical archaeology at that time. What it did have was a field school that funded participation for accepted students. As a result, I joined the Naco Valley field school in Honduras in 1977, and it changed my life as an archaeologist.

On this field school, as one of six undergraduates assisting three doctoral students and the faculty project director, I was able to assist in excavation of a Late Classic ball court at one site, help document excavations of a sixteenth-century town mentioned by Cortés, and record ceramics from a test excavation at a Formative Period site first discovered that season. After asking graduate students on the Naco project where to go to pursue Honduran archaeology,

I applied to the University of Illinois, Urbana-Champaign, where a doctoral student was doing her dissertation on a site near San Pedro Sula, the city where we lived that summer.

I arrived at Illinois with no theoretical focus in archaeology. My theoretical frameworks came from social anthropology, notably ethnography of Oceania and Indonesia where transaction of things creates and recreates social life at extensive and local scales. I trained in symbolic anthropology using structuralist methods, but also exploring the power symbols draw from their associations in worldly life. The archaeology I had been trained in previously, mainly culture history, had nothing as powerful to offer to explain how and why human societies took specific forms.

As I entered graduate school, I reached out to my former undergraduate professor about the chance of returning to Honduras. I learned that a new project was about to start in the San Pedro Sula area (Figure 16.1). I joined the Proyecto Arqueológico Sula as one of three doctoral students who worked on a systematic settlement survey that engaged up to a dozen undergraduates in periodic field schools and provided paid employment to 8–12 local workers. By the time our project was over, we had identified more than 500 sites in 2400 sq km. I conducted excavations in three, including my dissertation site, Cerro Palenque. I developed expertise in ceramics, defining a sequence of types for the valley, so that we could understand variation over time.

At Cerro Palenque, directing a team of eight people, I applied the then-new concept of household archaeology, where actions taking place in households were understood to be the economic engine of society and the means by which social identities were reproduced. I developed a way of looking at actions by people who constructed their identities and differential power in everyday practice. My project built on the work of the anthropologist Richard Newbold Adams, who proposed a model for how people recognized each other as more or less influential over fundamental aspects of life, creating social power. At Cerro Palenque, a settlement that expanded as Classic Maya cities were contracting, I thought it was possible to explain local developments

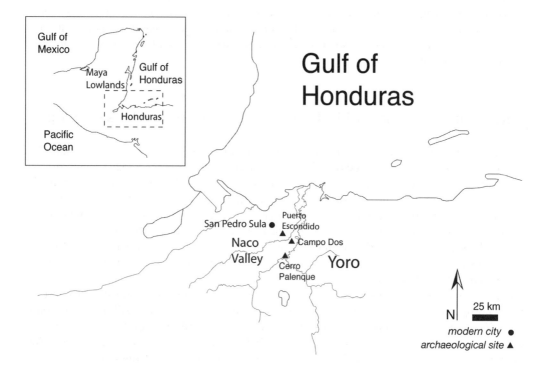

Figure 16.1 Map of northwestern Honduras showing places mentioned.

as the result of people, individually and in groups, creating social power by taking advantage of opportunities provided by changes in networks of which they were part.

Almost ten years later, after my first post-doctoral project I returned to the lower Ulua Valley. My intervening project explored heterarchy, or the existence of multiple hierarchies that constrained the development of absolute hierarchy (Joyce and Hendon 2000). The leading theoretical issue was still social power. I also incorporated feminist theoretical work that urged consideration of embodied experiences, difference, and subjectivity. The smaller, less densely populated valleys in Yoro provided less evidence of social difference. The lower Ulua Valley project promised a place to fully explore the implications of these theoretical approaches.

The Lower Ulua Valley Project

The Lower Ulua Valley project aimed to show how households were organized in different zones of one valley and how towns of different sizes and specializations interacted, exemplifying "horizontal complexity" in a society of "wealthy farmers," as an alternative to viewing the region as a backwater of hierarchical Classic Maya states (Joyce 2013).

Using data from our settlement survey, we identified two settlement patterns for the AD 500–1000 period. One group of sites, including Cerro Palenque, preserved cobblestone terraces that once supported residential buildings. Most of what we understood about everyday activities in these sites came from small and often shallow trash deposits. Features like hearths were rarely identified. In household archaeology terms, in these sites we encountered houses, but not "activity areas."

In contrast, sites on the river floodplain included large earthen platforms that had supported multiple buildings, repeatedly remodeled and sometimes buried by river floods. They preserved features like post holes, hearths, ovens, and storage pits representing the everyday activities of generations of residents. The greater preservation of traces of activities was a considerable advantage for household archaeology. Multiple episodes of remodeling, material signs of stability of occupation, allowed us to explore inter-generational persistence.

There was urgency in excavating these sites. Honduras was experiencing new economic development in the 1980s, following establishment of civilian government after decades of military rule. Development replaced cattle ranches and banana plantations that had preserved sites with small factories and housing tracts that destroyed them. We expected to rapidly build up data through extensive excavations at threatened sites.

The first site we excavated in summer 1993 proved this strategy would be productive. With input from the local representative of the Honduran Institute for Archaeology and History, we selected Campo Dos based on its imminent danger of destruction and the presence of household features, such as hearths. Our excavations, assisted by two doctoral students, eight undergraduates, and a team of six local archaeological laborers, documented a village where figurines and ceramics were produced as part of household-level rituals creating inter-village social ties between AD 700 and 1000 (Hendon, Joyce, and Lopiparo 2014: 57–76).

The 1993 season at Campo Dos was our only opportunity to excavate before development proceeded. As we considered where to work in summer 1994, we again consulted our Institute contact, who told us another site, CR-372 or Puerto Escondido, was being developed. We decided to conduct another one-season project there. We arrived with another group of undergraduates and doctoral students, planning to implement a program of household archaeology as we had at Campo Dos.

Finding an early village was not part of the research agenda.

Puerto Escondido: Pursuing the Classic House Compound

Because it was on land subject to military black-out on air photos, with limited access before the transition to civilian government, CR-372 was not recorded in our original settlement survey. It was already greatly transformed by bulldozing to level the area and cut streets for a new housing development. From the construction company, we obtained a contour map done prior to bulldozing. On it appeared at least four broad earthen platforms like those that supported clusters of residential buildings in other sites. We mapped in the excavations undertaken by our Honduran colleague, designating his excavations as Operation 1. Our own excavations would be Operation 2.

We walked the site to select our excavation location. Everywhere the bulldozer had exposed broken pieces of pottery, fragments of obsidian blades and flakes, and chunks of hard, fire-baked clay from hearths. The majority of the ceramics were identifiable as typical of the period between AD 500 and 1000. They represented all vessel forms we would expect in household contexts.

Our walk across the site began at the bulldozer cut where Operation 1 was located. As we walked west, we encountered an area where the map indicated the edge of a platform. Here, bulldozers had pushed soil to fill in lower areas. Continuing, the map showed a second, lower, broader platform. Here, river cobbles formed surfaces of small rectangular features exposed by the bulldozer, but not destroyed. These we recognized as likely supports for perishable houses. In no other place could we identify intact building features on the surface. Expecting to be able to spend only eight weeks on this site, we wanted to be sure our household sample was expanded. This seemed like an ideal area to begin work with our field school students.

Operation 2, as we hoped, produced evidence of residential occupation. We found storage pits full of trash and many burned features, likely hearths. We mapped every feature, screened excavated sediments, and collected soil for flotation. Refilled storage pits yielded large sections of partly restorable vessels, dating somewhat earlier than our intended focus: they suggested occupation no later than about AD 400. Bulldozers had removed all later house remains. Still, the *kinds* of features we encountered were similar to those from later household sites, so the main adjustment we needed to make to our research design was to expand it to include an earlier period, from AD 200–500.

Luckily for us, progress on the housing development stalled, and we were able to propose a second field season in 1995. We decided to initiate household excavations near the original Operation 1. Our team, now almost 20 undergrads, doctoral students, and recent PhDs, located our Operation 4 in an 18 m (E–W) by 24 m (N–S) block aligned with and stepped back from cuts made by bulldozers outlining streets for the housing development. Based on surface concentrations of ceramics and lithics, we located excavations in five areas, expanding to follow features. This judgment sample, designed to rapidly identify features typical of houses, worked: we excavated filled-in storage pits west of a zone of hearths, shallow unburned pits, and fragments of packed clay house walls. In the area of house walls, we encountered human burials, some disturbed by bulldozing. The features represented the remains of clusters of buildings whose standing walls had been cut horizontally by the bulldozers, removing most of their floors but leaving subsurface features partly visible.

Ceramics showed that use of these houses dated between AD 400 and 650, later than similar features in Operation 2. The rest of the artifact assemblage was just as rich as that recovered in Operation 2. Our obvious next move was to continue excavating below the disturbed houses, hoping to find evidence of earlier residences contemporary with those of Operation 2.

Unexpected Finds and Modified Research Goals

As we removed the last clay from house features on the eastern side of Operation 4 cut by bulldozing, we unexpectedly encountered a complete ceramic vessel, a small jar with a body modeled to resemble a squash. I had seen these before. I asked the excavators if there were any broken sherds in the surrounding fill that I could examine. Sensing something was up, they pulled out the sherd bag, and handed me a few large, well-finished, thick fragments with glossy black and gray surfaces.

What I held in my hands were the first examples of sherds reported from the Ulua Valley that could be identified as dating to before 800 BC. I had recognized the jar as similar to others preserved in the Peabody Museum at Harvard University, where I studied them in the late 1980s. These bottles were recovered in excavations in the 1930s at a site along the Ulua River called Playa de los Muertos, whose modern radiocarbon dates ranged from 600 to 200 BC.

Finding a Playa de los Muertos period village was exciting enough, but what we had was more. The thicker, glossy black and gray sherds were unknown in previous excavations in the Ulua Valley. Similar ceramics were found in caves in the highlands west and east, and in construction fill at Los Naranjos, located in mountains to the south (Joyce 2004). At Los Naranjos, these ceramics were associated with one radiocarbon sample dated to the eighth century BC.

The first complete bottle was soon joined by others, as we excavated a construction fill forming a large terrace with an eroded plaster surface. Discontinuity in use of the area was suggested between the time when the complete pots were buried, which had to be no later than 400 BC, and the earliest preserved houses, used after AD 400. I carefully examined all the sherds from the excavated sediments, and found none of the pottery I would expect in sites occupied during those eight centuries. Clearly not a house, the early terrace was constructed long before the period targeted in our research design. What was the right thing to do now?

Here it is good to remember that household archaeology is a programmatic approach to research concerning everyday activities. It is not, or should not be, an end in itself. Our reasons for engaging in household archaeology had become to understand how the societies of the Ulua Valley contemporary with Classic Maya city-states maintained a lower level of inequality, and a more widely shared standard of living, that allowed for stable occupation of villages and towns for many centuries. We used the concept of heterarchy to envisage how different social actors could have had authority in one area of life, but not in every area, providing checks on the exercise of social power. This represented, for me, a logical outcome of the fusion of feminist and social theory: our goal as anthropological archaeologists should be to contest the naturalization of the kinds of structures we see around us today, and take for granted, that historical analysis shows are just one way people have lived.

So our interests were not limited to understanding basic household maintenance tasks, but rather concerned how people, acting individually and as part of co-residential groups, built social ties, created and reinforced limited authority, and reproduced that authority over generations as part of identities at the scale of the residential group, the village, and the town. Ignoring the earliest site ever identified in the lower Ulua Valley because the features we identified were not residences would have been irresponsible, especially knowing the site was about to be destroyed or at least made inaccessible by construction.

Our entire project was guided by the desire to integrate a research agenda in a field practice aimed at sites being destroyed. What we needed was to ask what work on this earlier period might tell us about the everyday lives of people and the way authority was asserted and countered. Luckily, the site had something to say on this topic.

Puerto Escondido: Understanding Everyday Life in a Cosmopolitan Village

Thinking this would be our last season at Puerto Escondido, we quickly laid out a compact group of excavation units in the area where the cached pots were uncovered (Joyce and Henderson 2001). As they excavated, students noted the unusual character of the sediments on the eastern side of this block of 6 × 8 m, which looked burned and formed distinct shapes. We realized it *was* burned, the remains of a building of "wattle and daub" construction, clay covering a frame of sticks, preserved as fired clay with impressions of the framework. When we reached the bottom of this mass of fill, we uncovered a floor. Covering part of the floor were broken pieces of bowls and small jars, polished black and gray, many with deeply carved designs, some with red pigment rubbed into the carved areas after the pot was fired. Someone had had a feast, and ended it by burning down the house, burying whole jars in the fill, before encapsulating the whole thing in clay to form a large terrace.

We were running out of time. We knew we had to try to come back.

Based on the unprecedented age of the finds, the Institute persuaded the developers to hold off on further construction. We developed plans for a third field season, now with a new but related focus: understanding early village life at Puerto Escondido in relation to villages across Mexico and Central America. In 1996 and 1997, with funding from private foundations, and a smaller team of returning volunteers and local workers, we targeted the burned house and started an excavation in one 4 × 2-m area that would ultimately reach 3 m deeper, producing evidence of centuries of rebuilding of a domestic structure in the same place, with postholes and a hearth repeatedly re-established over multiple generations (Joyce 2007).

The carved designs on ceramics from the burned house floor were comparable to those of Mexico's Gulf Coast Olmec culture, so we began to examine all lines of evidence for participation by early residents of Puerto Escondido in long-distance social and economic exchanges (Joyce and Henderson 2010). Students analyzed samples of marble vessels and obsidian blades and flakes for undergraduate theses and doctoral dissertations. Project members completed geoarchaeological prospecting in the mountains. We found collaborators who tested sherds from pots and confirmed that some, dating as early as 1150 BC, had contained cacao (Joyce and Henderson 2007).

We continued to use the excavation methods we had initially adopted to document household-scale activities. These involved careful dissection of deposits, removing layers as small as 1 cm. This kind of excavation was unusual in Mesoamerican archaeology. Using this fine-grained excavation method totally transformed how we thought of sites: rather than layer-cakes of levels representing chunks of time, sites were products of activities that produced deposits and removed them, through human and natural agencies, at scales from the momentary to the geological.

We identified a specific historical question we needed to settle: was the deeply buried house, and its history and wealth, evidence of the common way of life in the early village? Or was this house the center of residence of a group within the early village that consolidated more authority than other contemporaries had? To respond, we sought funding from the National Science Foundation to use randomly placed test pits to see whether buried deposits from the older period could be identified in other parts of the site. If they were, we could expand excavations to produce comparable datasets from other sectors of the early village.

This final excavation season was delayed until 2000 by the devastation Hurricane Mitch caused in 1998. Our field crew was our largest yet, with just under 30 participants. Our randomly placed test pits did identify other locations with early remains, and we expanded excavation in three places, one in the area we originally explored in Operation 2. In each of the new excavations, we documented likely residential features and use of symbolic objects in household-based rituals (Joyce 2011).

The expansion of histories of village life was inherently important in this region, where conventional archaeological models expected development of social "complexity" to lag behind more "advanced" regions, like the Mexican Gulf Coast, or be a result of contact with other societies. Yet establishing that we had a very early village did not require repeated seasons of research and specialist analyses. Those were undertaken to explore theoretical concepts of heterarchy at the regional level and practice at the level of daily life.

Theories that equated complexity with constantly increasing hierarchy would have predicted concentration of control of resources in the hands of a small elite. We looked for the ways social differences were materially created, displayed, and correlated with differences in resource use that they potentially legitimated or naturalized. In contrast to theories that presented processes operating above the level of the everyday as determining constraints on action, we looked at the ways daily practices were creative and effective in changing the course of Puerto Escondido's history.

All the neighborhoods of the early village that we sampled used the same kinds of ceramic vessels and stone tools in daily practices, but the houses residents built of wattle and daub were sometimes finished in plaster, sometimes built on stone foundations, and other times had neither, making the dwelling a focus of differentiation in an otherwise relatively uniform community. Some neighborhoods used more imported materials than others. Not everyone used pottery with carved motifs like those we encountered in the burned house. These practices were independent of each other, as we would expect in an emerging heterarchical network where actors pursued different pathways of distinction. Residents of one neighborhood preserved a fragment of a close to life-size stone statue, suggesting the presence of individual people considered worthy of historical commemoration, not necessarily controlling the importation of goods or even the use of symbolic materials.

We persisted in our investigation of Puerto Escondido due to this potential as a case study of the complexity of complexity. It was that goal that drove us to explore different neighborhoods and examine practices independently of each other.

Reflections and Lessons Learned

Puerto Escondido diverted our regional-scale project on household variation away from understanding the period contemporary with Classic Maya city-states and redirected us to the much earlier relationship of Honduras to the Gulf Coast Olmec culture. Yet we maintained our core interest in understanding limited hierarchy as a product of everyday actions, perceptible at the scale of the dwelling through the application of fine-grained excavation methods.

We maintained a commitment to acting as a means of cultural resource management in a country with limited ability to document sites before urgently needed development projects were undertaken. Our selection of sites had to be flexible, and that ended up leading us to obtain better data for understanding our questions in a developmental framework. We understand more today about how heterarchy worked over thousands of years and can see moments when people in certain settlements pushed (unsuccessfully) to consolidate power in more limited hierarchies.

The shift to an earlier period made the information we produced significant to a wider community of archaeologists. The trade-off, given that Puerto Escondido is deeply buried, is that our time and effort produced less data on the spatial organization of activities. Our interpretations are based on more fragmented information than if we had continued with wide area excavations of house compounds in sites of the later period.

Is there a broader lesson here? Perhaps it is simply that a theoretical issue can inform a multitude of specific efforts in the field. We cannot force sites to produce the kinds of data we predict in our research design. We have to be prepared to answer the question, "how can this feature be understood from the perspective of my theoretical agenda?" Owing to the demands of funding agencies, we tend to invest most of our effort in defining specific data sets that we will produce to address specific questions. It is useful to be open to re-thinking our questions when the data refuse to behave.

We may even want to consider funding proposals as limiting, because they require more easily defined, answerable questions. I had no difficulty writing a proposal to the National Science Foundation that centered on assessing the strength of the three main models for the emergence of social complexity in Mesoamerica at Puerto Escondido. Yet, once we dated the initiation of plant cultivation, analyzed sources of imported obsidian, and inventoried the symbolic repertoire of incised pottery, stamps and seals, and sculpture, my work to "answer" this question was done. The potential the site offered, however, far exceeded those limited topics, and it would have been irresponsible to deconstruct long-preserved deposits without opening up new lines of inquiry to address how these materials came into being and what they did at this place in the past.

It took accidentally excavating an early Central American village for me to discover that. I don't regret responding to the challenge of the site. It expanded my understanding of inequality, social difference, and the long-term effects of repeated practice in ways that shaped my theoretical writing more than the theoretical writing shaped this fieldwork.

Paired Reading

Joyce, Rosemary A. and John S. Henderson. 2001. "Beginnings of Village Life in Eastern Mesoamerica." *Latin American Antiquity*, 12: 5–24. DOI: 10.2307/971754.

References

Hendon, Julia A., Rosemary A. Joyce, and Jeanne Lopiparo. 2014. *Material Relations: The Marriage Figurines of Prehispanic Honduras.* Boulder, CO: University Press of Colorado.

Joyce, Rosemary A. 2004. "Unintended Consequences? Monumentality as a Novel Experience in Formative Mesoamerica." *Journal of Archaeological Method and Theory*, 11: 5–29. DOI: 10.1023/B:JARM.0000014346.87569.4a.

Joyce, Rosemary A. 2007. "Building Houses: The Materialization of Lasting Identity in Formative Mesoamerica." In *The Durable House: House Society Models in Archaeology*, edited by Robin Beck, 53–72. Carbondale, IL: Center for Archaeological Investigations, Southern Illinois University.

Joyce, Rosemary A. 2011. "In the Beginning: The Experience of Residential Burial in Prehispanic Honduras." In *Residential Burial: A Multiregional Exploration*, edited by Ron L. Adams and Stacie King, 33–43. Archeological Papers of the American Anthropological Association, Volume 20. Malden, MA: Wiley-Blackwell.

Joyce, Rosemary A. 2013. "Surrounded by Beauty: Central America before 1500." In *Revealing Ancestral Central America*, edited by Rosemary A. Joyce, 13–22. Washington, DC: Smithsonian Institution Latin Center/National Museum of the American Indian.

Joyce, Rosemary A. and John S. Henderson. 2001. "Beginnings of Village Life in Eastern Mesoamerica." *Latin American Antiquity*, 12: 5–24. DOI: 10.2307/971754.

Joyce, Rosemary A. and John S. Henderson. 2007. "From Feasting to Cuisine: Implications of Archaeological Research in an Early Honduran Village." *American Anthropologist*, 109: 642–653. DOI: 10.1525/aa.2007.109.4.642.

Joyce, Rosemary A. and John S. Henderson. 2010. "Being 'Olmec' in Formative Honduras." *Ancient Mesoamerica*, 21: 187–200. DOI: 10.1017/S0956536110000052.

Joyce, Rosemary A. and Julia A. Hendon. 2000. "Heterarchy, History, and Material Reality: 'Communities' in Late Classic Honduras." In *The Archaeology of Communities: A New World Perspective*, edited by Marcello-Andrea Canuto and Jason Yaeger, 143–159. London: Routledge.

17

Slouching Towards Theory: Implementing Bioarchaeological Research at Petra, Jordan
Megan A. Perry

Project Summary

The Petra North Ridge Project (PNRP) is an interdisciplinary effort to explore the lives of first-century BC to fourth-century AD inhabitants of Petra, Jordan. This chapter explores the challenges and expectations of developing a new methodological approach, bioarchaeology, in addition to generating anthropologically-informed research questions in a region where archaeology has had a humanistic, primarily cultural-historical approach. As a result, applying theoretical perspectives developed in other parts of the world remains difficult because of the nature of the information generated from these projects. In addition, bioarchaeology in the Near East is underdeveloped, and comparative data are scarce. In order to fill these knowledge gaps and provide proper contextualization of the human skeletal data from Petra, the project described here necessitated the inclusion of students and professionals with field and laboratory specialties necessary for analyzing the diverse data produced by the excavation. In addition, it served as a field school for multiple institutions. As a result, the field crew of the project ranges from 35 to 45 individuals in addition to 15–20 employees from the local community. Therefore, the logistical and financial difficulties involved in overseeing a relatively large project in another country are addressed.

Short Biographical Account

I started working on archaeological excavations in Jordan in 1993 and very quickly fell in love with the country's history, landscape, and people. At the same time, I began developing a strong interest in bioarchaeology and entered a graduate program to that end in 1995. Even then I realized that, as a bioarchaeologist and anthropologically-trained archaeologist, I had a long road ahead of me. At that time, not only did Jordan lack any scientific, problem-oriented human osteological research, but anthropologically-oriented archaeological research had primarily focused on prehistoric periods, not the historical periods that interested me.

Starting from the ground up meant that, throughout my career, I have felt my theoretical sophistication lagged behind those of my colleagues working in other regions who can benefit from a longer history of bioarchaeological and anthropologically-oriented archaeological research. My early scholarship instead focused on gathering basic information. What factors affect preservation of human skeletal remains in Jordan? What kinds of mortuary features exist? How many burials can be expected in communal tombs? Where are they located? What kinds of data can we gather to establish a baseline for future comparative analyses?

Engaging Archaeology: 25 Case Studies in Research Practice, First Edition. Edited by Stephen W. Silliman.
© 2018 John Wiley & Sons, Inc. Published 2018 by John Wiley & Sons, Inc.

My long-term research goals involve understanding how human remains embody the individual, their lived experiences, their group identity, and the emotions and actions surrounding their death. I also was interested in how the diverse cultural influences on the Nabateans, who ruled the area from third century BC until the early second century AD, impacted these variables, and how they might have altered with the Roman annexation in AD 106. The detailed documentation and publication of these contexts, particularly in terms of the human skeletal remains, remains highly underdeveloped in this region. The skeletons themselves have been curated poorly, if kept at all. Thus, I needed to explore the mortuary contexts within which these bodies existed through a project that welcomed a bioarchaeologist's involvement in research design and implementation. Through a series of events, I ended up as co-director and bioarchaeologist of the Petra North Ridge Project, where I could finally engage in large-scale, methodologically-sound excavation of tombs within the Nabataean capital city.

Source of Project

As with most fundamental moments in my life, my involvement in the Petra North Ridge Project (PNRP) emerged through luck and circumstance (Figure 17.1). I was living in Amman in 1999, working on my doctoral dissertation and finishing a part-time position at the American Center of Oriental Research (ACOR) when its Associate Director, Patricia M. Bikai, invited me to assist her with the excavation of a first-century AD tomb that had been revealed during ACOR's excavations of the Ridge Church in Petra. With that, I became the Assistant Director of the project, which also included excavating and restoring a fifth- to sixth-century Byzantine chapel complex through 2002. We did not even need to explore funding sources during this period due to a substantial endowment to ACOR from USAID. It didn't matter that until then most of my research focused on later periods, in other parts of the country. The PNRP fell into my lap, and I loved it.

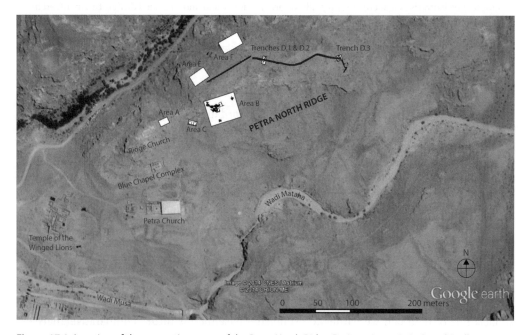

Figure 17.1 Location of the excavation areas of the Petra North Ridge Project. Areas A, B, C, and D all contain domestic areas, Area E the purported bath complex, and Areas B and F the tombs.

The good life of endowment-funded research ended in 2002. Dr. Bikai retired from ACOR and the field, and I went on to lay the groundwork for continued excavations on the North Ridge focusing primarily on the tombs. Our excavations had discovered that other shaft chamber tombs underlay the Byzantine structures, and many other tombs along the Ridge had been exposed through tomb looting and soil erosion. It was also important that I continue the Department of Antiquities permit to 1) transfer the permit into my name by having Dr. Bikai and I be co-directors, and then the following season, establish me as the director, and 2) keep the permit active to enable future large-scale research on the Ridge. I began my faculty position at East Carolina University in 2003, and that gave me the chance to seek internal seed grants to move this research forward. I received a small grant in 2005 to bring four graduate students with me to Petra to digitally map the archaeological features visible on the western end of the North Ridge, which included structures likely dating from the first century AD through the Ottoman era, relatively recent terracing systems, and the first-century BC to first-century AD tombs.

I was a tenure-track professor during this period and therefore still had to generate data and publish peer-reviewed articles while applying for federal grants for larger-scale excavation of the North Ridge. This balance is important, for it can be easy to doggedly focus on pursing one long-term research trajectory at the expense of creating a broader and more immediate research portfolio necessary for tenure and promotion. Therefore, it is essential to get involved in other projects or avail yourself of other datasets to generate publications while putting together a larger research project. In addition, keep a clear focus on how these different studies relate on a broader level to provide a coherent research portfolio. In graduate school, for example, professors may hand over data for you to analyze that you think may be completely unrelated to your longer-term project. The ability to link what appear to be disparate datasets into a broader research framework, and to synthesize what can appear to be a willy-nilly set of projects into a coherent intellectual activity, reflects an individual's ability as a scholar.

Theoretical Framework

Developing the theoretical framework was the greatest challenge in building the PNRP, primarily due to the limitations posed by current archaeological research in the region and the broad scope of the project. The PNRP in the pre-2002 years opened up the adventure of archaeological fieldwork and rural Jordan to diplomats, members of the royal family, expats, and other residents of Amman who rarely left the city's confines. However, its intellectual contributions to Petra's Byzantine history or Nabataean mortuary rituals were realized *ex post facto*. The PNRP's theoretical perspective mirrored that of most archaeological projects in the Near East – straight-up culture history (Childe 1929). Many project directors in Jordan, most of whom are not trained in anthropology, rarely have the incentive to develop a more sophisticated theoretical perspective beyond culture history primarily because they often do not have to seek external funding. A large number of projects instead receive continuous, often non-competitive funding from private individuals, government or non-profit organizations, field school tuitions, or their own institutions. Since the first step to a successful grant proposal is developing research questions, hypotheses, and alternate hypotheses, all informed by a disciplinary theoretical framework, these projects rarely spend their time seriously considering the theoretical framework of their specific project beyond it providing some information about people in the past.

The project's large scope also impacted the development of an overall theoretical perspective. I realized that, in order to get to the tombs, we had to excavate overlying structures that I hypothesized were Byzantine, based on the prevalence of Byzantine ecclesiastical structures on the Ridge. I felt that not having a specific research agenda for these overlying structures would be a red flag to the proposal's reviewers. Finally, the lack of published data on skeletal remains or mortuary contexts from Petra, and Jordan in general, made any bioarchaeological hypotheses I generated risky due to lack of comparative data.

In my first attempts at gaining external funding I attempted to combine the bioarchaeological and domestic components of the project through three research issues that tracked the occupational history of the Ridge: 1) Nabataean cultural influences as reflected in mortuary ritual, population genetics, and isotopic evidence of migration, 2) the biological impact of Roman annexation, by comparing the Petra skeletons to those in post-AD 106 cemeteries, and 3) the economic activities in the Byzantine period (thought to be a "dark age" in Petra's history). Grant reviewers with the National Endowment for the Humanities (NEH) and the National Science Foundation (NSF) both commented negatively on the broad reach of the project; they claimed that I was "trying to do too much" and that my focus was too "culture-historical." The first aspect could easily be alleviated by bringing on a co-director who also had the expertise to deal with the huge corpus of ceramic data that the tombs produced (see Bikai and Perry 2001). One of my mentors and a prominent ceramic typologist, S. Thomas Parker, just happened to be searching for a new field project in the Classical Near East, preferably one with a domestic component. We thus joined forces, with me focusing on the tombs and bioarchaeology, and Tom on the ceramics and occupational history and use of the domestic areas (Parker 2016; Perry 2016).

In general, even though I was trained in social theory and well-read on bioarchaeological studies in other regions, I still found it very difficult to go beyond culture history in my research development of the PNRP. I could almost sense the frustration of grant proposal reviewers over the next proposal iterations – "she has this great site, these interesting questions, very sound methods, yet the project is not theoretically-grounded." Parker and I managed to have a 2012 season funded by various smaller grants, but knew that we needed larger sources of funding to support such a diverse project. Thankfully, our 2014 and 2016 seasons were mostly funded by an eventually successful grant from the NEH, which not only does not have as much of an issue with culture history, but also found the combined bioarchaeological and domestic components of the project, framed as a means to reconstruct Petra's disease ecology, intriguing and unique. This rather outdated functionalist, systems-theory approach, however, did not impress the NSF, and again they questioned culture-historical nature of the project.

It was after the excavation of six tombs on the North Ridge by the end of the 2014 season that I realized how we could explore mortuary behavior at Petra using a theoretical framework that would be meaningful for archaeological investigations of death and body treatment. All of the tombs contained partially or completely articulated remains within commingled assemblages. I hypothesized that, while there was a general homogeneity in burial practices at Petra, each extended family utilizing a tomb expressed their unique identities through variations in mortuary behavior. This follows closely with Bourdieu's and Giddens' observations that individual agency can affect and is impacted by a larger social construction of behavior, which Giddens termed "structuration" (Bourdieu 1977; Giddens 1984). As noted by Joyce (2001), mortuary contexts provide a remarkably nuanced reflection of individual behavior in addition to larger social ideologies that make them particularly well-suited for exploring the construction and maintenance of identity. Our proposed method of detailed documentation of archaeological strata in complex tomb deposits would reveal tomb-specific mortuary behaviors usually out of archaeologists' reach. We also intended to reveal areas of homogeneity between the tombs, perhaps representing areas of ritual under larger social regulation.

A geospatial sciences colleague and I developed a method for geospatial analysis of the assemblages to determine the human and natural processes involved in their formation, but also identify cycles of mortuary behavior within the tombs that resulted in commingling. This focus on commingled assemblages enabled their proper analysis and better aligned them with current anthropological investigations into embodiment, identity, and commemoration. While we did not have the time to generate a successful grant application before we utilized this method during the 2016 season, I believe that the reviewers' comments and high scores generated by our proposal to the NSF meant we would have been selected for funding after one or two revisions. And no one accused this proposal as being too "culture-historical."

The lesson here is not that culture history is "bad." In underexplored regions, researchers first need to lay the groundwork by generating enough data to reveal patterns that can be explored further. Sometimes the lacunae of knowledge are so wide that the research focus of a project becomes unwieldy. In this case, culture history – figuring out the "who" and the "where" – helped us get through this stage before we could address the more intriguing "why" and "how." The issues of using an underutilized bioarchaeological perspective and melding it with the investigation of domestic areas meant it took almost 20 years to situate the project within a theoretical perspective relevant to anthropology at a global, diachronic level.

Methods

The multifaceted nature of the PNRP means that different specialists rely on particular methods for their data collection and analysis. Since I am the project's bioarchaeologist, I focus only on methods related to field recovery and analysis of the human skeletal remains. The types of data collection and analysis that have and will be performed are dictated by my theoretical perspective as well as needs and interests that emerge from colleagues and students. During the muddling early phases of the project, methods that I wished to use (and were familiar with) drove the perspective that I eventually had. However, once I had a theoretical perspective which involved identifying homogeneity in tomb-level versus site-level mortuary rituals, I sought out methods that would reveal the level of detail and types of data for this analysis.

The excavation techniques utilized by the PNRP follow standard operating procedure in the Near East: a modified Wheeler-Kenyon method of stratigraphic excavation (Kenyon 1939; Wheeler 1954). Our new theoretical focus in 2016 to illuminate individual-level and societal-level behaviors included the use of terrestrial laser scanning (TLS) and structure-from-motion (SfM) to document tomb strata and occupational surfaces in the domestic structures and geological sampling of tomb strata for microstratigraphic analysis. In order to complete the proper spatial analysis needed to reveal cycles of mortuary behavior that resulted in commingling, and rule out natural explanations, each bone or major artifact within each scan were given field identification numbers that were used to link geospatial information from the scans with attribute data from bone or artifact analysis through a relational database. Luckily, since much debris and fill had to be removed before any burial or occupation layers were reached, we had time to practice this data collection method in the field before their actual application. Patience was indeed a virtue in this process. In addition, I began micromorphological sampling of tomb strata to allow the assessment and identification of different formation processes occurring to create each tomb stratum (see Karkanas *et al.* 2012). Therefore, the field techniques began with what is standard in the region but evolved to include new methods to address our more specific research questions.

On the other hand, the bioarchaeological methods that I was interested in using drove the theoretical perspective of the earlier successful NEH grant. This has primarily been the case in my bioarchaeological work in Jordan. Skeletal remains – if they are collected – are not done so with any specific goal or to answer any specific research question within a particular theoretical construct. Therefore I am usually contacted to do basic documentation and collect any other data that I wish to. My dissertation had been to assess the impact of imperial interests of Rome and Byzantium in their eastern provinces, focusing specifically on health or patterns of mobility (Perry 2002). Thus, most of my bioarchaeological research has continued along this vein. The PNRP gave me the chance to collect data on individuals who lived before the Roman annexation of the region to continue this research focus. Therefore, my methods focused on documenting disease, diet, nutrition, and migration patterns. The first iterations of my proposals for major funding included the larger theoretical implications of understanding the biological impacts of imperialism, with mixed success. The expansion of the project to include the domestic areas shifted the application of these methods to understanding Petra's disease ecology in the 2012 NEH application. The skeletal biological data therefore served to establish the adaptive success of Petra's inhabitants within its political, social, and environmental contexts.

Our primary skeletal data included paleopathology and paleodemography to explore disease profiles, nutrition levels, and mortality and fertility patterns, and isotope analyses to assess population mobility and diet. We primarily relied on standard data collection protocol used in bioarchaeology (e.g., Buikstra and Ubelaker's *Standards for Data Collection from Human Skeletal Remains* published in 1994) so as to facilitate comparative studies, and sent our dental enamel and bone samples to established laboratories for isotope analysis. Our largest methodological hurdle for our skeletal analysis was how best to inventory the commingled, fragmented bones that comprised the PNRP assemblage. This remains a thorny issue in bioarchaeology (see Osterholtz *et al.* 2014), but recently a few databases and data collection standards have been developed and shared between bioarchaeologists facing these issues. I invited Anna Osterholtz, creator of a digital database, to join the project in 2014, where she could tailor her skeletal inventory method for the skeletal collection from Petra – which was not unique for Jordan and thus could be applied in other Near Eastern contexts.

Nature of Data

The research questions explored by the PNRP could never be answered without a team of specialists handling different aspects of data collection and analysis – a zooarchaeologist, a paleobotanist, a geologist, a ceramics specialist, a bioarchaeologist, a conservator, a small finds specialist, and a geospatial scientist. My co-director and I knew from experience that a project of this size could not rely on post-hoc assemblage of scientists, but needed people either in the field or able to implement remotely different procedures for organizing the different types of data recovered. Any excavation director has to be prepared for unexpected finds, however. For example, this past season we found museum-quality imported marble statues of Aphrodite and Eros, which not only required specialized conservation skills but also an expert on Greco-Roman marble statuary in the Near East. My problem as an archaeologist is that I tell myself that I will be able to write up this artifact or that interesting assemblage. Don't convince yourself that it is imperative that you study all aspects of your data, even on small projects. It can be difficult to wrangle multiple affiliates to adhere to publication deadlines, but worth it in terms of the quality of research and your time in the long run. If you can, build a small line-item in your grant budgets for post-field analyses to accommodate, for example, travel of another specialist to your lab or the excavation site. Use your contacts to reach out to specialists. Focus your research on your own specific interests.

Even analysis of the human skeletal data has involved multiple researchers. These data can be grouped into "core information" – that related directly to the research questions at hand – and "supplementary data" – that which can add something to the research agenda but are primarily driven by the interests of other parties or which emerged through initial investigations. Observations of bone lesions related to disease and malnutrition, isotopic investigations of diet and immigration levels, and assessment of age-related mortality patterns have been and will be combined with analyses of paleobotanical, zooarchaeological, and architectural data to understand whether or not Petra's ecological, political, and social context created a "healthy" environmental system, the focus of the NEH grant.

Our project is lucky in that the Department of Antiquities of Jordan generally agrees to loan human skeletal remains to researchers' institutions for study. Thus, we packed and shipped the boxes of human bone from Amman to the Bioarchaeology Laboratory at East Carolina University. The ability to take time to analyze the material, particularly without the usual travel expenses, has and will be invaluable for careful study of this complex assemblage. In addition, it will facilitate returning to the sample after the initial data collection to address new questions that arise through our analysis. I would say that this "big data" collection period probably is the most isolating period of the project. Communication between project co-researchers drops off as everyone is involved in the initial documentation. Many projects choose to have yearly meetings or seminars, often coinciding with a major conference, to provide updates and share new results. I think this is important to keep everyone on track and coordinated.

We are just over a year out of the field and have yet to assess whether or not our geospatial, micromorphological, and skeletal data will elucidate cycles of mortuary behavior as we initially hypothesized. The recovery of commingled deposits during the last few days of the season rushed 3D documentation through TLS, and while initial scans looked good while in the field, we can only hope they come together just as well in the lab. I regret not having a specialist on hand for the geomorphological sampling, as collecting these samples proved to be a challenge in the field – one of those instances where I thought, unwisely, "I can do it!" In addition, permits now are necessary to import the soil samples into the United States, and we need to find someone interested in doing the thin sections and analysis.

Reflections

My ultimate goals for the PNRP were to increase the comparative skeletal data and the visibility of bioarchaeology in Jordan. It helped that the project was situated in the capital city of an enigmatic kingdom where mortuary features appear so prominently on the landscape. Here, ANY dataset, no matter how small or imperfect, vastly increases our knowledge of ancient Jordan and contextualizes the small amounts of data that do exist. Consequently, projects that use new methods or data within a region or a discipline can create a large impact in essentially open territory. On the other hand, as noted above, the lack of baseline data makes it difficult to generate research questions specific to a region, or to know that the data recovered are appropriate for applying broader research questions explored elsewhere. In addition, it may be difficult to draw those with the needed expertise already embedded in another geographic area to a new research site. It can be an exciting yet lonely endeavor.

Lessons Learned

Many readers of this book likely will not be embarking on directing a large-scale archaeological field project. I have tried to focus on the difficult yet fulfilling task of breaking disciplinary and methodological boundaries through focusing on implementing an anthropologically-focused archaeological field project in the culture-historically entrenched Near East. Over the years, I have felt "left in the theoretical dust" by friends and colleagues working in regions with long-term and multiple bioarchaeological projects such as Peru, the lower Illinois Valley, or Sudan. As I have scrambled to create a cohesive set of data as a springboard for bioarchaeological research in Jordan, I have come to realize that being a trailblazer may mean sacrificing sophisticated theoretical frameworks and just focusing on moving dirt.

With that being said, each step of the research development process needs to include seeking relevance in current anthropological thought. The questions early in this process will be necessarily vague because of the high risk for not ending up with the data to answer them, which, frankly, does not interest large federal granting agencies. Don't take their possible rejection as a statement on the value of your research. Seek out alternate sources of funding, particularly from regionally-focused organizations that will look upon your research as new and exciting. Try not to directly compare your work to that of your colleagues, for they may have the freedom of working on already-excavated material and have colleagues exploring similar questions in their region. With effort you will be known for building or advancing a discipline in a hitherto unexplored region, which often opens more doors that generating new light on a previously explored question. Or at least that's what I've been told.

Paired Reading

Perry, Megan A. 2016. New Light on Nabataean Mortuary Rituals in Petra. In *Studies in the History and Archaeology of Jordan XII*, edited by Monther Jamhawi, 385–398. Amman: Department of Antiquities.

References

Bikai, Patricia M. and Megan A. Perry. 2001. "Petra North Ridge Project Tombs 1 and 2: Preliminary Report." *Bulletin of the American Schools of Oriental Research*, 104: 59–78.

Bourdieu, Pierre. 1977. *Outline of a Theory of Practice*. Cambridge: Cambridge University Press.

Childe, V. Gordon. 1929. *The Danube in Prehistory*. Oxford: Clarendon Press.

Giddens, Anthony. 1984. *The Constitution of Society: Outline of the Theory of Structuration*. Cambridge: Cambridge University Press.

Joyce, Rosemary A. 2001. "Burying the Dead at Tlatilco: Social Memory and Social Identities." In *Social Memory, Identity, and Death: Anthropological Perspectives on Mortuary Rituals*, edited by Meredith S. Chesson, 12–26. Archeological Papers of the American Anthropological Association 10. Arlington, VA: American Anthropological Association. DOI: 10.1525/ap3a.2001.10.1.1.

Karkanas, Panagiotis, Mary K. Dabney, Angus Smith, and James C. Wright. 2012. "The Geoarchaeology of Mycenaean Chamber Tombs." *Journal of Archaeological Science*, 39: 2722–2732. DOI: 10.1016/j.jas.2012.04.016.

Kenyon, Kathleen. 1939. "Excavation Methods in Palestine." *Palestine Exploration Quarterly*, 71: 29–40. DOI: 10.1179/peq.1939.71.1.29.

Osterholtz, Anna J., Kathryn M. Baustian, Debra L. Martin, and Daniel T. Potts. 2014. "Commingled Human Skeletal Assemblages: Integrative Techniques in Determination of the MNI/MNE." In *Commingled and Disarticulated Human Remains: Working Toward Improved Theory, Method, and Data*, edited by Anne J. Osterholtz, Kathryn M. Baustian, and Debra L. Martin, 35–50. New York: Springer.

Parker, S. Thomas. 2016. "The Petra North Ridge Project: Domestic Structures and the City Wall." In *Studies in the History and Archaeology of Jordan XII*, edited by Monther Jamhawi, 587–595. Amman: Department of Antiquities.

Perry, Megan A. 2002. "Health, Labor, and Political Economy: A Bioarchaeological Analysis of Three Communities in *Provincia Arabia*." PhD Dissertation. Albuquerque, NM: University of New Mexico.

Perry, Megan A. 2016. New Light on Nabataean Mortuary Rituals in Petra. In *Studies in the History and Archaeology of Jordan XII*, edited by Monther Jamhawi, 385–398. Amman: Department of Antiquities.

Wheeler, Mortimer. 1954. *Archaeology from the Earth*. Oxford: Clarendon Press.

18

In Archaeology, "You Get What You Get," and Most of the Time What You Get Is Unexpected: Investigating Paleoindians in Western North America

Ted Goebel

Project Summary

In field archaeology, even the best-reasoned expectations can fail to accurately predict outcomes. This is what happened at Bonneville Estates Rockshelter, Nevada, where a team of researchers developed a long-term, multi-disciplinary investigation of Paleoindian ecology and adaptation. After nine years of excavation, the variety of materials recovered led to a new interpretation of Great Basin Paleoindians at odds with the conventionally held view that they were highly mobile big-game hunters who tipped their spears with fluted bifacial points. Instead, the team found that the region's first human inhabitants exploited a diverse array of fauna and flora gathered from stable campsites, using various technologies including stemmed bifacial points and nets, typically made on local raw materials. Without a doubt the first Americans were quick to adapt to the diverse challenges their New World presented, a lesson students of archaeology will do well to follow as they develop and implement their own forays into human prehistory.

Introduction

Archaeologists do not have X-ray vision, so to recover evidence of past human activities we must excavate into the ground. This is the case whether we are conducting a survey in search of new sites, or investigating a previously known site considered to have an especially important story to tell. Excavation of the buried record provides us not only with perishable and more durable remains of past cultures, but also a three-dimensional context for interpreting chronology and spatial relationships. As a result, archaeologists have repeatedly developed and applied sophisticated models for predicting where sites of different ages and functions occur on a regional scale and where different kinds of archaeological features occur at a site scale. When digging is over, however, seldom have the predicted discoveries or hypothesized results materialized, and rarely have we accomplished what we actually set out to do.

This is one of the most important lessons I learned from my graduate advisor, the late Dr. W. Roger Powers, a professor of anthropology at the University of Alaska Fairbanks. During our first field season together in 1986 excavating the late Pleistocene Walker Road site in central Alaska, the lesson seemed to repeat itself constantly. My first 1 × 1 m excavation unit turned out to be practically sterile, while adjacent units were rich in 13,000-year-old artifacts. Roger's response was, "Ted, archaeology is like that – you get what you get." As the summer continued,

Engaging Archaeology: 25 Case Studies in Research Practice, First Edition. Edited by Stephen W. Silliman.
© 2018 John Wiley & Sons, Inc. Published 2018 by John Wiley & Sons, Inc.

it turned out to be one of the wettest on record for the Fairbanks area, and incessant rain slowed the excavation considerably, preventing us from completing even 50% of the field season's goal. Sitting around a fire on the last night of the summer, in response to our grumbling about how little we had accomplished, Roger simply mused, "You get what you get."

Roger's maxim replayed itself time and again during my years as a graduate student. The following summer Roger directed a few of us to survey for more early sites like Walker Road, but after spending several weeks digging a lot of test pits as much as 2 m deep, no new sites materialized. Roger's predictable response was "You get what you get – next time it may be better." Some years later, upon returning from a long dissertation trip in Siberia and telling Roger that one of the most important Paleolithic assemblages I had planned to study had not been available, he responded "Working in Russia is like that – you get what you get." But as our excavations at Walker Road continued, the positive side of Roger's archaeological maxim began to play out, too. By 1990, after four field seasons, we had excavated more than 100 m^2, and through those excavations we had actually "got" quite a lot: one of the largest assemblages of late Pleistocene stone tools still known from Alaska; two well-preserved hearth features filled with charcoal and calcined bone; and several well-defined activity areas, two of which we interpreted to potentially represent the spatial limits of some of North America's oldest dwellings. After years of hard work, Roger was right, and the information we had assembled turned out to be pretty important.

This is the problem all Paleolithic and Paleoindian archaeologists face. Early human sites are typically small, deeply buried, and imperceptible from the surface, and as a result extremely difficult to find and access. The investment of time and resources is always high, while frequently the return is not as anticipated (or desired). Sometimes, however, what we unexpectedly "get" in the field is remarkably positive, and it is these situations that make us return year after year, no matter how difficult the situation or how long the season. Let me explain with an example, our discovery and investigation of the incredibly well-preserved and unique Paleoindian occupation of Bonneville Estates Rockshelter, Nevada.

Exploring Bonneville Estates Rockshelter

Upon earning a PhD degree in Alaska, an academic job offer led me to Southern Oregon University, where I began to investigate Paleoindian archaeology in the Great Basin region. This path eventually led me to Bonneville Estates Rockshelter, a "dry cave" located in eastern Nevada, on the ancient shoreline of the now dry Lake Bonneville, about 100 miles west of Salt Lake City, Utah (Figure 18.1a, b). In the year 2000, my colleagues and I visited the shelter together for the first time to consider its potential for exploring hunter-gatherer adaptation to climate and environmental change in the Desert West. From past work we knew that protected sites like Bonneville Estates often contain well-preserved remains of ancient human cultures as well as plants and animals – not just stone tools and animal bones but also perishable articles like baskets, twines, sandals, dart and arrow shafts, seeds, nuts, and even desiccated human fecal matter (coprolites). Studies of these well-preserved records have allowed us to expand our understanding of the Great Basin Desert's prehistoric environments and cultures much further than in other more mesic settings where soil processes quickly break down buried organic material. We predicted that Bonneville Estates Rockshelter would contain such a record, given that it is one of the most prominent natural shelters along the western margin of the Bonneville Basin, a place where ancient humans were known to have frequented since the Ice Age. As we were to discover during the next several years of excavation, though, our work at Bonneville

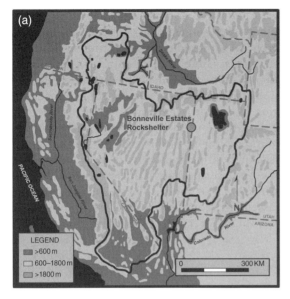

Figure 18.1 Map, photograph, and artifacts of Bonneville Estates Rockshelter in the Great Basin. (a) Map showing location of Bonneville Estates Rockshelter in the Great Basin; (b) View of the rockshelter; (c) Materials recovered from the excavation: 1, sage grouse bone with cut marks; 2–6, 8–11, stemmed-point fragments; 7, katydid carcass with hind legs removed; 12–15, needle fragments; 16–17, bone-bead preforms; 18, antler retoucher; 19, eyed needle; 20–22, twine fragments. Photographs by the author.

Estates was going to bring to light many unexpected revelations about Paleoindian behavior during the late Pleistocene.

The first surprise came during our initial excavation season in 2001. For many years, Bonneville Estates had been extensively looted by illegal digging, and our first task was to clean exposed profiles of looters' pits, so that we could quickly establish the shelter's geological and cultural stratigraphy. We found a series of well-preserved cultural layers with dart and arrow points typologically assignable to the entire Archaic sequence of the Great Basin's prehistoric record, from 8000 calendar years ago (cal BP) to historic times. These cultural layers were filled with plant debris, most of it anthropogenic and having been carried into the shelter by humans, but some of it biogenic, likely the product of collecting packrats, *Neotoma cinerea*. At the base of the early Archaic occupation we found a hard rocky layer that early investigators in the shelter had labeled as bedrock. To be sure, we traded in our trowels for rock hammers and began to pick away at the rock, after a few days realizing that it was not bedrock at all but compacted rubble from a lengthy period of rock fall from the shelter's ceiling. For our field school students, digging through this stratigraphic layer was no easy task, and in response to their repeated questions of "How much farther should I dig?" Kelly Graf and I repeatedly encouraged, "Keep going – let's see what we get." On the last day of the field school, student Gabe Ferley was the first to reach the bottom of the rock fall, exclaiming "I think I found charcoal!" What she had found turned out to be a well-preserved hearth feature full of bits of charred wood, a few stone flakes, and fragments of animal bones. Within a month we had a radiocarbon date on the hearth – it told us that Paleoindians had visited the shelter several centuries earlier than 12,000 cal BP, the very end of the Pleistocene.

Armed with this new discovery, during the winter of 2001–2002, we developed and submitted a proposal to the US National Science Foundation for a multi-year, interdisciplinary field project. Paleoindian archaeological sites were common in the Great Basin, but most occurred in surficial, open-air settings that were undatable, not in buried contexts like rockshelters that could be dated and could yield important information about subsistence and perishable technology. Accordingly, in the proposal we designed an excavation project that would ultimately provide one of the first glimpses into the lifeways of Great Basin Paleoindians during the late Pleistocene, a time of dramatic climate change, animal extinctions, and desertification. We fully expected that in a two-year excavation project we would find the first evidence from the region that, as in other areas of North America, Paleoindians were highly mobile hunters of soon-to-be-extinct megafauna, such as mammoth (*Mammuthus columbi*), bison (*Bison antiquus*), and possibly even horse (*Equus* sp.). We also expected their tool kits to be focused on hunting and centered on stone weapon tips like Clovis fluted points, some of the earliest spearpoint forms known for the Americas. When we resumed excavations in 2002, this model of Paleoindian behavior was definitely on our minds, and we had assembled a group of scientists who together would investigate the many facets of the rockshelter's record. Once again, though, what we expected to find was not what we got.

Theoretical Perspective

The Bonneville Estates research program was grounded in the theory of cultural ecology, the study of the interrelationship of humans and their environment. The Great Basin was a fitting context, given that pioneering anthropologist Julian Steward had formulated the concept of cultural ecology decades earlier while ethnographically studying the local Shoshone and Paiute peoples of Nevada and eastern California. Through years of painstaking research, Steward carefully documented the technological, subsistence, settlement, and social systems of these hunter-gatherers, exploring how their culture served as a non-biological (or "extra-somatic") means of adaptation, and, in a more general sense, how broadly similar natural settings (e.g., deserts) have led to the evolution of broadly similar human solutions to environmental problems (e.g., the Shoshone/Paiute adaptation in the Great Basin and the San adaptation of the Kalahari, Africa) (Steward 1955). Shortly after Steward's ground-breaking ethnographic work, archaeologist Jesse Jennings developed the related concept of the "Desert Culture," theorizing that humans in the Great Basin had always lived as the traditional Shoshone and Paiute people of the region, being well-adjusted to the desert environment since initial human colonization during the late Pleistocene (Jennings 1957).

However, by the time we had initiated the Bonneville Estates project in 2001, interdisciplinarily-minded paleoecologists and archaeologists had demonstrated with reasonable certainty that Nevada's desert environment had not always been the way it is today and that a series of climate shifts during the past 13,000 years had led to radical environmental changes in moisture, vegetation communities, and animal populations, implying that Jennings' Desert Culture model oversimplified the ancient human experience (e.g., Grayson 1993). To explore the complex interplay of environment and cultural evolution, contemporary Great Basin archaeologists including Robert Bettinger, Robert Elston, Robert Kelly, David Madsen, James O'Connell, and David Zeanah, for example, have been instrumental in the development of human behavioral ecology (and its application to archaeological problems), which attempts to explain the adaptive design (or "fitness") of cultural traits, behaviors, and life histories in an ecological context, and how such cultural variation represents an adaptive solution to the competing demands of environment and social interaction (e.g., Bettinger 1991). This is how we framed the objectives of the Bonneville Estates project: generally, to investigate how prehistoric Great Basin populations had adapted to climate and environmental change since the late Pleistocene; and specifically, to document the poorly understood Paleoindian adaptation of the region.

Methods

To reconstruct and explain human environments and adaptation, the Bonneville Estates project quickly morphed into a multi-disciplinary endeavor with five principal investigators (PIs) and numerous students conducting a variety of analyses. Inside the rockshelter, Kelly Graf, Bryan Hockett, and I directed excavations, which reached as much as 2 m in depth. Excavations were painstakingly slow, given the large volume of materials recovered from the shelter's 12 stratigraphically separate cultural layers. We eventually exposed more than 160 archaeological features, mostly hearths but also a few storage pits and intentional dumps of material. Graf directed the complex stratigraphic assignment of all features and other cultural remains, and as profiles were exposed, she described and mapped their stratigraphies, in the laboratory analyzing sedimentology and developing a radiocarbon chronology of cultural occupations. Hockett and David Schmitt conducted detailed zooarchaeological and paleontological analyses of preserved faunal remains, calculating number of individual specimens present (NISP) and minimum number of individuals (MNI) for each identified species and element. This included bones and teeth of animals as well as carcass parts of economically-important insects. Hockett's analyses also focused on taphonomy, investigating how the faunal assemblages accumulated, whether at the hand of humans or through the behaviors of other animals like carnivores or scavengers (e.g., felids, canids, and birds of prey like owls). Schmitt's analyses of microfauna complemented this by documenting environmental change in the region (Schmitt and Lupo 2012). David Rhode dry sifted, through a series of nested sieves, the hearth samples, separating plant macrofossils from bones, artifacts, and other materials, in addition floating tiny seeds from the smallest fractions of the nested sieves. Rhode's paleobotanical analysis focused on taxonomic identification, but like Hockett's studies, he considered taphonomic features preserved on seeds and other plant parts to determine the agency of accumulation (i.e., whether they were economically important and processed by humans, or the product of animal behavior, for example collecting packrats). My own research focused on the artifacts, performing typological, technological, and raw-material analyses of lithics, in collaboration with students Marion Coe (perishable materials like baskets and twine), Josh Keene and Aria Holmes (geochemical analysis of obsidian tools), and Joshua Lynch (use-wear analysis of projectile points). Together we sought to explore how studies of raw-material procurement as well as artifact form, production, and use could provide insights into the changing role of the rockshelter in the context of hunter-gatherer adaptation from the late Pleistocene through Holocene.

While excavations were underway inside the shelter, research was also conducted outside. Geologist Kenneth Adams described and mapped Bonneville Estates' geomorphic context, interpreting the shelter's physical environment. Palynologist Lisbeth Louderback extracted a 4 m long sediment core from a nearby spring and analyzed its fossil-pollen record to define changes in vegetation communities through time (Louderback and Rhode 2009). We also completed an archaeological survey of the hills surrounding the shelter, identifying additional sites and providing an areal context of the shelter's record. After all, we knew through Steward's early ethnographic work that the Great Basin's foragers had extensive territories, mapping onto resources scattered across the desert during different seasons of the year.

Results

Excavations inside the shelter continued from 2002 through 2009, much longer than we antici-pated, given complexities of the site's stratigraphy and large volume of Archaic materials found in layers above the Paleoindian occupation. By the end of the project we had supplemented funding with a second NSF grant, ultimately excavating $60\,m^2$ of the rockshelter's interior area, digging all $1 \times 1\,m$ units through the 12 Archaic and Paleoindian layers. Gradually over those nine years we uncovered an extensive Paleoindian occupation, finding late Pleistocene remains in nearly every unit excavated (Figure 18.1c).

In the Paleoindian deposits, we distinguished three stratigraphically separate cultural layers that together contained nearly 30 well-preserved hearth features. Graf's dating of charcoal samples from hearths indicated an age of 10,670 cal BP for the uppermost Paleoindian layer, 11,500–11,800 cal BP for the middle layer, and 12,200–12,900 cal BP for the lowest layer (Graf 2007). The oldest two hearths turned out to be synchronous with the age of the Clovis culture elsewhere in North America (12,600–13,000 cal BP), while all the other hearths post-dated Clovis and were contemporaneous with the presumed age of "Great Basin Stemmed" Paleoindian points in the Intermountain West.

The lithic assemblages from the Paleoindian occupations, however, featured seven Great Basin stemmed points and no fluted points (Goebel 2007). All were broken and most displayed evidence of impact breakage, demonstrating their use in hunting activities. Most, however, also displayed signs of reuse as knives after breakage, and overall the lithic tool assemblage contained twice as many flake tools – side scrapers, gravers, denticulates, and retouched flakes – than points. This variation in the tool assemblage suggested that Paleoindians were doing more at Bonneville Estates than preparing to hunt large game. It also suggested that mak-ers of stemmed points were the first humans to colonize this part of the Great Basin, not the makers of Clovis points.

Among the Paleoindian artifacts were several other unusual finds. From one of the early hearths came a tiny eyed needle carved from bone, and nearby were other tip fragments of nee-dles or small awls (Goebel *et al.* 2011). We also found seven small fragments of cordage/twine scattered around the Paleoindian living floor. These ranged in size from 1 to 5 cm long and 1 to 7 mm in diameter, and they were made on a variety of plant fibers and two of them were knot-ted. Their function is not known, but they could be net fragments. Like the diverse stone arti-fact assemblage, these perishable remains indicated a surprisingly broader array of technological activities than normally recovered from Paleoindian contexts.

Faunal remains abounded in the Paleoindian layers, and Hockett's analysis of them unveiled still more surprises. His first look at the emerging assemblage startlingly revealed sage grouse (*Centrocerus urophasianus*), a ground-feeding, terrestrial bird common today in the sagebrush steppe of interior western North America (Hockett 2007, 2015). Many grouse bones (NISP = 619, MNI = 18) showed signs of processing, including cut marks from stone tools and the systematic snapping of wing and leg bones. Remains of leporids (rabbits and hares) abounded as well, with most representing cottontails and pygmy rabbits (*Sylvilagus/Brachylagus*, NISP = 622, MNI = 59), and fewer, jackrabbits (or hares, *Lepus*, NISP = 218, MNI = 13). No bones of now-extinct fauna were recovered; instead identified remains of large mammals represented four extant species: pronghorn, mountain sheep, mule deer, and bison. Their numbers were rela-tively low (together, NISP = 12, MNI = 4), leading to an unexpectedly high small-game index of 0.89, meaning that only 11% of the fauna could be attributed to large mammals, the opposite of our expectations, given previous data from other Paleoindian sites in the American West sug-gesting a big-game-hunting focus.

Beyond the bones, however, there were other signs of a broader-than-expected diet. Around the early hearths, we encountered 21 desiccated carcasses of the western longwing katydid (*Capnobotes occidentalis*). Most were nearly whole but lacked hind legs, a pattern seen ethnographically in the Great Basin, where these kinds of insects (e.g., grasshoppers and crickets) have long been an important part of human diet, being processed through the removal of back legs to keep from damaging the throat (Hockett 2015). In addition, Rhode's analysis of vegetal contents of 11 Paleoindian hearths identified a series of charred remains of plants that might have been gathered by the shelter's earliest inhabitants (Rhode 2007). These included seeds of 15 different grasses, shrubs, and marsh plants, as well as saltbush fruits, cactus spines, and a possible lily bulb. Although many of these could have been brought into the shelter by packrats and other small rodents, some were not available within these small mammals' ranges, arguably suggesting that humans were responsible for their deposition in the hearths. Plant remains of this sort are extremely rare in Paleoindian sites; once again our findings defied the common characterization of Paleoindians as big-game hunters.

Another surprising development related to the procurement of raw materials for the production of stone tools, and what this told us about the scope of Paleoindian mobility. Commonly, early Paleoindians are portrayed as highly mobile hunters who had extensive territories thousands of square kilometers in size. This is based on the conveyance of valuable lithic materials like obsidian (volcanic glass) hundreds of kilometers, or even more than 1000 km in a few cases, from their geological sources. At Bonneville Estates, although finding that most of the obsidian in the assemblage originated from the Browns Bench source about 200 km north-northwest of the shelter, more than 75% of the lithic assemblage was made on locally available cherts and fine-grained volcanics like basalt (Goebel 2007). Even projectile points were often made on these local toolstones. Again the early inhabitants of Bonneville Estates defied expectations. Not only did they rely less on high-quality, hard-to-get obsidian than expected, but also they focused lithic procurement on local resources, together suggesting lower levels of mobility and longer durations of occupation of Bonneville Estates than predicted.

Reflections

What did we get after nine years of excavating at Bonneville Estates Rockshelter? In this case, careful research planning, hard work, and patience succeeded in bringing to light substantial evidence leading to a new understanding of the Paleoindian adaptation in interior western North America. Technologically, the Great Basin's earliest inhabitants appear to have made and used stemmed points, not fluted points, providing support for the theory that Clovis may not have been first, and that west of the Rocky Mountains a different population of Paleoindians existed that was distinct from Clovis. Moreover, early humans of the Great Basin produced a variety of tools that are not commonly seen in other Paleoindian contexts, for example bone needles and awls as well as twine for netting. Likewise, Paleoindians in some environments like the Great Basin did not focus subsistence on large, now-extinct fauna like mammoth and bison, but instead broadened subsistence to include a variety of small mammals, insects, and even plant foods. Levels of mobility were variable, too, so that in some environments, like the Bonneville Basin of Utah-Nevada, Paleoindian groups may have moved less, and when they did, their movements may have been shorter in distance than in other regions like the Great Plains. In other words, Paleoindians were intelligent, flexible, and quick to adapt technology, subsistence, and settlement to new circumstances as they explored and colonized North America's varied landscapes.

Lessons Learned

For me as a student a quarter-century ago, and for my own students today, one of the most fundamental lessons has been "you get what you get." No matter how much we prepare, and how well thought-out our research plan may be, we can never completely predict what we will find in the field. Sometimes what we get is really exciting and ground-breaking, as our experience at Bonneville Estates Rockshelter showed. However, even at Bonneville Estates, what we found was not at all what we expected, and the amount of time we spent excavating (nine years!) went well beyond our most liberal expectations. Often, variables outside our control – weather, bears, rattlesnakes, and most importantly the long-ago actions of prehistoric humans – can result in little new information after weeks and even months of field work.

To head off as many of these intangibles as possible, thereby minimizing the negative side of the adage "you get what you get," a well-formulated research design is paramount. Not only should a research design expertly present the theoretical orientation, questions, and objectives of the proposed project, but it should also describe and justify the materials and methods to be used to solve the problem. This justification should carefully predict the outcome of the research, and it should consider the possibility of failure. This is especially important for graduate students developing field-based theses or dissertations, especially when results will be based on new excavations or discovery of new sites. Not only are excavations and surveys expensive and time-intensive, but also expected outcomes often fail to materialize. Excavations take longer to complete than most advanced-degree programs prefer, and they require advanced research teams for their analysis. In today's archaeology, it is impossible for a student researcher to master all these analytical techniques. At Bonneville Estates Rockshelter, for example, given the complexity of the site and diversity of materials recovered, it would have been impossible for any one of our team to have completed the work single-handedly.

Simply put, because we do not have X-ray vision, and because we cannot foretell the future, students should avoid high-risk projects. Time is short, and funding for graduate research is scarce. Thesis and dissertation research should focus on previously excavated assemblages, or if fieldwork is required, it should focus on a tightly defined problem that can be efficiently solved. This is the only way to keep your advisor from remarking after a long frustrating field season, "You get what you get, and sometimes it's not good."

Paired Reading

Goebel, Ted, Bryan Hockett, Kenneth D. Adams, David Rhode, and Kelly Graf. 2011. "Climate, Environment, and Humans in North America's Great Basin during the Younger Dryas, 12,900–11,600 Calendar Years Ago." *Quaternary International*, 242: 479–501. DOI: 10.1016/j.quaint.2011.03.043.

References

Bettinger, Robert L. 1991. *Hunter-Gatherers: Archaeological and Evolutionary Theory*. New York: Plenum Press.

Goebel, Ted. 2007. "Pre-Archaic and Early Archaic Technological Activities at Bonneville Estates Rockshelter: A First Look at the Lithic Artifact Record." In *Paleoindian or Paleoarchaic? Great Basin Human Ecology at the Pleistocene/Holocene Transition*, edited by Kelly E. Graf and Dave N. Schmitt, 156–184. Salt Lake City, UT: University of Utah Press.

Goebel, Ted, Bryan Hockett, Kenneth D. Adams, David Rhode, and Kelly Graf. 2011. "Climate, Environment, and Humans in North America's Great Basin during the Younger Dryas, 12,900–11,600 Calendar Years Ago." *Quaternary International*, 242: 479–501. DOI: 10.1016/j.quaint.2011.03.043.

Graf, Kelly. E. 2007. "Stratigraphy and Chronology of the Pleistocene to Holocene Transition at Bonneville Estates Rockshelter, Eastern Great Basin." In *Paleoindian or Paleoarchaic? Great Basin Human Ecology at the Pleistocene/Holocene Transition*, edited by Kelly E. Graf and Dave N. Schmitt, 82–104. Salt Lake City, UT: University of Utah Press.

Grayson, Donald K. 1993. *The Desert's Past: A Natural Prehistory of the Great Basin*. Washington, DC: Smithsonian Institution Press.

Hockett, Bryan. 2007. "Nutritional Ecology of Late Pleistocene to Middle Holocene Subsistence in the Great Basin: Zooarchaeological Evidence from Bonneville Estates Rockshelter." In *Paleoindian or Paleoarchaic? Great Basin Human Ecology at the Pleistocene/Holocene Transition*, edited by Kelly E. Graf and Dave N. Schmitt, 204–230. Salt Lake City, UT: University of Utah Press.

Hockett, Bryan. 2015. "The Zooarchaeology of Bonneville Estates Rockshelter: 13,000 Years of Great Basin Hunting Strategies." *Journal of Archaeological Science: Reports*, 2: 291–301. DOI: 10.1016/j.jasrep.2015.02.011.

Jennings, Jesse D. 1957. *Danger Cave*. Society for American Archaeology Memoir No. 14. Washington DC: Society for American Archaeology.

Louderback, Lisbeth A., and David E. Rhode. 2009. "15,000 Years of Vegetation Change in the Bonneville Basin: The Blue Lake Pollen Record." *Quaternary Science Reviews*, 28: 308–326. DOI: 10.1016/j.quascirev.2008.09.027.

Rhode, David, and Lisabeth A. Louderback. 2007. "Dietary Plant Use in the Bonneville Basin during the Terminal Pleistocene/Early Holocene Transition." In *Paleoindian or Paleoarchaic? Great Basin Human Ecology at the Pleistocene/Holocene Transition*, edited by Kelly E. Graf and Dave N. Schmitt, 231–247. Salt Lake City, UT: University of Utah Press.

Schmitt, Dave N., and Karen D. Lupo. 2012. "The Bonneville Estates Rockshelter Rodent Fauna and Changes in Late Pleistocene–Middle Holocene Climates and Biogeography in the Northern Bonneville Basin, USA." *Quaternary Research*, 78: 95–102.

Steward, Julian H. 1955. *Theory of Culture Change*. Urbana, IL: University of Illinois Press.

19

Archaeologies of a Medieval Irish Castle: Thinking about Trim

Tadhg O'Keeffe

Project Summary

One of Ireland's most impressive medieval archaeological sites, Trim Castle attracts some 90,000 visitors every year. Decades of research have illuminated its history in considerable detail. Given this level of attention, it is precisely the sort of site from which graduate students steer clear when choosing research projects: how can a budding archaeologist hope to say something new about a site studied so comprehensively and for so long by experienced archaeologists? I show in this chapter that Trim Castle is by no means a closed subject, and I use it to demonstrate to graduate students or young researchers that "expert" opinions can sometimes be challenged by returning to basic principles.

Introduction

Fans of the 1995 movie *Braveheart* will have some familiarity with the site that is under the microscope in this paper. Trim Castle, located about 30 miles north-west of Dublin (Figure 19.1a, b), was adapted temporarily to play the role of the fortified town of York in northern England. *Braveheart* plays fast and loose with historical facts (Wallace did not attack York, for example), but casting Trim as a fortified English settlement was one of the movie's lesser sacrileges: a substantial English castle in Ireland, it was precisely the sort of place that symbolized colonial power, even oppression, among the native Gaelic people of medieval Ireland and Scotland.

Trim's celluloid fame is merely garnish on its greater fame as a heritage site. A large and visually striking fortress built by the single most powerful lord among the Anglo-Normans (or English) in Ireland following their invasion of AD 1169, it is one of the few Irish monuments of its period known to archaeologists outside Ireland. It is also, fittingly, one of the most comprehensively studied medieval monuments in Ireland thanks to a significant investment of money by the State's heritage service. In the early 1970s, when systematic archaeological research on Irish castles was in its infancy, excavations were carried out within the castle's enclosure. In 1993, the main building which visitors know as the "keep" – castle specialists prefer not to use that rather antiquated term any more, preferring the terms "great tower" or *donjon* – was purchased from private ownership by the State. There followed between 1995 and 1998 a more extensive program of excavation, carried out alongside conservation work on the standing walls, and it transformed even more radically our knowledge of the castle's history.

Engaging Archaeology: 25 Case Studies in Research Practice, First Edition. Edited by Stephen W. Silliman.
© 2018 John Wiley & Sons, Inc. Published 2018 by John Wiley & Sons, Inc.

(a)

(b)   (c)

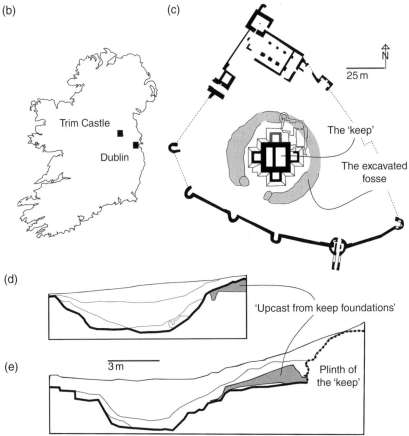

Figure 19.1 Trim Castle, Co. Meath (Ireland). (a) View from the south; (b) Location map; (c) Plan of the castle; (d, e) Excavated sections of the fosse.

Almost all of the work that has ever been carried out at Trim has been published by now, with the monograph by the site's most recent excavator, Alan Hayden, offering what many will regard as the definitive statement on the castle's archaeology and history (Hayden 2011). The conservation work yielded important architectural-historical information on the "keep" which has yet to be published, but there is a summary of its findings in the 2011 monograph.

Asking Questions: Trim Castle as a Research Project

A childhood fascination with ruined castles led me to choose a career in archaeology and to develop a specialty in medieval architectural history. This is not a niche interest. Humans are not just tool-makers; humans are builders. Understanding how and why buildings appear as they do, and understanding how behavior is often shaped by the built environment, are central to archaeology's mission. I had no involvement in the Trim project described above, but that is not to say that Trim is not a project of mine. As a university teacher, I have often thought and talked about the castle, both in the classroom and at the site itself, where my students and I are required to take – and listen to – the official guided tour in order to gain access to the "keep." And I have published some ruminations on aspects of its archaeology over the years. But I have never been involved in any conversations about the site's *official* interpretation and did not see any part of the monograph until it was published. Why, then, have I chosen to discuss Trim in this volume? There are three reasons.

The first reason is to make a very candid point about territoriality. Senior and experienced researchers can be very territorial, and start-of-career researchers can feel deterred from taking on topics closely identified with others. I would certainly not suggest that any such culture surrounds Trim Castle and its researchers (and do not take personally my exclusion from the conversation). Instead, I have chosen the castle to make the point that all subjects, including iconic sites, "belong" to all researchers who are interested in them.

The second reason is related. Trim Castle is one of those sites routinely, if only anecdotally, regarded as "done," a concept with which many professional archaeologists will be familiar. It is "done" in the sense that the investigations are over, with no further work planned. And it is "done" in the sense that historical and archaeological research has been published by the State in a peer-reviewed monograph, which means that the site's interpretation has been considered by those whom the State regards as the key people for the study of monuments in its care, and that the big questions about it have been answered to their satisfaction. Symbolizing this analytical "closure" is that prohibition, alluded to already, on visitors entering the castle's "keep" except in the company of an official tour guide who is trained to deliver a pre-prepared narrative on the site's history and archaeology. There are plenty of similarly "done" monuments around the world. Only a brave graduate student would dare to suggest a fresh study of such a monument. My own research on Trim has led me to query whether the castle's sequence is correctly understood. In the section below entitled "What is the sequence at Trim Castle?" I show how one does not necessarily need specialist knowledge to engage in debate about archaeological sites; one needs to be able to read archaeological sections and to be alert to their occasional ambiguities. My point in demonstrating this is to encourage new researchers to regard every site, even the "done" ones that have seen excavation, as capable of further research.

The third reason is that my engagement with Trim Castle is, anyway, part of some larger, career-long, research projects of my own. One particular project is to understand how architecture "worked" in medieval society in Ireland, a topic on which I have written a book intended mainly for students and start-of-career researchers (O'Keeffe 2015). Unlike the reading of stratigraphy, this *does* require more specialist knowledge. Achieving that understanding in the case of an archaeological site from a historically-documented period involves far more than simply collecting information from written sources that capture information on contemporary society. It is at least as important for the researcher to possess an awareness of how society and the social identities of individuals are constructed spatially and materially. This is one of archaeology's immutable theoretical propositions, and it can be understood by simply reflecting on how our own world works. The objects that we make and use, and the ways in which we make and use space, signify who we are in a relational sense: the social collectives to which we are attached are those with shared rules of behavior, which by their nature involve things and spaces that we understand sufficiently well to follow or desire to subvert. No less important again is the need for the researcher to recognize, and therefore negotiate, how earlier scholarship always says as much about its own cultural and intellectual milieu as it does about the subject of its enquiry. So, while I do not think of Trim Castle as a self-contained research project in itself, it is a site that I return to repeatedly, in part because it is such an important site in the exploration of that large research topic. I discuss this matter briefly in the section "How did Trim Castle 'work'?" below.

Viewing Trim Castle Through Three Lenses: History, Archaeology, Scholarship

Being a site that dates from a historically-documented period and is itself recorded in documents, Trim Castle has a history in the conventional sense: there are names associated with it, and specific events are known to have taken place inside it. As a general rule, archaeologists need always to exercise caution when dealing with documents which record such things, and more especially with historians' interpretations of those documents. It is easy to accept unwittingly that the discipline of history offers core "truths" that archaeology cannot actually challenge. Many historians certainly believe it and, anecdotally, are not slow to communicate it. They write with a level of confidence and methodological certainty that can intimidate start-of-career historical archaeologists for whom epistemological introspection – thinking about how we know what we (claim to) know – is part of the training.

Now, in Trim's case the written records, incomplete though they are, present a coherent story for which the archaeological evidence seems to provide an extremely good match. One of the medieval sources is a *chanson de geste*, which is a type of medieval epic poem intended to celebrate heroic deeds. The *chanson* in question is known as *La Geste des Engleis en Yrlande* (*The Deeds of the English in Ireland*), and it relates to the invasion that began in 1169. It tells us that a castle was started in summer 1172 at Trim by Hugh de Lacy, an Anglo-Norman lord from the England-Wales border region to whom King Henry II granted a large estate in Ireland after the invasion. The *chanson* indicates that it was a fairly modest fortress, built of earth and timber; castles built in a hurry in Europe in the eleventh and twelfth centuries to secure newly conquered lands were normally built of these materials. Hugh left Ireland for a short time not long after work began on the castle, and consigned its care to a fellow Anglo-Norman, Hugh Tyrel. That winter an Irish army, led by Ruaidrí Ua Conchobhair, the most powerful Gaelic-Irish king of the period, marched on the castle and destroyed it. Tyrel "refortified his fortress" in 1173. In 1174 de Lacy returned to Ireland and, according to one medieval chronicle, constructed a [new] castle at Trim in 1176. Exact dates given in certain medieval Irish chronicles are often "wrong" by a year or two, and the 1176 date may be one of them. The likelihood, most historians would probably agree, is that de Lacy started his new castle in 1174. Whatever the case, we can say that three different castles are attested to in Trim: the first lasted less than six months (summer to winter 1172), the second lasted just over a year (starting in late winter or spring 1173), and the third was started between autumn 1174 and winter 1176 and is the first phase of the stone castle that we see today. Later building work is recorded but that need not detain us here.

Most archaeologists agree on the physical and spatial development of Trim Castle (Figure 19.1c). In the excavations of the early 1970s part of a fosse (ditch) enclosing the "keep" was discovered. It was interpreted at the time as part of the fosse of the original 1172 castle. A decade later Terry Barry suggested that this original castle was of a type that archaeologists call a "ringwork castle," which is a type characterized by a circular or penannular bank and outer fosse to enclose and protect timber buildings (Barry 1983: 307–309). Tom McNeill (1990), an eminent Irish castle-scholar, argued that the fosse at Trim was later rather than earlier than the tower. In the 1995–1998 excavations by Alan Hayden the remainder of the fosse was excavated. Hayden accepted the description of it as a ringwork castle and attributed it to the 1173 castle, rejecting McNeill's view of a later date. He also found evidence that he interpreted as surviving from the short-lived 1172 castle, which he also regarded as having been a ringwork castle. The official view, then, as articulated in Hayden's monograph and repeated by the castle's guides, is that two successive ringworks preceded the stone castle, and that the fosse surrounding the "keep," which is one of the most striking features of the castle's plan, remains from that early period of Trim's history.

There is also a consensus that the "keep" was started by Hugh de Lacy after he returned to Ireland in 1174, that it was still being built when he was killed in 1186 (by an axe-wielding Irishman), and that it was largely completed by his son, Walter, by the start of the thirteenth century. The dates are derived from the historical record, but we have supporting evidence which is both architectural-historical and dendrochronological: the tower's design is consistent with a late twelfth-century date, while stubs of original timbers which were found embedded in its fabric during the conservation work produced matching tree-ring dates. The castle's stone curtain wall – the enclosure wall – is understood to have been built principally in two main phases, one stretch of it (to the north-west of the "keep") dating from the later 1170s and there-fore attributable to Hugh, and another (the curving stretch south of the "keep") dating from the early thirteenth century and attributable to Walter.

Two principal datasets, then, inform our understanding of this castle: the historical and the archaeological. But, to pick up a point made above, we should also consider Alan Hayden's monograph itself to be part of evidence as well, rather than just the conduit by which the most recent research on Trim has been made available. Much of the archaeological evidence – the deposits that were excavated – is mediated through the monograph, and has no existence independent of that monograph. The stratigraphic evidence is gone, as excavation is destructive, so the report is a record of what can no longer be seen, in the same way as the *chanson de geste* is a record of events that can no longer be witnessed. And just as the *chanson* – its structure, its language, its very existence – is embedded in late twelfth-century culture, the Trim Castle excavations and the monograph that reports them are themselves embedded in a cultural context. Even the idea of *scientific* excavation – archaeologists sometimes feel a need to use that adjective – is culturally-located. When I think about Trim Castle, therefore, I think of the content of the monograph in the same way that I think of the medieval textual records.

Moreover, while the monograph is presented as a history of the site, it can also be thought of as an actual part of the site's history. For example, by shaping how the castle is understood today, it has shaped how visitors are brought around the site, their footsteps effecting a selective, if miniscule, eroding of its surfaces. And, as another example, by implying that no further excavation work needs to be done on the castle, it is an agent of stasis, ensuring the castle remains as it is now, just as Ruaidrí Ua Conchobhair's attack of 1172 can be described as an agent of change back in 1172.

Question 1: What is the Sequence at Trim Castle?

In 2012 I was invited to write a review for a local historical journal of the Trim Castle monograph, published the previous year. Finding myself unconvinced about one key conclusion drawn in the report, I transformed my review into a short article (O'Keeffe 2013), and that article has, in turn, informed yet another article (O'Keeffe 2017). This chapter is another by-product of that invitation five years ago. This small production-line of publications originates in an observation that I made when reading the monograph: the sequence of late twelfth-century phases reported in the text of the monograph is not supported by the stratigraphy shown in the drawings. One does not need to be a specialist, nor does one need any theoretical awareness, to see that the stratigraphy as recorded in the cross-sections suggests a slightly different sequence.

In the monograph a number of layers are identified as "early Norman deposits pre-dating the keep," "upcast from keep foundations," and "late thirteenth- to early fourteenth-century deposits." The first of these pertains to the period of the 1172 and 1173 castles. The second pertains to the soil that was redeposited when the foundation trenches of the "keep" were being dug, so its deposition dates from the period 1174–1176. The third pertains to a later period, but it is relevant for dating purposes.

In four of the five relevant cross-sections published in the monograph, of which I have selected one as an example (Figure 19.1d), the cut of the fosse is *through* the material identified as upcast. But it should, if the narrative is correct, be sealed by that material. Work on the "keep" began in the mid-1170s, which gives us a *terminus post quem* for the cut of the fosse as recorded in those sections. The earliest fill in the sections, other than basal silt, is assigned a late thirteenth- or early fourteenth-century date, which gives a *terminus ante quem* for the cut. The fosse cannot be assigned, therefore, to either the 1172 or 1173 castles. Rather, according to this stratigraphy, it must have been dug after the "keep" was built, as McNeill had suggested.

Only one drawn section in the report suggests a different chronology (Figure 19.1e). Here, a small trickle of material identified as "upcast" is shown descending into the fosse. However, the cut of the fosse appears to be *through* "early Norman deposits pre-dating the keep." This would suggest that the fosse was cut between the initial phase of Anglo-Norman settlement (in 1172–1173) and the erection of the great tower (1174), which would allow us to identify it as a feature of the refortification of 1173. But it is only a trickle of suggested "upcast," and one wonders whether it should be allowed contradict the evidence of the stratigraphy in the other sections.

An additional problem surfaces with the suggestion of the official narrative that the fosse belongs to a pre-1174 castle. It is very shallow: it is no more than 3 m deep (less than 10 ft) from the top of its cut to the level of undisturbed soil or bedrock. It is also quite narrow: in places it can only have been about 5 m (16 ft) wide at the top. This would not have been a substantial monument. That is not the problem. The problem is that its earliest material-rich fill, in part abutting the cut, is assigned a date no earlier than the late thirteenth century. If the fosse does indeed survive from a pre-1174 castle, we need to believe that Hugh de Lacy, having decided to build a massive stone tower, was happy to leave open the shallow fosse of the older castle, that he and his son expected their stone masons to cart a huge volume of stone through its narrow entrance over a period of nearly 30 years, that those masons were able to set up their scaffolding and move about effectively within the confined space, and that the fosse was kept open until it was allowed fill (or was back-filled) with material a century later. This makes little sense. My conclusion is that, contrary to the narrative in the monograph, there is actually no strong evidence of one or two ringwork castles preceding the building of the great tower. The excavations of the 1990s did yield some evidence for timber building in the original castle or castles of pre-1174, but the stratigraphic evidence would indicate that the fosse around the "keep" was added later. I have suggested that it was dug in advance of a documented siege of 1224 (O'Keeffe 2017).

Why does all this matter? There is an intrinsic value in knowing the sequence of construction at this iconic site. No lives are lost if the sequence is incorrect; we just like to know. But the castle's value within comparative castle studies in Ireland and Western Europe is compromised by the presentation as fact of a sequence of phases that may actually be incorrect. It also matters for another reason, which I would not dare to suggest were I a junior researcher! I think that, based on Terry Barry's interpretation in 1983, the possibility of a late date for the fosse was simply not entertained in the 1990s excavation. Stratigraphy was dutifully recorded, but it was not examined to see if it corresponded to the narrative. There is a lesson in that, not just for excavators but for researchers looking at excavation reports. Interpretation is not over with publication, but enters another phase.

Question 2: How Did Trim Castle "Work"?

The sequence which I critiqued above is not only conveyed in the monograph; it also features, albeit briefly, in the official tour of the site. That tour brings one through the "keep," starting at the original first-floor level entrance and then ascending to the parapet. While the sequence of the earliest phase of Trim can be contested, the sequence of the post-1174 "keep" is fairly secure. One can see in its fabric the actual phases of construction. It is the account of how we understand the tower to have functioned that is somewhat problematic.

A fairly recent survey of the history of research on Irish castles by a leading Irish specialist in castle studies contained the following statement:

> The building of castles in medieval Europe arose from the need of the military elite of the time for strongholds in which they could house their armies and from which they could control their land grants under the feudal system of land tenure, which was military in origin. Thus, these fortifications were just as essential to the military aspect of feudalism as were knights and feudal armies... Possibly the most straightforward definition of a medieval castle [is] "a fortified residence which might combine administrative and judicial functions but in which military considerations were paramount."
>
> *(Barry 2008: 115)*

A number of other Irish castle specialists have made similar assertions about the fundamentally military nature of castles. Specialists in castle-archaeology outside Ireland, and especially in Britain, will raise their eyebrows at the confidence of the assertion that castles are fundamentally military things. Recent decades have seen a retreat from the strong militarist interpretation that dominated castle research when it first emerged in the nineteenth century. The traditional view, now widely challenged outside Ireland, held that medieval castles were essentially machines of war, the builders of which were engaged in an ongoing quest to create the optimal architecture of defense in event of attack or siege. Influenced as much by Sir Walter Scott's early nineteenth-century novel *Ivanhoe* as by any medieval testimony, traditional scholarship held, for example, that testosterone-fueled fighting men sometimes poured, or had poured upon them, boiling oil from the parapets.

Alas, the official interpretation of Trim Castle by the State agency that owns it is also overtly militaristic, judging by the guided tour. For a long time, in my recollection, even the arrangement of rooms inside the "keep" was explained to visitors in terms of the castle's garrison being able to retreat behind one door after another if attacked. This was a particularly egregious error: as one can see in the plan (Figure 19.1c), the interior of the "keep" is divided in two by a cross wall, and its purpose was not to provide a barrier against attackers but to separate the (public) hall of the castle, located near the door, from the (private) chamber of the castle, positioned further back. That particular misunderstanding has been eliminated from the tour, but the spirit of boiling oil has not.

Today, castle specialists are more likely to focus their attention on the other roles and meanings that castles had in the medieval world, and on how castle-architecture itself "worked" as a space of habitation for women and children as well as men, as an object of aesthetic appeal, and so on (see Johnson 2002). Some of the most interesting recent research has considered castles in the medieval imagination, exploring how "castle" was as much an idea – of literary provenance, and even with Biblical reference – as a physical object (see Wheatley 2004, for example). There is scope for this work on castles, including Trim, in Ireland too, and I have tried to pave the way (see O'Keeffe 2001, for example). For tourists who have no intellectual investment in the castle and how it is understood, stories of siege engines and boiling oil are fun. I still find myself biting my lip during the guided tour at Trim and wondering about the durability of myths and the difficulty of replacing them with more historically accurate – and ultimately more interesting – interpretations. The purpose of research is to inform. Trim has taught me to be patient, which is a lesson I would pass to younger researchers.

Final Reflections

I end with two closing reflections. First, researchers, especially when beginning as students, are usually pressed to identify key questions as the first stage of their research. They generally search for gaps in knowledge, and they frame their questions in a manner that suggests that those gaps can be filled by following certain strategies. But the process also works in reverse. Armed with contextual knowledge and familiarity with relevant literature, the researcher can sometimes identify answers to questions before those questions are even imagined, much less explicitly articulated. This particular relationship of question to answer is entirely valid. It is how my research on Trim has evolved. Second, research fields are crowded places, and new interpretations are not victimless: they are always made at the expense of older interpretations, some of which have been the foundations on which other scholars have built their careers. To be a researcher of consequence is to enter fearlessly into a contract with posterity. New ideas will, in time, become old ideas. It is a principle to be embraced, not feared.

Paired Reading

O'Keeffe, Tadhg. 2017. "Trim before 1224: New Thoughts on the *Caput* of de Lacy Lordship in Ireland." In *From Carrickfergus to Carcassonne: The Epic Seeds of Hugh de Lacy during the Albigensian Crusade*, edited by Paul Duffy, Tadhg O'Keeffe, and Jean-Michel Picard, 31–56. Turnhout, Belgium: Brepols Publishers.

References

Barry, Terry B. 1983. "Anglo-Norman Ringwork Castles: Some Evidence." In *Landscape Archaeology in Ireland*, edited by Terence Reeves-Smyth and Fred Hamond, 295–314. Oxford: British Archaeological Reports.

Barry, Terry B. 2008. "The Study of Medieval Irish Castles: A Bibliographic Survey." *Proceedings of the Royal Irish Academy,* 108C: 115–136. DOI: 10.3318/PRIAC.2008.108.115.

Hayden, Alan R. 2011. *Trim Castle, Co. Meath: Excavations 1995–8*. Department of Arts, Heritage and the Gaeltacht Archaeological Monograph Series 6. Dublin: Stationery Office.

Johnson, Matthew. 2002. *Behind the Castle Gate: From Medieval to Renaissance*. London: Routledge.

McNeill, T. E. 1990. "Trim Castle, Co. Meath: The First Three Generations." *Archaeological Journal*, 47: 308–336. DOI: 10.1080/00665983.1990.11077947.

O'Keeffe, Tadhg. 2001. "Concepts of 'Castle' and the Construction of Identity in Medieval and Post-Medieval Ireland." *Irish Geography*, 34: 69–88. DOI: 10.1080/00750770109555777.

O'Keeffe, Tadhg. 2013. "Trim Castle Uncovered: Some Thoughts." *Ríocht na Midhe*, 24: 160–168.

O'Keeffe, Tadhg. 2015. *Medieval Irish Buildings, 1100–1600*. Dublin: Four Courts Press

O'Keeffe, Tadhg. 2017. "Trim before 1224: New Thoughts on the *Caput* of de Lacy Lordship in Ireland." In *From Carrickfergus to Carcassonne: The Epic Seeds of Hugh de Lacy during the Albigensian Crusade*, edited by Paul Duffy, Tadhg O'Keeffe, and Jean-Michel Picard, 31–56. Turnhout, Belgium: Brepols Publishers.

Wheatley, Abigail. 2004. *The Idea of the Castle in Medieval England*. England: York Medieval Press.

Part III

Materials, Collections, and Analyses

20

Dr. Stage-Love, or: How I Learned to Stop Worrying and Love My Dissertation on Race, Pipes, and Classification in the Chesapeake

Anna S. Agbe-Davies

Project Summary

Using legacy collections of locally-made tobacco pipes I set out to transform the way historical archaeologists analyze these artifacts, in the process learning how pipes were made and distributed in the seventeenth-century AD English colonies of the Chesapeake Bay of the Eastern United States. Or maybe my goal was simultaneously much simpler (completing my PhD at the University of Pennsylvania) and more complex (an opportunity to contemplate the production of archaeological knowledge; the pipes were as good a vehicle as any), which is the basis for my hope that this chapter offers something for readers besides those in the middle of their graduate school journey.

Introduction: The Best Eight Years of Your Life

This subtitle, of course, is misleading. While the average archaeologist takes approximately eight years to complete a PhD from a US university, only a fraction of that time is spent conducting library research, obtaining and analyzing data, and typing the words to be reviewed and approved by one's committee. Furthermore, engagement with the ideas thus explored often extends well beyond, both before and after, the period of matriculation in a PhD program. "The dissertation" has a life cycle, much like a living organism, in which the document itself is merely one stage.

If anyone had told me at the outset that I'd spend 20 years thinking through the materials of my own dissertation, I would have felt some combination of surprise/despair/anticipatory ennui. But I am here to tell you that a dissertation research program, *or indeed any other*, is as much about the journey as the destination. In fact, the moment of arrival will likely be completely eclipsed by sights along the way. The dissertation leg of my project's journey was approximately three years long. But to treat that span as the beginning and end of the project belies my actual experience. The way I thought about the manufacture and distribution of clay tobacco pipes in early colonial Virginia when I received my degree bears only a passing resemblance to the way that I thought about it when I took the first steps toward developing a research design or when I published a book drawing heavily on the analyses in my dissertation, or now.

And while I'm at it: PhD students often hear, "write your dissertation as a book." Fine advice, but it's also okay to write it as a dissertation! Wanting a dissertation to also be a book is like wanting a caterpillar to also be a butterfly. Who's to say which form is the creature's "real" state?

Engaging Archaeology: 25 Case Studies in Research Practice, First Edition. Edited by Stephen W. Silliman.
© 2018 John Wiley & Sons, Inc. Published 2018 by John Wiley & Sons, Inc.

Each one has a purpose. A dissertation exists in part because it forces engagement with certain processes, creating particular kinds of experiences.

From where I stand, archaeology is a scientific discipline producing new knowledge about the past, but it is also a way of being-in-the-world. To the extent that it is one of a range of strategies that we as humans use to manage, make sense of, and use our surroundings, archaeology is a kind of meta-practice: a practice about [past] practices. The doing of archaeology is, I argue, as important as the knowing. This does not diminish the importance of great discoveries, but rather humanizes our endeavors.

Inspiration

My project was inspired by debates I encountered upon entering the vibrant archaeological community in the Chesapeake region of the United States, an important center in the development of historical archaeology, "archaeology [that] studies the transformation and nature of the Modern World" (www.sha.org). These debates were often longstanding and cut to the heart of major issues in the discipline. In the early 1990s, attention increasingly turned to the problem of ethnicity in the archaeological record. Colonial Williamsburg, where I worked as a field technician, had emerged as a key place to research African-American archaeology.

Leland Ferguson's (1992) *Uncommon Ground* had made a big splash a couple of years before, with its analysis of Colono Ware, pottery produced in contexts of colonialism and enslavement, where the worlds of African, European, and Native people collided from the late seventeenth through the nineteenth centuries across the southeastern United States. Ferguson concluded that these ceramics often represented the handiwork of African-descended people. This, along with Matthew Emerson's (1988) similar argument regarding locally-made clay tobacco pipes, ran counter to the conventional wisdom that the pots and the pipes were colonial-era extensions of enduring Native ceramic traditions. Whichever artifact was under discussion, conversation ran pretty hot. I figured out quickly that the irreconcilable interpretations (pipes-as-Native versus pipes-as-African) had hardened into positions that spoke past each other, seldom referencing the same assemblages, using consistent methods, or employing compatible theoretical concepts.

I really can't say what drew me to the pipes more than the pots. Perhaps it was their aesthetic qualities – the pipes are sometimes highly decorated. Maybe it was the time period they permitted me to examine, falling into a niche between the early seventeenth-century emphasis of sites like the settlement at James Fort and the mid- to late eighteenth-century focus in Williamsburg. Delving into the literature I found that the emphasis on the racial identity of the pipes' makers was longstanding. No less a figure than J.C. Harrington, lead archaeologist at Jamestown in the infancy of historical archaeology, perhaps best known for his method for dating historic sites using pipe stem bores, posed the question in an early article on Jamestown's pipes. What could explain the enduring appeal of such a question? How could it remain unresolved for so long? With the field at an impasse I saw an opportunity to make a mark.

My interest in intercultural spaces, like the colonial Chesapeake, predated any notion of studying archaeology, let alone becoming an archaeologist. I had gone to college planning to major in International Relations, the only thing I knew to call this curiosity. Fortunately for me, I happened upon "Introduction to Archaeology" in my first semester. So later, as a novice field tech, I seized opportunities to engage these issues via small-scale projects directed by my mentors and supervisors. Upon leaving employment for graduate school, related themes began to guide my own work.

My interests could have been channeled into further engagement with debates over the ethnic/racial identity of the pipemakers. But that discussion covers only a fraction of what can be done with the pipes and their role in the construction of race in seventeenth-century Virginia. As my horizons as a social scientist expanded – and I had more opportunities to critically inspect the social structures of the discipline itself – I came to wonder not only "who made these pipes?" but "why do we care 'who made these pipes?'" Casting about for a way to reframe the analysis, I tweaked the "who." Rather than indicating a racial or ethnic category, it instead pointed to workshops or groups of allied producers in relation to the owners of labor in the colony. This new "who" did not speculate on the nature of that relation or the cultural genealogy of their practice. Rather, it probed the social relations of pipe production and consumption. I focused on Jamestown, the colony's first English capital, along with its hinterlands in the years surrounding an upheaval now commonly called Bacon's Rebellion. In that era, did land- and labor-owning elites control the trade in pipes as they did so many other forms of production? The dissertation, having settled this question, allowed the book (spoiler alert) to become a more wide-ranging exploration of the problem of classification – how we know which pipes, or which collectives of people for that matter, are for our purposes "the same?"

What emerged was an effort to understand how artifact classifications and racial classifications shape past and present meanings of social worlds. The project examined both practices within a seventeenth-century colony and a twentieth- or twenty-first-century discipline, using artifacts produced at the very moment when racial social structures were taking new forms. The pipes were *a lens through which* to examine this problem. What mattered were the people associated with the pipes. Generally, how do social systems work? Specifically, how did seventeenth-century Virginians construct and maintain their social worlds? And especially, how do the mechanisms they devised continue to shape the lives of people living in the United States today? With apologies to René Magritte, this was not a pipe.

The project truly began to take shape in a seminar in archaeological method and theory I took midway through my graduate coursework. My research paper for Jeremy Sabloff's course was a review of the literature on the type concept. Here I found a language for the aspects of local pipe research that had troubled me. Here, too, I read Walter Taylor's (1983) *A Study of Archeology* all the way through for the first time. His comments on typology are apposite, but he appears here because he reiterated for archaeologists Clyde Kluckhohn's explanation of the relationships among technique, theory, and method, which underlie the remainder of this chapter.

Techniques are what we as researchers apply to things-in-the-world (texts, artifacts, persons) in order to render them as data (Taylor 1983 [1948]: 8). Theory gives us the language for describing what those data might mean. Methods allow us to apply the data to specific problems. James Deetz writes in terms of *observation*, *explanation*, and *integration* (Deetz 1967: 8–9). His shift from objects to actions gives me handles to grasp in the following attempt to show this project moving through stages dominated by one of the three – data, theory, or method – even though in reality these stages were overlapping and their sequence non-linear.

Observation

When it came time to examine the data, I was pleasantly surprised to discover that the information proved robust enough to stand up to my hypothesis. Given what I knew about social organization in seventeenth-century Virginia it seemed plausible that, like many trades, the large-scale production of pipes was controlled by, if not directed by, land- and labor-owning elites. But using the pipes, I actually discovered a total disconnect between the social and economic ties among land- and labor-owners and the distribution of distinctive pipe production styles.

It was heartening, really. Virginia in the seventeenth century was a difficult time and place to say the least. The written record reveals heartbreaking levels of exploitation and suffering.

The archaeological record clearly shows the harsh living and laboring conditions, with few creature comforts. And yet, people persisted. Elites may have dominated society and most sectors of the economy, but they did not, or could not, appropriate trade in these locally-made tobacco pipes.

Another surprise was that the analysis generated far more data than I could ever use in the dissertation. I had begun the project worried that I might not have enough to write about but ended up sidelining whole swaths of data because there was not room for it all. Believe me, the vision I had for the project was only partway realized by the document I produced to attain my degree. I'd been duly warned: the dissertation, far from being one's life's work, was only a first salvo. It doesn't need to be *comprehensive*, but rather *completed*. Some of the material that couldn't find a home in the dissertation eventually found its way into the book.

One reason that I had such a wealth of data was that I did not rely on specimens from my own excavations. In hindsight, a project based on legacy collections was a logical extension of a longstanding love of museums. Like many archaeologists, I suspect, I'm something of a pack rat, and I find collections of *things* strangely compelling. Accuse me of being old-fashioned or reactionary (it wouldn't be the first time), but a part of me misses the old style of archaeological exhibit: row upon row of neatly labeled and sorted objects, the better to contemplate the sheer volume and diversity of the material to be inspected. Of course, there are consequences for reducing the world's variety so tidily.

Be that as it may, using existing collections ensured a large, representative, and predictable (at least in terms of sample size) dataset: nearly 5000 pipe fragments from six structures at Jamestown and five plantations in James City County, Virginia. Many of the sites had been owned or occupied by members of extended family networks, in some cases by the very same individual. I restricted the sample to sites occupied in the second half of the seventeenth century, focusing more tightly when possible on the decades surrounding Bacon's Rebellion. The narrow time frame was essential if I were to successfully argue that the variations I observed were not simply due to change over time. The significance of that specific time slice was twofold.

First, the seventeenth century was when many of England's American colonies developed the legal and ideological framework for modern slavery. Virginia is often presented as a prototype for the social structures that came to dominate what is now the United States, for example, in Audrey Smedley's (1993) *Race in North America: Origin and Evolution of a World View*. A direct challenge to authoritarian administration by a royal governor, Bacon's Rebellion was also sparked by changing ideas about humanity, citizenship, and race. Second, historians had shown that during Bacon's Rebellion allegiances were shaped by existing social networks. The conflict would strengthen ties among allies and deepen cleavages between rival elites. If they controlled the pipe trade, then all else being equal assemblages from sites owned by allies should draw from similar sources of pipes, while assemblages from antagonists' households would have fewer variables in common. So in addition to limiting the time frame, I also included assemblages from households on both sides of the conflict. How, then, to determine which pipes were alike?

This question signaled a new stage in my thinking. My undergraduate self had a model of scientific study extrapolated from high school lab courses: one selects a pre-established protocol and applies it. Initially, archaeology seemed to me to be the application of well-understood principles to novel datasets. Every problem already had a (single) tailor-made solution; the work of the archaeologist was to deploy it. Even when I began background research, my goal was to develop an improved (read: universally-applicable) technique. What I thought we in the Chesapeake needed was a better (that is, more comprehensive) classification system for these pipes. In other words, we needed a technique. But, the further in I got, the more obvious it became that what we really needed was a reorientation to classification itself (a method, and at some level, a theory).

The work proceeded in a "grounded" fashion. It began with the data. Instead of starting with a general idea of how the world works (a theory) and using it to understand a new sample, the theory and method would grow out of the material I proposed to study and the questions that I wished to answer. Since my problems differed from those dominating the scholarship of the moment, it made little sense to adopt the same techniques (and resulting data) or methods (and associated arguments) that were being used to address questions about ethnic or racial identity and affiliation.

Explanation

Given my concern with the emergence and transformation of the modern world, the precepts of world-systems theory were attractive. World-systems theory gets a bad rap in part because it is often read as a theory of power, especially political power. I see it, fundamentally, as a theory of relations. It challenges us to reconsider our unit of analysis, asserting that the societies and cultures of the anthropological and archaeological imagination are fragments of a much larger whole. Therefore, treating our categories (Native, European, African; Algonquian, English, Yoruba) as inherently stable and self-contained impedes our comprehension of them. So the other side of the world-systems theory coin is a critical concept of ethnicity.

My lodestone was, and remains, Fredrik Barth's (1969) classic introduction to *Ethnic Groups and Boundaries*, in which he articulated a theory of ethnicity as relational rather than essential. The description was equally applicable to race as currently understood – a social category with profound implications for relations among groups. I was surprised to discover how difficult it was to get fellow researchers to think about ethnicity and race as anything other than, respectively, narrower and broader categories within a taxonomic system not unlike that devised by Linnaeus in 1758, albeit without his belief in the significance of biological variables (Figure 20.1a).

Coincidence or not, the taxonomic typology underlay *both* the essentialized social categories of historical archaeologists *and* the classification schemes used to analyze the pipes (Figure 20.1b).

Figure 20.1 Diagrams of classificatory systems. Interestingly, we could read the archaeologist's focus on decoration as analogous to the way that earlier concepts of "race" relied on superficial features to create categories presumed to be internally homogeneous and externally heterogeneous.

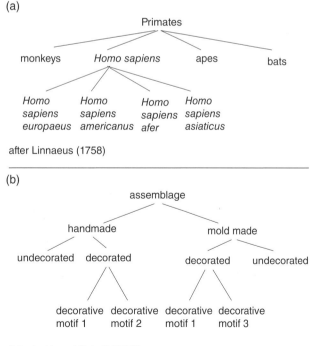

Pipes might not be people – to adapt the archaeological truism – but they were classified in analogous ways. So among the outcomes of that aforementioned graduate seminar paper was a deep dive into the literature on classification and systematics (the set of concepts and strategies used to create units of meaning and analysis). The exploration revealed that, for all its dominance, the taxonomic typology is not the only game in town.

The limitations of taxonomy are likewise laid bare when we consider the classification system known as "race." Empirical data teach us that race is a system of social structures and relationships rather than a set of categories to which people belong due to their possession of (trivial) biological characteristics. Critical race theory (Crenshaw *et al.* 1995) is a framework for examining the processes that create those social structures. Just as critical race theory makes transparent the processes of category creation and maintenance for humans, I wanted something similar for the pipes, a *critical systematics* (Agbe-Davies 2015: 19–21). A critical systematics would define artifacts not in terms of their essential qualities (trivial or otherwise), but consider these attributes in relation to others, without buying into the reality or permanence of the categories into which given objects fell. The meanings of these categories were explicitly conceptualized as a function of their perception by an analyst, in Peirce's terms the interpretant (Peirce 1994).

I had encountered Peirce's ideas about language early in my graduate career, though I left town too soon to participate in conversations about how his semiotics help us understand meaning as made with material culture (Preucel and Bauer 2001). Most germane to my work with the pipes was his concept of an index, in which a sign is related to its object by co-presence or effect (e.g., smoke as a sign of fire). Previous explanations of the pipes hinged on the origins and meaning of their decorations, treating both the pipes and the decorations as symbols, signs that are related to their objects by law or convention (e.g., smoke as a sign that a new pope has been chosen). The focus on decoration also meant that only a small subset of pipes were examined; undecorated or highly fragmented artifacts were excluded. Furthermore, because these decorations were treated as symbols – signs having meanings specific to particular historical contexts – interpretations required a decision, far from certain, about which symbol system ("Native," "European," "African") might be relevant. A method that could get around that conundrum would be valuable, indeed.

Integration

Traditional artifact classification is frequently typological or paradigmatic. Even exploratory data analyses aim to associate attributes with one another, usually to discover categories-of-thing. Instead of beginning with a plan for sorting individual pipes into classes based on their (mostly decorative) characteristics – and an argument about which (classes of) people produced the pipes – the data and the research question drove a search for alternative methods. What do relational categories look like, methodologically? With *modal analysis* each variable is analyzed separately, with the artifacts grouped and regrouped multiple times, according to their different attributes. The method accommodates fragmentary specimens, since categories are not based on the co-occurrence of attributes. *Modes* share a great deal with the concept of *clines* in biological anthropology which, incidentally, are presented as a way to understand human variation that does not rely on a notion of categorical "races." Difference is fleeting and relational; it is produced rather than essential.

Variable-by-variable analysis greatly preceded the technological tools to implement it with ease. We can look at least as far back as Irving Rouse's (1939) approach, which has become much more feasible with the ready availability of computerized databases. And indeed, building the database in which I recorded the pipe fragments' attributes was essential to my understanding of the problem. In wrestling with the inadequacy of previous pipe classification schemes for my research problem that it became ever clearer that there could be no universal classification scheme for these objects. What distinguished my method was a theory of non-hierarchical classification built into the structure of the database itself.

So it's difficult to say, as authors in this volume have been asked to do, whether methods or theory drove this project. Developing the methodological framework and designing and implementing the technique of data recording were by far the most time-consuming parts of the project. But they were deeply interesting – in fact the part I cared about most – and what has stuck with me well beyond the dissertation's completion. Methodological conversations are what keep us a coherent discipline, as archaeologists, despite the many differences among the phenomena we study and the meanings we think they have. Methods are arguably more essential than theory, if we wish archaeology to remain an empirical discipline. However, as important as methodology is to the advancement of archaeological practice, it makes for pretty dull reading. It's important when the communication aims to demonstrate an ability to develop and execute a research project (i.e., a dissertation). It is less so if the purpose is to communicate the results of that research project more broadly.

Reflection

I'm not sure that this research project had the effect that I had intended. Certainly, I did not introduce a new classification scheme for the analysis of locally-made clay tobacco pipes. Part of my process was arriving at a grounded critique of that very goal. The project provided an opportunity to engage with big picture questions having to do with the nature of knowledge, the workings of social power, and the history of ideas. Likewise I confronted the task of synthesizing the aims of a scientific archaeology with those of a critical/reflexive archaeology.

To the extent that I sought a new understanding of power relationships in seventeenth-century Virginia, the project succeeded. New knowledge about the organization of craft labor was added to our picture of life in the early colonial Chesapeake. Unlike so much else in the colony, elites did not control the trade in local pipes. But I didn't stop there. That insight arrived at in 2004 continued to live in my brain. It shaped new projects that came along in the interim. And it was that new research, along with the time to mull things over, that made the book stage (nearly ten years on) a very different kind of project.

Part of what has sustained me as this project wended its way through various life-stages was maintaining a flexible concept of what it might become. The basic aim was to explore theories of difference, both social and material. What made the project so satisfying, and what sets archaeologists apart from others who may explore similar questions (e.g., philosophers), is the way that these explorations were grounded in empirica (Archer and Bartoy 2006).

Concepts and data from linguistic, biological, and sociocultural anthropology all contributed to the framing and execution of this project. I even made forays – admittedly not very far! – into systematic biology and cognitive psychology. Your sister fields may not be the same as mine, but surely there is a great deal to be gained by becoming conversant in scholarship outside of one's own subfield and spatio-temporal specialization. This effort includes two challenges: maintaining an open mind and knowing when to stop reading and start writing.

Writing a dissertation, like all forms of communication, is an inherently social act. It is essential to remember this, even at the outset, even if the negative messages of the world convince you that "no one's ever going to read this." Readers, like other interlocutors, get you outside of your own head. So it is in that spirit that I offer my one piece of advice: find people (not your committee) with whom to share your dissertation. Readers will push you to explain yourself more thoroughly and reading their writing in return will refresh your brain and open windows onto new intellectual worlds. They will help you move your project to the next stage.

As I tap out these words I am sitting with two members of my summer writing group who have helped shape this chapter since it first saw the light of day. I need them, not only for the accountability – they're expecting this conclusion from me next week – but also to stand in for you, dear reader, from whom I am separated in time and space, and can only hope to reach with these words on this page.

Paired Reading

Agbe-Davies, Anna S. 2015. *Tobacco, Pipes, and Race in Colonial Virginia: Little Tubes of Mighty Power.* Walnut Creek, CA: Left Coast Press.

References

Agbe-Davies, Anna S. 2015. *Tobacco, Pipes, and Race in Colonial Virginia: Little Tubes of Mighty Power.* Walnut Creek, CA: Left Coast Press.

Archer, Stephen N. and Kevin M. Bartoy. 2006. "Introduction: Considering Methods and Methodology in Historical Archaeology." In *Dirt and Discussion: Methods, Methodology, and Interpretation in Historical Archaeology*, edited by Stephen Archer and Kevin Bartoy, 1–9. New York: Springer.

Barth, Fredrik. 1969. "Introduction." In *Ethnic Groups and Boundaries: The Social Organization of Cultural Differences*, edited by Fredrik Barth, 9–37. London: Allen & Unwin.

Crenshaw, Kimberlé, Neil Gotanda, Gary Peller, and Kendall Thomas, eds. 1995. *Critical Race Theory: The Key Writings That Formed the Movement.* New York: The New Press.

Deetz, James. 1967. *Invitation to Archaeology.* Garden City, NY: The Natural History Press.

Emerson, Matthew Charles. 1988. "Decorated Clay Tobacco Pipes from the Chesapeake." PhD Dissertation. Berkeley, CA: University of California at Berkeley.

Ferguson, Leland G. 1992. *Uncommon Ground: Archaeology and Early African America, 1650–1800.* Washington, DC: Smithsonian Institution.

Peirce, Charles Sanders. 1994. "Division of Signs" (Volume 2, Book 2, Chapter 2). In *The Collected Papers of Charles Sanders Peirce.* Electronic edition. Available at http://pm.nlx.com/xtf/view?docId=peirce/peirce.02.xml;chunk.id=div.peirce.cp2.11;toc.depth=1;toc.id=div.peirce.cp2.11;brand=default and https://colorysemiotica.files.wordpress.com/2014/08/peirce-collectedpapers.pdf.

Preucel, Robert W. and Alexander A. Bauer. 2001. "Archaeological Pragmatics." *Norwegian Archaeological Review*, 34 (2): 85–96.

Rouse, Irving. 1939. *Prehistory in Haiti: A Study in Method.* Vol. 21, Yale University Publications in Anthropology. New Haven, CT: Yale University Press.

Smedley, Audrey. 1993. *Race in North America: Origin and Evolution of a Worldview.* Boulder, CO: Westview Press.

Taylor, Walter W. 1983 [1948]. *A Study of Archeology.* 3rd ed. Carbondale, IL: Center for Archaeological Investigations.

21

Lessons Learned in Seriating Maya Pottery

Lisa J. LeCount

Project Summary

Ceramic seriation is one of the most basic techniques that archaeologists rely upon to place material remains in time. Doing seriation, however, is thought to be simple given pat textbook examples or to be "old school" since radiocarbon provides more precise dates. It is also rumored to be just plain unnecessary because chronological schemes were developed years ago for most regions. All of these notions are far from the truth. In this chapter, I discuss my research at the ancient Maya sites of Xunantunich and Actuncan (Mopan Valley, Belize) and the trials and tribulations of seriating pottery attributes that appear to be unchanging over long time spans. I describe my successful seriation of Late Classic (AD 600 to 900) pottery at Xunantunich and then my ongoing work at Actuncan, which peaked during the Late Preclassic (400 BC to AD 300). While seriations are critical in determining when Xunantunich and Actuncan rose and fell from political prominence, they also illuminate the taken-for-granted technical processes within the *chaîne opératoire* of ancient Maya pottery manufacture.

Introduction

I would have never guessed that my most frequently cited contribution to Maya archaeology would be my study of pottery seriation and chronology building for the eastern periphery of the Petén in Belize and Guatemala (LeCount *et al.* 2002). Seriation was just a mandatory task I had to do for my dissertation research before I could address more anthropologically interesting questions concerning feasting, gifting, and identity among elites and commoners at the provincial capital of Xunantunich in the Mopan Valley (LeCount 1996). There already existed a classification system at the site of Barton Ramie about 20 km downstream from Xunantunich developed by James Gifford (1976), one of the founders of the type-variety method. Researchers routinely called his book, *Prehistoric Pottery Analysis and the Ceramics of Barton Ramie in the Belize Valley,* the "bible" because it was considered a true and trusted account of pottery types by phase. Unfortunately for me, his data had some serious gaps, particularly in the Late Classic, a 200-year long time period when Xunantunich both rose and fell from political power between AD 600 and 900. I needed a more fine-grain chronology to document the timing of political events and place household contexts within a temporal framework. Only then could I get on with the more important job of comparing pottery styles and forms across status groups before and after the collapse.

Engaging Archaeology: 25 Case Studies in Research Practice, First Edition. Edited by Stephen W. Silliman.

Twenty years later I face the same problem at Actuncan, a site that rose to power in the Late Preclassic period. Before I can investigate how the first Maya kings institutionalized authority and the roles households played in this process, I must continue to refine Gifford's chronology. My experiences are not unusual. Although tried-and-true classification systems and chronologies established in the mid-twentieth century may work well enough for some questions, archaeologists increasingly demand more precise temporal frameworks and innovative classification schemes to answer anthropological questions.

Textbooks will invariably state that "[t]he first, and in some ways the most important, step in archaeological research involves ordering things into sequences" (Renfrew and Bahn 2010: 107). Without an understanding of how things are arranged in time, the two other fundamental dimensions of archaeology – space and form – cannot be studied productively. In Colin Renfrew and Paul Bahn's *Archaeology Essentials*, dating methods are divided into relative and absolute techniques, but based on their descriptions it is clear that absolute dating techniques are considered the most pertinent in today's high-tech world. Relative dating techniques including stratigraphy, seriation, and typological sequencing are explained in seven pages, while 18 pages are devoted to absolute methods including calendars, dendrochronology, radiocarbon, potassium-argon, and other chronometric techniques. In particular, seriation is described in a single page and illustrated by the changing popularity of New England tombstone designs (the famous death's head, cherub and urn and willow) in the eighteenth and nineteenth centuries. American automobile and European axe types are shown in relative sequences. According to Renfrew and Bahn (2010: 108), "most of us can mentally arrange them into a rough chronological sequence," presumably based on intuition. When compared to chronometric methods that require radioactive instrumentation and calibration, relative dating techniques look simple and frankly, primitive. But if relative dating is so old school, why I am wasting my time doing it?

The point I want to make is that it is impossible to do archaeology generally and absolute dating specifically without relative methods. Most archaeologists work with relative dating methods every day in the field, while absolute dating is done after considerable time and effort has been spent analyzing stratigraphy, classifying pottery, and organizing proveniences into cultural strata. Only then do we understand which samples may help us establish an absolute *time frame* for architectural, occupation, or ceramic sequences. Therefore, relative and absolute dating methods go hand-in-hand because absolute dating relies on the basic work of relative methods. Further, most of us don't actually date remains directly, unless we work with volcanic rock, fossils, or bone. Rather, the vast majority of archaeologists indirectly date pottery, architecture, or lithics using carbon samples. Some of these samples may be found *in situ*, like burned food remains in a pot, but most are collected from soil matrices of excavation units. It is not the samples themselves that are the objects of inquiry; rather it is their associations with archaeological remains that allow us to construct chronologies in absolute time. Stratigraphy and seriation underpin this process by first ordering things in a sequence, a process that is fundamental to archaeological practice with or without the application of absolute dates.

Ceramic Seriation: The Basics

Seriation techniques come in many forms, but today, archaeologists rely on frequency seriation. Ceramics are often seriated because they are abundant on ceramic-bearing sites and are stylistically diverse. In a nutshell, the technique relies on the popularity principle. It is assumed that each style begins as an innovation that gradually increases in popularity and then slowly fades away, a phenomenon that can be charted using the changing percentages of styles through time. James Ford nicknamed the shape of the popularity curve a "battle-ship curve" because the bar graphs of changing percentages look like ships seen from an airplane. Later, these illustrations came to be known as Ford Diagrams. For this technique to work, assemblages are arranged in rows by proveniences, and the percentages of each style within an assemblage are placed in columns. It doesn't matter if styles are attributes or types, but their percentages must sum to 100% within a provenience. Collections can come from survey or excavations, from a single site or multiple ones, but for a fine-grained sequence many collections are required. The only trick to doing a frequency seriation is to make styles behave like ships passing in the night; in other words, you must align the rows so that as one style moves slowly out of sight with diminishing popularity, another comes into view.

I prefer to seriate pottery collections from stratified deposits, a technique called interdigitated percentage stratigraphy. Lee Lyman, Steve Wolverton, and Michael O'Brien (1998: 239) suggest that archaeologists

> regularly confuse frequency seriation with a technique for measuring the passage of time based on superposition – percentage stratigraphy – and fail to mention interdigitation as an important component of some percentage-stratigraphic studies. Frequency seriation involves the arrangement of collections so that each artifact type displays a unimodal frequency distribution, but the direction of time's flow must be determined from independent evidence. Percentage stratigraphy plots the fluctuating frequency of types, but the order of collections is based on their superposition.

The term interdigitation denotes the use of data from several excavation units. When ordering interdigitated proveniences on the chart, you cannot willfully violate the law of superposition by placing collections out of stratigraphic order to make the battleship curves behave properly. Because of this rule, interdigitation percentage stratigraphy often results in ugly Ford Diagrams because reality is messy. Minor fluctuations in the frequencies of styles within assemblages can be caused by small samples or ancient cultural practices that skew the deposition of pottery. However, one advantage of the method is the ability to create a tightly-dated ceramic chronology. At Xunantunich, I coupled 22 radiocarbon dates taken from the same stratified units in which I did my ceramic seriation to date Classic-period styles with great accuracy (LeCount *et al.* 2002).

Archaeologists often ask me how I know what to seriate. They've read how I refined Gifford's Late and Terminal Classic chronology using microseriation of attributes, particularly those on Mount Maloney Black Type bowls and jars. Through time, the angle of Mount Maloney bowl lips changed orientation from vertical (90°) to beveled (45°) to horizontal (0°) in a continuous fashion; similarly, jar necks flared outward over time. I recognized the pattern after looking at thousands of Mount Maloney rim sherds from the provincial capital of Xunantunich and its hinterland farming community of San Lorenzo. Gifford recognized the bowl lip patterns, too, but did not have large enough collections to verify the trajectory. To confirm the pattern, I spent three years looking for stratigraphic sequences in which to seriate bowl lips and other pottery styles. San Lorenzo's collections were key to building a fine-grain seriation. The site's farmers remodeled their houses on a regular basis, and these numerous, small-scale additions generated layers of deposits filled with materials found around their homesteads. Because of these activities, temporally diagnostic ceramics were relatively unmixed in the deposits. On the other hand, Xunantunich's civic buildings were constructed when leaders commissioned new monuments; consequently, construction was sporadic, strata were thick, and ceramic diagnostics were highly mixed. Understandably, fine-grain rather than coarse-grain deposits are best for seriation.

The value of the Mount Maloney microseriation is the fact that it works in almost all contexts. These sturdy black-slipped vessels comprise the most common type of pottery found in households and civic buildings, making up between 20 and 50% of recognizable types in collections. They were the proverbial pots and pans of the Classic Maya, and everybody had lots of them. Their abundance means that small, poorly preserved, non-elite household collections can be dated even without the presence of beautiful pots that the ancient Maya are known for. The Classic Maya are world renowned for their polychrome vases and plates painted with hieroglyphic texts, complex scenes, and calendar dates. Commissioned artisans working in palace schools made these unique pieces for royalty, and we know a lot about them: where they were made based on their chemical signatures, who commissioned them because kings depicted on them were name-tagged, and when they were made since palace schools had short lives (Reents-Budet 1994). These characteristics made them the perfect index fossil. However, most of us will never find one unless we dig royal tombs; and even then it's not guaranteed. On the other hand, Mayanists find literally tons of domestic pottery consisting of plain wares, monochrome wares slipped in cream, red, orange, and black, and a few nicely incised and painted types. Besides being abundant, common pottery types were long lived, often resulting in extended battleship curves, while palace school types appear as blips on the radar.

Most of my colleagues prefer to work with pottery types, and wonder why I choose to seriate attributes of the pots themselves, such as lip orientation or slip color. Types, defined by the co-occurrence of attributes, are certainly easier to talk about. They condense variation by overlooking minor inconsistencies within types and accentuating differences between them. As named entities, they have become canonized as facts, and archaeologists spend a good deal of time learning how to pick them out of the morass of pottery variation that can overwhelm a person. Young students think they have earned the title "Archaeologist" after they learn their ceramic types, and old archaeologists have come to rely on favorite types as broad temporal and spatial markers. I don't dislike types. In fact, I use them every day. Some, like Mount Maloney Black, are highly consistent in slip color, surface treatment, and paste composition because they were produced in workshops that manufactured fairly standardized vessels. However, even standardized types display stylistic variation because production contexts and technical choices are not static across time or place. By focusing solely on finding types, ceramicists often lose sight of important variation they display.

You might find it surprising to know that I think about theory quite a bit while sorting and seriating ceramics. There is, of course, the classic Ford-Spaulding debate to think about. Am I discovering emic, cultural categories of pots that ancient people had in mind or am I constructing etic, analytically useful variables only a ceramicist could love? Because I favor attributes rather than types for my analyses, you might think I prefer analytical categories. However, I suggest this dichotomy is too overdrawn. If attributes pattern strongly across time or place, it suggests they must have been meaningful to ancient people. The French theory of *chaîne opératoire* developed by André Leroi-Gourhan suggests that attributes reflect the techniques (tools and gestures) and the manufacturing sequence shared by those who master their production. As such, they strongly correlate with social groups through learned or transmitted cognitive structures and behavioral practices. Like types, attributes can be used to understand the maintenance of cultural practices and the construction of social boundaries, but at a level in which specific decisions are made.

Ceramic Seriation in the Mopan Valley

I came to work with the Xunantunich Archaeological Project (XAP) in Belize after political turmoil in Peru forced me to look for a new project to do my dissertation research. Unlike other graduate students who worked on XAP, I hadn't taken a field school in the Maya lowlands or spent years studying the literature. I accepted the opportunity to be the project's ceramicist because I was desperate. I didn't know the pottery types, but neither did the other students. I learned them by studying Gifford's bible, deciphering J. E. S. Thompson's (1942) pre-Gifford ceramic typology from his work at the site, and showing senior archaeologists pottery I carried around in my pockets. I started building a type collection by curating examples in plastic shoe-boxes and wooden trays sorted by type. As I looked through my constantly growing collections, I was astounded by the variation in Classic pottery and questioned my ability to recognize Gifford's types. I observed attributes he never mentioned in his type descriptions, especially lip, feet, and base forms, as well as paste composition. These attributes later became the basis of my microseriation work. However, I also noticed continuity through time in many of his types, an initially casual observation that was confirmed in my interdigitated percentage stratigraphy seriation results. My seriations have led to an increase in the number of temporally diagnostic attributes known for Classic-period phases and greater reliability in assigning collections to phases especially in domestic contexts.

Although I am best known as a ceramicist, my primary interests have always been ancient politics and economies. After securing a tenure-track position at a major university, I developed the Actuncan Archaeological Project (AAP), which investigates the roles households played in the rise of Maya kingship in the Preclassic period. Actuncan, located about 2 km north of Xunantunich, has a rich history of occupation spanning two millennia from 1000 BC to AD 1000 and deep, complicated stratigraphy to prove it (annual reports, papers, and articles available at http://llecount.people.ua.edu/). One of the most dynamic time periods is the Late Preclassic to Early Classic transition, when Actuncan became the most architecturally impressive center in the region. Actuncan South is dominated by a triadic temple complex rising 28 m above its plaza. It connects to Actuncan North by a wide road that opens into a large formal space containing a ball court, palace, and pyramids. Elite residential compounds are located on the eastern side of this space, and a commoner settlement is situated to the north. Since 2000, I and my project members have tested all households, including a noble palace, and civic monuments including an E-Group, the earliest known civic-ceremonial complex among the ancient Maya. Although I love to dig, over the years I have come to rely on my graduate students for the day-to-day field operations while I do project business. I also find that my expertise is required in the lab, where I continue to do most of the ceramic analysis.

The timing of Actuncan's rise to power means that I am confronted with a new chronological problem. The Late Preclassic to Early Classic transition (BC 400 to AD 300) is the most problematic part of Gifford's ceramic sequence. It is subdivided into three complexes (Barton Creek, Mount Hope, and Floral Park) that despite continued research still remain inadequately described and dated. One problem is that the Floral Park and Mount Hope complexes overlap in time during the latter part of the period now called by many, the Terminal Preclassic. In many areas of the lowlands, Floral Park and similar diagnostics associated with the Protoclassic and Holmul I Sub-complexes are found only in ritual contexts and at a restricted number of sites (Brady *et al.* 1998). This suggests to some researchers that the fancy bowls and dishes that make up the complex are special-purpose serving wares, which co-occurred in time with the multifunctional pottery of earlier complexes, in my case, the Mount Hope Complex. There is no such disagreement about Barton Creek, the earliest of the Late Preclassic complexes, which is widely recognized as a relatively homogeneous complex made up of bold waxy red, black and cream slipped vessels, plus striated and unslipped plain wares.

A second problem is the recognition of diagnostic attributes indicative of Terminal Preclassic pottery. During this time, potters developed new surface treatments (glossy polishes), slip colors (brown and orange), and decorations including negative resist, positive painting, and the first polychrome types. Unfortunately, these innovations also resulted in hybrid attributes. For instance, semi-waxy or almost-glossy surfaces and colors such as brownish-orange or brownish-black make categorization very subjective. The difference between glossy and waxy surfaces is based on feel, while color is a continuous spectrum. The question is where you draw the line in each case, and researchers see and feel them differently. Finally, some types have very long lives, especially a waxy type called Sierra Red that spans the Late Preclassic to Early Classic transition. Apparently, waxy red pottery was "doxa" to the Preclassic Maya, in other words a highly valued tradition that resulted in biased choices of color and shine within the *chaîne opératoire* of ancient manufacture.

Rather than bemoan the fact that Preclassic Maya ceramic styles do not perform as index fossils the way Gifford intended, we can use them to our advantage since frequency seriation is a technique that deals effectively with changing styles over time. To seriate the Late Preclassic to Early Classic pottery, I decided that the first step should be charting the frequencies of wares – combinations of surface treatment, slip color, and paint technique. These attributes make up the basis of Gifford's types, but without the additional details of formal or stylistic modes that appear sporadically in collections dominated by body sherds. In the field lab, I coded the counts of each ware, as well as other variables into a Microsoft Access database for hundreds of Actuncan proveniences over the course of two field seasons. But for the seriation I settled on 36 lots associated with deeply stratified floor and fill deposits in three elite domestic structures (Structures 41, 40, 29), two commoner households (Groups 1 and 5), and two civic structures within the E-Group (Structures 23 and 26). The E-Group lots were included because Structures 23 and 26 contained many construction episodes dating to the target period. I did all the coding for this seriation project given the subjective nature of the attributes. Back from the field and in the comfort of my air-conditioned office, I loaded my data into Tim Hunt and Carl Lipo's Frequency Seriation Tool 3.0 software (Lipo 2001; Lipo *et al.* 1997). It does the tedious work of calculating frequencies of styles by row and creating a Ford Diagram, but you must manually place proveniences into a stratigraphically correct, interdigitated sequence in the database to produce an array of pleasing battleship curves.

Seriation, no matter how you do it, is accomplished by a trial-and-error process. After the first run of the software, many of the proveniences with small sample sizes did not seriate. They contained only a few dominant surface treatments like unslipped plain ware, waxy reds, and little else. So I lumped together lots that came from the same analytical unit such as floor, fill, or feature contexts to increase sample sizes. I had a similar problem with minor styles, so I combined black and brown slip colors since they often graded together on the same waxy or glossy sherds, as well as red and orange slips on waxy sherds. Although I believe the Maya understood these colors to be different, their choices about how to render them are challenging to understand unless you have whole, well-preserved vessels. I also removed styles such as unslipped plain ware and other surface treatments that did not change in frequency over time and therefore did not help my efforts. I found that I had to have around 50 diagnostic sherds to feel confident about achieving the expected range of variation within the style universe. I reran the program more than 20 times shifting the order of proveniences and lumping or removing attributes until they formed battleship curves. In the end, my Ford Diagram contained 15 proveniences and 13 diagnostic styles, about half of what I started with (Figure 21.1).

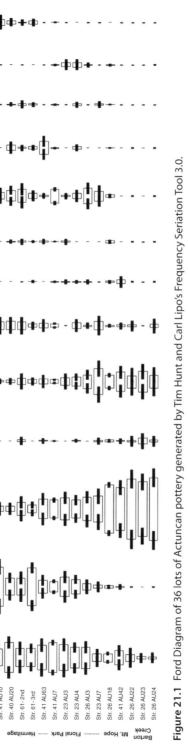

Figure 21.1 Ford Diagram of 36 lots of Actuncan pottery generated by Tim Hunt and Carl Lipo's Frequency Seriation Tool 3.0.

If James Gifford were alive today to see my Ford Diagram, he would feel vindicated. Although I did not seriate his types, my ware seriation validates much of his chronology. In Late Preclassic times, there was a developmental trajectory from a small set of slipped waxy wares to increasingly innovative surface treatments, slip colors, and paint techniques. By the Early Classic period, polished, slipped, and painted styles were rapidly replacing waxy wares. These innovations can be traced by their *terminus post quem* "starting points" on Figure 21.1. But the more important finding is the fact that waxy red wares consistently declined through time. Starting in the Barton Creek Complex red waxy wares dominate the assemblage at 75 to 65% of diagnostics, but frequencies fall to 60 to 50% in the Mount Hope Complex, then to 30 to 20% in the Floral Park and finally to 15 to 5% in the Hermitage Complex. This pattern means that rather than relying on the presence of rare elite or ritual vessels to identify chronological phases we can use the frequency of a common pottery style for this task.

Conclusions

Only time will tell if my waxy red ware seriation will be as useful to archaeologists as my Mount Maloney microseriation. Next field season I will test out my pattern on new collections to see if it produces reliable results. I also will begin coupling these data with other variables, such as Gifford's types and formal attributes, using nonmetric multi-dimensional scaling to construct a more comprehensive relative dating scheme. Once completed, it can be integrated with the project's 35 radiocarbon dates derived from the same excavation units from which the ceramic chronology was built. Although the final scheme is a few years away, at this point in the research process I have achieved what I set out to do.

My advice to those who wish to embark on a similar seriation project is to develop a good eye for pattern. When I first started working with Xunantunich ceramics, I spent a month just breaking sherds to look at temper, paste, and texture. I drew hundreds of rim profiles and illustrations, each on a single piece of graph paper keyed to an ID number written on the sherd. There, I also recorded slip, paint, and paste colors using a Munsell color chart and other notes, which I placed in a notebook organized by ceramic type and form. But by far the most useful strategy for me was building my massive type collection, which I continue to develop and refer to on a daily basis in the field. Researchers come to see it from all over the Maya lowlands because the proof of the pudding (my seriation) is the ceramics themselves.

My experiences also have taught me that seriation is not just another data management task divorced from anthropologically interesting questions. It reminds me that good archaeology is based in the fundamentals of time, space, and form. To explore and explain the past requires comparisons between things that are known to be either temporally similar or divergent. To do otherwise is to make something look more significant than it really was. It also informs my understanding of the taken-for-granted technical processes within the *chaîne opératoire* of pottery manufacture. The color, shine, and feel of pottery were deeply held values among the ancient Maya, and understanding these preferences enriches our view of this astonishing civilization.

Paired Reading

LeCount, Lisa, Jason Yaeger, Richard M. Leventhal, and Wendy Ashmore. 2002. "Dating the Rise and Fall of Xunantunich, Belize: A Late and Terminal Classic Lowland Maya Secondary Center." *Ancient Mesoamerica*, 13:41–63. DOI: 10.1017/S0956536102131117.

References

Brady, James E., Joseph W. Ball, Ronald L. Bishop, Duncan C. Pring, Norman Hammond, and Rupert A. Housley. 1998. "The Lowland Maya 'Protoclassic': A Reconsideration of Its Nature and Significance." *Ancient Mesoamerica*, 9: 17–38. DOI: 10.1017/S0956536100001826.

Gifford, James C. 1976. *Prehistoric Pottery Analysis and the Ceramics of Barton Ramie in the Belize Valley*. Memoirs of the Peabody Museum of Archaeology and Ethnology, Harvard University 18. Cambridge, MA: Peabody Museum of Archaeology and Ethnology, Harvard University.

LeCount, Lisa J. 1996. "Feasting, Gifting, and Displaying Wealth among the Late and Terminal Classic Lowland Maya." PhD dissertation. Los Angeles, CA: University of California Los Angeles.

LeCount, Lisa, Jason Yaeger, Richard M. Leventhal, and Wendy Ashmore. 2002. "Dating the Rise and Fall of Xunantunich, Belize: A Late and Terminal Classic Lowland Maya Secondary Center." *Ancient Mesoamerica*, 13: 41–63. DOI: 10.1017/S0956536102131117.

Lipo, Carl P. 2001. *Science, Style and the Study of Community Structure: An Example from the Central Mississippi River Valley*. British Archaeological Reports, International Series, no. 918, Oxford: British Archaeological Reports.

Lipo, Carl, Mark E. Madsen, Robert C. Dunnell, and Tim Hunt. 1997. "Population Structure, Cultural Transmission, and Frequency Seriation." *Journal of Anthropological Archaeology*, 16: 301–333. DOI: 10.1006/jaar.1997.0314.

Lyman, R. Lee, Steve Wolverton, and Michael J. O'Brien. 1998. "Seriation, Superposition, and Interdigitation: A History of Americanist Graphic Depictions of Culture Change." *American Antiquity*, 63: 239–262. DOI: 10.2307/2694696.

Reents-Budet, Dorie. 1994. *Painting the Maya Universe: Royal Ceramics of the Classic Period*. Durham, NC: Duke University Press.

Renfrew, Colin and Paul Bahn. 2010. *Archaeology Essentials: Theories, Methods, and Practice*, 2nd ed. London: Thames & Hudson.

Thompson, J. E. S. 1942. *Late Ceramic Horizons at Benque Viejo, British Honduras*. Carnegie Institution of Washington Pub. 528. Contributions to American Anthropology and History, No. 35. Washington, DC: Carnegie Institution.

22

The Bones from the *Other* Tell: Zooarchaeology at Çatalhöyük West

David Orton

Project Summary

Çatalhöyük needs little introduction to students of Eurasian prehistory. Situated on the Konya Plain, Turkey, the 21 m depth of densely-packed, superimposed house remains – replete with wall paintings, cattle-horn installations, and underfloor burials – that make up the Neolithic tell settlement of Çatalhöyük East Mound (ca.7100–5950 BC) have caught the imagination of archaeologists and laypeople alike, ever since they were first excavated by James Mellaart in the 1960s. Much less well known, however, is the nearby West Mound (ca.6100–5600 BC). A little smaller, a little later, and considerably less thoroughly researched, Çatalhöyük West is at best a footnote in accounts of the site. This chapter describes my experience as the zooarchaeologist for the Çatalhöyük West Mound Project (WMP) from 2006 to 2016. My role was to provide specialist support to a field project – a loose remit allowing me to refine a research agenda in response to developments in the field. As such there is no tidy, hypothesis-driven research design to set out here. Likewise, analysis is still underway so there are no neat conclusions. Instead, this chapter focuses on challenges encountered along the way.

Site Background

Çatalhöyük is a large Neolithic settlement in Central Anatolia, consisting of two *tells* (Figure 22.1), artificial mounds built up by centuries of human activity. The site was the earliest known settlement in the region when first excavated in 1961–1965 by James Mellaart, whose findings brought international attention: layer upon layer of close-packed mudbrick houses, elaborate wall paintings and cattle-horn installations (*bucrania*), underfloor burials, and spectacular figurines. Subsistence centered on cereal crops plus domestic sheep and, it appeared, cattle, the latter featuring prominently in symbolism. Although there are now earlier known Neolithic settlements in Central Anatolia – for example Aşıklı Höyük in Cappadocia – Çatalhöyük remains important for understanding the spread and development of farming, and the social organization of early village communities. Research resumed in 1993 led by Ian Hodder – effective founder of the post-processualist school – who saw the iconic Neolithic site as the perfect case study to demonstrate that his theoretical ideas could be fruitfully applied in practice.

Engaging Archaeology: 25 Case Studies in Research Practice, First Edition. Edited by Stephen W. Silliman.
© 2018 John Wiley & Sons, Inc. Published 2018 by John Wiley & Sons, Inc.

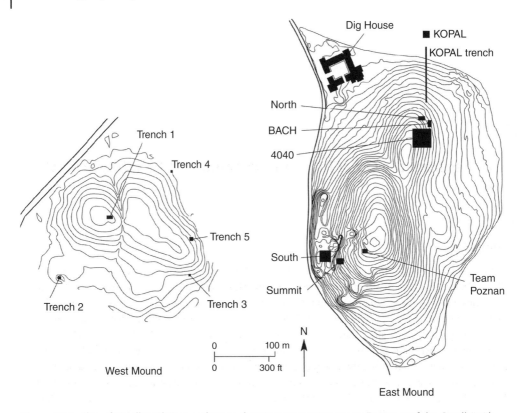

North

Figure 22.1 Plan of Çatalhöyük East and West, showing excavation areas. Courtesy of the Çatalhöyük Research Project.

The larger East Mound was the main focus of research both by Mellaart and by Hodder's Çatalhöyük Research Project (ÇRP; see Hodder 2011, 2014). At 21 m high and circa 13 ha in extent, it was occupied for over a millennium (ca. 7100–5950 BC), supporting a population in the thousands for much of that period. Much less is known about the smaller (ca. 6 ha) West Mound, only 200 m away. Traditionally considered Chalcolithic rather than Neolithic due to the presence of painted property, Çatalhöyük West has few of the "classic" Çatalhöyük features. The shift in location has often been taken to suggest a sudden disruption to life at Çatalhöyük, circa 6000 BC, perhaps due to conflict or climate change (see Biehl *et al.* 2012).

Aims

Ideally, any research project should start with clearly defined aims. This was the case for the Çatalhöyük West Mound Project (Biehl *et al.* 2012), which set out to understand social change on the Konya Plain around the turn of the seventh to sixth millennia BC by comparing lifeways at Çatalhöyük West with results emerging from the latest levels of Çatalhöyük East (the Polish-led "Team Poznań" (TP) excavation area). As the zooarchaeologist, I was expected to contribute to this research agenda as appropriate, but there were no specific questions or hypotheses beyond this loose remit. The upside was that I had considerable freedom to refine my aims in response to developments both in our West Mound excavations and in the East Mound research. On the downside, I went into the project with little idea of exactly what I was looking for.

In practice, two more specific aims crystallized over time: (1) to understand the depositional processes behind some very odd building infills in our main trench, and (2) to test the hypothesis that herding and hunting practices actually changed very little across the transition from the East to West mounds. The first is fundamentally taphonomic and entailed close collaboration with the rest of the WMP team; the second meant working with the main East Mound zooarchaeological team.

Methods

The principal methodology involved in my research at Çatalhöyük was conventional zooarchaeology – that is, morphological analysis of animal bones and teeth. This included the standard suite of analyses: taxonomic identification, metrical analysis, sex and age-at-death assessment, and taphonomy (the study of what happened to animal remains after death – from butchery and consumption, through deposition, to preservation in the ground – by looking at which bones are present and what physical traces of damage they retain).

All of this was conducted as part of a multidisciplinary team that included specialists (mostly graduate students) in ceramics, lithics, architecture, and – eventually – archaeobotany and bone tools. Later in the project we also sampled bones for radiocarbon dating and proteomic identification, which are described in more detail below. Finally, my role involved facilitating further biomolecular analyses, in particular aDNA (ancient DNA) and stable isotopes, by external collaborators, though little has yet to emerge from this.

Theoretical Background

Çatalhöyük is often associated with the post-processual movement effectively founded by its director, but, like many, I believe this label to be obsolete. The "theory wars" that wracked Anglophone archaeology from the 1980s had petered out by the 2000s, and we are now in an era where rigorous scientific methodology and critical cultural analysis are as often allies as rivals. In my view the history of the Çatalhöyük Research Project is a microcosm of this wider development, but that is another story. In any case, researchers at the site are free to bring their own theoretical outlooks to the project; indeed pluralism is an explicit part of Hodder's approach.

My own theoretical stance has unsurprisingly shifted over a decade of research, inevitably affecting my approach to the Çatalhöyük data. Back in 2006 I was a graduate student railing against both the materialism of traditional, subsistence-obsessed zooarchaeology that reduced animals to resources, and the idealism of some recent work that reduced them instead to symbols. Inspired by the *human-animal relations* literature and people like Tim Ingold, Arek Marciniak (coincidentally director of the TP team at Çatalhöyük), and Nerissa Russell (then co-director of the East Mound faunal team), I was distrustful of many routine quantitative techniques in zooarchaeology – seeing them as simplistic abstractions – and saw taphonomy and detailed contextual analysis as the key to a relevant *social* zooarchaeology.

As time passed, however, I realized this was short-sighted: all that "boring" metrical and age-at-death data really is very useful, whatever one's theoretical stance. Nor does a view that animals are *more* than just calories mean that their role in human subsistence is not an important object of study. This realization was prompted partly by the experience of writing up my PhD and partly by working with a Çatalhöyük faunal team that held similar theoretical views moderated by far more experience of actual research. Indeed, over the years I have swung back to the view that animal remains in prehistory are *usually* a better source of information on broad subsistence trends than on subtle questions of cultural identity or human-animal relations, though I remain interested in both. All this caused my priorities to shift over my decade at Çatalhöyük.

Getting Involved

Like many archaeology students, I initially heard of Çatalhöyük during first-year undergraduate lectures on the Neolithic. Being determined to study the Palaeolithic, I paid little attention. Two years later I completed my degree at Cambridge and moved to York for a specialist master's program in zooarchaeology. My interests shifted, and by 2005 I found myself back in Cambridge, embarking upon a PhD on hunting in the Balkan Neolithic, particularly Serbia. Suddenly Çatalhöyük became an analog from which to draw ideas and inspiration. I attended a lecture at University College London by Louise Martin, then co-director of the zooarchaeology team at Çatalhöyük, and was excited to hear about the discovery – published that year (Russell *et al.* 2005) – that the famous "domestic" cattle were in fact wild aurochsen, hunted by the site's occupants and disproportionately used in feasts and installations. This was just the kind of pattern that I was interested in exploring within my PhD.

It therefore came as a very pleasant surprise to receive an unexpected email from a visiting lecturer at Cambridge, Peter Biehl. Peter would be starting an excavation project at Çatalhöyük, he wrote, focusing on the West Mound, and he needed a zooarchaeologist for his team. Someone had apparently recommended me, and would I be interested in taking the role on? I knew I shouldn't get distracted from my doctorate, but there was only one possible answer.

In summer 2006, therefore, I travelled to Turkey for my first season at Çatalhöyük. At this point I had no idea how long my involvement would last: Peter's West Mound project (WMP), co-directed by Eva Rosenstock, was set for a few years in the first instance, with continued funding uncertain, while my PhD was due in 2008. In fact, I ended up working at the site for ten years: as a student, post-doc, and eventually lecturer. But Çatalhöyük was never my PhD topic, nor a post-doctoral project. Rather, it became a decade-long side-project.

Settling In

Starting out at Çatalhöyük can be a bewildering experience due to the sheer number of different people and projects involved. Apart from the main ÇRP, there have been numerous subsidiary field projects over the years, including our WMP. When we arrived in 2006, the Polish TP team were just leaving, the Istanbul University crew was hard at work in their IST trench, and a new team from the local Selçuk University were investigating Late Antique activity around the site. Alongside the field teams are specialists in numerous branches of archaeological science and artifact research: at a recent estimate, 160 researchers across 32 specialties have contributed to the current state of knowledge regarding Çatalhöyük East (Hodder 2014: 18), while a typical season might peak at 120–130 people on-site simultaneously.

All this activity requires a substantial infrastructure, and the ÇRP has constructed an extensive dig-house (visible in Figure 22.1) complete with visitor center, seminar room, and a suite of laboratories, plus accommodation, a kitchen/canteen, and storage depots. Researchers (or their projects) pay a daily charge to cover these overheads. I would be working in the dedicated "faunal" laboratory, alongside the main zooarchaeological team.

There are some important prerequisites for any new zooarchaeological project. First, a recording protocol must be established – a process involving numerous seemingly arcane decisions that can make a huge difference to the research potential of the data. Should you prioritize speed or detail? Which bones are "diagnostic"? Should "non-diagnostic" fragments be measured and recorded individually or *en masse*? How much detail will be recorded regarding breakage, butchery, preservation condition…? The list goes on, and there are as many recording systems as there are practicing zooarchaeologists – probably more, in fact, since it is common to tailor one's system to a specific project.

Second, one must assemble sufficient reference material to enable identification of all the species that might reasonably be expected (see, for example, Baker and Worley 2014). Physical reference skeletons are ideal, but in practice are almost always supplemented by published identification guides, photographs, and recently also 3D models. Where logistics, legislation, or permit conditions prevent bones being taken off-site, as at Çatalhöyük, a field reference collection/library needs to be built up from scratch.

At Çatalhöyük, all of this was taken out of my hands. The zooarchaeology team already had a well-established recording system and associated database. This involved a Microsoft Access front-end, with the database itself hosted on a server accessed via wireless network – allowing multiple researchers to enter data simultaneously. Key context information was pulled straight from the main excavation database to inform each "Faunal Unit Description" – an initial assessment of the bones from each stratigraphic unit – while team leaders also had remote access to the Finds Register, allowing them to manage the locations of bones in the depot.

Likewise, the team had built up an impressive field laboratory with modern reference skeletons for most of the major species expected at the site, albeit with a few problematic gaps (pigs, for example, are hard to come by in a relatively conservative region of Turkey). This was supplemented by an extensive library of reference manuals and papers, all in hard copy at that point, though much subsequently digitized. Recording equipment and laboratory consumables were taken care of: sample bags, balances, calipers, a measuring box for large bones, and even a flatbed scanner for recording butchery marks requiring only a shallow depth of field. Ordinarily I would have had to arrange to bring all of these supplies and equipment with me from the United Kingdom, or find local suppliers.

As a member of the faunal laboratory, working under the ÇRP umbrella, I was expected to use the existing database for my West Mound bones. It would have been foolish not to: employing the same protocol made my results fully compatible with hundreds of thousands of bones already recorded for the East Mound and earlier West Mound excavations. On the downside, the system was at the complex (hence slow) end of the spectrum, requiring considerable training. Louise Martin gave me an introduction in London beforehand, but nonetheless my first season at Çatalhöyük was spent familiarizing myself with the database and coding systems by working on East Mound units, supervised by the team leaders.

In fact, I continued working on East Mound bones until the 2008 season. Both mounds at Çatalhöyük are dotted with post-Chalcolithic burials, dating from the Hellenistic through to Selçuk (early Islamic) periods, which must be excavated and documented with due respect, even when one's real objective is earlier. Because our main trench, T5, encountered many of these burials and other "late" features, secure Chalcolithic deposits were not available for more than two seasons. While our pottery and lithics specialists could begin work using diagnostic specimens from mixed deposits, this is not possible with bone.

Frustrating as it was, this was a useful exercise. Apart from becoming proficient in site protocols, I gained insight into the East Mound zooarchaeology, had the valuable experience of participating in analysis and publication (Russell *et al.* 2013), and took many methodological and interpretative ideas back to my doctoral research. Had this been a PhD or time-limited post-doctoral project, however, the delay would have been crippling.

Going West

From the 2008 season, securely Chalcolithic bones landed on my desk in ever-increasing numbers, and my research began in earnest. My first realization was that the typology of bone deposits that had developed over the years for the East Mound, and that I had gained a feel for, did not carry across to the West. On the East Mound, abandoned buildings were typically rapidly filled with relatively sterile rubble in preparation for rebuilding. "Room fills" thus usually contain a low density of animal bones, mostly redeposited from elsewhere. Richer faunal material is encountered in "middens" – representing day-to-day deposition – and special "feasting deposits," both typically found between buildings (Martin and Russell 2000).

In Trench 5 we encountered only infilled buildings. The fills of those buildings, however, bore no relation to their East Mound equivalents. Some units were extremely rich in cultural material, with bones often better preserved than anything at Çatalhöyük East. Limited fragmentation indicated light, even wasteful, processing; lack of weathering or dog gnawing suggested rapid burial; and frequent *in situ* articulations showed that subsequent disturbance had been minimal. So "fresh" did some deposits look that there was suspicion they might be Hellenistic intrusions, until the first radiocarbon dates came back firmly Chalcolithic. Other units contained raw and partially worked antlers and scored and split bones, suggesting raw material caching and/or *in situ* craft working.

Species representation also stood out. Sheep and goat are the most common finds throughout the sequence at Çatalhöyük, but cattle and wild equids were also frequent in the East Mound units I had previously encountered. The T5 bones, by contrast, were over 95% sheep/goat by NISP (Number of Identified Specimens, i.e., fragment count). At first glance this fit the narrative of a radical break in settlement at Çatalhöyük: a shift in subsistence base coinciding with the move to the West Mound.

As I was coming to grips with the West Mound remains, however, a new picture of change was emerging on the East Mound. Rather than a millennium of continuity, it was increasingly clear that a significant change in subsistence base and social organization occurred around 6500 BC. Cattle now appear to have become domestic at this point, based on body size and age structure, though it remains uncertain whether local aurochsen were domesticated or (more likely) domestic cattle imported from elsewhere. Meanwhile the relative frequency of sheep and goat increased dramatically, such that the new domestic cattle were much less economically important than their wild predecessors. Compared with the new results for the upper levels of Çatalhöyük East, the T5 data now seemed – at least superficially – to emphasize *continuity* between the mounds, with the most obvious breakpoint in subsistence patterns occurring centuries before the move.

Two research questions thus started to emerge. First, what consumption and deposition practices underlay the infilling of the T5 buildings, particularly the bizarrely fresh deposits? Second, was there continuity in sheep and goat herding practices, as well as sheer numbers, across the transition between East and West?

Priorities, Priorities

Animal remains are typically amongst the most frequent finds on archaeological sites, and it is thus rare for *all* the bones from an excavation to be recorded, at least on large sites. Rather, analysts usually attempt to study a representative, stratified sample, ideally capturing the variation within and between phases, areas, deposit types, and so on. At Çatalhöyük this process was facilitated by a triage system, with many units "assessed" prior to full-scale recording. Bones were laid out and assessed qualitatively for composition, condition and coherence, and given a lengthy "Faunal Unit Description" (FUD) in the database before being graded as A1–A5. A1 units were top priority for recording; A2s would probably be recorded eventually; A3s maybe not; and units given A4–A5, which were typically either mixed-phase or heavily redeposited, were consigned straight to the depot. Metrical data were also recorded at this stage from all but the least secure units.

I initially embraced this process, putting a lot of time into writing detailed FUDs in keeping with my interest in consumption/deposition practices and context-level taphonomy. In hindsight, while this was perhaps a worthwhile exercise in ordering my own thoughts about formation processes, I might have done better to concentrate on getting more bones into the database. When I came to start systematically reviewing formation processes within the T5 building infills, alongside the other West Mound specialists, I primarily relied on collating quantitative taphonomic data from fully-recorded units, rather than consulting the FUDs. Moreover, all this careful description of unit coherence wasn't generating the basic data on species frequencies, body size, or age-at-death necessary to address the emerging hypothesis about continuity/change in herding strategies. In later years I adapted the assessment system accordingly, adding a count of "diagnostic zones" per species and recording all mandibles for age-at-death, but also concentrated more on fully recording units.

In any case, each season produced more bone than I could record or even assess, and when excavation in T5 finished in 2013 I had a substantial backlog. Going into our study seasons in 2014–2015, with the project monograph due in 2017, I had to decide on priorities: should I study a good sample from each space, or record *all* bones from key buildings while neglecting others? The former should give a more representative sample of subsistence data; the latter would be better for reconstructing infilling processes. I settled upon a hybrid strategy: writing-off some spaces almost completely, studying a sample from most, but focusing efforts on recording all the bones from our best-preserved building (B.98).

Branching Out: Collaborations and Specialist Analyses

As the hypothesis of continuity in herding practices between mounds crystallized, so did two problems. First, any assessment of change-over-time requires a solid absolute chronological framework, which was not yet in place. Second, the notorious difficulty of distinguishing sheep from goat bones undermined any detailed analysis of changes in their relative frequencies and herding patterns.

Until recently, neither the West Mound nor the uppermost levels of the East Mound had many published radiocarbon dates. An intensive dating was underway on the East Mound, but the WMP needed to make its own arrangements – an expensive proposition at roughly €250–€450 per sample. The best material for dating in T5 was the abundant articulated animal bone – ideal because it's very unlikely to be residual – and the task of designing, funding, and executing a dating program thus fell to me. Funding came from the NERC Radiocarbon Facility, a UK-based scheme to which I had previously made successful applications in support of my PhD. We were lucky: 16 out of 18 samples produced results, all within the expected window but a little earlier than anticipated. Coupled with some surprisingly late dates from the TP area, published in 2015, these showed that our T5 deposits probably dated to *just* after the East Mound was abandoned, while the West Mound as a whole almost certainly overlapped with the East by one or more centuries (Orton *et al.* 2018). My T5 faunal data could thus be juxtaposed directly with the later East Mound sequence, but we were clearly not looking at a sudden break in occupation.

To deal with the sheep/goat identification problem I turned to a recently developed molecular barcoding technique: Zooarchaeology by Mass Spectroscopy (ZooMS: Buckley *et al.* 2010). Based on analysis of collagen, the main protein in bone, this permits taxonomic identification of tiny fragments of bone at much lower expense than aDNA. ZooMS doesn't necessarily provide species-level identification but can easily distinguish between sheep and goats. Since studies of herd management rely heavily on age-at-death data from mandibles, I applied ZooMS to a large sample of sheep/goat mandibles from both mounds.

Funding came from a British Academy Small Research Grant, a program which awards up to £10,000 and is useful for junior researchers due to unusually broad eligibility criteria. This was enough for about 320 ZooMS samples, plus travel costs, part of the overhead charges for the two sample-collection seasons (2014–2015), and a student research assistant. At the time of writing the final results have just come through, with 98% of samples successfully identified to species level. Worryingly, more than 10% of the original morphological identifications need to be corrected. Analysis in terms of herding strategies is yet to come, but it appears that goats became markedly more common at Çatalhöyük West.

Regional Meta-Analysis

In 2011 the faunal team was contacted by Ben Arbuckle, an expert on prehistoric Central Anatolian zooarchaeology. Together with archaeological open data champions Sarah and Eric Kansa, Ben was starting an ambitious project aimed at charting the spread and development of animal husbandry across Anatolia, while showcasing the benefits of data sharing. Unlike typical archaeological meta-analyses, which make use of published or archived data, researchers would submit raw data to be compiled and analyzed together in a truly integrative study, a challenge given the diversity of recording systems noted above. The data would then be made freely available on the Open Context platform.

The benefits of open data in archaeology are contentious, but for me the clinching argument is transparency: if raw data are not available, how can other researchers evaluate one's conclusions? More pragmatically, anything that facilitates other researchers using your research – and giving you formal credit for it – cannot be bad for a young researcher trying to build their profile. While I haven't always lived up to this view in practice, I wasn't going to miss the opportunity to participate in such an innovative project. Meanwhile the latest tranche of East Mound zooarchaeological results was shortly to be published, and the team were happy for the data to be used. The task of cleaning and decoding our vast faunal database for sharing/publication fell to me, taking ten solid days, but the effort paid off. We produced an interesting paper (Arbuckle *et al.* 2014) which has subsequently been cited as much as an example of data sharing practice as for its contribution to Anatolian prehistory. Equally importantly, it was extremely helpful to collaborate directly with zooarchaeologists working on other sites in the region. Finally, getting the West Mound data "out there" helped to assuage a growing sense of guilt at not having produced substantial interim reports on my work.

Looking Back

It's hard to write conclusions about a project which has not (quite) concluded. Although data collection is finished, I am still bringing these data to bear on the two main research objectives. With regard to the herding continuity hypothesis, early indications from age-at-death, metrics, and ZooMS are that, contrary to superficial impressions from taxonomic frequencies, there *were* some fairly significant changes in sheep/goat herd management, but these require further analysis alongside the East Mound data.

This was not a textbook project. In retrospect I should have engaged more with the intellectual and regional context from the outset, refined my questions/hypothesis earlier, and built more regional collaborations. My principal regret, however, is not spending enough time in the trench, getting a feel for the contexts from which the bones derived. The great advantage of a field laboratory is the opportunity for back-and-forth dialogue between excavators and specialist analysts, with the latter able to observe and participate in excavation. I would urge any novice zooarchaeologist or other specialist to seize this opportunity with both hands when it arises.

A final lesson that I think can be learned from my Çatalhöyük experience is not to be scared of deviating – a little – from your core research. Side-projects *can* become a millstone around your neck, but chosen wisely they can also provide opportunities, insights, and inspiration that feed back into your primary research far more than they distract from it.

Paired Reading

Orton, David C., Jana Anvari, Catriona Gibson, Jonathan Last, Amy Bogaard, Eva Rosenstock, and Peter F. Biehl. 2018. "A Tale of Two Tells: Dating the Çatalhöyük West Mound." *Antiquity*, in press.

References

Arbuckle, Benjamin S., Sarah Whitcher Kansa, Eric Kansa, David Orton, Canan Çakırlar, Lionel Gourichon, Levent Atici, Alfred Galik, Arkadiusz Marciniak, Jacqui Mulville, Hijlke Buitenhuis, Denise Carruthers, Bea De Cupere, Arzu Demirergi, Sheelagh Frame, Daniel Helmer, Louise Martin, Joris Peters, Nadja Pöllath, Kamilla Pawłowska, Nerissa Russell, Katheryn Twiss, and Doris Würtenberger. 2014. "Data Sharing Reveals Complexity in the Westward Spread of Domestic Animals across Neolithic Turkey." *PLoS ONE*, 9. DOI: 10.1371/journal.pone.0099845.

Baker, Polydora and Fay Worley. 2014. *Animal Bones and Archaeology: Guidelines for Best Practice.* Swindon: English Heritage.

Biehl, Peter, Ingmar Franz, Sonia Ostaptchouk, David C. Orton, Eva Rosenstock, and Jana Anvari 2012. "One Community and Two Tells: The Phenomenon of Relocating Tell Settlements at the Turn of the 7th and the 6th Millennia in Central Anatolia." In *Tells: Social and Environmental Space*, edited by Robert Hofmann, Fawzi-Kemal Moetz, and Johannes Müller, 53–65. Bonn: Habelt.

Buckley, Mike, Sarah Whitcher Kansa, Sarah Howard, Stuart Campbell, Jane Thomas-Oates, and Matthew Collins. 2010. "Distinguishing between Archaeological Sheep and Goat Bones Using a Single Collagen Peptide." *Journal of Archaeological Science*, 37: 13–20. DOI: 10.1016/j.jas.2009.08.020.

Hodder, Ian. 2011. *The Leopard's Tale: Revealing the Mysteries of Turkey's Ancient Town*. London: Thames & Hudson.

Hodder, Ian. 2014. "Çatalhöyük: The Leopard Changes Its Spots. A Summary of Recent Work." *Anatolian Studies*, 64: 1–22. DOI: 10.1017/S0066154614000027.

Martin, Louise and Nerissa Russell. 2000. "Trashing Rubbish." In *Towards Reflexive Method in Archaeology: The Example at Çatalhöyük*, edited by Ian Hodder, 57–69. Cambridge: McDonald Institute.

Orton, David C., Jana Anvari, Catriona Gibson, Jonathan Last, Amy Bogaard, Eva Rosenstock, and Peter F. Biehl. 2018. "A Tale of Two Tells: Dating the Çatalhöyük West Mound." *Antiquity*, in press.

Russell, Nerissa, Louise Martin, and Hijlke Buitenhuis, 2005. "Cattle Domestication at Çatalhöyük Revisited." *Current Anthropology*, 46: S101–S108. DOI: 10.1086/497664.

Russell, Nerissa, Katheryn Twiss, David C. Orton, and Arzu Demirergi. 2013. "More on the Çatalhöyük Mammal Remains." In *Humans and Landscapes of Çatalhöyük: Reports from the 2000–2008 Seasons*, edited by Ian Hodder, 213–258. Los Angeles, CA: UCLA Cotsen Institute of Archaeology.

23

Disrupting Fixed Narratives: Researching Colonial Dress and Identity in Museum Collections

Diana DiPaolo Loren

Project Summary

My research on colonial dress and adornment in New England stems from my interest in investigating the lived experience of individuals within colonial contexts. Clothing and adornment artifacts speak not only to how individuals covered their body but also to the manner in which they lived within and reacted to colonial strictures and structures. I conduct this research in museum collections focusing on how assemblages of clothing and adornment artifacts "fit" together. Here, I highlight my investigation of one category of material culture, which is part of this larger research agenda. Researching museum collections is sometimes a challenging task. At times, information on object history, provenance, and supporting documentation can be limited, which is especially true with older collections. Additionally, archaeologists must also navigate through issues of provenance and stewardship in addition to the study of the material and cultural aspects of the object itself. Despite these challenges, museum collections can provide unique insights on different artifact assemblages as well as historical collection practices.

Conducting Research on Seventeenth-Century Stone Molds and How Museums Shape Narratives

Seventeenth-century stone button molds recovered from New England contexts are the focus of my chapter. I should note that I am still in the process of researching these collections, and my interpretations here are a work in progress. This research into one specific object category is part of a larger study on dress, identity, health, and the body as materialized and performed through clothing and adornment in the seventeenth-century New World. Examining the archaeology of clothing and adornment as it relates to dress and identity poses some challenges. In New England, whole pieces of seventeenth-century clothing are rarely recovered from the archaeological record, and there are few, if any, pieces of seventeenth-century clothing extant in museum collections. Rather what is found in the archaeological record are items that were part of larger items of clothing, such as fasteners for clothing (e.g., buttons and buckles) or adornment, including glass beads or parts of jewelry. Also considered artifacts of dress and adornment are the items and tools used to fashion the body, including hair combs and wig curlers and tools used for making and mending clothing, such as thimbles, needles, lead fabric seals, and stone molds.

Engaging Archaeology: 25 Case Studies in Research Practice, First Edition. Edited by Stephen W. Silliman.

My larger research on dress and the body includes all forms of material culture related to clothing and adorning the body. To consider the fully dressed body and how that body interacted with the world, assemblages of artifacts are more telling than just a single item. For example, the confluence of shell and glass beads along with sleeve buttons and shoe buckles in an eighteenth-century household context suggests some of the items of clothing that may have been worn by individuals that lived in that residence. The size, color, and number of shell and glass beads may suggest that they were used as jewelry or embroidered on clothing. Sleeve buttons may suggest tailored shirts, while the kind of shoe buckles (fancy or plain) suggest how some residents may have ornamented their leather shoes. Historical and archival information are folded into to this research to gain insight on how different combinations of clothing were worn in relation or opposition to sumptuary laws and social expectations as well as suggest how items may have been worn in unexpected ways, such as buttons worn as earrings and glass beads that were woven into hair.

Research into clothing and adornment in distinct historical contexts also necessitates analysis on singular object types, such as I discuss in this chapter. Here, my focus is on stone button molds, a relatively rare item only primarily available in museum archaeological collections. I became interested in button molds as they were a relatively understudied artifact of clothing and adornment in colonial New England but did occur as I considered larger assemblages of clothing and adornment artifacts. As most buttons used for closures on clothing in seventeenth-century New England were made in England and shipped to the Americas in bulk lots or on fashioned clothing, what accounted for button molds in collections? The recovery of this tool from seventeenth-century contexts suggests that people were making buttons rather than depending solely on resources from England. The local production of buttons in seventeenth-century New England is an interesting aspect to this research on clothing and adornment, suggesting ingenuity and creativity of colonial peoples living in New England. But who made and used button molds? What does the presence of these rare items signify in the larger context of dress in seventeenth-century New England? The answer to these questions is related to provenance of button molds, their interpretation in museum catalogues, and primary and secondary source research on seventeenth-century dress.

Museum collections can be daunting locations to conduct research as museums contain their own silences regarding object history, provenance, and supporting documentation. The location of an object in museum storage, rather than in the field, necessitates certain attention to issues of provenance and stewardship in addition to the study of the material and cultural aspects of the object itself. The movement of an artifact or group of artifacts from the field involves museum practices (i.e., collections catalogue and inventory, accessioning, archival and object documentation, and curatorial interpretation) that add not only to the object's biography but also to the ways in which we view and understand them today (see Byrne *et al.* 2011; Gosden and Knowles 2001; Stewart 1993; Thomas 1991). Despite these challenges, museum collections are incredibly rich contexts for engaging with archaeological material.

In this chapter, I outline my research process using museum objects, highlighting some of the challenges in working within collections and collection documentation. I start with a discussion of dress and embodiment followed by a short history of dress in seventeenth-century Massachusetts as a way to ground my research into stone button molds. I then turn to methodological considerations of researching museum collections: how to access them and what to consider with regard to how they have been catalogued in the past and how they can be considered in the present. I end with some reflections on the process of engaging archaeological collections in this research and how certain research pathways continue to shape my continued explorations on colonial dress.

Some Theory and History Regarding Dress

Everyone has a different journey to approaching their research topic. In my own backward glance, different experiences and events seem to foreshadow my current study. My background in art and making things seem to fit with my current position as museum curator and my fascination with material culture. In considering the topic of dress, however, what resonates (at least in this moment) is my parochial school uniform: that hunter green polyester jumper (girls weren't allowed to wear trousers in my school), rayon shirt with Peter Pan collar, green polyester knee socks, and, God help me, hunter green saddle shoes. I hated the restrictions of that uniform, one meant to erase the individual and shape her to the institution. Graduating from high school meant freedom not only from the institution, but also the uniform that constricted my body and my perception of self. Clothing was an integral aspect of that lived experience; clothing, body, and self were intertwined in that place.

When I consider colonialism, my personal history reminds me of the laws, strictures, and agency of the individual and their body in relation to the institution. Thus, I situate the body at the center of my research on dress in the colonial world. The body was the corporeal space in which identity was created, materialized, sexualized, and embodied in the early modern world; it marked where you fit within colonial empires and the boundaries of exclusion and inclusion specific to the landscape in which you lived (White 2012). Dress, which includes both clothing and bodily adornment, was a means by which identity was materialized and embodied (Loren 2010). Dress communicated identity, differentiated self from other, and served to ally oneself with a particular interest group. Even today, how one covers and adorns the body is a powerful statement of political and personal identity. The color, fabric, and fit of clothing, along with adornments, posture, and manners, together convey multiple meanings, such as information on status, gender, bodily health, and religious beliefs. While dress can be purposeful, it can also be mandated and policed, as is demonstrated by the sumptuary laws and other social expectations of dress that emerge from the archival record. Dress was also manipulated in different contexts. As Sophie White (2012: 5) articulates, "sartorial identities were not fixed but malleable"; dress was a mutable form of communication to allow for social movement and simultaneously blurring imperial categories.

Dress did not mirror identity; rather identity was constituted with material culture and colonial peoples socialized material goods in daily practice. My focus is on embodiment, in particular how one experiences the world, performs identity, and mediates social exchanges (Crossland 2010; Harris and Robb 2012; Joyce 2005). Clothing doesn't just live on the surface of one's body, but becomes an extension of one's body as they experience the world. So then, artifacts of clothing and adornment are extensions of the body itself, enabling the performance and embodiment in and through colonial contexts. It is not enough to say that bodies and worlds constitute one another, as one must account for the numerous and differential ways that peoples and things intersect over time and within communities. Harris and Robb (2012) explain how historical individuals embodied different perspectives simultaneously, in different contexts "sometimes apparently seamlessly, sometimes with tension" (Harris and Robb 2012: 674). For example, my identity as a museum curator is embodied and communicated when I wear a white lab coat (the wearing of which is mandated by museum protocol), while I can simultaneously wear jewelry that signals my cultural beliefs (a *cornicello* or little horn to ward off the evil eye). These embodiments of identity occur at the same time, linked to a specific context. I can remove a layer (that white lab coat when not working with museum collections) and add others. Following this logic, colonial identity was mutable even while it was mandated and policed. The material culture used to constitute identity was similarly manipulated to refashion identity in a variety of contexts.

This theoretical approach suggests that dress was a fluid practice, shaped by local historical contexts. Yet, does this understanding of dress apply to seventeenth-century Massachusetts? How did the colonial population employ dress in their embodiment of different identities? This research necessarily includes an examination of the historical context through primary and secondary historical sources to understand the role of material culture in the past. Yet, the goal is not to simply identify material culture, but rather to consider points of intersection and disjuncture between different textual and material sources. Where do they diverge from one another and when they diverge, what does this suggest about the materialization of identity through dress?

In the mid-1630s, English Puritans founded the Massachusetts Bay Colony in present-day New England amongst existing Massachusett, Narragansett, Niantic, Nipmuc, and Wampanoag communities. Adherence to Puritan ideology was regulated through the production of Massachusetts Bay Colony laws, which stipulated the comportment, action, and dress of Puritans. Bay Colony sumptuary laws loudly enforced a modest and conservative style of dress among all inhabitants, a style that would indicate, at a glance, who you were by what you wore. The language of dress as a means of identity communication was not only important for Puritans, but also among Native American communities among them.

Puritan missionary efforts to convert indigenous peoples included the development of Praying Towns: communities for Christianized Native Americans who were to live, pray, dress, and comport themselves as Puritans and encourage ceasing long-standing Native American practices of long hair, loose fitting clothing, and body adornment with beads. Native American responses to proselytization efforts were varied; some were convinced that Christian conversion was necessary for survival, while other individuals vocally and materially rejected conversion efforts. So, for some Native Americans, English-style clothing bespoke of one's spirituality, while others wore English-style clothing to create alliances with, or in some cases, confuse Puritans. Coats then embodied a certain identity when worn: that of the Christian or Christianized Native American.

Clothing meant to transform the unconverted into a Christian was also used to deceive the viewer as the same clothing could be used not only to disguise one's allegiance but also mock and pose a threat to Puritan rule. This suggests that Native American individuals were aware of the nuances in the language of clothing in the Puritan worldview and the importance of context when performing identity through dress. For example, in Mary Rowlandson's 1682 autobiographical account of her captivity during Metacom's Rebellion, she makes reference to the dress of Weetamoo, a female Wampanoag sachem, noting that "She had a kersey coat, and covered with girdles of wampum from the loins upward. Her arms from her elbows to her hands were covered with bracelets; there were handfuls of necklaces about her neck, and several sorts of jewels in her ears. She had fine red stockings, and white shoes, her hair powdered and face painted red" (Rowlandson 1828: 63–64). While Rowlandson was shocked by this, Weetamoo's dress, however, embodied her status and power as she fought to maintain and protect her community and their traditions in the face of English colonization. Historical accounts then suggest that a coat, and the buttons used to close it (which were perhaps made using a button mold), was a laden item by which to embody, communicate, and refashion identity in seventeenth-century New England in relation to imperial constructs.

In the museum, however, the categorization of the archaeologically-recovered material culture of a coat – namely the lead or pewter buttons – are based on a somewhat narrow reading of the historical and archival record. Coats were worn by English and Christianized Native Americans rather than non-Christian Native Americans who presumably did not wear coats. While historical accounts suggest some fluidity regarding practices of dress in the seventeenth century, in museums buttons are often interpreted to be European items because of their location of manufacture and the presumption of who wore them. But what about button molds used to produce buttons for coats? Surprisingly, these items are often catalogued as a tool for Native Americans. Button and button mold are then attributed to two different historical groups, fixing a certain interpretation of who used these items. Thus, museum cataloguing processes often counter notions of sartorial fluidity and manipulation discussed in historical accounts through the application of static categories to define material culture.

Below, I consider how these museum practices then influence historical and contemporary interpretations, specifically with regard to stone molds. Keep in mind, however, that historical descriptions on all kinds of artifact categories are archived through time in the museum and questioning these descriptions was not part of museum practice until recent decades. When working within collections, and particularly in older collections, it is important to question descriptions along with provenance and provenience. What a priori assumptions regarding function and meaning are ascribed to the objects over time simply through the process of cataloguing? How have these functions and meanings been reproduced through time?

Button Molds in the Museum, Thoughts on Looking and the Disruption of Narratives

In my role as museum curator at the Peabody Museum, I am fortunate to have access to a substantial collection of archaeological and ethnographic material from colonial New England. Some of the material is the result of the Museum's ongoing excavations on seventeenth-century Harvard College, while others are collections that have been in museum storage for decades or even a century. Some of those collections are the result of systematic archaeological excavations that have a rich associated archive of field notes and photography, while others are singular finds, accessioned into the museum collections with little or no information on provenience or provenance. As I mentioned previously, my work begins with examination of assemblages of clothing and adornment artifacts. Sometimes, these assemblages are from systematic excavations. Yet in this research, singular finds also have relevance in understanding the scope of dress and adornment practices within certain contexts. In looking at seventeenth-century European-manufactured buttons that were used as fasteners for coats with a focus on the location from which those buttons were recovered, I became aware of tools for making buttons locally: the stone button mold.

I originally came across stone button molds in former Peabody Museum director Charles Clark Willoughby's 1935 *Antiquities of the New England Indian*s as I was researching clothing and adornment artifacts in New England. Willoughby's publication made me aware of distinct artifact type in the museum's collection, which at that time was not fully catalogued. When researching museum collections, I suggest tracking down older publications as they may contain information and illustrations of lesser known and under-catalogued collections. I encountered the molds in storage much like Willoughby did in the 1930s. Willoughby's concerns with the collections were regarding diversity and function of particular artifact types. While I share some of his same concerns regarding inventory, identification, and cataloguing, I am also interested in the legacy of interpretation, how objects acquire layers of interpretation over time while they are located within a museum collection.

So while it is important to note the hand of the collector in creation of specific collections, it is equally important to emphasize how the museum's cataloguing schema has affixed cultural attribution to colonial material culture. In particular, it is worth noting that museum practice for categorizing archaeological collections as either "Native American" or "European" has remained almost unchanged in many museums since the 1950s (Byrne *et al.* 2011; Thomas 1991). These classificatory tendencies limit and narrow our interpretations of the nuanced ways in which colonial peoples acquired, used, and constituted identity with material culture. As mentioned previously, it is important to examine not only the object itself, but the documentation that accompanies the object, so that the history of interpretation of the object in the collection can be more fully understood. It is that legacy of interpretation that fixes the object in a historical place and time, impacting how we know it today.

An early colonial-period stone mold in the Peabody's collection provides an example of the power of museum classification categories on interpretation. In 1892, James Baker, an avocational archaeologist, recovered a stone mold from a field in Lincoln, Massachusetts, and in 1924, he donated the object to the Peabody Museum (Figure 23.1). A physical examination of the object indicates that it is a simple one-sided mold. Molten lead or pewter was poured into the indentations, and the cast items could be easily removed once cooled. The reverse side of the stone mold is incised with an image of an individual wearing an English-style fitted coat.

Further physical examination of the mold indicates the kinds of clothing artifacts that were made from it. One side of the stone is carved with hollows for a ring, a small buckle (likely a knee buckle frame), and two rounded buttons: one shallow 1 cm button and the other a deeper 2 cm button. The size of buttons produced would be consistent with buttons used for fastening seventeenth-century fitted wool coats and waistcoats manufactured in England and shipped to the New World. These sizes and styles of pewter or lead buttons cast from these molds are consistent with other buttons that have been recovered from both Christian and non-Christian

BUTTON MOLD

PART OF A STONE MOLD FOR CASTING LEAD OBJECTS, PROBABLY MADE BY WHITES AND USED BY THE INDIANS.
LINCOLN, MASSACHUSETTS, C. FIRST HALF OF 17TH CENTURY
COURTESY PEABODY MUSEUM OF ARCHAEOLOGY AND ETHNOLOGY, HARVARD UNIVERSITY

Figure 23.1 Both sides of a slate mold from Lincoln, Massachusetts, and exhibition label. *Source:* ©President and Fellows of Harvard College, Peabody Museum of Archaeology and Ethnology, PM# 24-7-10/94279. Courtesy of the Peabody Museum of Archaeology and Ethnology, Harvard University, PM# 2015.0.2.

contexts in New England. Thus, while measurement suggests clothing, it in no way indicates who wore that clothing.

There is little associated museum documentation of the mold and almost nothing is known of its provenience beyond "Lincoln." A letter dated 1892 indicates that the object was brought to Peabody director Frederic Ward Putnam for identification and that Putnam indicated that "the excavations rings etc are really moulds…I think that the Indians had no knowledge of melting lead until after contact with the whites." In 1932, Willoughby went on to discuss the molds as Native American tools for casting lead. In the mid-twentieth century, an exhibition label for the object indicated that the mold was "made by Whites and used by Indians." In 1984, R. J. Barber (an avocational archaeologist) published an image of the mold in the *Bulletin of the Massachusetts Archaeological Society,* arguing that, based on Putnam's comments, a Native American was responsible for the manufacture of this object, as well as its adornment. Curators at the Peabody took issue with this interpretation, stating that because of the unclear provenience of the object, the ethnicity of the maker could not be determined. The interpretation of the mold as a Native American item, however, is one that sticks.

The Peabody collections have a number of stone button molds, and I first understood them to be solely Native American items based on locale of collection and categorization of the object. Yet, a search for similar items in New England museums through online databases, inquiries to collections managers at other museums, and reviewing published sources (including NAGPRA notices) have indicated that while stone molds have been recovered from a variety of Native American contexts, others have been recovered from English and/or multicultural contexts (Loren 2014). I recently contacted the Peabody Essex Museum in Salem, Massachusetts, to examine a stone button mold in their collection (E67–335). The mold in the Peabody Essex collections was recovered from Danvers, Massachusetts. Similar to the mold at the Peabody Museum at Harvard discussed above, the mold at Peabody Essex Museum was a singular find and donated by a collector in 1891. It is a simple single-sided mold from which small rounded buttons could have been cast. The molds at the Peabody Museum at Harvard and the Peabody Essex share a lack of provenience information. In both cases, only the city from which it was recovered is listed, with no site information to indicate that it was recovered from a Native American Praying Town or English household or community.

The attribution of both these molds as Native American, while contested and tenuous, is the predominant interpretation for these and other stone button molds recovered in New England. This is an interpretive legacy that needs to be challenged. Historical accounts indicate that coats were important for many different members of the Massachusetts Bay Colony: Native American and non-Native American, converted and unconverted. A survey of archaeologically-recovered molds in museum collections suggests that they were recovered from numerous locations, both Christian and non-Christian contexts.

Lessons Learned and Reflections on Museum Collections

All of the button molds that I have studied are part of museum collections, and if not for those collections, I would not know about the existence of these colonial tools linked to dress and embodiment of identity. In the process of researching museum collections, however, it is important to be mindful of rigid categorical systems. While best practices in museums call for strict categorization to maintain collections, it is crucial to also acknowledge objects and stories that are not present, and the ways in which the remnants of those daily practices are represented or not in archaeological, textual, and visual records. When I started researching stone molds several years ago, I was influenced by the predominant museum interpretation of these items as Native American. Their location on Native American sites indicated to me the ways in which different community members made buttons for a coat worn in reaction to Massachusetts Bay Colony sumptuary laws. This interpretation, while highlighting the important role of clothing in the lives of seventeenth-century Native Americans, however, did not fully attend to the intersection of different historical accounts and the diverse recovery locations of molds in museum collections. This shortcoming in my research in being attentive to religious and gendered identities has been further amplified as I examine button molds in collections beyond the Peabody Museum at Harvard and in further interrogation of historical sources.

English-style coats were worn as a sign of religious conversion in some communities, but also worn by the unconverted to facilitate diplomatic relations as well as signal power. Coats were worn by Native American men and women, and in the case of the latter, in ways that flew in the face of Puritan conventions and laws. Puritan settlers also wore coats to signal religion and status: ministers wore a plain and somber fashion, while those of greater means wore more embellished fashions. The button mold was a tool used to create buttons that would be attached to a coat, to replace those that were lost as well as in the construction of a new coat. The ways in which that coat was used to embody identity by different individuals in seventeenth-century New England was far more diverse than museum categories would suggest.

Buttons, when attached to a fitted coat and worn in combination with distinct objects of adornment or other articles of clothing, permitted the wearer to embody a specific identity. The single button mold, then, becomes a meaningful symbol in the social power of dress: it enabled one to fashion self and express religious, gendered, and social identities in different colonial spaces. The recovery of these tools in New England contexts suggests some of the nuanced sartorial needs and practices of both seventeenth-century Native Americans and English residents, converted and unconverted, in the Massachusetts Bay Colony, enabling a more elastic understanding of what it meant to be colonial.

Paired Reading

Loren, Diana DiPaolo. 2014. "Casting Identity: Sumptuous Action and Colonized Bodies in Seventeenth Century New England." In *Rethinking Colonials Pasts through Archaeology*, edited by Neal Ferris, Rodney Harrison, and Michael V. Wilcox, 251–267. Oxford: Oxford University Press.

References

Byrne, Sarah, Anne Clarke, Rodney Harrison, and Robin Torrence, eds. 2011. *Unpacking the Collection: Networks of Material and Social Agency in the Museum*. New York: Springer.

Crossland, Zoe. 2010. "Embodiment and Materiality." In *The Oxford Handbook of Material Culture Studies*, edited by Dan Hicks and Mary C. Beaudry, 386–405. Oxford: Oxford University Press.

Gosden, Chris and Chantal Knowles, eds. 2001. *Collecting Colonialism: Material Culture and Colonial Change*. Oxford: Berg.

Harris, Oliver J. T. and John Robb. 2012. "Multiple Ontologies and the Problem of the Body in History." *American Anthropologist*, 114: 668–679. DOI: 10.1111/j.1548-1433.2012.01513.x.

Joyce, Rosemary. 2005. "Archaeology of the Body." *Annual Review of Anthropology*, 34: 139–158. DOI: 10.1146/annurev.anthro.33.070203.143729.

Loren, Diana DiPaolo. 2010. *The Archaeology of Clothing and Bodily Adornment in Colonial America*. Gainesville, FL: University Press of Florida.

Loren, Diana DiPaolo. 2014. "Casting Identity: Sumptuous Action and Colonized Bodies in Seventeenth Century New England." In *Rethinking Colonials Pasts through Archaeology*, edited by Neal Ferris, Rodney Harrison, and Michael V. Wilcox, 251–267. Oxford: Oxford University Press.

Rowlandson, Mary. 1828. *A True History of the Captivity and the Restoration of Mrs. Mary Rowlandson*. London: Carter, Andrews, and Company.

Stewart, Susan. 1993. *On Longing: Narratives of the Miniature, the Gigantic, the Souvenir, the Collection*. Durham, NC: Duke University Press.

Thomas, Nicholas. 1991. *Entangled Objects: Exchange, Material Culture and Colonialism in the Pacific*. Cambridge, MA: Harvard University Press.

White, Sophie. 2012. *Wild Frenchmen and Frenchified Indians: Material Culture and Race in Colonial Louisiana*. Philadelphia, PA: University of Pennsylvania Press.

24

Reverse Engineering in Prehistory: The Neolithic Bow of La Draga, Spain

Juan A. Barceló, Vera Moitinho de Almeida, Oriol López-Bultó, Antoni Palomo, and Xavier Terradas

Project Summary

La Draga is an archaeological site in the northeastern Iberian Peninsula dating to the Early Neolithic era, more than 7000 years ago. Given the extraordinary preservation of objects made of wood and vegetable fiber, this site offers an exceptional window on a period in human history when agriculture and herding were used for the first time in Europe to produce food and new means of living. In this chapter we concentrate on a single kind of object: archery equipment. We do so not only because these represent an important kind of tool, but also because the way we have researched them involves a combination of detective work, forensic research, and state-of-the art computer technology. It is our view that only by "reversing" the prehistoric engineering, in the same way that modern designers do with objects, we can learn how people lived in the deep past. In our efforts to "revive" prehistoric societies, we sometimes need both state-of-the-art modern computer technology and the careful work of archaeologists, as the roster of authors of this chapter attest.

The Archaeological Site

In northeastern Spain, the archaeological site of La Draga is located on the eastern shore of the "Estany de Banyoles" (Banyoles Lake), a small lake 40 km from the current Mediterranean shoreline and 40 km south of the Pyrenees in northeastern Catalonia. The fact that the site is now partially covered by the waters of the lake has favored the extraordinary state of conservation of posts and timber structures, objects made of wood, vegetable fibers, and many other organic materials.

Following the site's discovery in 1990, the archaeological excavations carried out to date under the direction of Raquel Piqué, Toni Palomo, and Xavier Terradas have documented a habitation level, which corresponds to occupation by an Early Neolithic small population linked to the Cardial Culture (Bosch *et al.* 2011; Palomo *et al.* 2014). Numerous radiocarbon dates have been obtained from samples of wood, seeds, bone, and charcoal, placing the earliest occupation between 5300 and 5000 BC. The location of the site does not seem to have been chosen at random and corresponds to a pattern that is repeated in Early Neolithic occupations in the western Mediterranean. These are wetland locations, on the shores of lakes, lagoons, or marshes, yet close to agricultural land – that is, in areas with great ecological diversity.

Engaging Archaeology: 25 Case Studies in Research Practice, First Edition. Edited by Stephen W. Silliman.
© 2018 John Wiley & Sons, Inc. Published 2018 by John Wiley & Sons, Inc.

Through the dozens of wooden objects of all types and sizes preserved, the life of the earliest farmers of Iberian Peninsula appears before our eyes (López 2015; López *et al.* 2012; Palomo *et al.* 2013). We can learn how plants were cultivated thanks to the wooden digging sticks. We can suggest how wood was worked by artisans because we discovered the earliest carpentry tools (adzes, wedges, etc.). We have inferred what they ate and how they ate because we have evidence of food (seeds, plant remains, animal bones) and artifacts related to food cooking and processing such as hearths, charcoal, knives, pottery, wooden bowls, baskets made from aquatic plants, spoons, spatulas, and more. Although farming is well evidenced, hunting was also important in their lives, as revealed by hunting weapons such as bows, arrows, and spears.

In this case study, we deal with bows. And we do so for several reasons. First, this is a unique find for such an old chronology; not many prehistoric bows older than 7000 years have been recovered given the highly perishable nature of wood. Second, hunting was still an important economic activity for the first farming communities, and it deserves more research attention. Third, archery is a very complex activity, and when we understand how prehistoric people manufactured and used their bows and arrows, we understand a lot about their technological knowledge and cognitive capabilities. Finally, the best preserved of all bows from La Draga revealed an unexpected use, an amazing discovery made thanks to the latest technology and sophisticated experimental approach.

Research Questions

For a majority of people visiting museums, past objects are something they see in a showcase, but seem too old and strange for being more than an occasional curiosity. Archaeologists do not see dusty stones or incomprehensible chunks of timber; we see the remains of what once were instruments, tools that allowed people to survive. The problem is that those relics from a forgotten past do not speak by themselves. We need to find a way of hearing what they tell us today about what people did in the past. The real challenge is then explaining existing perceivable phenomena in terms of long past causes.

Why are the Neolithic bows from La Draga the way they are, and what action(s) or process(es) happened in the past to produce what we see in the present as the preserved bow? In this case study, the easiest answer is that these pieces of wood have a distinctive appearance and materiality for the sake of their proper functioning: shooting projectiles. Nevertheless, arriving at such an apparently simple conclusion is not as easy as it seems.

More than a reinvention of Indiana Jones, modern archaeologists work like detectives who try to solve a murder, investigating whether the suspicious butler had the motivation, the opportunity, and the knowledge about how to murder the house owner. Our corpse in this case is a prehistoric object made of wood, with its form, size, visual appearance, materiality, and context of discovery. And the people we are looking for, responsible for the manufacture and use of those items, are the artisans who made them from a tree branch and the persons who used them to kill an animal and to obtain food for their families. That said, the days of Sherlock Holmes are gone, and modern detectives use new technologies, some of them taken from the archaeologist's toolkit and some of them (microscopes, 3D scanners, advanced analytical software, and many others) from the forensic investigator's toolkit.

For researching how prehistoric bows were produced and used in the past we have followed a "reverse engineering" approach. This expression often relates to industrial design and modern technology, but it relates equally well to an investigation of the remote origins of human behavior. It has been defined by the process of extracting missing knowledge from anything human-made, by going backwards through its development cycle and analyzing its structure, function, and operation (Wang 2011). In our case, it implies documenting and measuring the form and the material properties, and then, by real-world or virtual experiment, trying to evaluate the implied functional behavior (Barceló and Moitinho de Almeida 2012).

More than a mere inductive exercise to build up to some conclusions about material and design choice in a cultural context, by "reversing" the prehistoric engineering approach to design a bow in Neolithic times we have approached this problem deductively – that is, with expectations about human technological behavior and economic efficiency to see how such choices would have been made in this case. We intend to understand archaeological artifacts by explaining the particular causal structure in which they are supposed to have participated. In other words, we look for an answer to the question "how did *S* work in the past?" where *S* is a goal-directed system in which the material entity whose function we are interested in appears. To solve it, we need to integrate causal and functional knowledge to see, understand, and be able to manipulate past use scenarios, because this knowledge reflects the causal interactions that someone in the Neolithic had or could potentially have had with needs, goals, and products in the course of using archery equipment. Functional analysis appears then as the reproduction of some mechanical behaviors in a specific context for the accomplishment of a particular purpose. In this sense, we focus on the interaction between task and instrument, between what ancient people could do in the past and what we know today about what they might have intended to do. Then, by integrating all observed and measured properties in a computer system and executing the program, we have appreciated the function of prehistoric bows interactively, by observing the deformations that happen on the model when submitted to simulated forces according to the potential use of the bow. The causal effect of such forces can be efficiently represented algorithmically using physical and mechanical equations.

The Neolithic Bows from La Draga and the Nature of Archery

Three pieces of wood from the La Draga site have been classified so far as possible as bows because they have the form we usually associate with the idea of an instrument for shooting arrows. The best preserved artifact is 1080 mm long, has a maximum width of 25 mm in the medial area, and is 15 mm thick. It is made of yew, like the other bows, and preserved in fragmented state. In this case, both surfaces, the dorsal and ventral, were heavily degraded by contact with the organic sediment of the archaeological matrix. However, one end is well preserved because it was in contact with carbonated sands. It can be observed from this end that one side of the bow corresponds to the cortical surface of the last growth ring, while the other shows work traces. This side has facets of rough carving left by stone tools used for its manufacture, although the edges of these facets were smoothed by polishing. Despite the generally poor state of preservation it is possible to observe that small branches have been removed. Both ends are pointed, and no other additional modification was made to fix the bowstring. The tip of one end has a small fracture while the other is slightly crushed, as can be seen from the disintegrated fiber at the tip. The bow displays a section between convex and plano-convex and a curved profile, of which the dorsal side is convex and the ventral is concave (López 2015; Moitinho de Almeida 2013; Piqué *et al.* 2015).

These characteristics are important because they set the context for bow use and function. The behavior of the bow-arrow-archer system (i.e., interior ballistics) and the arrow in flight (i.e., exterior ballistics) are of great complexity (Bergman *et al.* 1988, Zanevsky 2011). The overall performance of a bow-and-arrow system depends on several parameters: bow length, brace height, string length, draw, and mass of arrow; as well as on three functions of distributions of bending stiffness, mass along the bow, and form of the bow in its unstrung situation. Furthermore, the energy which an archer can put into a bow and the quality of the shooting are also limited by the characteristics of the archer's own body and skills. Nonetheless, reduced to its simplest terms the usual prerequisite of a bow is that it is capable of shooting an arrow.

Consequently, given that the design of the bow by its prehistoric artisan was characterized by the combination of form, material, and manufacturing techniques, among other constraints, how was its performance in the past determined by the overall design?

Replicating Prehistoric Bows

Toni Palomo has considerable experience in experimental archaeology, researching abilities of prehistoric artisans. He has produced flint tools, pottery vessels, and even metallic objects that look exactly like original prehistoric ones. He has even reconstructed the prehistoric huts at the La Draga site. He has been able to do those reproductions by adhering to the methods and technologies from the past. The most important aspect of his work, however, is that he does not reproduce ancient artifacts for their mere appearance, but rather for understanding prehistoric manufacturing in an experimental way. Modern archaeology needs this experimental approach – reproducing ancient behavior under laboratory controlled conditions – to understand what people might have done in the past constrained by affordances of the materials available.

In collaboration with Jürgen Junkmanns (2013), a specialist in ancient archery, Palomo has built real-world replicas of La Draga preserved archery equipment, reproducing all of the details of what the rest of the research team assumed prehistoric artisans did. In all cases, we have recorded the time needed for each task (e.g., cutting, splitting, carving and drying the stem; scraping and polishing the wood; and notching and balancing the bow) to obtain an estimate of the quantity of labor necessary in ancient times to make their hunting instruments. The total estimated time for producing a bow using Neolithic technology and procedures established from archaeological data is between four and six hours, taking into account that obtaining the proper raw material and the drying process to gain the necessary mechanical properties can take 15 days. Surface traces observable in the replica coincide with those observed on parts of the archaeological artifacts. The surface was stripped of its bark and its twigs removed, but was used rough without any further polishing or transformation. The other side was carved and polished.

Archery is today an Olympic sport. It is also one of the hot events of the Prehistoric Olympic Games, a gathering of archaeologists and others without any formal training in archaeology who meet to compete in ancient activities that we practice as sports. We are not the best archers in modern times, but we have done our best to use the real-world replica to throw replicated arrows, and we have performed some ballistic tests while doing so. This experimentation has allowed us to tentatively interpret the longest and best preserved bow from La Draga as a learning instrument – a teenager's bow (Moitinho de Almeida 2013; Piqué *et al.* 2015). At just 1080 mm, it can only produce a draw weight of 24 lbs at 20 inches, able to shoot arrows of 19 grams at a maximum distance of 92 m.

This has been a totally unexpected and quite revelatory discovery. We thought that we had remains of full-sized adult instruments, but our replica and experiments suggest that they were not completely efficient instruments, but simplified approximations to the size and strength of a juvenile archer. Of course, one might argue that this explanation can be the consequence of using bad replicas or a result of our deficient training in shooting arrows with a self-made bow. Therefore, to minimize such possible errors, we have produced a complete and detailed computer simulation of what is mechanically possible using the preserved wooden bows from La Draga.

Computer Simulation Experiments

To go beyond mere replication we should test whether the efficiency of the bow was related to its form or to the specific properties of yew wood and how the overall geometry of such an object would react to distinct woods, forces, and magnitudes. It implies measuring physical parameters such as stress, strain, and deformation. Nevertheless, to measure the resistance of the bow, we first have to bend the object until the point of permanent deformation and then to the point of breakage. But, of course, we cannot do that with a precious heritage item, and we do not recommend it even with replicas that have taken significant time and effort to reproduce.

Given such limitations to experimental work, the directors of the archaeological project (Piqué, Palomo, and Terradas) contacted a specialist in computer applications in archaeology, Juan A. Barceló, who designed an innovative approach to archaeological experimentation based on computer simulation. The idea was to build a "digital model" of the prehistoric bow and then draw the virtual bow and pull a virtual projectile back in the bowstring to place the back of the virtual bow under tensile stress and the belly of the bow under compressive forces that could be simulated within the computer.

A computer model of the archaeological object was created using a close-range 3D structured light scanner known as SmartSCAN3D Duo System. These digital surface models have allowed an in-depth qualitative and quantitative study of their form, size, and aspect, as well as tool marks (splitting, rough down, and other tool signatures) produced during the different steps of the elaboration process, and use-wear (breaking, smashing, erosion, starches, and sanding). Then, we converted the 3D digital surface model into a solid model (also known as finite element, FE), defined by the exterior surface, the interior volume, and the material properties of the bow. Finally, we used computer simulation methods – more specifically, finite element method/analysis (FEM/FEA) – to test and analyze our hypothesis. This is complex technical work that requires specific training, which not many professional archaeologists actually have. Vera Moitinho de Almeida's PhD was on the implementation of computer experiments of reverse engineered archaeological objects to investigate the efficiency of bows. Oriol López' PhD investigated those digital models to understand how the original wood was transformed into suitable bows (Moitinho de Almeida 2013; López 2015).

When simulating on the computer how the bow was deformed, we took into account the form and material properties of the artifact, and defined the bow's *use* as the exertion of control over freely manipulable external matter with the specific intention of first, altering the physical properties of another object, substance, surface, or medium (the target, which may be the object user or another organism) via a dynamic mechanical interaction; or second, mediating the flow of information between the tool user and the environment or other organisms in the environment. In this way, causal relationships between parts of tools, and their corresponding effects on other physical objects, help us understand how we can use them and why they are efficient. The direction of the force applied has a strong impact on the proportion of the total draw force which is applied in a particular direction during the simulation. The original load direction was maintained in the deformed geometry and the time the wood was in tension was also taken into account (Figure 24.1).

Since the relational force-draw length affects the bow's performance, it is one of the most important factors to be controlled when simulating how the bow was used in the past. The area under the force-draw curve determines the bow's efficiency for propelling an arrow, which can be measured by the fraction of available potential energy transferred into kinetic energy of the arrow. Furthermore, the shape of the force-draw curve, which depends primarily on the dimensions and geometry of the bow, indicates the possibility of the bow becoming difficult to control or breaking. The maximum distance along the path made by the limbs in response

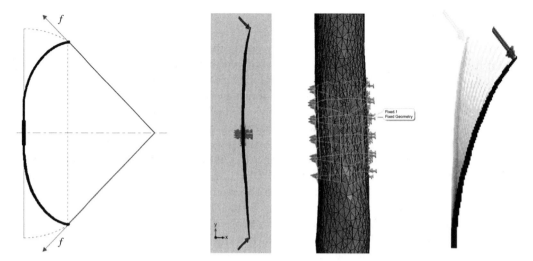

Figure 24.1 Simulation results for the La Draga bow. Support diagram for the simulation tests of a bent bow, side view (left). Finite element model of artifact D/12 JF/JG-81: Location of initial applied loads (center left); detail of the area with fixed geometry (center right). Detail of the upper limb of the finite element model subjected to various loads applied across 13 steps in 1 second to the back side of the nock (right) (Moitinho de Almeida 2013). *Source:* Moitinho de Almeida (2013). Reproduced with permission of J. A. Barceló.

to variations in force and wood species has been simulated, not the actual draw length of the bow as that depends on the string's length, type, and manufacture.

In measuring fracture strength it is important to distinguish between the strength of the wood from which the artifact is made and the actual failure limit of the artifact as a whole, which is also dependent on both form and dimension. By changing the material parameters of each wood species in the digital model, we have confirmed that some woods are more prone to fracture at extreme tensional stress than others. The results of these simulation studies indicate that it is necessary to exert higher forces on ash, pine, oak, and elm wood species to fully bend the bow. Yew and willow are the wood species which require the lowest force, while being capable of achieving greater displacement of the arrow. The advantage of yew wood over the other wood species was confirmed by its ability to store higher strain energy while undergoing lower stress. Its superior toughness and high resilience allow the bow to withstand greater displacements under lower forces and to achieve higher ranges compared with bows made from other species.

Lessons Learned

Not any piece of wood that seems to our modern eyes to have been a prehistoric bow was in fact such an instrument. A careful functional study should be implemented, which involves making real-world replicas and digital models. We have discovered that these Neolithic bows were made with a segment of yew wood, which seemed to take advantage of the unique properties of sapwood and heartwood parts. The belly was made from heartwood, which is better suited to handle compressive stress, and the back face from sapwood, which is very strong and elastic under tensile stress. Our results suggest that this material could have been selected on the basis of how well it fitted the requirements for this particular artifact.

In our case, the best preserved bow seemed to have been not only an instrument for hunting but also for learning to hunt (Moitinho de Almeida 2013; Piqué *et al.* 2015). Careful comparison of experimental results with the modern replica and computer simulations suggests that measurements taken from the middle portions of two of the preserved bows at La Draga site indicate that both handles would be too small to fit the hand of an adult. The former could eventually fit the hand of a teenager, while the latter would fit the hand of an 11 year old. We have also drawn attention to the peculiar marks on the belly of the middle portion, particularly on one of its sides, which may eventually indicate the contact area between bow and arrow, such as the location of the grip. These marks, which are clear in the digitized 3D model, could occur as a result of the archer's lack of technical skill to nock the arrow (i.e., to set an arrow in a bow), where an incorrect dynamic spine (i.e., the arrow's stiffness) would result in an unpredictable contact between the arrow and the bow.

Well beyond the interpretation of prehistoric hunting instruments, we have learned that the functional explanation of archaeological items is much more difficult than expected. Archaeologists usually draw functional explanations on the basis of their experience in the present. Our study reveals that visual analogy is not enough for proper explanations of human life in the past. We need to know the physics of human behavior and physical constraints on the size, form, visual aspect, and materiality of ancient objects. We argue that the knowledge of the way past artifacts were created and used in the past should reflect the causal interactions that someone had or could potentially have had with needs, goals, and products in the course of using such elements.

More than integrating knowledge of physics with the appearance of the archaeological object in a deductive way, we have interacted with real-world replicas and digital models to discover in a proper way what the ancient inhabitants of this Neolithic settlement had and could do with it. We have explored alternatively the studies of possible deformations on the object as a result of manipulations with it, which has involved the study of elasticity and resistance to breakage; deformation and damage due to the continued use of the instrument; and the *dynamic* aspect of artifacts, which refers to the object's diverse response in different use scenarios.

This work has convinced us that a better comprehension of archaeological artifacts could happen by bringing quantitative 3D digital methods and techniques, computer simulation, and real-world experiments to technological and functional analysis. We have stressed that archaeological analysis should involve establishing and exploiting constraints: between the user/producer and the artifact, the user/producer and the environment, and the artifact and the environment. Investigating prehistoric or ancient artifacts through reverse engineering and experimentation may provide new insights into the complex dynamics of certain human behavior in the past. Experimental replication, 3D digital models, and computer simulation helped us understand how artifacts were manufactured and used.

After nearly four years of work, we have learned a lot about what archaeologists should do to better understand technology and functionality. If readers are interested in following a similar path with their own data, we recommend a multidisciplinary approach. First of all, ask the proper questions: archaeological materials are what remain of past instruments, and they should be regarded not as something to be seen in a museum, but as something that did some work in the past and gives information about the people that made and use them. Second, proceed scientifically, measure rather than merely describe, and physically experiment rather than simply tell a history. Go to the basics of mechanisms and try to understand the affordances of raw materials and the shape and form of objects when working with them. You need to learn to think differently (experimentation, replication, computer simulation), to use a new language (mathematics), and to find new ways of expressing knowledge (computer programs and models), but the results are compelling. Of course, the truth is not within the computer, and no one can ever understand everything that people did in the past. There are many mechanisms that cannot be reduced to physical movement and the driving of forces; consequently many cognitive aspects of human behavior cannot be explored in that way. In any case, fascinating new work is already under way for understanding the many fundamental aspects of human behavior and cognition in the past.

Paired Reading

Piqué, Raquel, Antoni Palomo, Xavier Terradas, Josep Tarrús, Ramón Buxó, Ángel Bosch, Julia Chinchilla, Igor Bodganović, Oriol López, and María Saña. 2015. "Characterizing Prehistoric Archery: Technical and Functional Analyses of the Neolithic Bows from La Draga (NE Iberian Peninsula)." *Journal of Archaeological Science*, 55: 166–173. DOI: 10.1016/j.jas.2015.01.005.

References

Barceló, Juan A. and Vera Moitinho de Almeida. 2012. "Functional Analysis from Visual and Non-Visual Data. An Artificial Intelligence Approach." *Mediterranean Archaeology and Archaeometry*, 12: 273–321.

Bergman, C. A., McEwen, E., and Miller, R. 1988. "Experimental Archery: Projectile Velocities and Comparison of Bow Performances." *Antiquity*, 62: 658–670. DOI: 10.1017/S0003598X00075050.

Bosch, Ángel, Julia Chinchilla, and Josep Tarrús. 2011. *El poblat lacustre del neolític antic de la Draga. Excavacions 2000–2005*. Girona: CASC – Museu d'Arqueologia de Catalunya (Monografies del CASC, 9).

Junkmanns, Jürgen. 2013. *Pfeil und Bogen. Von der Altsteinzeit bis zum Mittelalter*. Ludwigshafen: Verlag Angelika Hörning.

López, Oriol. 2015. "Processos d'obtenció, transformació i ús de la fusta en, l'assentament neolític antic de la Draga (5320–4800 cal BC)." PhD Dissertation. Bellaterra: Universitat Autònoma de Barcelona.

López, Oriol, Antoni Palomo, and Raquel Piqué. 2012. "Woodworking Technology and Functional Experimentation in the Neolithic Site of La Draga (Banyoles, Spain)." *Experimentelle Archäologie in Europa*, 11: 56–65.

Moitinho de Almeida, V. (2013). "Towards Functional Analysis of Archaeological Objects through Reverse Engineering Processes." PhD Dissertation. Barcelona: Facultat de Filosofia i Lletres, Universitat Autònoma de Barcelona.

Palomo, Antoni, Raquel Piqué, Xavier Terradas, Oriol López, Ignacio Clemente, and Juan F. Gibaja. 2013. "Woodworking Technology in the Early Neolithic Site of La Draga (Banyoles, Spain)." In *Regards croisés sur les outils liés au travail des végétaux*, edited by Patricia C. Anderson, Carole Cheval, and Aline Durand, 383–396. Antibes: Éditions APDCA.

Palomo, Antoni, Raquel Piqué, Xavier Terradas, Ángel Bosch, Ramón Buxó, Julia Chinchilla, María Saña, and Josep Tarrús. 2014. "Prehistoric Occupation of Banyoles Lakeshore: Results of Recent Excavations at La Draga Site, Girona, Spain." *Journal of Wetland Archaeology*, 14: 58–73. DOI: 10.1179/1473297114Z.00000000010.

Piqué, Raquel, Antoni Palomo, Xavier Terradas, Josep Tarrús, Ramón Buxó, Ángel Bosch, Julia Chinchilla, Igor Bodganović, Oriol López, and María Saña. 2015. "Characterizing Prehistoric Archery: Technical and Functional Analyses of the Neolithic Bows from La Draga (NE Iberian Peninsula)." *Journal of Archaeological Science*, 55: 166–173. DOI: 10.1016/j.jas.2015.01.005.

Wang, Wego. 2011. *Reverse Engineering: Technology of Reinvention*. Boca Raton, FL: CRC Press.

Zanevskyy, Ihor. 2011. "Mathematical and Computer Model of Sport Archery Bow and Arrow Interaction." *International Journal of Computer Science in Sport*, 10(2): 54–70.

25

Learning about Learning in Ice Age France through Stone Tools: An Intersectional Feminist Approach without Gender
Kathleen Sterling

Project Summary

Stone artifacts are the most abundant objects in the archaeological record and sometimes the only artifacts that are preserved, but all too often lithic analysis relies heavily on metrics and interpretation through lenses of adaptation and efficiency, a tendency that only increases as we look further back in time. With this legacy, it can be difficult to imagine using lithic analysis to contribute to nuanced, human interpretations of past life, particularly of the Pleistocene. Attempting such an approach fits well with a feminist science standpoint, but executing this kind of research requires some creativity. This chapter describes how I attempted to discuss social relationships in late Ice Age France using theories of learning applied to lithic data for my PhD dissertation. The two cave sites I analyzed were used by hunting and gathering peoples in the French Pyrénées. One site was intensively occupied and the other lightly so, but both had a broad range of material culture beyond stone tools including bone tools, personal ornaments, and visual imagery. I was able to identify different levels of expertise, but not in the fine detail I had hoped.

Biographical Note

My first archaeological experience, as a high-school student, was excavating a small Archaic campsite in the United States. As I learned about other times, places, and ways of life as an undergraduate, I found that my interest in mobile hunting and gathering peoples grew stronger, and I wanted to go further back in time. My undergraduate adviser gave me a copy of "Archaeology and the Study of Gender" by Conkey and Spector (1984), and this opened my eyes to not just the possibility, but the necessity of doing archaeology as a feminist. Later, I had the chance to pursue my graduate studies with Meg Conkey as my adviser. Feminism and anti-racist action have been important to me for as long as I can remember. This comes as no surprise since I am a mixed-race Black woman, but choosing deep prehistory as the setting for research that employs these standpoints may seem surprising. Bringing a Black feminist or intersectional feminist perspective to the study of some of our most iconic human ancestors can lead to changes in the ways in which we view these ancestors and thus ourselves.

Engaging Archaeology: 25 Case Studies in Research Practice, First Edition. Edited by Stephen W. Silliman.
© 2018 John Wiley & Sons, Inc. Published 2018 by John Wiley & Sons, Inc.

The Project

The project I describe here was my dissertation project. My area of interest is late Pleistocene modern humans, particularly 20,000–10,000 years before present. This is the end of the last Ice Age, when all people on earth lived through gathering and hunting wild foods. They are popularly described as "cavemen" – whether or not they lived in caves, and though they were not just male or adults – and as "natural." While anthropologists might be critical of this conception of human groups, it remains part of the structure of public education and academia. Anatomically-modern human hunter-gatherer groups past and present are found in natural history museums; paleoanthropologists use living and recent gatherer-hunters as analogies to understand multiple species of prehistoric hominins; and social psychologists and others have long looked to the peoples of the Pleistocene and early Holocene for examples of what is inherently good, bad, or basic about human beings (Sterling 2011). Because Ice Age cultures are used this way in both public and academic discourse, whether we like it or not, it is crucial that archaeologists flesh out this picture in a way that does not sacrifice the complicated, nuanced reality of human life in favor of safe but dull artifact-focused systems. The messiness of cultures is not only much more interesting than tables and graphs of flake attributes, but it is also truer, and makes for better science.

I had begun to make contacts with French researchers as an undergraduate through my adviser, and learning French helped me advance my undergraduate honors thesis research and field experiences. My graduate adviser had also researched the French Magdalenian period for decades, and she helped me extend and strengthen the connections that would later allow me access to archaeological collections and lab space in a French university. I was interested in lithics from my very first archaeological experiences, and this is a category of artifacts that is abundant, preserves well, and has the potential to inform us on multiple aspects of daily life. So, throughout graduate school I planned to do my dissertation research analyzing lithic data from Magdalenian France, but I wanted to find an approach that would be empirical and feminist.

Since lithics have been a very masculinist part of archaeology, there were no models and little inspiration. As a student I learned a variety of analytical techniques that could be applied to stone tools, but ideas seemed quite limited about what to do with the numbers and descriptions. Some researchers were doing interesting things with more recent, often historic, lithic collections, and others were asking questions about cognitive development in extinct human lineages, but few took up social questions in the vast middle. In Europe, the "type fossil" remains influential as a guiding concept, even if stone tools are not fossils. This means that if you have a certain type of tool or a certain ratio of tools, you have a certain culture. It serves as an "index." Yet, other than providing chronocultural identification, artifact style is still too often seen as almost entirely following function. As anatomically-modern humans in the late Pleistocene, their technology is seen as being advanced, but without space or desire for personal or cultural expression. Adaptation and efficiency are assumed among Ice Age humans; their lives were seen as so precarious and difficult, so close to disaster that they could not have behaved in a way that was anything less than optimal or environmentally adaptive. The fact that stone tool assemblages look different through time and space is not due to the constant invention of new things to do with those tools; it is due to varying cultural norms. Lithics are the most abundant and well-preserved artifacts of Ice Age Europe, and because their manufacture involves subtracting material, we can see many of the choices or mistakes people made.

Archaeologists have judged raw material choices in the same way. The arbitrary limit of 50 km typically demarcates the local from non-local, regardless of terrain. If non-local materials were recovered at a site, one of the first questions asked would be whether that material was there through trade or direct procurement. This is quite a difficult question to answer without considering other evidence, and in the context of mobile societies the determination of what is local can vary over the course of the year. However, if archaeologists could discern dependence on any given material as judged by the quantity of material at the site and by how much of the reduction process took place onsite, they would develop an explanation that fits within the adaptive/efficient approach. That is, if the material is considered local, this demonstrated an efficient use of energy. If the material is non-local and closer material exists, it may be more difficult to explain, but typically the distant material would be described as higher-quality, justifying the energy expenditure on the procurement end with energy gains in production. Finally, if that did not make sense, since Paleolithic peoples did use raw materials that we do not consider "high-quality," perhaps the better sources were not known to them or they faced some other barrier to getting that material.

Another central assumption, one that is less explicitly stated after more than 30 years of feminist archaeology, is that stone tool production and use are primarily male tasks. Lithicists and experimental knappers are primarily men as well. However, there is no reason why this should be the case. Flintknapping does not typically require simply strength or force, but knowledge of angles and precision. Women past and present can produce stone tools, though it requires access to materials and practice. Many archaeologists learn to knap in groups, usually during an excavation project or at the lab, and these circles can be somewhat unfriendly to women, limiting our opportunity to participate in a learning community and to network. Last, even if we rely on the stereotypical belief that men are the hunters in society, stone tools are not used only, or even mostly, for hunting. Lithics occupy a privileged place in Paleolithic archaeology, not just because these are the most abundant materials, but because we associate them with men. In turn, male archaeologists have historically had privileged access to these materials. This environment would appear to be a difficult, but potentially fruitful, one in which to engage in feminist research. There is a great deal of room for lithic research that addresses social questions, but why has that so rarely happened? If the reason relates to limitations of the data, then it would be risky to try different kinds of analysis.

When I began to think about a potential dissertation project, I knew that I would analyze lithic material from late Paleolithic France, but I also was determined to take a feminist approach. Feminist science argues that by paying attention to and reducing androcentric biases, science is made better (e.g., Haraway 1988; Harding 1987), contrary to those who would argue that feminism has no place in science. Taking a feminist approach in archaeology does not mean looking for women; if we cannot find women in the past then we almost certainly cannot find men either. People made, used, and disposed of stone tools in cultural settings, but ignoring the people is a flawed way to attempt objectivity. At the same time, it is difficult to say meaningful things with limited data.

Inspiration came in an article about the Magdalenian site of Étiolles, in the Paris Basin. The analysts had nearly every stage of lithic production at the site and excellent horizontal and vertical control that allowed them to trace how pieces were moved within the site (Pigeot 1990). They were also able to convincingly argue for different levels of expertise at different stages of production and, less convincingly, for inherited socioeconomic differentiation. This latter argument was left out of later publications, but while a few details of the interpretation changed, the main arguments remained the same: they had evidence of different skill levels and apprenticeship at the site. However, the authors argued that this kind of approach could not be applied at other sites unless those sites were like Étiolles, with the complete or nearly-complete production sequence available and artifacts that appear to be exactly where they were left 10,000 years ago.

Needless to say, very few sites fit these criteria, but surely learning, if not apprenticeship, took place at most sites that were used more than ephemerally. Learning through doing is a lifelong process, and all material culture production must be learned. Lithic production is a reductive process, in which each step determines the possibilities that follow, and many of the traces of that reduction are preserved on the objects as scars. I thought that many of the attributes the Étiolles researchers had recognized as those of experts, novices, and learners could be identified in a large lithic collection, and that these stages of learning would be related to social position. Differential access to knowledge is universal, and engaging in certain material practices is part of one's identity. Therefore, I decided it was worth trying to identify different levels of skill.

As I began to research other work in this area, I found that there were indeed other attempts to look at apprenticeship in flintknapping, but these focused primarily on the cognitive abilities of extinct hominins. This work is fascinating, but I was not interested in gauging skill in order to say something about the brain. Because I focused on anatomically-modern humans in the past, I began with the assumption that their cognitive abilities were the same as those of living humans. There had also been research that highlighted learning in more recent periods or used other materials such as ceramic, but these models were of limited use.

My adviser at the University of California, Berkeley introduced me to the work of Jean Lave, an anthropologist in the School of Education. Lave has done considerable work on apprenticeship from an ethnographic perspective and, along with Étienne Wenger, developed the concepts of situated learning and communities of practice (Lave and Wenger 1991). Situated learning considers the ways in which learning occurs within specific contexts. This approach does not need to be limited to classrooms or formal master–apprentice relationships. Communities of practice are formed by people engaging in similar practices. Members of the community agree broadly on how practices are done, who is and is not a member of the community, and this is reinforced and transformed through their interactions and shared language. Members change the community and its values, and they are in turn changed by membership in the community for as long as they belong to it. People are members of multiple, often overlapping communities of practice, and their positions as central or legitimate peripheral participants can vary. How people learn to be members of their society and how they occupy those roles throughout their lifetimes could tell us a great deal about them. One difficulty, however, is that anthropological approaches to learning and apprenticeship available in the early 2000s when I began my research all came from ethnographic contexts. Although these approaches were materially-focused with real implications for archaeological research, they benefited from discussions between the analyst and the teachers and learners, and the anthropologists also had the possibility of engaging in participant observer research and participating in the community of practice. An archaeological approach would necessarily be limited by the lack of those methodologies, but the knowledge and skill that archaeology brings to the analysis of material culture and technology could offer different insights to these questions.

The Data

The sites I chose to analyze for my dissertation were two Magdalenian sites in the central French Pyrénées. Because I had been participating in a regional survey project in the Pyrénées for several years, I was very familiar with that context, and I had developed relationships with people who controlled access to various collections. I chose two sites to keep data collection manageable while allowing for comparison. I looked at one "room" in the cave of Enlène, known as La Salle des Morts, which dates to approximately 14,000 years ago. This site was dense with material culture; some areas had more artifacts than sediment! A relatively small excavated area of the cave yielded tens of thousands of stone tools. Besides stone tools and faunal remains, there was a broad variety of bone, antler, and ivory objects including needles and awls, spear throwers, beads, and spear points. Many engraved stone plaquettes had been placed on the floor of the cave, and a small corridor connects this cave to another cave in the system that reveals very little evidence of use as a living site, but has extensively painted and engraved walls. The other site was Les Églises, dated to about 12,000 years ago. This site yielded a much smaller collection, although superficially similar in composition including stone and bone tools, faunal remains, parietal art, and grooved animal teeth (presumably for suspension). While only 2,000 years and less than 50 km separated these two sites, they had been assigned to different phases of the Magdalenian based on their lithic technology. Enlène belonged to what we call the Middle Magdalenian and Les Églises to the Upper or Late Magdalenian. Site functions seemed to differ as well. Enlène contains a much greater diversity and density of material culture that goes beyond possible differences in length of occupation. Les Églises seems to have been visited briefly and seasonally, primarily for ibex hunting and salmon fishing. This site is at a much higher elevation where seasonally ibex had been present and overlooks the Ariège River where freshwater salmon run.

When I obtained the collections, they were mostly already sorted, though sorted differently. Enlène was sorted by technological type: blades, burins, flakes, and so on. I disagreed with some of the categories, and it may come as a surprise to non-lithicists that we cannot always agree on something that seems so basic. Les Églises was sorted into raw material types. The vast majority of objects were produced in two different materials, approximately half each, with a handful of other materials.

One of the key questions I needed to address was whether or not a community of practice of flintknappers had been present at each site, and I thought that seeking recurring patterns in production could help answer this question. I was unsure what attributes would be useful in finding patterns, so I began recording standard data such as size, raw material, number and nature of dorsal scars, cortex, platform type, and termination. Because the objects from Enlène were sorted by technical type, I developed a routine that sped up the process. I also recorded any interesting observations and photographed several objects, some under the microscope, if they seemed to show anything that could be interpreted as expertise or lack thereof. I sorted the objects within the raw material types at Les Églises into technical categories and repeated the process with that collection. The result was quite a lot of quantitative data that I used in basic statistical analyses such as correlation. This proved to be largely unnecessary, since variables that showed strong correlation (e.g., $r = 0.9$) should have been obvious without the statistics. For example, a relationship exists between platform size and type and overall flake size due to the physics of flintknapping. The collection of those quantitative data was long and time-consuming, and if I were to start the project again I would probably collect less quantitative data.

However, the close observation required to collect those measurable data resulted in a wealth of qualitative data, and it was primarily in those that I found ways to discuss learning and skill. At Enlène I could identify evidence of high or low expertise based on similar judgments at Étiolles, my observation of and discussion with flintknappers, and my own practice as a flint-knapper. While an expert can make mistakes and a novice can get lucky, it is in the accumulation of actions that we see the opposite ends of the spectrum of skill. Beginning knappers typically understand what they want to achieve, but they do not always have the ability to execute their plans. One of the signs of this is repeated blows to a location that cannot produce the desired product, which inflicts damage that negatively affects the quality of the core. Novices often continue to strike at a core when success is no longer possible, while an expert knows when continuing is futile, either due to problems with the material or mistakes. Expert knapping can be seen through the execution of a series of steps that lead to successful production, or the execution of difficult techniques that lead to a higher likelihood of success. It is the middle range of expertise that is most difficult to identify. Once knappers move beyond novice knowledge, they will have varying levels of ability to execute difficult techniques, and while mistakes and futile attempts will be reduced, they will not be eliminated. This is, of course, where many members of the knapping community of practice should be found.

At Enlène I found strong evidence of a community of practice of knappers. Experts were evident in what reached practically virtuoso levels of production. There were very precisely faceted platforms for bladelet production, well beyond what was necessary, and the removal of bladelets as small as a millimeter in width to re-center a scar to produce a bladelet. These finely-worked details assured success, but went above and beyond what was necessary for successful production. If we imagine this knapping taking place inside the cave, this would have been done by the light of a hearth, lamp, or torch, and for anyone to observe this work they would have to be very close and presumably have the consent of the knapper. Not just anyone would have access to this type of knowledge, although someone may have been able to reverse-engineer the techniques if they had a certain level of knowledge. Besides the experts, novice production was also frequent, as seen in striking platforms that had been repeatedly bashed with far too much force and too little accuracy. In addition, I was able to refit a handful of objects at Enlène, which is another considerably time-consuming technique, but unlike at Étiolles refitting did not provide any additional insights. Also unlike Étiolles, many stages of the production process were missing at Enlène.

Les Églises was quite different. It seemed unlikely that a community of knappers was present at the site, and if individual members were there, their skills were not as valued as at Enlène. Raw material choice was much more important than what was done with that material. The material held meaning to its users, perhaps because it represented the place it came from rather than for any explanation of "efficiency" or "adaptiveness." I am hesitant to deem any raw material as "poor," since what a modern knapper values may not be what a prehistoric knapper valued, but half of the material used at Les Églises would be considered poor by most knappers' standards. This material is riddled with fissures at right angles, resulting in blocky, cubic chunks. The flakes produced from this material had to be heavily modified to suit their purposes. The other half or so of the material was of acceptable quality, and the products of that material were what you would expect to find at a Late Magdalenian site, including numerous bladelets not produced in the other material. However, the same level of attention to detail cannot be seen at Les Églises as it was present at Enlène. The people at Les Églises satisfied their technical needs, but did not seem to be interested in doing much more than that. This might be due in part to the limited amount of time the site seemed to have been occupied, but it might also reflect a different attitude toward lithic production.

Reflections and Lessons Learned

In the end, I was able to identify experts and novices in lithic production, though I recorded much more data than I needed to. By considering knapping within the broader context of the site I was able to discuss social relations to some extent, and I believe that a learning-centered approach may be a way to consider the difficult biocultural category of childhood, an area

I would like to pay more attention to in the future. This work would not have been possible in the limited amount of time available for dissertation research and writing if the collections had not been already curated, and I encourage students to use museum collections whenever possible both to save time and money, but also to make use of these valuable and underused resources. I wish I had known sooner what kinds of data collection would be most useful because I would have been able to use my time differently.

As I write this, one of my graduate students is attempting a similar project, although the context is quite different. His materials come from a Northeastern Native American open-air site, but while he does not have any more ethnographic information than I did, a great deal of work in communities of practice and learning in archaeology has taken place since I did my dissertation. My student has a strong background in cognitive psychology, and while I did not find those approaches useful to address my questions, he is finding some utility in them. Despite my experience, it has been difficult to advise him on the most challenging aspect I faced, which was how much and what kind of quantitative evidence to collect. Because the kind of lithic production he is analyzing is so different from the collection I had, the same categories do not apply. However, sometimes we must accept the very real conclusion that collecting too much data is much safer than collecting too few, for we can more easily slim a dataset to better address a question than we can go back and augment it.

My student is still collecting data, so he has not yet performed any statistical tests. We will see later what we can learn from the quantitative data. In his qualitative observations he is also seeing both ends of the spectrum of expertise. In addition, despite the different technological traditions in Magdalenian France and Early Woodland New York, many of the signs of expertise levels are the same. In both cases novices repeatedly bashed platforms, and experts were able to execute a complicated series of gestures that produced the desired product or quit when that was no longer possible. He has also identified stylistic differences in the assemblage that do not seem to be differences in expertise, but perhaps represent two individuals at the site. These two highly-skilled styles were found near each other, and novice production took place a few meters away. Again, the middle range of skill is hard to identify, but I hope that the combination of spatial, observational, and statistical analyses may help my student identify knapping between the beginning and expert levels.

What my student's and my projects share, and what I believe applies to anyone who wants to take this approach, is that you have to develop a highly detailed understanding of the technology you are studying and reject supposedly common-sense notions of efficiency and adaptation which can lead you to see things that are not there. This knowledge does not necessarily have to come from engaging in the practice yourself, but this can be very helpful. When time is an issue, as it is for someone writing a thesis or a dissertation, or on the tenure-track, manageably-sized collections are a must since it is more likely that you can develop the required intimate knowledge of the collection. Looking at technology as interwoven with learning in social context is just one way to investigate a *peopled* past and not just a material past, and this was a way that satisfied my intersectional feminist commitments without having to focus on gender as the primary category of identity.

Paired Reading

Sterling, Kathleen. 2011. "Inventing Human Nature." In *Ideologies in Archaeology*, edited by Reinhard Bernbeck and Randall H. McGuire, 175–193. Tucson, AZ: University of Arizona Press.

References

Conkey, Margaret W. and Janet D. Spector. 1984. "Archaeology and the Study of Gender." *Advances in Archaeological Method and Theory*, 7: 1–32. DOI: 10.1016/B978-0-12-003107-8.50006-2.

Haraway, Donna. 1988. "Situated Knowledges: The Science Question in Feminism and the Privilege of Partial Perspective." *Feminist Studies*, 14: 575–599. DOI: 10.2307/3178066.

Harding, Sandra G. 1987. *Feminism and Methodology: Social Science Issues*. Bloomington, IN: Indiana University Press.

Lave, Jean and Étienne Wenger. 1991. *Situated Learning: Legitimate Peripheral Participation*. Cambridge: Cambridge University Press.

Pigeot, Nicole. 1990. "Technical and Social Actors: Flintknapping Specialists and Apprentices at Magdalenian Etiolles." *Archaeological Review from Cambridge*, 9: 126–141.

Sterling, Kathleen. 2011. "Inventing Human Nature." In *Ideologies in Archaeology*, edited by Reinhard Bernbeck and Randall H. McGuire, 175–193. Tucson, AZ: University of Arizona Press.

26

How Not to Write a PhD Thesis: Some Real-Life Lessons from 1990s Michigan and Prehistoric Italy
John Robb

Project Summary

This chapter describes the process of putting together a PhD thesis, a process about half careful "research design" and about half random circumstance and contingency. The thesis used skeletal data on health, diet, and lifestyle to track the development of inequality in Italy over a 6000-year span from the Neolithic through the Iron Age. I discuss not only the kind of research design needed for archaeological research, but the reflexes and soft skills needed to carry research through to completion.

Introduction

Research is a deeply personal form of work. There are really two sides to surviving – and even excelling at – research. One is designing a sound project which is feasible and will make an original contribution to your field. This serves as the bread and butter staple of graduate courses in "research design." But the other is knowing *how* to go about research. This involves a lot of "soft skills" which are rarely formally taught. It is more like training to be a Jedi than designing a project. If you are lucky enough to have a supervisor who thinks about such things, they can guide you; otherwise, you usually fall back on your instincts, for better or worse.

My PhD project was a 10-year random walk through the hazard-strewn plains of graduate life. I skirted the Craters of Badly Flawed Research Design, bungee-jumped off the Cliffs of Where Are My Data Coming From?, breathed deeply the noxious fumes of the Permanently Broke and Depressed Volcano, and barely squelched my way out of the Bog of Never Finishing. I survived it (and even found a job afterwards), but luck was on my side. The thesis itself had serious design flaws and immediately vanished into the oblivion it deserved.

How do you successfully make it through a PhD or master's thesis or any other kind of archaeological research project? On one hand, there is a lot of luck in it. On the other hand, you make your own luck. I did some important things wrong and somehow got away with it, and I did some important things right without realizing it. This guide – all the examples are based directly on my own experience, plus those of friends, colleagues, and students – distils some of the important things which might help you make it through your research journey.

Engaging Archaeology: 25 Case Studies in Research Practice, First Edition. Edited by Stephen W. Silliman.
© 2018 John Wiley & Sons, Inc. Published 2018 by John Wiley & Sons, Inc.

The Backstory

I spent ten years in doctoral research at the University of Michigan. Michigan at that time had one of the top graduate programs in anthropological archaeology, with famous professors, worldwide expertise, and hegemonic networks encircling the globe. Not unrelatedly, it was the citadel of 1970s–1980s New Archaeology. Gender and post-processual archaeology were beginning to get up momentum elsewhere, but most of our professors regarded them as dangerously postmodern and stuck to a straightforward agenda of positivism, social evolution, and formal political structures.

Formulating a Project

The heart of a project is a research design. Sometimes one falls into a ready-made, water-tight project, but for many, particularly students, formulating a sound research design is a protracted process which fills a year or more with anxiety. The basics are not rocket science. For most anthropological archaeologists, you want to investigate an Idea, using a Method, on materials from an Area/Region. Hence the ponderous titles we give theses and books: "Social complexity, feasting, and power: Faunal remains from prehistoric Georgia" or "Did Neandertals love? Comparative ethology and the Middle Palaeolithic settlement record." To a generative linguist, the formula would be "[IdeaTopic]: a [Method] study of [PlaceTime]."

In my case, after five years in the relaxed graduate school environment of those days, it dawned upon me that perhaps graduate school was not a permanent state of existence and I should apply myself to some concrete project and move on someday. By then I had been dig-hopping in the Neolithic of southern Italy for several years. The archaeology was interesting in a Puebloesque way, I knew marginally more about it than about anywhere else, and it seemed politically and logistically a lot easier to work in than (say) the Near East, where several of my advisors worked. So it seemed like a promising PlaceTime. I had also learned how to analyze human skeletons, which gave me a Method. What about an IdeaTopic? If you worked in pre-state societies in a 1980s social evolutionary school, you had only two big stories – the origins of farming and the origins of inequality. The former was out, mostly because the local Mesolithic was very poorly known, which made studying the Mesolithic-Neolithic transition difficult. I was also incapable of lithic studies. Besides, everyone knew that the Neolithic began in the Near East far earlier, and what happened in Europe was just its later spread, which sounded far less interesting. Inequality, in contrast, probably came about indigenously and was certainly important. The poor are always with us; so, how did they get there?

The challenge in forging a research topic is painfully tugging the three components into connection. Most of us build outwards from a home turf in one element. We've dug in Arizona for years but don't know what conceptual issue we want to study; we know isotopic analysis but don't know where we want to work; we're fascinated by cognition but don't know how or where you actually study it. As we start to flesh out a plan, we find fearful gaps between these components. Student Sue wants to study prehistoric landscapes, but most of the data available date to later periods; should she change regions or change her period of interest? Candidate Charles is fascinated by ideas of technological agency and wants to use lithic analysis, but the available collections are blenderized, undatable assemblages from surface survey; should he give up on the concept or find different data?

In my case, the plan was to find out how inequality developed in prehistoric Italy, a completely traditional New Archaeology problem. To do so, I was going to look for patterns of health, consumption, activity, and violence in skeletal remains. Again, this was a straightforward New Archaeological approach; most skeletal markers of social relations had been developed exactly for studying big social transitions such as the origins of farming (Cohen and Armelagos 1984), and the current cutting edge work was Mary Powell's study of skeletons from Moundville, Alabama, to find out whether elites had better health than common people (Powell 1988). So it looked straightforward: I was going to hunt up lots of prehistoric Italians and compare skeletal data on how they lived and died with contextual data on their status using things like grave goods. This would tell me whether inequality in prehistoric Italy was accompanied by real differences in living conditions rather than just prestige.

At the core of every successful project is a question, the most basic statement of what you want to know. Archaeological analysis is grounded in a linkage between concept and material which allows us to look at concrete data and draw some general conclusions. This is true whatever your theoretical paradigm is. To take a classic New Archaeology example, if you argue that settlement hierarchies mirror political hierarchies (Steponaitis 1978), you can then ask a question which works both to make a theoretical contribution:

> "Does inequality increase with environmental change?"

And which, on the flip side, can be answered empirically:

> "Is there more settlement hierarchy in my survey data in period A than in period B?"

The same is true in Postprocessualese: if you establish a linkage between visibility and spiritual power (Tilley 1994), then you can ask theoretically:

> "Are monuments placed to construct ancestral landscapes?"

While also asking empirically:

> "Are the megalithic tombs in my survey area placed where they command the biggest viewsheds?"

Thus, a research question has to work at two quite distinct levels, that of general ideas and that of the concrete nuts and bolts of actual data. If a research question works at an abstract level but not at a concrete level, it poses a question you won't be able to answer with your data. If it works at a concrete level but not when phrased in abstract nouns, it won't make a contribution to knowledge beyond your specific materials. (The Abstract Noun Test is also critical in publishing. Generally speaking, if you can't express what your article is about in abstract nouns applicable to anywhere rather than concrete nouns which describe only your own field setting, editors will shunt your article to purely regional journals where people actually care about your site.) In my case, the abstract research question was, "Was early political inequality accompanied by differential work, health, and consumption?" The nuts-and-bolts version, which put it in terms which I could answer with a graph or table, was "are there more signs of stress and disease in periods when there was more inequality?"

Your research question is your lifeline. A research question provides continuity through the project, while transforming to meet different needs as you go through the opus. Typically, it begins as an abstract question of general significance, and then is successively translated into regional and methodological terms. By the middle of the project, it consists of a concrete

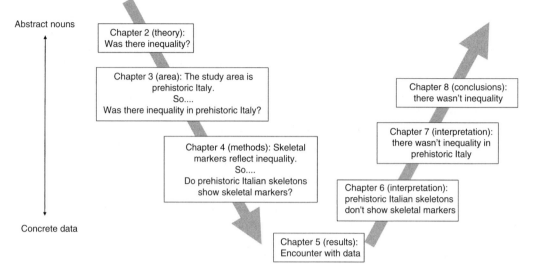

Figure 26.1 Diagramming a research question. The research question provides continuity throughout a project such as a PhD thesis; note how it both remains the same but also changes as the work progresses.

question you can answer with a table full of sherds or animal bones, a GIS database, or a lab result. And once you answer this, stunning the reader with ground-breaking charts and graphs in the "results" section, the rest of the work gradually draws it back to the general level, drawing the general conclusions for the big picture interpretation (Figure 26.1).

The Research Design Encounters Reality

At least, that's how it is supposed to work. My research design held together just long enough to get funded by the Wenner-Gren Foundation, to whom I remain eternally grateful, and to get me into the field. Then it began to unravel.

It had four basic problems, covering everything from cash to concepts. One was simply practical. My grant funding covered some research, but it would not cover a year's worth of hotels, pasta, and train fares for gathering data in Italy. What saved the day was serendipitously finding a year's work on the staff of the University of Michigan's junior year abroad program in Florence. Going to Florence was a decision which branched outwards to open new research possibilities. In return for free room and board, at nights I kept an eye on undergraduate art history students living in the Renaissance villa the university rented. During the days I studied skeletons in Florence anthropological museum, and when the students went home between terms I foraged for skeletons in museums further afield.

Other problems were less tractable. I hadn't thought enough about samples. The kind of work I wanted to do assumed that you had analyzable whole skeletons and that their grave goods and burial treatment mapped out their social status clearly – like Powell's Moundville study. In Italy, this happened in the Iron Age (ca. 900–400 BC), and by immense luck the Florence museum had large, well-preserved Iron Age collections. But Neolithic (6000–3500 BC) burials occur in small numbers and rarely have burial goods, and Copper (3500–2400 BC) and Bronze Age (2400–900 BC) depositions usually involve commingled bones from collective tombs, which makes studying their health a challenge. In the end, I tried finessing this problem by a combination of assiduously chasing handfuls of Neolithic burials wherever I could find them and using statistical methods which enabled coarse-grained, lowest-common-denominator comparisons between periods with different kinds of collection (Robb 1997). But the results could not be anywhere as fine-grained or conclusive as I originally hoped.

Methodologically, my project depended upon several critical assumptions. All projects do. Such assumptions are often called "linking arguments" or in Binfordian terms, "Middle Range Theory"; they give you the bridges to get from actual data to abstract terms. One assumption was about linking inequality in life and skeletal markers. If inequality in life had no relation to skeletal markers, then studying skeletons wasn't going to tell me anything about social inequality. The rather bullish 1980s literature on the topic suggested that inequality usually results in poorer health and generalized "stress." Since then, it has turned out that the relationship is more complicated. Inequality certainly leads to major health gaps in the modern world, but it may not have done so in the past. It depends upon well-off and poor people having different exposure to disease, but even in a clearly class-stratified ancient city such as Rome, rich and poor people lived mostly in the same environment as far as air, water, and bacteria were concerned, and there wasn't an effective medical establishment for the rich to run to when they got ill. Moreover, skeletal measures of diet and health were a blunt instrument, particularly before methods such as isotopic analysis became routine. So skeletal biomarkers of childhood stress might tell me about extreme cases, such as if poor people were starving in childhood, but they might not tell me about finer variation in diet between rich and poor.

On the conceptual side of the "inequality equals differential health" equation, it turned out that inequality is much more complicated than I had been taught. Standard New Archaeology approaches mostly reckoned up the number of levels of social hierarchy and concluded that a society was either "egalitarian" or "stratified." But skeletons respond to concrete actual life circumstances. So what did such summary designations of political structure actually mean on the ground, in terms of actual behavior, food consumption, and so on? At the time, I was also reading anthropological theories which suggested that inequality was far more complex. It might be ambiguous or consist of multiple, contradictory principles; it might be an ideal which had little to do with on-the-ground behavior; or it might depend upon symbolic context. And what about gender: was it an important part of inequality? Prehistoric Europe proved ground zero for such theoretical problems. The kind of unambiguous, across-the-board stratification I had been taught to look for only turns up very late and patchily in Europe, and major 1980s theorists who tried to map social evolutionary schemes onto the European sequence quickly realized that we did not have a simple increase in the amount of inequality so much as shifts between different kinds of inequality (Robb 1999).

Habits of Mind and Intellectual Footwork

So, in hindsight, the kind of inequality in prehistoric Europe rarely resulted in different enough lifestyles to leave much differences in "elite" and "non-elite" skeletons. In 1990, people hadn't realized these problems yet and were willing to give me benefit of the doubt to carry out my research. But when it came to interpreting the results, it was a mess. Nobody told me to do two things which should be standard advice for graduate students:

- Don't be rigid; adapt. Producing a coherent work is more important than sticking with the specific combination of idea, method, and area/region you started with. That is, it's better to wind up with two out of three of these and a project that hangs together than to insist on your original plan. Should I have shifted areas to find somewhere with larger numbers of single burials for all my periods? Possibly. Should I have shifted to non-skeletal methods for getting at prehistoric inequality? In the end, I did. Several chapters of my thesis created a reconstruction of evolving inequality based on settlements, burial evidence, material culture, and art which had nothing to do with skeletons (Robb 1994, 1999), but this did not happen in a planned, efficient, or graceful way.

- Test the connections between them with a pilot study, early on. Before finalizing your design, use your method and materials to get a small dataset together and take it all the way through to interpretation to see if the central axis of the research will work. This would have revealed the problems discussed above in time to create a much sounder thesis.

What saved the day – at least in making sense of my data – were two things. The first involved intellectual habits, not research design. Graduate school and later professional life can give you serious tunnel vision. You face pressure to ignore everything that does not bear directly on your research. But this doesn't give you the tools to think outside the box you have defined for yourself. Should you go to hear a visiting speaker on some random topic that has nothing to do with your work? Should you spend a week or two dig-hopping on a colleague's field project in a completely different area from yours? These take time away from your core work, but they also act as intellectual cross-pollination. They let you pick up ideas, questions, and methods you didn't know existed, a new way of presenting data, a new concept or buzzword. As one example, while our professors were pretending that post-processualism and gender archaeology didn't exist, some of us were reading it, going to papers at annual conferences on it, and talking over how it might open new doors. With my thesis, such scouting around the intellectual terrain gave me confidence that when my results didn't match expectations, it wasn't because the work was a failure. It was because the idea of inequality I was using was too simple, and indeed a bit parochial within the social sciences, and there were other languages I could use to talk about my results. And talking with others is where you learn the craft of academe. I learned much more in graduate school from my peers than from my professors. Gossiping, drinking coffee or beer, sitting around the shared office listening to each other's research agonies and kicking around solutions, you learn the broader intellectual terrain, how to solve problems, what resources are around, and how people in different parts of the field see the world differently. A good deal of continuously reformulating my project so it did not get derailed by its own design flaws happened in such discussions. This was also instrumental in understanding how the Italian academic and museum world worked and getting access to collections. In all this, it is also worthwhile to err on the side of generosity; a bit of time helping someone fix a problem, lending a hand with a colleague's fieldwork, or assisting someone with a translation always repays you in terms of knowledge, experience, and cooperative networks.

The second thing that saved me was something simple and obvious, but following it will save a lot of heartbreak. When formulating a research question or "hypothesis," one is always tempted to phrase it in terms which contrast the new, sexy answer with the old, boring answer:

Research Question (H1): My Brilliant New Idea is right. (In my case, skeletal changes show that there was prehistoric inequality.)

This inevitably casts the conventional wisdom as the dull, old null hypothesis:

> H0: The Conventional Wisdom is right. (Skeletal changes don't demonstrate social inequality in prehistoric Italy.)

The problem is that this builds your research in a way which has only one "right" answer. You then spend several years fervently hoping that your research will come up with the result you want, and dreading that it won't. If you don't find a neat pattern where all the elite burials have healthy skeletons and all the poor ones are diseased and traumatized, your research has no "result" or story line, your thesis is a failure, and you've wasted several years.

Instead, mostly by luck or instinct, I had asked the question in a way which allowed different possible outcomes to be interesting: "was political inequality accompanied by differential work, health, and consumption?" This meant that, if it turned out that health and political status were correlated, I could discuss this as a new way of studying how inequality developed. But if they weren't, as turned out to be the case, I could find something to say about the reasons why; maybe it could help me problematize inequality and how it relates to health and lifestyle in new ways (Robb *et al.* 2001). Never pose a research question which has only one "right" answer. Indeed, the ways in which reality does not cooperate with your hypothesis are almost always more interesting and informative than finding what you expected to find. Instead, write a research question where there is something interesting and productive to say about *all* the various outcomes. Your research will inevitably give you lemons; plan ahead for lemonade.

Your Research, Your Self: Intellectual Comfort Zones

As the above story suggests, what got me through my thesis was not the research design, but a combination of luck, intellectual footwork, and reflexes. One rarely taught fact is that this mostly has to do with how you interact with your research. Every researcher has a comfort zone. We all short-cut some tasks, avoid others, and wallow in others longer than we need to. Many researchers cling tenaciously to their home turf. We love field archaeology or lab work for its own sake, and learn just enough theory to scrape through a degree. Or we're happiest playing with ideas filched from Continental social theorists, and we learn just enough about the archaeological setting to scrape through the "area" chapter. Or maybe the comfort zone has to do with the tasks we like and hate. Some students love polishing their database and filling in gaps, but wince when you ask them to cut to the chase and say what it means. Others can spin out their own ideas by the hour, but never quite make it to the library to properly fill in the scholarly underpinning it needs to go public confidently. Comfort zones are deeply limiting in the long run. To finish a project all the way to a thesis, article, or book you can feel proud of, and, importantly, to make it in the highly competitive market after finishing a degree, you need to combine all the skills, solo. The key here is self-awareness. Think about *how* you work, not just about *what* you do. What is your comfort zone? What are your strengths? What do you avoid doing, and why? Once you understand your academic comfort zone, moving out of it is never as hard as you fear, and realizing you can do so is tremendously empowering. If you get something wrong (and everybody does), reflect on why and learn the relevant lesson; you'll know you're making progress when you make new mistakes rather than repeating old ones.

Beyond this, most of us have a Monster Under The Bed, some aspect of our research we find deeply worrying or threatening. Do you find yourself dreading specific questions you fear you can't answer? Denying possible methodological flaws which might prevent you from using a key procedure, or data problems which might make your sample vanish? Avoiding giving talks on your work or submitting draft chapters for fear they will expose you to criticism? Doctoral Candidate Danielle wrote brilliantly, but she never turned her fragments into a whole text. An underlying insecurity meant that putting closure on a piece of writing meant it was ready to be judged by others, so her fledgling work never left the safety of the nest. Graduate Student Greg was so oppressed by a sense of hurry that he never did his methodology and area literature reviews more than superficially, and he avoided works which suggested that his methods might be more complicated than he wanted them to be, which added to his insecurity when he met specialists. When other scholars questioned the stratigraphy of Learned Loretta's key site, she simply refused to entertain their views. This kept her work safe in her mind, but it got her a reputation for dogmatism, and it filled her with anxiety whenever she presented her work. Among young researchers, the two biggest underlying anxieties are (1) fears that some dreadful flaw in your method or data will be revealed and your project will evaporate and (2) "Imposter Syndrome," the worry that everyone else is a real scholar but you will be exposed and humiliated sooner or later.

Most graduate students and new scholars suffer from these worries in some form, and they are almost always dark fantasies rather than realistic assessments. In my case, one fear was that skeletal remains might not in the end be able to reveal inequality, which in turn would knock out the methodological basis of the project. (This turned out in fact to be partly the case!) Fortunately, I did not simply go into denial and insist that the bones had to mean what I wanted them to, but it took several anxious years to realize that social inequality and skeletal inequality could be different things attested by different evidence, and how they related could actually vary historically in interesting ways. Then there were the psychological points of weakness. As someone with no previous background in archaeology, I felt far out of my depth among the other graduate students, who had all been digging for years, had big professional networks, and knew their research areas like the back of their hand. Only years later did I realize that, among my colleagues, every single one of us was secretly terrified by all the others, for different reasons! Trust the people who let you into grad school; if they thought you belong there, you belong there. If you identify a major worry, tackle it head on. If there is a real problem, you're going to have to deal with it sooner or later, and there is almost always a way of adapting your research plans to accommodate it. And don't get sucked into competing. Academia is rarely a zero-sum game; a lot of it depends on shared information, cooperation, and group problem-solving, and you will be in it with mostly the same people for three or four decades.

Conclusions: Surviving a Research Project, and Maybe Even Winding Up on Top

In the end, my research delivered the minimal goals for a research project: I learned some important things about my topic, and, mostly by making mistakes, I learned how to be an independent researcher. (I still work on both interpreting skeletons socially and the intricacies of emerging inequality, and I've gained the middle-aged confidence that when the expected answer doesn't work, it is probably because the disciplinary expectations are wrong, not my results.) But rather than the punchy study of social change I had envisioned, I wound up with an unwieldy monster of a thesis. It had 100+ tables of skeletal data which had little relation to the theoretical question, and hundreds of pages of social reconstruction of ancient society based on other people's published work which made zero use of these painfully acquired data. As soon as the ink was dry on my committee's signatures, the opus fell apart into article-sized chunks on completely different topics. Someone taking a good hard skeptical look at it might have saved me a lot of time and worry, and got me out with a better thesis. If nobody else does this for you, do so for yourself.

Perhaps the clearest lesson from my doctoral work is this: research design is important, but the intangible skills, reflexes, awareness of your comfort zones, and *savoir faire* to carry it out are equally important. Hence a lot of my guidance is not about an abstract research process; they are actually personal guidance about how you interact with your research and your colleagues.

Graduate school can be exciting. You learn about fascinating things, you become an expert, and you take the first step towards an academic career. But it can also be much more stressful than "real life." There is no royal road to getting a graduate degree or pursuing research in general. Creating new knowledge and learning to be a researcher involves blood, sweat, toil, and tears. But the guidance above will help you carry out your plans more productively and with less trauma, and with the psychology and professional footwork of someone who can do independent research for the long haul. They will say: "The Force is strong within this one!"

Paired Reading

Robb, John, Renzo Bigazzi, Luca Lazzarini, Caterina Scarsini, and Fiorenza Sonego. 2001. "Social 'Status' and Biological 'Status': A Comparison of Grave Goods and Skeletal Indicators from Pontecagnano." *American Journal of Physical Anthropology*, 115: 213–232. DOI: 10.1002/ajpa.1076.

References

Cohen, Mark and George Armelagos, eds. 1984. *Paleopathology at the Origins of Agriculture*. New York: Academic.

Powell, Mary. 1988. *Status and Health in Prehistory: A Case Study of the Moundville Chiefdom*. Washington, DC: Smithsonian Institution Press.

Robb, John. 1994. "Gender Contradictions, Moral Coalitions and Inequality in Prehistoric Italy." *Journal of European Archaeology*, 2: 20–49. DOI: 10.1179/096576694800719256.

Robb, John. 1997. "Violence and Gender in Early Italy." In *Troubled Times: Osteological and Archaeological Evidence of Violence*, edited by Debra L. Martin and David W. Frayer, 108–141. New York: Gordon and Breach.

Robb, John. 1999. "Great Persons and Big Men in the Italian Neolithic." In *Social Dynamics of the Prehistoric Central Mediterranean*, edited by Jonathan Morter, Robert H. Tykot, and John E. Robb, 111–122. London: Accordia Research Center.

Robb, John, Renzo Bigazzi, Luca Lazzarini, Caterina Scarsini, and Fiorenza Sonego. 2001. "Social 'Status' and Biological 'Status': A Comparison of Grave Goods and Skeletal Indicators from Pontecagnano." *American Journal of Physical Anthropology*, 115: 213–232. DOI: 10.1002/ajpa.1076.

Steponaitis, Vincas. 1978. "Locational Theory and Complex Chiefdoms: A Mississippian Example." In *Mississippian Settlement Patterns*, edited by Bruce D. Smith, 417–453. New York: Academic.

Tilley, Christopher. 1994. *A Phenomenology of Landscape: Places, Paths and Monuments*. Oxford: Berg.

Index

Page numbers in *italics* refer to figures.

Engaging Archaeology: 25 Case Studies in Research Practice, First Edition. Edited by Stephen W. Silliman.
© 2018 John Wiley & Sons, Inc. Published 2018 by John Wiley & Sons, Inc.